Information Systems Foundations:
THE ROLE OF DESIGN SCIENCE

Information Systems Foundations:

THE ROLE OF DESIGN SCIENCE

Dennis N. Hart and Shirley D. Gregor (Editors)

THE AUSTRALIAN NATIONAL UNIVERSITY

E PRESS

Published by ANU E Press
The Australian National University
Canberra ACT 0200, Australia
Email: anuepress@anu.edu.au
This title is also available online at: http://epress.anu.edu.au/is_foundations_citation.html

National Library of Australia
Cataloguing-in-Publication entry

Author: Information Systems Foundations ('The role of design science') Workshop (2008 : Canberra, A.C.T.)

Title: Information systems foundations : the role of design science / edited by Shirley D. Gregor and Dennis N. Hart.

ISBN: 9781921666346 (pbk.) ISBN: 9781921666353 (eBook)

Notes: Workshop held at the Australian National University in Canberra from 2-3 October, 2008.
Includes bibliographical references.

Subjects: Management information systems--Congresses.
Information resources management--Congresses.
System design--Congresses.

Other Authors/Contributors:
Gregor, Shirley Diane.
Hart, Dennis N.

Dewey Number: 658.4038

All rights reserved. No part of this publication may be reproduced, stored in a retrieval system or transmitted in any form or by any means, electronic, mechanical, photocopying or otherwise, without the prior permission of the publisher.

Cover design by Teresa Prowse

Cover ilustration by Jackson Gable

Printed by Griffin Press

This edition © 2010 ANU E Press

Contents

Preface ix

Philosophical Foundations

1. Identification-interaction-innovation: a phenomenological basis for an information services view 3
   Dirk Hovorka, Matt Germonprez

2. How critical realism clarifies validity issues in theory-testing research: analysis and case 21
   Robert B. Johnston, Stephen P. Smith

Theory and Method

3. Building theory in a practical science 51
   Shirley Gregor

4. Incommensurability in design science: which comes first—theory or artefact?............................ 75
   Michael Davern, Alison Parkes

5. An exploration of the concept of design in information systems 91
   Judy McKay, Peter Marshall, Greg Heath

6. Evaluating information systems: an appropriation perspective 121
   Justin Fidock, Jennie Carroll, Anita Rynne

Applications

7. On using materiality in information systems development: a research brief 145
   Andrea Carugati

8. How IS design can contribute to a major climate
   change mitigation project 165
   *Walter Fernández, Birgitta Bergvall-Kåreborn,
   Michael Djordjevic, Keith Lovegrove,
   Javier Fernández-Velasco, Mishka Talent*

9. An intelligent agent-assisted logistics exception
   management decision support system:
   a design-science approach 189
   Shijia Gao, Dongming Xu

10. Thinking beyond means–ends analysis: the role of
    impulse-driven human creativity in the design of
    artificially intelligent systems...................... 213
    Dongming Xu, Yonggui Wang, Sukanto Bhattacharya

11. An information systems design theory for an RFID
    university-based laboratory 233
    Samuel Fosso Wamba, Katina Michael

Design Science in IS

12. An assessment of DSS design science using the
    Hevner, March, Park and Ram guidelines 255
    David Arnott, Graham Pervan

13. Design science in IS research: a literature analysis 285
    Marta Indulska, Jan Recker

Workshop Chair

Shirley D. Gregor, ANU

Program Chairs

Shirley D. Gregor, ANU
Susanna Ho, ANU

Program Committee

Jörg Becker, University of Münster, Germany
Andrea Carugati, University of Aarhus, Denmark
Joseph Davis, University of Sydney, Australia
Walter Fernandez, Australian National University, Australia
Erwin Fielt, Telematica Instituut, Enschede, Netherlands
Steven Fraser, Australian National University, Australia
Eleanor Gates-Stuart, Australian National University, Australia
Tom Gedeon, Australian National University, Australia
Sigi Goode, Australian National University, Australia
Peter Green, University of Queensland, Australia
Dennis Hart, Australian National University, Australia
Pertti Järvinen, University of Tampere, Finland
Robert Johnston, University College Dublin, Ireland
Nigel Martin, Australian National University, Australia
Craig McDonald, University of Canberra, Australia
Peter Marshall, University of Tasmania, Australia
Liam O'Brien, National ICT Australia (NICTA), Canberra, Australia
Nicholas Pratt, ESSEC Business School, France
Michael Rosemann, Queensland University of Technology, Australia
John Venable, Curtin University, Australia
Xiaofang Zhou, University of Queensland, Australia

Preface

This volume contains the papers presented at the Information Systems Foundations Workshop, 2-3 October, 2008. This workshop was the fourth in the ANU series of biennial workshops, originally inspired by one held in 1999 by Kit Dampney at Macquarie University, and focussing on the theoretical foundations of the discipline of information systems.

The theme of the 2008 Workshop was 'Answering the Unanswered Questions about Design Research' and it once again allowed researchers and practitioners in the field of Information Systems to come together to discuss some of the fundamental issues relating to our discipline.

Information Systems is still a quite young field of study that, perhaps uniquely, is a peculiar juxtaposition of the technological, in the form of computing and communication technology, and the non-technological, in the form of the humans and organisations that design, implement and use systems built with that technology. Indeed, it is this fact of "design" that was the focus of the 2008 workshop and which tempts one to put information systems into the same sort of category as disciplines such as, for example, architecture, accounting or engineering where artefacts (which may be physical or conceptual) destined specifically for human use and activities are envisaged and created ex nihilo, as it were. But even so, it may be argued that information systems remains different from these and other similar areas in at least one important sense for, once an architectural, engineering or accounting artefact is completed it is typically just that – complete. But most information systems are never "complete". They are instead usually dynamic by being modified, adjusted, extended or otherwise changed over the course of their existence in continuing response to altered needs and circumstances. This has and still does present a problem, for how does one go about successfully designing an artefact of this nature? Moreover, on what theoretical foundations should such design be based? Design sciences are not, as are the natural and most other human sciences, aimed at understanding and explaining the phenomena of the world as presented to our senses but rather enabling intervention in the world through the designed artefact in such a way as to achieve certain desired outcomes. Accordingly, it is to be expected that the principles as well as the practices of the design sciences in general and information systems in particular will differ from those of other sciences, and it was towards these issues that the 2008 workshop was directed.

Typically the information systems foundations workshops give authors an opportunity to present papers and get feedback on ideas that might be regarded as too new or risky for publication in conventional outlets. There have been some good outcomes from this approach, with revised papers going on to find a wider audience in mainstream journals. As the workshop is deliberately kept small, and there is only one stream of papers, all paper presentations are typically attended by all participants, which often leads to ongoing and vigorous discussion.

The papers presented here were accepted after a double-blind review process and we thank our program committee and reviewers for their assistance. We also acknowledge and thank the sponsors of the workshop: The National Centre for Information Systems Research (NCISR), the School of Accounting and Business Information Systems at the ANU and the Enterprise Information Infrastructure Network of the Australian Research Council.

Finally, we would like to thank the keynote speakers at the workshop – Richard Baskerville, Juhani Iivari and Alan Hevner – whose presence, expertise and participation added greatly to the value of the event for all concerned. All in all, therefore, the Workshop provided a stimulating and productive as well as an enjoyable couple of days for both the authors and attendees, and we hope that the papers that form this volume will provide similar stimulation, provoke similar productive outcomes, and perhaps provide some enjoyable reading as well, for a wider audience than those who were able to attend the Workshop itself.

Dennis Hart

Shirley Gregor

Preface

The Papers

The papers in this book are organised into four sections entitled 'Philosophical Foundations, 'Theory and Method', 'Applications' and 'Design Science in IS', reflecting the wide range of topics relating to Design Science that were addressed in the 2008 Workshop.

The philosophical foundations section contains two papers, each of which puts forward a different and challenging new perspective to the Information Systems discipline. The first, by Hovorka and Germonprez, essentially argues that service-based information systems in fact do (and should) undergo not only the usual design stage (or stages) recognized by traditional systems development methods but also potentially multiple "secondary" design phases where their users identify, through a continuous evolutionary process of interaction and innovation, initially unknown or unforseen possible services that the system can provide for them. That is, systems undergo continuous re-design by their users throughout their lives. This, the authors term an "information services view" and they argue strongly that a new, user-centred phenomenological philosophical stance focussed on understanding the interchange or "conversation" that continuously takes place between users and the technology that supports them is essential to the development of contextually relevant, flexible and adaptable information systems and services. The second paper in the philosophical foundations section, by Johnston and Smith, tackles the issue of validity in information systems research, claiming that the usual empiricist/realist notions (either explicit or implicit) that underlie most research in the discipline lead to a lack of clarity and understandability when it comes to the construct, internal and external validity of such research. They then go on to argue that if critical realism is adopted instead as the philosophical base on which information systems research is founded then these difficulties disappear and, moreover, that such an approach is more in tune with how validity issues are normally regarded and treated by researchers in actual practice anyway.

When most of us encounter the term 'theory' we tend naturally to think of something akin to theories in the natural sciences like physics or biology rather than in fields like architecture or art. Consequently Gregor, in the first paper of the theory and method section, focusses on what 'theory' and especially 'theory building' might in fact mean, as well as the principles upon which such building should be based, in a practical and design oriented discipline (and information systems in particular) that is concerned with the design and construction of artefacts for human benefit and use. In a related discussion in the second paper, Davern and Parkes, ask the rhetorical question "Which comes first, theory or artefact", not so much as to answer it one way or the other but rather to highlight, through consideration of a system development in which they were involved, that not only are theory development and artefact construction interlinked and cyclic but also that expectations from the former might be incompatible ("incommensurable") with experiences from the latter. What, they then ask, might be the implications for theory, and indeed artefact design, if this turns out to be the case?

The third paper in the theory and method section is by McKay, Marshall and Heath and, through a consideration of the concept of "design" across a number of disciplines other than information systems, argues for a broadened understanding of what design is – especially to include its non-technical, human- and socially-centred aspects, which they contend are too often downplayed or even ignored in much of current "design science" literature within IS. The last paper of the theory and method section links, interestingly enough, to the first in the philosophical foundations section in that, exemplified by experiences with an Australian Army system and viewed through a theoretical "technology appropriation cycle" lens, it argues that users' evaluation of systems evolve significantly over time, as do their choices of whether and how to appropriate various technologies available to them. Recognising this, according to the authors, means expanding our view of what design is, as well as when it occurs in the process of systems development.

In the applications section there are five papers dealing with design-related issues in a variety of settings. The first of these, by Carugati, describes the development of a system for a shipyard in Denmark and, on the basis of this experience, argues for the importance of graphically simulating the material environment of the users as an integral part of the system design and development process. The second, by Fernandez and colleagues, addresses information system design and development issues that have been highlighted through their work on a climate change "BioSolar" project, which has occurred in a multi-national, multi-disciplinary, multi-stakeholder and therefore project managerially complex context. Gao and Xu, in their paper, discuss the development of a logistics exception management system using intelligent agents from a design science perspective while Xu, Wang and Bhattacharya adopt a similar approach to the design of artificially intelligent systems. Finally, in the applications section, Wamba and Michael describe their work towards the development of a university RFID laboratory.

The final section of the book, containing two papers, concerns design science and research based upon it in the information systems discipline at large. Firstly, Arnott and Pervan present a comprehensive analysis of the role and quality of design science in decision support journal papers published over the last 16 years, using the design science research guidelines articulated by Hevner et al (2004) as their basis, and finding that there are several aspects in which significant improvement to the conduct of design science research is needed. Lastly, in the final paper of the book, Indulska and Recker undertake a very similar analysis to that of Arnott and Pervan but without limiting themselves to a subset of the discipline and taking as their sample design science related papers published in five major information systems conferences since the appearance of the Hevner et al (2004) paper. Their findings, consistent with those of Arnott and Pervan, are that much design science research in information systems is significantly lacking in methodological quality and rigour. Naturally, such a result is a cause for concern, but of course this should not be taken to indicate that design science as an approach to information systems development and as a basis for research should be called into question. Rather, it represents a challenge to the information systems research community to execute its design science research better and more rigorously, thereby not only improving the quality of the research itself but also its applicability to the practice of information systems development at which the results of that research should ultimately be directed.

Dennis Hart

Shirley Gregor

Hevner, A.R., March, S. T., Park, J., Ram, S., (2004), "Design Science in Information Systems Research", MIS Quarterly, Vol. 28, No. 1, 75-106.

Philosophical Foundations

1. Identification-interaction-innovation: a phenomenological basis for an information services view

DIRK HOVORKA
BOND UNIVERSITY

MATT GERMONPREZ
UNIVERSITY OF WISCONSIN

Abstract

In this chapter, we challenge the received view of design research in light of an information services view. We argue that, in relation to the work of Orlikowski and Iacono, an information services view describes a unique class of information systems (IS), in which users are able to identify, interact and innovate with information service systems. To better support this phenomenon, we propose a phenomenological approach to better understand participant interaction and redesign of recombinant services in the secondary design phase. We suggest four design metaphors that will shape our perception and design approach to this emerging class of cognitive- technical systems.

Introduction

As with many technical information systems advances, research in service-oriented information systems (IS) has examined individual factors and technical specifications that provide insight into a technology-oriented, practical perspective of complex socio-technical systems. This research philosophy is representative of the 'product view of design' (McKay and Marshall 2007) that has come to dominate design-science research. Hevner et al. (2004:109) succinctly summarise this approach in the claim that the goal of design-science research is 'the development and evaluation of technologies'.

In response, recent research has included development of design-science theory focused on Heideggerian environments (Germonprez et al. 2007) and interpretative epistemology in design theorising (Neihaves 2007). These approaches build on earlier conceptual research by Dourish (2001) and Winograd and Flores (1986) and this new perspective is well articulated by McKay and Marshall (2005:6), who state: 'Design researchers are not merely designing an artefact to solve or ameliorate a problem: They are also charged with conducting research into some aspect or dimension of the design activity relevant to a particular problem solving space.'

Traditional information systems could be characterised as monolithic, rigid systems with crisp input/output interfaces, static ontological commitments, fixed functions and designer-controlled coupling of system goals and operators with the world. This has led to 'brittleness in adapting systems to new purposes as practices develop and change' (Dourish 2001:131). As information systems have evolved, there has been a shift towards tailorable systems in which users can align with their own tasks, goals, use patterns and metaphors (Germonprez et al. 2007).

The *information service view* (ISV) represents a coherent view of service-oriented socio-technical systems that make up a new class of information systems. This class defines a new problem space for the creation of information environments that are mutable, loosely coupled and emergent. Meta-category views of information technologies are presented in prior research (Orlikowski and Iacono 2001:130) and provide a set of conceptualisations that 'challenge us to engage more seriously and more explicitly with the material and the information technology artefacts'. This research contributes a meta-category of service-oriented systems about which we can 'theorize about the meanings, capabilities, and uses of IT artefacts, their multiple, emergent, and dynamic properties, as well as the recursive transformations occurring in the various social worlds in which they are embedded' (Orlikowski and Iacono 2001:133). In constructing the ISV, we challenge the received view of IS design research and suggest that an interpretative epistemological stance (for example, phenomenology, hermeneutics) could be fruitful in design theorising regarding a new class of information systems.

Challenging the 'received view' of design

The emphasis on technical factors in the design of socio-technical systems has recently been criticised for neglecting the philosophical foundations of design research (McKay and Marshall 2007; Niehaves 2007). First, and perhaps foremost, the received view of design-science research is strongly positivist, with an emphasis on 'artefacts' (Hevner et al. 2004)—a 'pervasive view that design science is about "things" and the things or artefacts of interest in IS are technical systems' (McKay and Marshall 2005:2). The oft-stated goal of design research is to discover 'knowledge that allows prediction of the behavior of some aspect of the phenomenon' (Vaishnavi and Kuechler 2005) or to develop 'predictive theory about the utility (effectiveness, efficacy, etc.) of applying the technological solution' (Venable 2006:12). In addition, the accepted rationale for design evaluation is to rigorously demonstrate functional measures of utility, quality and efficacy (Hevner et al. 2004) of the artefact and reduce errors in the outcome measures.

One outcome of this rhetoric is a tendency to reify strong views of artefacts and outcome measures as concrete external structures. The rhetoric of the received view of design science contributes to the construction of facts by shaping our perception and our experiences (Brown 1976) This has the effect of reinforcing a Cartesian object–subject dualism that separates actor cognition from actor action and presents the artefact as an external object to be thought about and acted on (Introna and Whitaker 2002).

In the design-science literature, there is an emphasis on theories that 'predict or explain phenomena that occur with respect to the artefact's use (intention to use), perceived usefulness, and impact on individuals and organizations (net benefits) depending on system, service, and information quality' (Hevner et al. 2004). Our knowledge of design is based on 'an explanation of why an artefact is constructed as it is and why it works and explanations are usually regarded as a desirable part of a theory specification, assisting with their communicative purpose and the facilitation of human understanding' (Gregor and Jones 2007). Very little research has, however, examined design from the *perspective of the user* to understand how the user interacts in the secondary design phase of the system, what goals are accomplished or what meanings are created through the recombinant design.

What faces us now is the reality that many of our information systems have multiple design states, including an initial design phase and multiple secondary phases, in an evolutionary trajectory of human-system-service interactions. Current design research has not addressed secondary design phases. We are still rhetorically constrained in a goal-oriented view of IT artefacts, hoping to identify and specify successful and innovative systems that could be optimised for specific problem domains within an organisation. We model and evaluate these systems in accordance with important but limiting performance criteria that are not reflective of all current interactions.

The ISV recognises that there are, at minimum, two states of design: one state is where the service is distributed to users and another is where users discover the service, interact with the service and redesign the service system to fit their changing contexts. It is in the secondary design states that we have to consider movement away from attempting to: 1) model systems; 2) apply classic, goal-oriented outcome measures; and 3) reduce error. These three issues are invariably intertwined such that models allow us to identify outcomes in which error reduction can occur. This positivist approach to IS research—although valuable across numerous systems—breaks down in the secondary design phase. The speed with which tailorable systems and their available components are identified, interacted with and then disbanded or abandoned suggests the classic model-outcome-error approach is not well suited for design or evaluation of these systems. This research is intended to provide an alternative philosophical foundation to help researchers understand the secondary design phase and thus be better prepared to design the primary design state of these information environments.

The information services view

To define the ISV, we conducted field research at four organisations that were in the process of developing and implementing a service orientation. Our research reveals that the participants each have different conceptualisations regarding the definitions, functions and goals of IS 'services'. The field studies were used to identify what designers considered critical issues in the initial design of service-oriented systems. Initial examination of the field research data indicates that this class of technologies represents a new view of the IT artefact—the *information services view*. This research summarises different views that make up the ISV with the goal of explicating the philosophical underpinnings that will allow for better understanding of this class of information system. In addition, we are able to serve both research and practice, speaking to the respective research and practice cycles, the knowledge transfer between the two and their associated outcomes.

The class of information systems in the ISV incorporates the distinction between the initial *design* and the *ways of doing design* and requires that attention be paid to the different experiences, perceptions, intentions and goals that the user will draw on to recombine services and redesign the system. An ISV emphasises a phenomenological *potential for action* in which the user continually tailors information services to create meaning, as well as develops uses in new contexts or for new tasks (Germonprez et al. 2007). An ISV moves away from a predominant approach in systems design to over-engineer the IT artefact through a restricted set of data structures, interfaces and reporting systems, which can result in constraints on work practices. An ISV specifies that system users are function-oriented actors who envision desired goals and identify meaning and value through the action of creating and configuring recombinant information services. This suggests that designers of the initial state of service-oriented systems do not need to know how their services are going to be used, but instead should develop a reflective environment in which users' thinking, goal identification and the identification of meaning are supported. This view represents a shift in design from the provision of a fixed, designer-controlled service set to design of 'a space of potential for human concern and action' (Winograd and Flores 1986:37).

Prior research has generally conceived of services as enterprise legacy system and application integration (Lee et al. 2003), providing information (for example, about the weather) or affecting the world (for example, an e-commerce service) (Fensel and Busler 2002). In the ISV, services are defined by the function they fulfil for the user, not through prescriptive ways they are to be used. The ISV shifts the focus of services to action and recreation of meaning by the user, thereby allowing new services and functions to emerge. Table 1.1 summarises the key categories of differing views and their descriptions, in addition to specific component issues that are being addressed by practitioners at these organisations.

Table 1.1 Key category issues in the initial design of an ISV

Key category of an ISV	Description
Service identification, distribution and discovery	How services are built, managed, and discovered; how services are recombinant
Governance of services	How services are guaranteed, how services transcend business units/who pays for services; access control to services, internally and externally
Services as data	Creation and provision of meta-data; archiving of data. Commensurability and accuracy of data
Services as innovation	User-defined and structured information systems assembled from provided services for relevant domain of action

The nature of services and the continuous process of design and redesign require that we challenge the received 'product view' of design science and re-examine the philosophical foundations that will support the cognitive-interactive-technical components of emerging information service systems. The data summarised in Table 1.1 suggest the emergence of a new class of IS and require us to recognise the importance of secondary design. This suggests an 'interactionist' perspective of IS design that draws on Dourish (2001), Winograd and Flores (1986) and interpretative design epistemologies from Introna and Whittaker (2002), McKay and Marshall (2005, 2007) and Niehaves (2007). By examining the observed phenomenon of tailorable, mutable and recombinant computing practices through the interactionist perspective, we propose that design science would benefit from alternative epistemological and ontological commitments not provided in the 'received view of design science'.

It is important to note that these issues are representative of technical developers and managers involved in the initial design of an ISV, not the participants in secondary states of what a technology could become once in use. Service-oriented technologies inherently have a dual design: the primary initial design as developed and provided to users and the secondary design, where users modify the technology in the context of use (Germonprez et al. 2007). We observe, however, that innovation, recombinant services, secondary design and commensurability of data are key issues. From these initial design observations, we suggest that the unique interactions of the information services orientation are characteristic of a new class of information systems and that an *information service view* will provide a coherent framework for research and development.

In seeking an expanded philosophical foundation, we build on this approach and explore the secondary states of an ISV. In particular, we propose three philosophical foundations, based on the field study findings regarding the initial design.

Seeking an expanded philosophical foundation

Much of the recent discussions regarding the philosophies underlying design science has focused on the relative merits of positivism versus interpretativism and the need for a broader philosophical base for design (McKay and Marshall 2005, 2007; Niehaves 2007). In addition, there is argument regarding the status of design science as a new 'paradigm' (Hevner et al. 2004; Niehaves 2007) and whether design theories are necessary or even possible (Venable 2006). These discussions follow in a long line of research into design theory for specific classes of systems, anatomy of design theory and history of design (Gregor and Jones 2007; Mumford 2006; Walls et al. 1992).

These philosophical discussions in IS retain, however, one common element: the subject/object dualism of the user and artefact. Recognition of the phenomenon that users interact with their information services and technology and engage in secondary design activities in the context of use has revealed a new problem space for researchers and designers. Recent work by Germonprez at al. (2007) on tailorable technologies and Gregor and Jones (2007) on mutable systems has identified the need for an underlying design philosophy that will embrace the processes of interaction with their inherent creation and communication of meaning in the world. Many emerging services and technologies fulfil functions and are used in ways not predetermined by developers. In referring to behavioural science, Hevner et al. (2004:76) state that 'it seeks to develop and justify theories (i.e., principles and laws) that explain or predict organizational and human phenomena surrounding the analysis, design, implementation, management, and use of information systems'. We contend that users of these systems can no longer be viewed as factors in an input-process-output model but must be considered as intentional actors capable of independent action. Technology has become highly embedded in our lives and users have become secondary and tertiary designers of systems that are intended to be modified in the context of use. We have to recognise that users are an integral part of the evolving states of a technology and, furthermore, how technology is continually specified, tailored or disposed of is often outside the realm of what designers can model, predict or optimise. Explanation and prediction (Gregor 2006) have been the emphasis in prior research in design science. Rather than relying on explaining and predicting outcomes or behaviour, we suggest that *understanding* the goals, action-as-meaning and behaviours of users of this new class of IS will better enable us to create the information environments with which they are interacting. Acceptance of this distinction will require a fundamental shift in the philosophical basis for our foray into design research, away from a positivist stance to a phenomenological approach to the discovery of meaning.

This research draws from four primary sources to develop a philosophical framework—all based around the findings regarding the initial design. The hope is that this framework will support understanding the secondary design phase and will inform the designers of the primary design state. The field data summarised above suggest three practice-based areas in which the ISV differs from prior conceptualisations of systems philosophically: identification, interaction and innovation.

Fundamental shift

In many areas of IS design, there has been a call for design of adaptable technology that can react to a volatile and changing world. The design research literature has only begun to explore the participant action required to interact with this class of technology or the design of information environments that support these actions. The implications for user behaviour and outcomes and the evaluation of the emerging 'interactionist' cognitive technological systems have also received minimal research attention. The fundamental philosophical basis for this research is an interpretative stance that emphasises understanding over explanation in design research. Interpretative research is based, in part, on the idea that 'because social theories are theories of intentional objects, they pose problems for analysis which cannot be grasped merely from an understanding of theories of physical things' (Fay and Moon 1996:29). We suggest that for a researcher to gain his or her own comprehension of the observed human subjects' understanding, the researcher should adopt a phenomenological stance to 'understand participants' perspectives and views of social realities' (Introna and Whittaker 2002:57). Johann G. Droysen (1858) is credited with making the distinction between 'explanation', which is the task of natural sciences, and 'understanding', which is the task of the human sciences. Dilthey (1989:332) was instrumental in describing the distinction by defining understanding as 'the process by which mental life comes to be known through an expression of it given to the senses'. From this perspective, one 'understands the aims and purposes of an agent, the meaning of a sign or symbol and the significance of a social institution or religious rite' (von Wright 1971:6). Phenomenology was identified early in the history of IS as a means of determining 'the structures of meaning that give sense and significance to our immediate experience' (Boland 1984:194) and has been used in recent IS (Introna and Whittaker 2002; Monod and Klein 2005) and human–computer interaction (Svanaes 2001) research. By utilising the 'phenomenological reduction' to 'bracket out' the researcher's own theoretical attitudes, and by 'supposing that something has to be "real" or "concretely existing" to be experienced' (Husserl 1964:154), the researcher can come to *understand* the nexus of relationships that make up the essential, subjective meanings held by the human participants in the phenomenon that he or she is researching. This shift to understanding the experiences of the participants becomes more relevant as we recognise the actions that are occurring in the secondary design phase of tailorable services. In using semiotics to examine design, Purao (2002) states that the design researcher simultaneously arrives at an interpretation (understanding) of the phenomenon and the design of the artefact. But in the case of the secondary design phase in the ISV, the designer is the user and the user is the designer. It is the user-as-designer's experience we are seeking to understand.

This shift to a phenomenological epistemology for design research leads to incorporation of the work of Martin Heidegger (1927), who proposes that meaning is embedded in the world and it is revealed through user interaction. Suchman's (1987) work on situated action and recent writings of Dourish (2001) and Ciborra (2002) have argued that foundational philosophy adopted by computer science and IS researchers has proven inadequate when describing the ways that computers and people interact. In the majority of computer-based research, users are treated as surveyors of an external world and that meaning is constructed based on continual survey. The 'embodied interaction' perspective of Dourish (2001) and the recent literature on tailorable systems (Germonprez et.

al 2007; Mansfield 1997; Morch and Mehandjiev 2000) recognise, however, that as users interact with technology through reflection and action, users create, reveal and communicate meaning in the world.

Three important cognitive technical views of services are described below and demonstrate how epistemological commitments selected to produce understanding, rather than explanation, can avoid traditional model-outcomes-error design and instead focus on identification-interaction-innovation. It is from these new identified philosophical bases that we can support the secondary design phase. We no longer are constrained by IT as product/artefact, but instead we dissolve the user–artefact dualism to understand the secondary design phenomenon from an interactionist perspective.

Identification

The identification of services is a new design challenge for a participant that requires support in the realisation of an ISV. Discovery and identification of services and their accompanying meta-data can be accomplished through technical means in the form of directory services or portals. Detailed meta-data might be required so that users can determine the accuracy, validity and commensurability of different services. In addition, well-defined interface descriptors and documentation will permit transparent recombination of services. Identification was introduced as a critical component of contextual design—a design consideration that parallels the secondary design of tailorable technologies (Beyer and Holtzblatt 1997). Contextual design emphasises the importance of discovery and identification as precursors to system understanding. From understanding comes interaction and from interaction comes innovation and development of a system.

Furthermore, a goal of strong service identification lies in capturing services in the long tail (Anderson 2006). In the long-tail theory, services that hit a small market will remain unseen. Before an ISV, services that were determined to hit only a small segment of an organisation would remain hidden and unidentified to the whole. Interaction and innovation would occur only with services that had large organisational exposure. The long-tail theory suggests that in a market supported by emerging service-based technologies, the entire tail of all services should be explored—not merely those with the highest, predetermined potential impact. If we encourage individuals to interact and innovate in unknown and unforeseen ways, we need to open support to the entire spectrum of all available services. The entire tail of organisational services is critical in the realisation of an ISV and is critical for interaction and innovation.

Interaction

The primary focus of the concept of 'embodied interaction' is that 'embodied phenomena are those that by their very nature occur in real time and real space' (Dourish 2001:101), and that our phenomenological being-in-the-world 'is found in the world in which we act' (p. 116). Dourish integrates different phenomenological stances to argue for the importance of understanding 'not just what the system *can do*, but rather, what it *really does do* for people…what decisions people make about when and how to use the system…what sort of information it contains' (p. 133). In addition to shifting from explaining the features or form (and the accompanying performance measures) of a service system to understanding what function the system fulfils, we must also examine inter-subjective communication between participants through their action of using the services. The secondary design phase supports sharing of how 'people develop and communicate shared ways of using software systems and the ways of doing their work with software systems' (Dourish 2001:133).

From the same philosophical roots, Introna and Whittaker (2002) argue that researchers interested in participant experience should recognise that thinking or cognition is action. We are never separate from our thinking and our thinking is always situated in the world.

The concept of 'possibilities for' accompanies a phenomenological approach that means that every interaction with the system opens the horizon of possibilities for the next action. The desired state of interaction is one of *situated being-in-the-worldness* (Heidegger 1962; Introna and Whittaker 2002) and is when the artefact becomes present at hand and reflects the intentions of the user. Introna and Whittaker (2002:163) pose the following analogy regarding 'the intentional arc':

> In leaving her office to go to a meeting in another building, she does not need to make a decision to exit her office, she does not need to visualize the door, the handle, and the movements required to open it, she does not need to determine the shortest route to the door; she does not need to coordinate them in a coherent set of thoughts and actions in order to leave her office…Thus she simply gets up and walks out to the meeting.

The 'user' does not withdraw from the (inter)action to think before engaging in the action; rather the situated use of recombinant information services is the cognition. Introna and Whittaker (2002) describe recalling how to use a tool as a non-random collection of actions or 'fiddling' thereby allowing re-emergence of meaningful use. This is the same type of discovery or creation of meaning that participants in services-related systems experience as they create mash-ups, tag-clouds or access services containing user-enhanced information.

Innovation

The ISV explicitly recognises that designers and service providers cannot articulate coupling of the system to the world by defining what it is intended to do and what the consequences of use will be. Rather users will create new structural couplings in alignment with their domain of action (Winograd and Flores 1986). From these real-world problem settings we can extract the areas of concern, which represent a broad set of categories that helps define an ISV. An ISV shifts the focus of services to action and recreation of meaning by the user, thereby allowing new services and functions to emerge. Intrinsic to an ISV is the idea that 'the users and the designers do not, in fact, share the same model of the task domain' (Dourish 2001:131) and that services 'will often be used in ways that were not anticipated in their design' (Winograd and Flores 1986:53). From an information services view, the user, rather than the designer, makes decisions about the relationships among services, types and relevancy of data and outputs and what things functionally go together as representations of the real world (Hovorka 2005).

Design metaphors for the information services view

Our thinking about service-oriented information, what constitutes services, how users really perceive the recombinant actions of service use and re-creation of service configurations must be greatly strengthened by further observation. It is clear, however, that the ISV represents a new class of 'IT artefact' in relation to the classes identified by Orlikowski and Iacono (2001) and that secondary design and interaction by participants are becoming crucial elements in the way systems are used to communicate and innovate. We propose that design researchers need to frame the initial design activities of these interactionist cognitive technical systems in different rhetorical terms and with different metaphors so that we can better understand how users interact with the 'life world' offered by the service-based systems. We also believe that metaphor can play an important role for users of service-oriented systems, making them more approachable and therefore more interacted with. By this interaction, empirical testing and evaluation can emerge through which refinement to the foundations of identification, interaction and innovation can be made.

Madsen (1989) argues that metaphor can be used to perceive a situation in a new way to provoke invention of future artefacts and that metaphors from our experience are used to understand new environments. Brown (1976:172) states that 'metaphor allows each system to be perceived anew from the viewpoint of the other'. As design inherently produces new environments, the metaphors by which designers and participants understand the systems are crucial. Introna and Whittaker (2002:166), in framing IS evaluation, suggest the notion of a 'conversation, as it includes the essential elements of situated directedness and ongoing dialectical movement (to and fro) as an exemplar of cognition and action'. In the secondary design state, this is an apt metaphor for the ISV, as the user is simultaneously *acting on* and *acting with* system components, engaging, distancing and reengaging, and communicating with components, other users and service designers/providers.

This research is not at a stage where principles for design, rules or guidelines are appropriate. Rather we lay out some comments regarding the secondary design phase that occur across a range of contextual and use settings that warrant consideration in the initial design phase.

Information services as a communication medium

An interactionist perspective emphasises the coupling and creation of meaning with the world and the sharing of that meaning with other participants. On the surface level, many of the service technologies (such as Web 2.0, RSS, wikis, cloud-tags, Twitter, and so on) provide inherent communication/collaboration in direct channels with other participants. At a deeper level, however, the services must supply feedback to the participant during the exploration of re-combinatorial characteristics of the service orientation. The service system must be initially designed to communicate to the participant what it *has done* and *might do*. Note this does not include what the system *can do*, as an explanatory communication, since this would require the design of the initial state to foresee all possible future actions. As the horizon of possibilities emerges, the participant must have clear signals about how to realise the desired structural coupling. This can be done through the principles of existing tools, recognisable conventions and components and established metaphors (Germonprez et al. 2007). In addition, we need to change the rhetoric from *design* to *disseminate*. In their lived action of secondary design, users are not experiencing a formal design action that they then describe to others. Rather, they are engaged in identification of goals and interaction with the services through selection, re-creation and dissemination of the resultant innovation through the action of creation. This subtly changes the design metaphor from product design to communicative action (Habermas 1987), which opens a new domain of applicable theory.

Information services as continual re-creation

The traditional rhetoric of the received design-science view shapes the perception of 'IT' and 'service' as fixed, finished objects that can be optimised. The research goal is to design, model, service and evaluate systems/services in relation to a set of preconceived goals and operators. In this way, we can manipulate the system so that we explain the greatest variance in a specific selection of performance measures.

In contrast, the ISV and its interactionist perspective suggest that the secondary design states cannot be fully predicted, modelled or well explained. Standard organisational impact and traditional performance measures might not be the best means of evaluating services and systems. It is well recognised that systems 'will often be used in ways that were not anticipated in their design' (Winograd and Flores 1986:53). The creation of tailorable technologies, information environments and loosely coupled services are all attempts to support secondary design of services and systems so that participants do not experience breakdowns or mismatches where technologies require them to disengage from being-in-the-world. By re-creating systems in accordance with their own tasks, tools, use patterns and metaphors, participants maintain a 'skilful conversation' with the services, other participants and themselves.

Information services as evolution

The trajectory of services systems is driven by functional fit—that is, what things go together in the world (Hovorka 2005). Those services that are adaptable, mutable and that lend themselves easily to re-combinatorial process can mutate and evolve to fill functional niches for a wider, and longer, tail of participants. Unlike biological evolution, in which 'mutations' are random, information services and their supporting technologies are functionally oriented designs. Like biological evolution, the components that contribute to some goal can be inherited by future services and systems. The secondary design phase can be a powerful force for service evolution as 'it can create new ways of being that did not previously exist and a framework for action that would not previously have made sense' (Winograd and Flores 1986:177). As technologies and services proliferate, and as participants select, interact, disseminate and disengage from services, it is important to understand these processes in the larger scope of the participants' entire information life world.

Information services as interaction

The interactionist perspective invites reflective evaluation along the lines suggested by Introna and Whittaker (2002). Reflection has long been an issue surrounding systems that engage and encourage the user to look, touch and work with parts in the creation of a larger whole. From Heidegger (1927) to Winograd and Flores (1986) and Dourish (2001), researchers have considered the reflective component critical if we are to interact with and ultimately innovate on component parts. Information services adhere to this in that a single service is functional but a collection of services can be unique. To move from a single-function service to a contextually oriented, unique and innovative set of services in the production of a new information system requires knowing what a service is, what it can do and how it can be combined. In short, it requires interaction.

Conclusion

This research outlines a preliminary philosophical foundation for a new class of information systems. In doing so, we challenge the conventional design-science approach by seeking to understand, rather than explain, what participants are really doing with service-oriented systems, from the user's own perspective. We suggest that an interpretative approach, based in phenomenology, will provide insight into the meaning of the creation in which users participate when they redesign service-oriented systems in a secondary design phase. Essential in this new understanding is the change from a subject/object dualism of user–artefact to an interactionist perspective in which participants are engaged in a 'conversation' with services and technologies. By clinging to, and reifying, the subject/artefact dualism, we could continue to design and evaluate information systems via techniques that satisfy our desire to explain variance and reduce error. In doing so, however, we would fail to see the ready-at-hand engagement observed in the continual creation, consumption and disengagement of service-oriented information systems. A coherent information services view allows us to describe the creative and reflective information environments in which the user is actively involved in a continuous process of separation, reflection and re-engagement.

References

Anderson, C. 2006, *The Long Tail: Why the future of business is selling less of more*, Hyperion Publishers, New York.

Beyer, H. and Holtzblatt, K 1997, *Contextual Design: Defining customer-centered systems*, Morgan Kaufmann, San Francisco.

Boland, R. 1984, 'Phenomenology: a preferred approach to research in information systems', *Research Methods in Information Systems. Proceedings of the IFIP WG 8.2*, Manchester, pp. 193–201.

Brown, R. 1976, 'Social theory as metaphor: on the logic of discovery for the sciences of conduct', *Theory and Society*, vol. 3, pp. 169–94.

Ciborra, C. 2002, *The Labyrinths of Information*, Oxford University Press, UK.

Dilthey, W. 1989, *Introduction to the Human Sciences: An attempt to lay a foundation for the study of society and human history*, Second edition, Wayne State University Press, Detroit.

Dourish, P. 2001, *Where the Action Is: The foundations of embodied interaction*, MIT Press, Cambridge, Mass.

Droysen, J. G. 1858, 'Grundrisse der Historik', in R. Hubner (ed.), *Historik, Vorlesung über Enzyclopädie und Methodologie der Geschicht*, Munich.

Fay, B. and Moon, B. 1996, 'What would an adequate philosophy look like?', in M. Martin and L. C. McIntyre (eds), *Readings in the Philosophy of Social Science*, MIT Press, Cambridge, Mass., pp. 21–35.

Fensel, D. and Busler, C. 2002, 'The web service modeling framework WSMF', *Electronic Commerce Research and Applications*, no. 1, pp. 113–37.

Germonprez, M., Hovorka, D. and Collopy, F. 2007, 'A theory of tailorable technology design', *Journal of the Association for Information Systems*, vol. 8, no. 6, pp. 315–67.

Gregor, S. 2006, 'The nature of theory in information systems', *MIS Quarterly*, vol. 30, no. 3, pp. 611–42.

Gregor, S. and Jones, D. 2007, 'The anatomy of a design theory', *Journal of the Association for Information Systems*, vol. 8, no. 5, pp. 312–35.

Habermas, J. 1987, *The Theory of Communicative Action. Volume II: Lifeworld and system*, T. McCarthy (trans.), Beacon, Boston.

Heidegger, M. 1927, *Being and Time*, State University of New York Press, Albany.

Hevner, A., March, S. and Park, J. 2004, 'Design science research in information systems research', *MIS Quarterly*, vol. 28, no. 1, pp. 75–106.

Hovorka, D. S. 2005, 'Functional explanation in information systems', *Proceedings of the 11th Americas Conference on Information Systems*, Omaha, Nebr.

Husserl, E. 1964, *The Idea of Phenomenology*, Nijhoff, The Hague.

Introna, L. D. and Whittaker, L. 2002, 'The phenomenology of information systems evaluation: overcoming the subject object dualism', *Proceedings of IFIP WG 8.2*, Barcelona, pp. 155–75.

Lee, J., Siau, K. and Hong, S. 2003, 'Enterprise integration with ERP and EAI', *Communication of the ACM*, vol. 46, no. 2, pp. 54–60.

McKay, J. and Marshall, P. 2005, 'A review of design science in information systems', *16th Australasian Conference on Information Systems*, Sydney, pp. 1–11.

McKay, J. and Marshall, P. 2007, 'Science, design, and design science: seeking clarity to move design science forward in information systems', *18th Australasian Conference on Information Systems*, Sydney, pp. 1–11.

Madsen, K. H. 1989, 'Breakthrough by breakdown: metaphors and structured domains', in H. Klein and K. Kumar (eds), *Systems Development for Human Progress*, Elsevier Science Publishers, Amsterdam.

Mansfield, T. 1997, 'User-tailorability in a locale-based collaboration system', *Proceedings of Group '97*, Phoenix, Ariz.

Monod, E. and Klein, H. K. 2005, 'A phenomenological evaluation framework for cultural heritage interpretation: from e-HS to Heidegger's historicity', *Americas Conference on Information Systems*, pp. 2870–7.

Morch, A. and Mehandjiev, N. 2000, 'Tailoring as collaboration: the mediating role of multiple representation of application units', *Computer Supported Cooperative Work*, vol. 9, pp. 75–100.

Mumford, E. 2006, 'The story of socio-technical design: reflections on its successes, failures and potential', *Information Systems Journal*, vol. 18, pp. 317–42.

Niehaves, B. 2007, On epistemological diversity in design science—new vistas for a design-oriented IS research?, Twenty-Eighth International Conference on Information Systems, Montreal.

Orlikowski, W. and Iacono, C. 2001, 'Desperately seeking the "IT" in IT research: a call to theorizing the IT artifact', *MIS Quarterly*, vol. 12, no. 2, pp. 121–34.

Purao, S. 2002, *Design research in the technology of information systems: truth or dare*, GSU Department of CIS Working Paper, Georgia State University, Atlanta.

Suchman, L. 1987, *Plans and Situated Actions: The problem of human–machine communication*, Cambridge University Press, New York.

Svanaes, D. 2001, 'Context aware technology: a phenomenological perspective', *Human Computer Interaction*, vol. 16, pp. 379–400.

Vaishnavi, V. and Kuechler, B. 2005, Design research in information systems, viewed July 2008, <http://isworld.org/Researchdesign/drisISworld.htm>

Venable, J. R. 2006, *The Role of Theory and Theorizing in Design Science Research*, DESRIST, Claremont, Calif.

von Wright, G. H. 1971, *Explanation and Understanding*, Routledge, London.

Walls, J. G., Widmeyer, G. R. and El Sawy, O. A. 1992, 'Building an information system design theory for vigilant EIS', *Information Systems Research*, vol. 3, no. 1, pp. 36–59.

Winograd, T. and Flores, F. 1986, *Understanding Computers and Cognition: A new foundation for design*, Ablex Publishing, Norwood, NJ.

2. How critical realism clarifies validity issues in theory-testing research: analysis and case

ROBERT B. JOHNSTON
UNIVERSITY COLLEGE DUBLIN

STEPHEN P. SMITH
MONASH UNIVERSITY AND UNIVERSITY OF MELBOURNE

Abstract

Much discussion of research validity in information systems (IS) draws on the empiricist tradition, which presents an impoverished account of reality, making it difficult to formulate issues of validity that are pertinent to a practitioner-oriented discipline. This is particularly true for external validity, which refers to the applicability, or relevance, of research to phenomena in the broader environment of practices, but also for construct and internal validity, which seek to establish rigour in human-centred practical research. Discussions of validity are often supplemented with implicitly realist notions that are not compatible with the espoused empiricism. We argue that critical realism presents a number of insights that profoundly clarify a discussion of validity in practitioner-oriented theory-testing research. We reformulate the notions of theory testing and research validity from the critical realist perspective and illustrate them using a description of a controlled experiment. Important new insights are gained into establishing each kind of validity.

Introduction

Ensuring that research is valid is an enduring theme in the information systems (IS) domain, as evidenced by the large number of articles in our premier journals that focus only on that topic and the amount of column space in more conventional theory-testing articles that purports to demonstrate that the work is valid in some way. In research that comes from the 'positivist' tradition in IS—such as laboratory experiments, surveys and theory-testing case studies—discussions of research validity typically draw either implicitly or explicitly on the empiricist position of quantitative social science for their justification. Because empiricism formulates the process of research only in terms of the domain of *theory* and the domain of *empirical data* and barely admits the existence of an independent ontological domain beyond the experience of the senses that we might identify with the 'real world', discussions of validity drawing on this tradition have difficulty formulating research validity issues in a way that would be appropriate for IS, which is principally a practice-based research domain. This is particularly true for external validity, which refers to the applicability, or relevance, of research conducted in contrived or bounded research situations to phenomena in the broader environment of practices, but it is also true of construct and internal validity that seek to establish the rigour of human-centred practical research in which many important constructs are socially constructed or experiential.

As a consequence, IS researchers tend to supplement the apparatus of empiricism with realist notions that are in fact incompatible with the ontology of hard empiricism (Mingers 2004b; Smith 2006). Discussions of research design issues for the IS field are therefore often quite opaque because the theoretical bases for them are neither entirely explicit nor completely consistent philosophically. We diagnose the root cause of this difficulty in discussing validity issues to the poverty of empiricism as a framework for these discussions and the uncontrolled way in which writers on research methodology try to compensate for this poverty with naive realist notions—or else with notions from ontologically incompatible constructivist or interpretivist traditions.

In this chapter, we want to show that new clarity can be brought to the formulation of the traditional validity issues of theory-testing research in IS by explaining the fundamental principles of each issue in the language of the critical realist philosophy of Bhaskar (1975, 1993, 1998), Niiniluoto (1999), Sayer (1992), and others. Critical realism has an ontology that admits a number of useful categories with which to formulate validity issues, and additionally has an epistemology that recognises the socially constructed nature of both the socio-technical practices that are the focus of IS research and the IS practice itself. With critical realism, it is possible to distinguish between the theory to be tested and the generative mechanisms to which the theory refers as causes of the events that are observed in both the contrived and the bounded circumstances of the research study (the 'laboratory'), as well as in the broader ambient circumstance to which research questions are supposed to apply (the so-called 'real world' of practice). These new ontological categories and distinctions profoundly simplify and clarify a discussion of construct validity, internal validity and, particularly, external validity in theory-testing research. We will show this by a detailed exposition of validity issues from a critical realist position and exemplify the analysis by applying it to a real laboratory experiment conducted by the authors.

We understand that nowadays most IS researchers would reject the stronger forms of empiricism described below. Actual research practice and pedagogy provide recipes for ensuring validity, which move beyond that framework and include many of the insights that we find follow from a critical realist perspective (Mingers 2000; Smith 2006). Our point is that these extensions lack an adequate philosophical foundation as long as empiricism continues to be the framework used for their exposition. Consequently, precise analysis and justification for validity procedures cannot be given. This is especially true for external validity where empiricism provides little guidance. Our argument is that critical realism provides such a precise alternative foundation.

Our argument proceeds as follows. In the next section, we outline briefly the epistemology of empiricism. The goal here is not to present a detailed critique of those philosophies. Rather, we wish to demonstrate the poverty of this position for discussion of research validity. We then outline critical realism to identify how this position allows the problems of theory testing and research validity to be reformulated with new clarity, with that approach systematised in the following section. Building on these principles, we describe an actual controlled experiment that illustrates the theoretical analysis and explicates the steps that might be taken to ensure and justify validity according to the new critical realist formulation. We conclude with a summary of the arguments and their broader implications.

The standard empiricist view of theory testing

Inquiry in the natural and social sciences is influenced heavily by the empiricist world view, which holds that all valid knowledge is empirical and so ultimately derived from sensory experience (Hamlyn 1967; Hooker 1975). Hume's scepticism—to the effect that no knowledge can be established conclusively by reason alone (and that even belief in an external world and/or the existence of the self are not justifiable)—has been particularly influential in the development of scientific methods (Fogelin 1993) and is the foundation for the hypothetico-deductive approach that is so prevalent in the natural and social sciences (Rosenberg 1993).

Positivism is an extreme extension of empiricism that rejects all claims of knowledge except those derived empirically. In this view, because the only meaningful form of knowledge is empirical (and ultimately derived from the sensory experience that informs direct knowledge), the ultimate aim of science is to maximise empirical knowledge (Hooker 1975). In keeping with Hume's view that what we think of as a causal relationship is merely a regularity in perceptions (a constant conjunction of events), to a positivist, a statement that one event causes another is equivalent to saying that one event is always followed by another. As a result, the (highly influential) positivist view of scientific inquiry is that the proper role of theory is for predicting patterns based on objective observations (because causation cannot be proved).

Theory testing, from an empiricist standpoint, finds its ultimate expression in Popper's (1959) falsificationism, which holds that because we can never prove a theory definitively, a scientific hypothesis must be evaluated in terms of whether it is in fact false. Theory testing, in this view, means assessing observational evidence to determine whether: 1) observations are consistent with an a priori hypothesis; and 2) this correspondence is systematic and unable to be explained plausibly by chance factors alone (the null hypothesis). This model of theory testing is illustrated in Figure 2.1, which shows the relationship between the empirical and theoretical domains under that paradigm. Note that this figure shows a more nuanced view of the research process than is possible using Hume's modern empiricism and is (arguably) a reflection of the neo-empiricist view of research (see Greenwood 1990).

The shortcomings of this philosophy—particularly that it tolerates only an impoverished view of the world—have been dealt with at length (Klein and Lyytinen 1985; Kolokowski 1972; Mingers 2004b; Smith 2006; Williams 1975), so are not the focus of our discussion. For the purposes of this discussion, however, two points should be noted regarding Figure 2.1. First, on a strict reading of empiricism, only empirical and theory categories enter the empiricism paradigm. Limiting the objects of inquiry in this way implies that the objective of science is merely to gather and predict data and not to explain at any deep level the mechanism that enabled those experiences (because nothing beyond experience can be analysed validly).

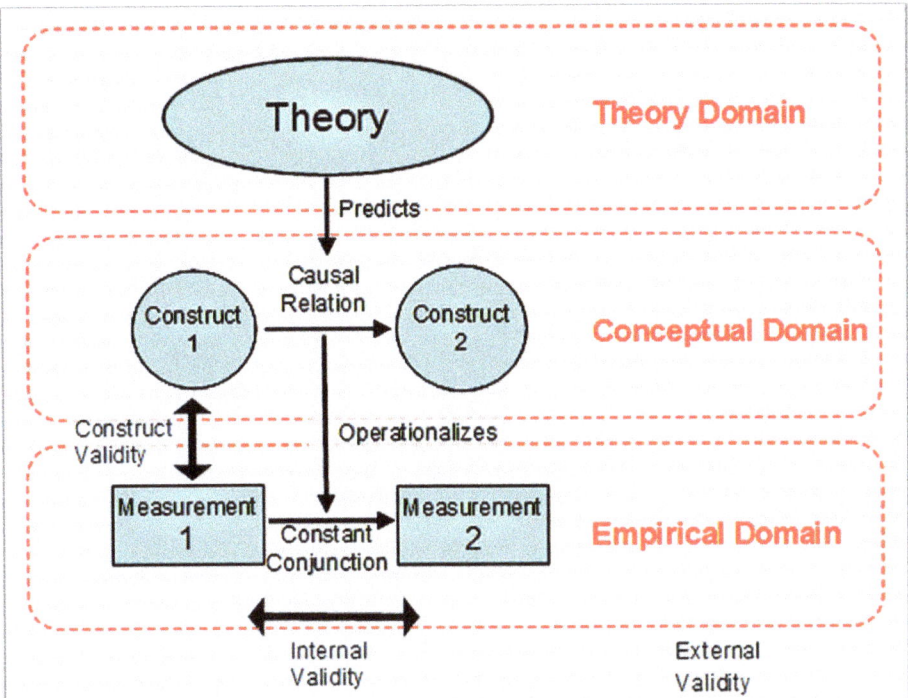

Figure 2.1 Research process and validity according to the positivist research tradition

After Neuman (2005)

Second, limiting the research focus to a comparison of experience with theory means that construct validity, internal validity and external validity must all be concerned primarily with empirical issues. The relationship between the data and the laboratory for each of these forms of validity is illustrated in Figure 2.1 and explained next.

Construct validity, for the empiricist, is concerned with the relationship between data and concepts described in theory. In that view, construct validity is established by demonstrating that parts of the measure are consistently related but distinct from other measures. Cronbach and Meehl (1955:283) (who created the term) define a construct as a 'postulated attribute of people assumed to be reflected in test performance'. To validate a construct, 'a nomological net surrounding the construct must exist' (Cronbach and Meehl 1955:291) so that the researcher can assess the strength of evidence that the label attached to a measure is an accurate description of the construct actually measured (for example, examine the correlation between the data collected and one or more variables that are believed to be related to the construct of interest). In other words, construct validity is the amount of correspondence between an unobservable concept and measurable indicators of that concept's properties.

Because the emphasis of validation is on the strength of the evidence within a nomological network, assessment of validity, in research practice, tends to stress the statistical structure of the construct (especially coherence and differentiation) while neglecting issues to do with meaning.

Internal validity is concerned with showing that there is a 'constant conjunction' between the empirical events observed as patterns. For an experiment, this means demonstrating that the constructed environment forms a closed system by virtue of the experimental controls. To the extent that closure can be demonstrated, the observed event sequences can be attributed to the research intervention because alternative explanations will be untenable.

External validity is whether the researcher can 'infer that the presumed causal relationship can be generalized to and across alternate measures of the cause and effect and across different types of persons, settings, and times' (Cook and Campbell 1979:37). Applying a pattern or rule to settings beyond those that have been observed is problematic from an empiricist perspective, however, because the reasoning process required (applying observations to unobserved phenomena) violates fundamental principles of empiricism. Specifically, empiricism requires the assumptions of any model to have been tested empirically before being included in that model. Constructing any argument about the validity of assumptions outside the specific data set examined (or other known data sets) ultimately requires, however, the use of inductive reasoning—a form of analysis that empiricism regards as invalid because the validity of inductively derived assertions cannot be tested directly through observation.

The limitations of the empirically centred conception of validity are reflected in the obscurity of discussion of this issue in positivist-oriented IS literature. For example, Lee and Baskerville's (2003) lengthy discussion about non-statistical forms of generalisability essentially proposes pragmatic work-arounds to some of the more serious validity constraints that a strict empiricist approach imposes on a practice-focused discipline (also see various critiques on validity-related issues in research: Boudreau et al. 2001; Klein and Lyytinen 1985). From these discussions and the standard definitions of validity terms presented above, it is clear that construct validity is problematic in IS research because many constructs we would like to measure have socially constructed or experiential aspects, and there is no way to assess the correspondence between a measure and a behaviour or other observable phenomenon. Moreover, in circumstances in which it is possible to observe an outcome (for example, technology use), because of the close relationship between data, measures and constructs, empiricists tend to conflate a trait with the test for that trait, resulting in theoretical properties of a construct being defined (at least partially) in terms of data values (Bunge 2006).

Internal validity is relatively straightforward to achieve in experimental studies. In a practice-oriented research field, however, it is highly problematic for many research methods, including theory-driven surveys, case studies and action research. In non-manipulative research, the only evidence of constant conjunction is the rather weak similarity between observed and predicted association, which provides little reason to believe that one variable is causally related to the other. Because the environment is not a closed system, demonstrating internal validity, in these cases, really requires additional evidence that the observation is not a chance association—for example, via time series data.

The epistemological status of external validity is problematic for researchers in a practice-focused discipline such as IS. Because our focus is on informing practice, we typically collect data about events in order to build theories and make recommendations that are potentially of assistance to practitioners. A limited set of environments is available to us in any given project, of course, but lessons drawn from the data are rarely restricted to just what was observed. Indeed, an important test of the success of any theory is whether it is useful for solving related (but non-identical) technology-related problems or assisting with managing resources in other (unobserved) environments. Empiricism falls short, because it does not really allow for the type of reasoning required to make the generalisations about the applicability of assumptions to unobserved objects that is required for a researcher to claim external validity (Lucas 2003).

Studies of the actual methods used by researchers in mathematics, IS and other disciplines indicate widespread departures from strict empiricist requirements, creating an implicit tension between 'ideal' and actual practice (see Bealer 1992; Maddy 1992; Smith 2006). In IS research in particular, these differences indicate that IS researchers already view aspects of the research process in transcendental realist terms (Mingers 2004b; Smith 2006), so critical realism could be a more accurate formulation of what researchers really believe and practice. We argue that conceptualising validity only in terms of the relationship between theory and observation has led to a great deal of confusion about validity issues in IS research—particularly external validity—because IS researchers tacitly deviate from the espoused empiricist tradition in realist directions (Smith 2006), so are unable to explain some research practices in strict empiricist terms. The more sophisticated realist position we expound in the next section illuminates this issue and provides a set of conceptual tools that helps address many of the problems that IS researchers have trouble dealing clearly with from the espoused empiricist position. In addition, by reformulating validity using a sophisticated realist philosophy, we are able to demonstrate that validity is not primarily an empirical issue.

Brief outline of critical realism

Bhaskar's (1993, 1998) philosophy of critical realism—as its name suggests—is a realist philosophy, which is to say that it claims that a world outside and independent of our conscious perception exists (reality) and that only some aspects of this world are objectively knowable via our senses. Our senses are not always completely reliable, of course—for example, we can be fooled by illusions and we can misinterpret sense data. Nevertheless, because reality is independent of our senses, when we misperceive an event, the occurrence and properties of that event are independent of our perception and understanding and the cause of the event operates even if we are not aware of its operation.

Bhaskar (1975) distinguishes between transitive and intransitive objects of knowledge in the world. Intransitive objects are the 'real things and structures, mechanisms and processes, events and possibilities of the world; and for the most part they are quite independent of us' (Bhaskar 1975:22). That is, the existence of an intransitive object does not depend on our knowledge or perception of it. Transitive objects, on the other hand, include theories, paradigms, models and methods. These objects are subjective and their existence is dependent on human activity (if people suddenly ceased to exist, transitive objects would cease to exist).

These distinctions between what happens and what we perceive and between an event and the underlying (but possibly unobservable) mechanism that caused that event are the key aspects of critical realism that we will explore here. In the language of critical realism, they form three views on reality: the real domain, the actual domain and the empirical domain. The actual domain is the easiest to describe. This is the domain of events: someone forms an intention to sell shirts via an Internet-based store, a consumer visits that store, and so on.

The empirical domain—an anthropocentric concept—is what people can experience. Things in the actual world, such as events, cannot be perceived, but events leave empirical traces, and we can perceive those traces. That is, the sensing of an event is not the same as the event (which can occur regardless of whether we can sense it). In addition, limitations on our senses mean that we might not perceive all traces (that is, of the things in the empirical domain that we can experience, we will experience only a subset), and the subjective and perspective nature of perception means that experiences will vary from one person to another and from one setting to another.

Behind events are structures and generative mechanisms that have enduring properties. In non-technical terms, a generative mechanism is the causal power that gives rise to something or the reason that something *is*. Bhaskar (1993) refers to generative mechanisms as *alethic truths*—the underlying processes that give rise to both actual and empirical events and the phenomena that scientists seek to identify. Explaining this concept, Groff (2000:411) writes, 'To be the alethic truth (y) of x is to be the causal structure, or generative mechanism, that gives rise to x'. The hierarchy of ontological categories, then, is that enduring generative mechanisms and structures are part of the overarching category of the real. These mechanisms and structures instantiate actual events (and non-events), which leave empirical traces that can be observed or otherwise experienced. Therefore, mechanisms, events and experiences are all real. Events and experiences are also actual (because they are instantiations of the generative mechanisms). Finally, experiences are obtained via empirical traces of actual things, so experiences are also empirical. The nested relationship between these three domains of the real—representing the stratified ontology of critical realism—is illustrated in Figure 2.2, derived from Mingers (2004b:94, Figure 1).

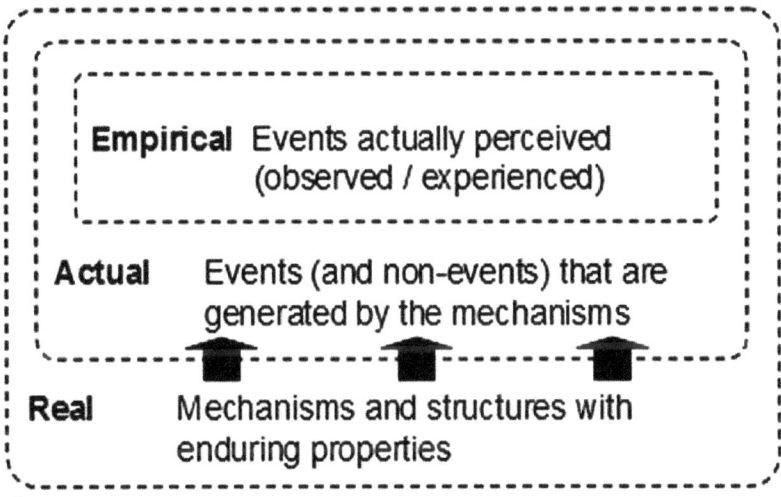

Figure 2.2 The three domains of the real (stratified ontology of critical realism)

After Mingers (2004b:94)

From the critical realist perspective, understanding the real domain is the proper role of science. To develop theory, from this perspective, is to explain *why*, but from a transcendental perspective. That is, the focus is not usually on the specific event observed, but on what that event tells us about enduring underlying causal relationships (generative mechanisms) that lie beyond common experience (the empirical domain). Scientific investigation, in this view, involves manipulation of the environment to trigger or manipulate the operation of a generative mechanism in order to produce particular actualised outcomes. For example, a researcher could manipulate the environment surrounding a particular class of decision process to answer the questions why someone would want to buy a shirt online and what makes a shopper select one online vendor in preference to another. Further, because critical realism distinguishes between the cause, the event and data about that event, any causal explanation must explain patterns of events independently of any particular event or data about that event. In the language of critical realism, these causal forces are known as generative mechanisms.

Having covered the essential characteristics of generative mechanisms (and other real entities), it should be noted at this point that empiricists hold that causality is a relation between two events, but explain why particular events are related though dispositions held by objects (a trait exhibited only when certain conditions that obtain or realise that property occur). A standard example is that a wine glass is fragile, but this property is not realised ordinarily, only when an enabling circumstance occurs, such as when the glass is dropped (Singer 1954). So the empiricist's idea of a disposition is a bit like a generative mechanism. Because all relationships between events are disposition based, there is, however, no conceptual terminology available to an empiricist to distinguish between a test for an event and properties of that event, leading to an almost inevitable conflation of a trait with the test for that trait—for example, saying that a property of an acid is that it turns blue litmus paper red (Bunge 2006:244).

With this background, we can now see how this philosophical orientation applies to objects of knowledge in the natural sciences, in which an event and empirical traces of that event can be explained and predicted by a generative mechanism. The proper job of the natural scientist, according to Bhaskar, is to attempt systematically to identify the entities responsible for an event and to describe the generative mechanism. He argues (Bhaskar 1975:195–6) that these principles also apply to the social sciences, in which the objects of inquiry are socially constructed entities, such as social structures (Durkheim's major work *Suicide* [1897] is cited as an exemplar for the social sciences), but also that the transitive nature of the structures examined in the social sciences (compared with the intransitive structures examined in the natural sciences) creates a number of ontological and epistemological issues. For example, ontologically, social structures do not exist independently of their effects, are localised in time and space and hold only for particular contexts—and epistemologically, social science is self-referential in the sense that, like the phenomena studied, it is itself a social practice (Mingers 2004a). Bhaskar argues, however, that these structures nevertheless exist independently of the researcher and the research activity and it is in that sense that the real, actual and empirical domains can still be examined. Furthermore, the fact that the structures are dependent on humans does not make them unreal or any less worthy of study. For example, languages are clearly transitive, but we also know that they are separate from the people who use them. Their structures, changes in them and even their very existence are types of events that must have been produced by generative mechanisms. The job of the social scientist is also therefore to explain the structures, objects and generative mechanisms.

Implications of critical realism for theory testing in IS

The threefold stratified 'naturalist' ontology just presented differs substantially from positivism and interpretivism—the dominant espoused research paradigms in the IS discipline (Smith 2006)—but also offers profound insight into the nature of the research activities we, as a practice-oriented discipline, undertake. We will now describe principles of critical realism in the context of IS research, and with reference to Figure 2.3, and show how these principles assist our understanding of validity issues in research. A description of how these principles were applied in a particular research project follows and is summarised in Table 2.1.

First, critical realism distinguishes between theory and the generative mechanism that the theory describes. Both theories and the generative mechanisms that they describe are real. Theories are transitive and are located in the social practice of science. Generative mechanisms are intransitive and located in the domain to which the theory applies, which in turn can be partly natural and partly social. The distinction between a theory and the generative mechanism to which it refers is, however, the key to understanding how the implications of critical realism for theory testing and validity differ from those of empiricism.

Strictly speaking, IS has few, if any, theories that can be said to truly describe a generative mechanism (at least, there is nothing comparable with widely applicable theories in the natural sciences, such as Einstein's theory of relativity). Most theories, instead, describe regularities between research entities located within the *actual* domain. For example, many pre-existing theories have been used to explain the phenomenon of technology adoption (including diffusion theory [Rogers 1995], the theory of planned behaviour [Ajzen 1991], and so on), while others have been developed specifically for that purpose (including the Technology Acceptance Model [Davis 1989] and its variants). These theories have particular built-in assumptions, apply from particular perspectives (for example, end-user, developer, manager) or apply under particular circumstances (for example, voluntary versus mandatory use), so are intended to explain *particular* instances of the phenomenon, rather than all possible occurrences.

Information Systems Foundations: The Role of Design Science

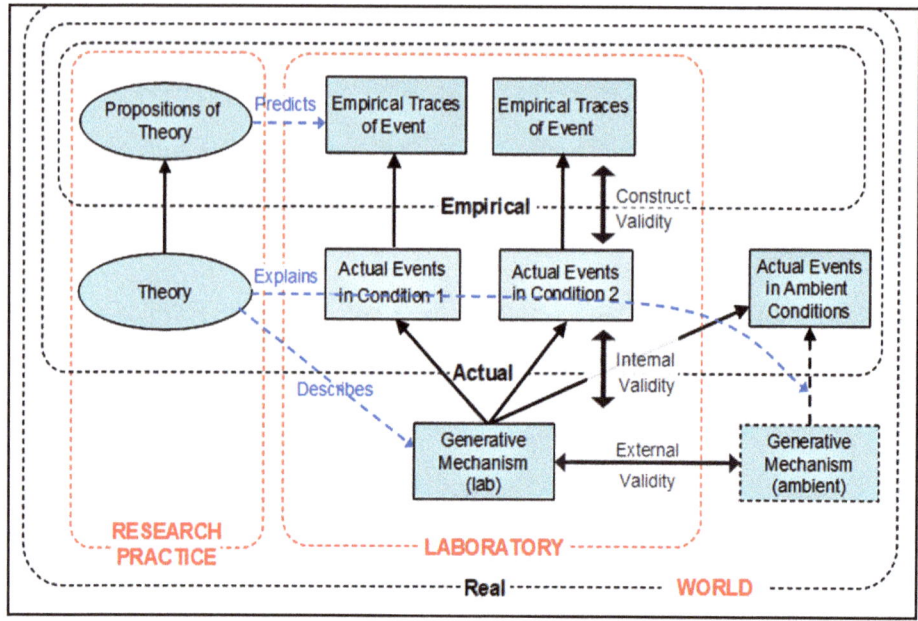

Figure 2.3 **Research process and validity interpreted according to critical realism**

This leads to the second principle: that critical realism distinguishes the actual consequences of the generative mechanism in specific circumstances from the generative mechanism itself (because, as shown in Figure 2.2, the actual is an instantiation of the mechanism in the real). So an actual consequence—say, user acceptance in a particular situation (employment or personal use)—is different from the generative mechanism underlying that outcome.

The third principle is that critical realism distinguishes between an actual instance (what happened) and empirical traces of the actual (our perception of what happened). For example, voluntary acceptance by a user of a personal organiser is distinct from the empirical traces via which we can obtain knowledge of that process (measures of ease of use, usefulness, intention, and so on).

Theory testing, in this view (and principle four), is concerned with showing that the generative mechanism explains phenomena observed in the problem domain (which is broader than explaining the empirical). In critical realism terms, this can be stated more specifically: theory testing means showing that the generative mechanism that the theory describes produces the actual events that constitute the research domain to which the theory applies (see Figures 2.2 and 2.3). For example, in the *user acceptance of IT* domain, we as researchers would like to explain the generative mechanism responsible for phenomena in the user acceptance domain, so explain all possible instantiations of that mechanism, which can be experienced via empirical traces. In other words, theory testing is concerned with systematically connecting the posited generative mechanism to the set of possible actual events in the domain of interest. The approximate equivalent in physics is that the task of a theory of relativity is primarily to explain that a certain conception of gravity explains the planetary orbits, not the position of the points of light we see in the sky (although it does that too). The empirical—observations of the celestial positions of the planets—is how we gain access to the actual orbits. In contrast with the empiricist position, however, critical realism asserts that this access to the actual is not entirely via the senses but also via theory (which is a significant point in the later section when we discuss construct validity). This focus on explaining the actual (the relationship between a generative mechanism and an actual instantiation) is radically distinct from hard empiricism in which it is merely the empirical that needs to be explained, and it is largely for this reason that critical realism views empiricism as an impoverished research philosophy.

Table 2.1 Principles of critical realism for discussing research validity

Principle 1	Critical realism allows a distinction between a theory and the generative mechanisms (causal influences) that the theory describes
Principle 2	Critical realism allows a distinction between generative mechanisms and the particular events that they cause in particular circumstances
Principle 3	Critical realism allows a distinction between the actual events we would like to explain and the empirical traces of these events that we can observe
Principle 4	Under critical realism, theory testing is showing that the generative mechanism that the theory describes produces the actual events that constitute the research domain to which the theory applies

Implications of critical realism for validity

The research approaches implied by the threefold stratified ontology therefore differ in important ways from those considered valid under the empiricist view of the world. Moreover, because the focus of the research becomes the generative mechanism underlying events (rather than the observations of the events), to some extent at least, concepts of validity in research are turned on their head compared with the empiricist's view. For an empiricist, *construct validity* refers to the correspondence between observations and the theoretical construct, whereas for a critical realist, construct validity is concerned with whether empirical traces give information about the actual events occurring in the laboratory that are purportedly caused by the generative mechanism (that is, whether the observations are a manifestation of the actual phenomenon of interest). Internal validity for the empiricist refers to whether observed changes can be attributed to the research intervention rather than other possible influences (primarily by excluding or measuring the effect of other factors that might produce the effect examined). For the critical realist, on the other hand, internal validity is concerned with establishing that the generative mechanism is the cause of the actual events observed in the study or laboratory. Finally, although for the empiricist external validity is a contentious concept, it is nevertheless generally conceptualised as the extent to which the relationships found in the data can be generalised to other types of people, settings and times (that is, generalised from specific observations to events in other situations). From a critical realist perspective, such a conceptualisation is bogus, because it conflates the empirical traces with the event and the event with the mechanism. The critical realist view of external validity, therefore, is that it represents the likelihood that the generative mechanism that caused the actual events in the laboratory also causes the events that occur more widely in the problem domain (within the broad research boundary). These distinctions are summarised in Table 2.2.

Table 2.2 Concepts of validity in empiricism and critical realism

	Empiricism	Critical realism
Construct validity	Whether the measure is consistent with the theoretical description of the construct.	Whether data that are empirically available give valid knowledge about the actual manifestation of the purported generative mechanism in the laboratory.
Internal validity	Whether observed changes can be attributed to the research intervention rather than other possible influences.	Whether actual events are manifestations of the particular generative mechanism in the laboratory circumstance.
External validity	Whether the researcher can infer that the presumed causal relationship generalises to and across alternative measures of the cause and effect and across different types of people, settings and times.	The likelihood that similar or related events that occur (or might occur) in other settings are caused by the generative mechanism that caused the actual events in the laboratory.

The overall objective of assessing these three forms of validity for the critical realist is to establish the extent to which the generative mechanism can be said to cause the actual events in the problem domain, with each form of validity operating in a different space within the three domains of the real. Construct validity establishes that the data (which are all that we have direct sensory access to) that are empirically available give valid knowledge about the actual manifestation of the purported real generative mechanism in the laboratory. Internal validity establishes that these actual events are a manifestation of the particular generative mechanism under laboratory circumstances. Finally, external validity establishes that actual events in the broader research boundary can be accurately predicted from the proposed generative mechanism. Note that these issues can also be extended to research approaches that are not laboratory based (such as a survey, field experiment or positivist case study) by interpreting the term 'laboratory' to mean the bounded and (semi-)controlled domain of empirical data collection.

It is also worth noting the new clarity that this formulation gives to external validity. In this view, forming hypotheses to be empirically tested is merely a stratagem for manifesting the purported generative mechanism in the controlled environments of the laboratory. But the task of showing that this generative mechanism also explains the actual events in the broader research domain (often incorrectly referred to as the 'real world') is no longer concerned primarily with the limited empirical traces of these actual events as they might manifest in that broader domain, but rather with showing that the broad phenomena to be explained by the research are actually explained by the same mechanism that were invoked in a contrived and controlled way in the laboratory.

Case illustration of application of validity principles

To exemplify how the application of critical realism principles can strengthen IS research, we refer to a study carried out by the authors (Smith et al. 2008) on consumer responses to product evaluation support technologies. This discussion of the research adopts a critical realist perspective. Using that study as a reference point, we illustrate the methods that might in fact be required to establish validity under this new view.

Overview of study

The specific problem analysed in the study was the impact on the product evaluation phase of a purchase transaction of a class of consumer-oriented software tools, called Virtual Model technology, with which a consumer could build a virtual self and then change the appearance of that self in a virtual dressing room (for example, change their hairstyle or try on virtual shirts, jeans, sunglasses and other wearable items). Consumer responses to different implementations of this concept were compared with responses to the more traditional catalogue-style interface to answer the specific question of whether customers who used a virtual model interface while evaluating felt more informed and whether feeling informed about a product led to a more positive attitude towards the online store.

In posing that question, we asked implicitly whether providing increasingly sophisticated technology was the best way to deliver effective customer support online, arguing that the technological determinism assumed by that development approach was untenable. Based on established theories from the consumer decision-making literature, we predicted that how a consumer perceived the product being evaluated (the object of the task) would cause that person to actively seek different information. In other words, we predicted that the outcome of the evaluation task would be determined by the *fit* between the type of information provided and the type of information sought by the consumer, rather than the fit between the technology and the task (as task-based theories commonly cited in the IS literature would suggest, including cognitive fit [Vessey and Galletta 1991] and the Task-Technology Fit model [Goodhue and Thompson 1995]).

The investigation of these ideas was operationalised via a controlled experiment in which participants assessed products online using either a basic catalogue or a description supplemented with a virtual model display. Unrelated systems at two live e-stores were used in the experiment and responses were collected from evaluations of four separate products. Verbal responses throughout each evaluation were recorded, providing rich accounts of attitudes and thoughts, and each participant also completed a survey to provide quantitative data about the experience.

Critical realism perspective of research

Using this brief description of the research method and aims, we are now able to illustrate the application of our argument to this research situation and to discuss how validity as conceived from the critical realist conception can be achieved through research design in practice. The explanation in the paragraphs following mirrors the content of Figure 2.4.

In the centre bottom of Figure 2.4, we show two entities: 1) the informational affordance of the web store (its potential to provide information of a certain kind); and 2) the information-seeking attitude of the user (which, we argue, determines the information they will find useful). Because, from a critical realist perspective, information is real (Mingers 2004b), the informational affordance of the web store is an intransitive real thing. It is, however, a potential that is actualised only in a certain circumstance—namely, when it is encountered by a user seeking that type of information. On the other hand, the information-seeking attitude of the user is entirely subjective, so would be classified as a transitive entity. Despite this, it would be viewed as real by critical realism because it has the potential to cause empirically observable effects (clicking the 'order' button, for example). The information affordance of the web site and the user attitude are not, however, actual in themselves because they do not actually produce a specific effect until certain circumstances obtain—namely, that the end-user with a particular attitude to the product encounters the web-store display that provides information relevant to that attitude. Consequently, these two entities are part of the generative mechanism that produces the actual effects that we predict will be empirically observed in the laboratory and occur more widely in the broader research domain (online apparel shopping).

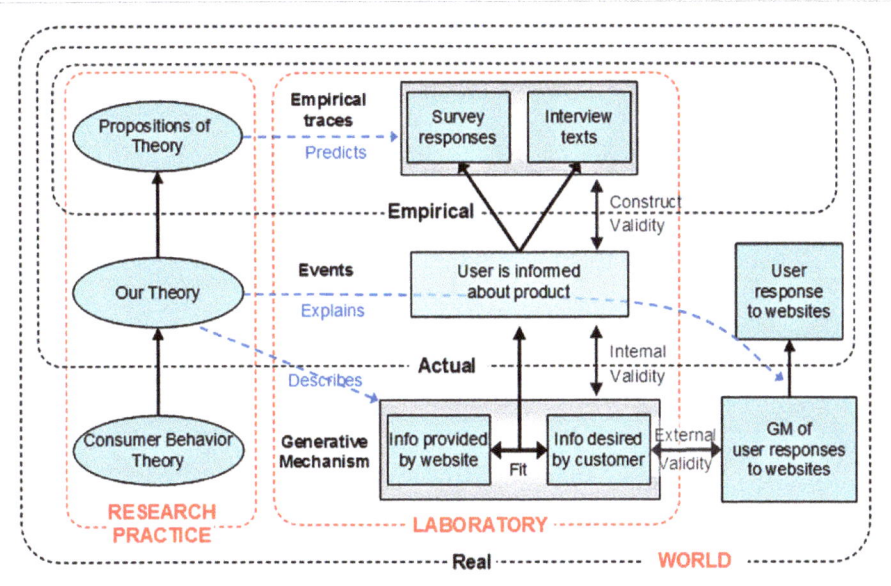

Figure 2.4 Research constructs and validity for the research example in Smith et al. (2008)

At least, this is what the theory that we developed and that we are testing proposes, and that theory itself is an actual instantiation of more general theories in the domain of consumer behaviour research. This theory domain is real because it has observable effects, such as the production of our previous research papers. It is a real domain of human practice and thus transitive. Critical realism, however, distinguishes between our actual theory and the generative mechanism to which it refers, the actual effects of that generative mechanism in particular circumstances (the user's experiences) and empirical traces of these events observed in the controlled situation (the questionnaire responses and taped oral responses of the experimental subjects).

According to our argument, the objective of testing our theory is to collect evidence that the generative mechanism to which the theory refers explains the events that occur in the broader domain to which our theory applies—namely, online apparel shopping. The research stratagem that our experiment employs is to make predictions about the nature of the empirical traces that should be observed of events that occur in rather controlled circumstances to carefully selected potential customers under careful manipulation of the web sites they encounter. We make these predictions by a process of logical deduction about how our purported generative mechanism will actualise itself under the conditions in the laboratory (hypothesis generation) and how we would expect the empirical traces of these events to be observed (operationalisation). Finally, we seek to design the experimental situation so that the conclusions we draw from comparing the empirical traces produced in the experiment with those predicted from our theory validly allow us to have confidence that the mechanism that produced this agreement in the controlled situation also *explains* phenomena that regularly occur in the broader domain of the research, and thus to answer the research question 'Under what circumstances, and why, would providing Virtual-Model technology to consumers lead them to use an e-store?'

Exemplifying the validity issues

A critical realist perspective of our research question is that a specific type of event—a customer having an experience with a product information display in the field—arises from the putative mechanism described in our theory. Observing this event and explaining the underlying causal mechanism is the point of the research. To do so, however, we need to ensure that requisite conditions for triggering that event are present and also that we can disambiguate the trigger and event from other parts of the environment. To evaluate this problem, therefore, we perform an experiment that (in idealised form) proceeds as follows

- we take two information resources that provide different types of information
- we take two groups of users who each seek one of the two types of information
- we show them each type of information
- we ask each person to use that information to evaluate a product as though considering buying that item
- we collect (self-reported) answers to predefined questions from each person that are designed to reveal whether the event of interest occurred.

It is important to note that testing hypotheses is *not* the main point of the exercise, but rather to observe what events occur and determine why. In addition, having a priori theory is also not critical except that, in experimental research, it is hard to ensure that the environment will trigger the event of interest or to observe the event and triggering conditions without a strong theoretical base. For example, we could record observations about an event and later find it is predicted by a theory (or even develop the theory). That approach is not as definitive as predicting something new and then observing it (hypothesis testing), but is quite common in the physical sciences (including geology, evolutionary biology and cosmology). Regardless of the point at which theory is developed, being able to make any claims about the operation of the generative mechanism requires addressing validity issues, particularly ones concerning construct validity, internal validity and external validity. These will now be discussed.

Construct validity

In the terminology of critical realism, construct validity is an assessment of whether the partial and perspectival empirical data collected under research conditions are empirical traces of the actual events of research interest that operate below the empirical surface. Both the empirical data and the actual events are considered real. In contrast, under strict empiricism, construct validity describes the connection between the empirical data collected (the measure) and the theoretical conception of the construct. When the actual events occur in the natural world (for instance, inventory is moved from one place to another), relating empirical traces to actual events is a rather straightforward problem of physical measurement. Many of the events we wish to observe in IS research are, however, either social constructions of the relevant communities of practitioners (such as agile software development practices [Meso and Jain 2006]) or experiences of individual people (such as 'feeling informed', in our case). In both these cases, critical realism still holds that the events are real but that now they are in the transitive domain of the social. In the first case, we need to establish that what we measure corresponds with actual occurrences within the community of practice that produces and uses the social construction, and in the second case that what we measure gives an indication of a certain mental state within a particular person (subject), which we consensually agree to be a certain experience. Consequently, establishing construct validity in these cases will require establishing a valid connection between what can be observed empirically (say, an answer to an interview question) and what some community agrees (consensually) to be the actual event, occurrence or experience. The community might be practitioners, consumers, the general public or researchers, depending on the nature of the event being measured.

The key difference in this formulation of construct validity from that under empiricism is that here empirical traces are related to real events (perhaps socially constructed or experiential events) rather than to theoretical ideas. An important insight is that since the domain of actual events is under-specified by their empirical traces, construct validity cannot be established simply by statistical analysis of the empirical traces themselves. Other procedures must be employed to demonstrate the connection of what is measured to what is occurring in the separate ontological domain of the actual—that is, to uncover the meaning of the data for actual events.

For the specific case we are examining here, we want a measure of how informed someone feels about an item after examining relevant product information, but we also want to ensure that we gather data that help us to assess the meaning of that measure—did we measure the right thing? We performed standard construct validation procedures on all experiential measures used in the survey by asking surrogate consumers to group rate and group propose questions in relation to the experience the question purported to measure. That created a line of evidence that when a certain empirical trace (a certain answer to a question) was observed, the underlying event had been experienced by the subject. We also asked the subject to talk aloud about what was experienced when a given product representation was viewed. This provided a second and independent empirical trace (speech, language) of the actual experience of the subject—albeit one with its own validity issues that were of a largely hermeneutic nature and that were addressed with standard content analysis techniques.

Internal validity

Internal validity means establishing that the actual events that occur in the controlled domain are caused by the generative mechanism that the theory proposes. That is, internal validity is established through: 1) explanation of the mechanism; 2) confirmation that the mechanism has operated as described; and 3) elimination of alternative explanations (for example, experiment procedures and measures that point to other possible causal mechanisms). In other words, testing is explanation. Testing can involve prediction, but not necessarily—particularly if the objective is historical analysis. It is worth noting that under this revised conceptualisation of internal validity, theory testing can employ a strategy similar to the hypothetico-deductive method, but the chain of logic does not have to be from theory to data to be valid; rather, provided the generative mechanism can be explained, assessment might in fact be validly driven by data. It is common in formal research practice to seek explanations from data in this way even when controlled experiments are performed, but because of the influence of empiricism in IS, research is usually written up as though hypotheses were derived from theory before observations. This is because empiricism requires prediction to precede observation to eliminate the possibility that the regularities observed in data might be spurious. In critical realism, identification of a consistent generative mechanism can provide an alternative guarantee.

In terms of our case, a defensible association between the event observed and the causal mechanism must be given to demonstrate internal validity. The generative mechanism we proposed was the fit between the information provided by a given style of product representation and the type of information the subject was seeking given their attitude to the product. The events we observed (as indicated by both the patterns of answering the survey questions and the verbal description of the subjects' own experiences) were shown to be consistent with the operation of this generative mechanism at least in a well-defined statistical sense. Indeed, the patterns of survey answers were predicted ahead of time and triangulated by the self-reporting data. We still, of course, need to eliminate explanations involving alternative generative mechanisms (for example, controlling treatment order, eliminating brand-recognition bias, recruiting consumers who have not used the systems previously, and so on). Because the aim is to explain the actual, if, however, we observe the result that we predicted, we also need to establish whether it occurred as a result of the mechanism described.

Bear in mind, however, that in critical realism terms, the manipulations are at the empirical level. Manipulations, therefore, are not the actual variables that are involved in the dynamics of the generative mechanism; they merely instantiate the initial conditions required for the generative mechanism to play out its dynamics. If the conditions are set in one way, these dynamics should lead to the consumer feeling informed. Set another way, they will lead to a different feeling (perhaps indifference). Further, the real entity that is the concern of the study—*information affordance*—is not directly observable through the real, but can be manipulated by changing the web interface viewed. This is why part of the task of demonstrating internal validity must be to show that the manipulation controls the variable: in our case, that to present the virtual model is, in fact, to make available a certain kind of informational affordance.

External validity

External validity means establishing that the generative mechanism that explains events in the 'laboratory' is also the generative mechanism that causes the actual phenomena of the broader domain of practice about which research questions are usually formulated. This means the researcher must establish that the event assessed (experimental treatment) invokes the same generative mechanism that operates in the ambient situation.

To achieve this goal, both the treatments and people (and other parts of the laboratory environment) should be good surrogates for the real-world phenomenon that we are claiming to investigate. This is the key to external validity—a point that seems to be missed often by researchers in our discipline, which accounts for many of the ultimately irrelevant studies that have been published that are *internally* valid but not *externally* valid and which is the motivation behind some extended discourses on this problem, including Lee and Baskerville (2003) and Seddon and Scheepers (2006).

In the context of our case, external validity means creating a controlled situation that invokes the same generative mechanism that is found in the real world. For example, given the choice between developing technologies ourselves and using live web sites, external validity considerations suggest building treatments around live sites (if we developed our own, we would not be sure that responses were governed by the same mechanism). Other considerations include whether the products examined are representative of the products that are available online (again, the use of live stores addresses this issue), whether the laboratory task itself is representative and whether the people are representative of the general population of Internet shoppers who could be subject to the generative mechanism of interest. This last point is crucial. Because our research is human centred, we must ensure that the humans involved are close surrogates for the users of the technology under study, otherwise the effect of the generative mechanism might not be the same. Therefore, recruitment (and screening) procedures are vital, as are more subtle population-related issues, such as ensuring that each participant evaluates only products that are personally relevant (for example, people who do not wear prescription eyewear should not evaluate eyeglass frames, only people who actually wear jeans should evaluate jeans, and so on) and the motivation of the participants during the study (many experiments involving decision making have no real consequences for the decisions taken, which is very different from the real world).

The point of reference in these considerations is that, conceptually, the environment that we create for the purposes of the experiment is a controlled form of the world, in terms not just of populations, but of the causal mechanisms that are at work at any given time. We therefore must ensure correspondence between what is done in the laboratory world with what is done outside it, in terms of both the population involved and the tasks performed. By ignoring underlying causal mechanisms, empiricism tends to direct attention to the former at the expense of the latter.

Final discussion

Overall, therefore, if we can establish these three types of validity, we can be said to have tested theory, which is to show that we assessed the operation of the generative mechanism described in our theory and can therefore explain the operation of that mechanism in situations outside the specific (laboratory) setting of the study. Theory testing, in this view, differs markedly from requirements informed by empiricism. In that view, we would need to show that: 1) the treatment design operationalises the theoretical construct—*the information affordance of the resource*; 2) the *information-seeking attitude of the user* varies independently of the treatment design (there is no demand effect); and 3) the measure operationalises the *feeling informed* construct. We would then need to show that our design had excluded potential confounds (internal validity) and the presence of a statistically significant association between the manipulations and the outcomes (in the manner predicted). Ironically, the actual event of being informed (the focus of the study) does not enter into this prescription. Moreover, it cannot enter into our considerations because it is not observable and is thus not an empirical entity. But, more importantly, because empiricism allows theory to be formulated in terms of expected values of the concepts, the actual event is redundant at the theory level.

The difference in the critical realism requirements—described under the various forms of validity—and empiricist requirements is significant. First, critical realism sees construct validity as a relation between the dependent variable operationalisation and the actual event that is supposed to occur, not between data and theory. Second, internal validity is concerned with whether the generative mechanism is responsible for (actually causes) the actual event, which is indirectly detected from the empirical traces, not with the logic of theory deduction (although this is important). Third, external validity refers to whether the events in the experiment are caused by the same mechanism that causes the phenomenon of interest in the field and thus whether the experiment provides evidence that the putative generative mechanism causes the effects in the field, which is the aim of theory testing. The empirical level is really of relevance only in the laboratory where a test of predictions is the issue. Consequently, inferential statistics are *not* the major concern when assessing external validity.

Conclusion

In this chapter, we have reformulated the notions of theory testing and research validity from the perspective of critical realism. Compared with an impoverished empiricist account of validity for practitioner research, critical realism brings important new ontological categories and distinctions to the problem. These include the notion of generative mechanisms distinct from theories, the distinction between generative mechanisms and their actual effects in particular circumstances and the distinction between these actual effects and the empirical traces that we observe.

Applying critical realism to each key validity issue has provided important new insights. Construct validity concerns whether the partial and perspectival empirical data collected under research conditions are generated by, and describe in an adequate form (for the purposes of the research), the actual events of interest that operate below the empirical surface. Consequently, the researcher must be concerned with establishing that the data collected represent the underlying actual variables both structurally and meaningfully. Since the category of the actual is distinct and larger than the empirical, this cannot be established entirely by analysis of empirical data, but is now seen as a theory-laden process.

Internal validity means establishing that the actual events that occur in the controlled domain are caused by the generative mechanism that the theory proposes. This requires the researcher to compare the events that follow from the purported generative mechanism with those revealed by the empirical data—as in the hypothetico-deductive method—but also to ensure alternative possible generative mechanisms for the events are eliminated.

External validity involves establishing that the generative mechanism that explains events in the 'laboratory' is also the generative mechanism that causes the actual phenomena of the broader domain of practice about which research questions are usually formulated. This means that the research manipulations that occur in the controlled research situation should invoke the same generative mechanism that produces the phenomena we wish to explain. Furthermore, since many variables that constitute these events are socially constructed or human centred, subjects must respond to the generative mechanisms in ways similar to practitioners.

Our systematic exploration of the consequences of critical realism for validity provides several novel contributions to theory compared with those derived from empiricism alone. External validity is essentially undefined under hard empiricism since the latter does not support a concept of an external world of practice to which the concept refers. This has led IS researchers to supplement empiricism in ad hoc ways with realist notions, with confusing results. The notion from critical realism of generative mechanisms and the new interpretation of theory testing bring new clarity to this issue and validity in general. The notion that the generative mechanisms that are invoked in contrived research situations must equate with those that operate under ambient circumstance is particularly novel and important. It provides a new razor by which research can be judged as relevant and important to practice.

In addition, critical realism underlines the limited extent to which research validity can be established by statistical manipulation of data alone. Empirical data give limited information about only the actual events that occur in the contrived or bounded research situation. Accessing the domains of actual events and real generative mechanisms is an essentially theory-bound process. Similarly, although comparing empirical data collected with predictions is a valid internal validity stratagem, external validity is not at heart an issue of statistical generalisation from those data.

The significance of this work for research practice lies in the way that important principles and practical procedures for conducting valid theory-testing research can be systematically derived and justified from a well-developed realist philosophical framework that embraces the complexities of socio-technical practice-based research.

References

Ajzen, I. 1991, 'The theory of planned behavior', *Organizational Behavior and Human Decision Processes*, vol. 50, no. 2, pp. 179–211.

Bealer, G. 1992, 'The incoherence of empiricism', *Proceedings of the Aristotelian Society*, vol. 66, pp. 99–138.

Bhaskar, R. 1975, *A Realist Theory of Science*, Alma Book Company, York.

Bhaskar, R. 1993, *Dialectic: The pulse of freedom*, Verso, London.

Bhaskar, R. 1998, *Critical Realism*, Routledge, New York.

Boudreau, M.-C., Gefen, D. and Straub, D. W. 2001, 'Validation in information systems research: a state-of-the-art assessment', *MIS Quarterly*, vol. 25, no. 1, pp. 1–16.

Bunge, M. 2006, *Chasing Reality: Strife over realism*, University of Toronto Press, Ontario.

Cook, T. D. and Campbell, D. T. 1979, *Quasi-Experimentation: Design & analysis issues for field settings*, Houghton Mifflin, New York.

Cronbach, L. J. and Meehl, P. E. 1955, 'Construct validity in psychological testing', *Psychological Bulletin*, vol. 52, no. 4, pp. 281–302.

Davis, F. D. 1989, 'Perceived usefulness, perceived ease of use, and user acceptance of information technologies', *MIS Quarterly*, vol. 13, no. 3, pp. 319–40.

Durkheim, E. 1897, *Le suicide: étude de sociologie*, F. Alcan, Paris.

Fogelin, R. J. 1993, 'Hume's scepticism', in D. F. Norton (ed.), *The Cambridge Companion to Hume*, Cambridge University Press, UK, pp. 64–89.

Goodhue, D. L. and Thompson, R. L. 1995, 'Task–technology fit and individual performance', *MIS Quarterly*, vol. 19, no. 2, pp. 213–28.

Greenwood, J. D. 1990, 'Two dogmas of neo-empiricism: the "theory-informity" of observation and the Quine-Duhem thesis', *Philosophy of Science*, vol. 57, no. 4, pp. 553–74.

Groff, R. 2000, 'The truth of the matter: Roy Bhaskar's critical realism and the concept of alethic truth', *Philosophy of the Social Sciences*, vol. 30, no. 3, pp. 407–35.

Hamlyn, D. W. 1967, 'Empiricism', *The Encyclopedia of Philosophy. Volume 2*, Collier Macmillan, New York, pp. 499–505.

Hooker, C. A. 1975, 'Philosophy and meta-philosophy of science: empiricism, Popperianism and realism', *Synthese*, vol. 32, no. 1, pp. 177–231.

Klein, H. K. and Lyytinen, K. 1985, 'The poverty of scientism in information systems', in E. Mumford, R. Hirschheim, G. Fitzgerald and T. Wood-Harper (eds), *Research Methods in Information Systems*, Elsevier Science, Amsterdam, pp. 131–61.

Kolokowski, L. 1972, *Positivist Philosophy: From Hume to the Vienna circle*, Penguin Books, Harmondsworth, UK.

Lee, A. S. and Baskerville, R. L. 2003, 'Generalizing generalizability in information systems research', *Information Systems Research*, vol. 14, no. 3, pp. 221–43.

Lucas, J. W. 2003, 'Theory-testing, generalization, and the problem of external validity', *Sociological Theory*, vol. 21, no. 3, pp. 236–53.

Maddy, P. 1992, 'Indispensability and practice', *Journal of Philosophy*, vol. 89, no. 6, pp. 275–89.

Meso, P. and Jain, R. 2006, 'Agile software development: adaptive systems principles and best practices', *Information Systems Management*, vol. 23, no. 3, pp. 19–30.

Mingers, J. 2000, 'The contribution of critical realism as an underpinning philosophy for OR/MS and systems', *Journal of the Operational Research Society*, vol. 51, no. 11, pp. 1256–70.

Mingers, J. 2004a, 'Critical realism and "multimethodology"', in S. Fleetwood and S. Ackroyd (eds), *Critical Realist Applications in Organisation and Management Studies*, Routledge, London.

Mingers, J. 2004b, 'Real-izing information systems: critical realism as an underpinning philosophy for information systems', *Information and Organization*, vol. 14, no. 2, pp. 87–103.

Neuman, W. L. 2005, *Social Research Methods: Qualitative and quantitative approaches*, Sixth edition, Allyn and Bacon, Milwaukee, Wis.

Niiniluoto, I. 1999, *Critical Scientific Realism*, Oxford University Press, New York.

Popper, K. R. 1959, *The Logic of Scientific Discovery*, Hutchinson, London.

Rogers, E. M. 1995, *Diffusion of Innovations*, Fourth edition, The Free Press, New York.

Rosenberg, A. 1993, 'Hume and the philosophy of science', in D. F. Norton (ed.), *The Cambridge Companion to Hume*, Cambridge University Press, UK, pp. 64–89.

Sayer, R. A. 1992, *Method in Social Science: A realist approach*, Routledge, London.

Seddon, P. B. and Scheepers, R. 2006, 'Other-settings generalization in IS research', *Proceedings of The International Conference on Information Systems (ICIS)*, Milwaukee, Wis.

Singer, E. A. jr 1954, 'Dialectic of the schools (II)', *Philosophy of Science*, vol. 21, no. 4, pp. 297–315.

Smith, M. L. 2006, 'Overcoming theory–practice inconsistencies: critical realism and information systems research', *Information and Organization*, vol. 16, no. 3, pp. 191–211.

Smith, S. P., Johnston, R. B. and Howard, S. 2010, 'Putting yourself in the picture: an evaluation of virtual model technology as an online shopping tool', *Information Systems Research*, Articles in Advance. http://isr.journal.informs.org/cgi/content/abstract/isre.1090.0279v1

Vessey, I. and Galletta, D. 1991, 'Cognitive fit: an empirical study of information acquisition', *Information Systems Research*, vol. 2, no. 1, pp. 63–84.

Williams, K. 1975, 'Facing reality—a critique of Karl Popper's empiricism', *Economy and Society*, vol. 4, no. 3, pp. 309–58.

Theory and Method

3. Building theory in a practical science

SHIRLEY GREGOR
AUSTRALIAN NATIONAL UNIVERSITY

Abstract

The aim of this chapter is to consider the problem of theory building in a practical science and in information technology (IT) and information systems (IS) in particular. Theorising in IT design disciplines (practical science) is differentiated from theorising in other scientific fields in essential ways. Two modes of theorising are distinguished for design disciplines: an *interior mode* with the *how* of artefact construction studied and an *exterior mode* with the *what* of existing artefactual phenomena studied. Eight principles of theorising are advanced for theory building: 1) artefact centrality; 2) artefact purposefulness; 3) artefacts as systems; 4) design research variants; 5) differing logics; 6) types of theory; 7) mid-range theorising; and 8) interior and exterior modes for theorising. The implicit claim is that consideration of these principles will improve theorising in design disciplines—for both design researchers and researchers using more traditional methods. Some illustrative applications are provided in support of this claim.

Introduction

A tension between pure and applied branches of knowledge has long been recognised and can be traced back to the distinction between *epistêmê* and *technê* by the Greek philosophers. More recently, a distinction has been drawn between the paradigm of 'science' and that of the 'artificial sciences'. The science paradigm can be categorised by terms such as *epistêmê*, pure science or the explanatory sciences, while the 'sciences of the artificial' paradigm has invited labels such as *technê*, applied science, prescriptive science, design science, technology and even on occasion art or craft. The distinction between the two paradigms rests on the characteristics of the traditional sciences, which concern 'what is', and the sciences of the artificial, which concern 'what could be'—the development of *artefacts* through human agency (Simon 1996). The traditional-science paradigm represents the dominant mode of thinking in the philosophy of science and it is comparatively rare to find any comprehensive account of how knowledge and theory might be developed in applied branches of knowledge, including those that deal with technology, such as information systems (IS) (see O'Hear 1989). The purpose of this chapter is to help redress this imbalance, by considering how theory can and should be developed in the artificial-sciences paradigm, with a focus on fields of study concerning information technology (IT).

This chapter considers theory generation in both an *interior* mode—in the design and development of the inner environment of artefacts—and an *exterior* mode, in which the artefacts are theorised about in their outer environment. These two modes are seen as two sides of a coin; they are intertwined and both contribute to the development of theory concerning artefacts in the sciences of the artificial. This chapter differs from prior work in that it applies not only to researchers who personally develop artefacts and theorise about the results in the interior mode (as in some conceptions of 'design science'), but to researchers who carry out more traditional theorising in the exterior mode in a manner common in mainstream journals. An implication of the chapter is that theorising in both modes can be improved by taking account of underlying principles that arise from the unique characteristics of the fields of study that concern IT artefacts.

Figure 3.1 is provided at this point as an orienting device for the argument in the remainder of the chapter, in which the perspective it represents will be explained in more detail. It shows the interior and exterior modes of theorising within an IT design discipline as well as the connections to reference theories in other design disciplines and in the science paradigm.

Although research and theorising in relation to design science are increasingly dealt with (for example, Hevner et al. 2004; March and Smith 1995; Simon 1996; van Aken 2004, 2005; Venable 2006), the question of theory building is still relatively unexplored. Further, discussion of theory building in the artificial-science paradigm is complicated by the fact that theory building in general is poorly understood. In reviewing the literature on the activities that go on during theory construction, Weick (1989:517) notes that 'the literature on this topic is sparse and uneven and tends to focus on outcomes and products rather than process'.

3. Building theory in a practical science

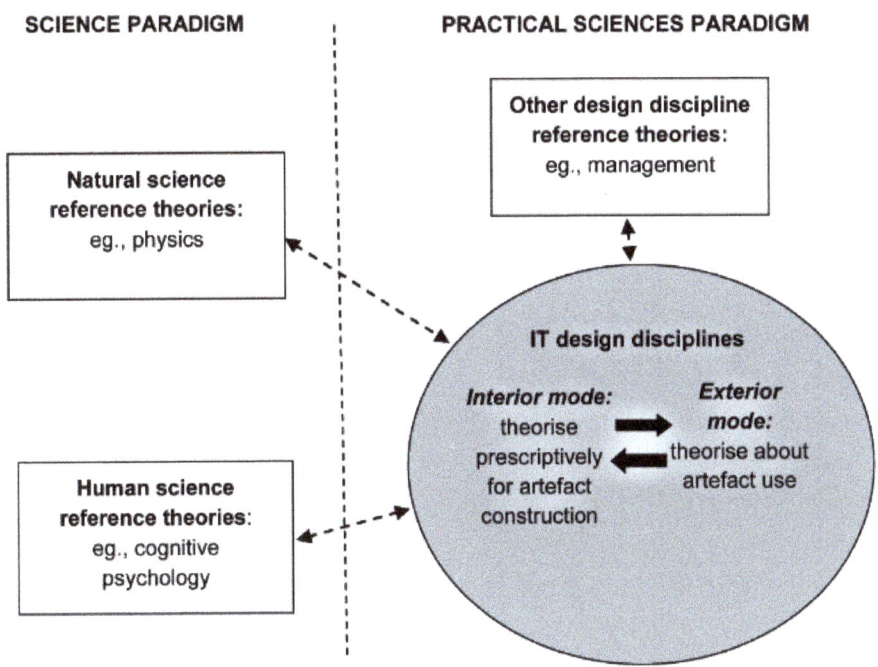

Figure 3.1 A framework for understanding theory building in IT as a practical science

In discussing theory building, we are studying a human activity, undertaken by researchers whose aim is to contribute to human knowledge. A broad view of theory itself is adopted. Theory is seen as knowledge that has some degree of abstraction and generalisability and consists of statements about relationships among constructs within some specified boundaries. The type of statements made can depend on the type of theory. Congruent with Gregor (2006), five interrelated different types of theory are recognised: Type 1—theory for analysing; Type II—theory for explaining; Type 3—theory for predicting; Type IV—theory for explaining and predicting; and Type V—theory for design and action. Here, we consider all five types of theory from within the perspective of the sciences of the artificial.

The terms 'sciences of the artificial', 'artificial-sciences paradigm' and 'design paradigm' are used in this chapter in the sense used by Simon (1996) to refer to the disciplines that are concerned with artificial, human-made phenomena, including administration, engineering, medicine, business, architecture and art. Strasser (1985) offers the alternative term of 'practical sciences' for these fields. The term 'design science' is used for the subset of research activities that more directly concerns the design and construction of particular artefacts (as in Hevner et al. 2004; March and Smith 1996).

The contribution of this chapter is that it brings together thinking about theory building in the design paradigm that has, until now, been relatively piecemeal. The chapter has practical relevance in that it focuses on building theory that concerns the design, construction and use of artefacts in some way—knowledge that has real-world utility. The chapter has implications for research practice in that it assists researchers by clarifying some of the issues around theory building itself—a thorny problem for both new and experienced researchers and one that is particularly poorly addressed from an applied-science perspective.

The focus of the chapter is on artefacts that relate to IT (computers) and the computing disciplines—identified as computer engineering, computer science, IS, IT and software engineering (CC2005 2005). Much of the discussion, however, is couched in terms that apply to IS. The artefacts that are of interest are of many types and include both products (databases, electronic markets, web sites) and processes (IT management strategies, modelling methods) (see Gregor and Jones 2007).

The chapter proceeds as follows. The next two sections provide further discussion of the two paradigms of science and artificial science and some underlying ideas for theory building in general. In the next section, the unique features of the IT discipline that cause its theorising to have distinct characteristics are presented, followed by eight principles that it is argued underlie this theorising. These principles were derived analytically from the characteristics of the discipline and a study of prior literature. Some concluding remarks end the chapter.

Two paradigms

The issue of the relationship between the pure and applied fields of human inquiry has a distinguished lineage, as shown by the attention the Greek philosophers devoted to the problem. Loosely understood in modern terms, *epistêmê*, or knowledge, was distinguished from *technê*, or practice. Aristotle spoke of *epistêmê* in terms that could be equated to the modern understanding of scientific knowledge. That is, scientific knowledge concerns objects that do not admit of change; these objects are eternal and exist from necessity (Parry 2007). In this treatment, scientific knowledge implies a deductive system with the relations among terms both invariable and necessary. On the other hand, *technê* concerns the bringing into existence of something that could either exist or not exist—that is, the contingent. Further, each *technê* aims at some end—for example, health is the end of medicine. A close relation between *technê* and *epistêmê* is also recognised, although not without some ambiguity. Again using the example of medicine, Aristotle spoke of medicine as an *epistêmê* because the physician studies health, but also as a *technê* because the physician produces health.

The distinction between pure and applied branches of knowledge has continued, although the close interrelationship among the two has also continued to be recognised. Nevertheless, it is probably fair to say that the philosophy of science as a whole has been fairly firmly rooted in *epistêmê*-type thinking, rather than concerning itself with the knowledge that relates to *technê*. For example, Nagel's work *The Structure of Science* (1979) makes practically no reference to applied science or to technology. As late as 2003, Scharff and Dusek produced an anthology of readings—the *Philosophy of Technology*—in order to address a perceived 'widespread failure to question the relation between contemporary technology and modern science' (p. x). The argument developed in this chapter is that the neglect of applied science and technology in the philosophy of science has meant that some important aspects of thinking about how knowledge and theory are developed for the sciences of the artificial have been overlooked.[1]

It is helpful to look at some of the distinguishing features of the two paradigms (see Table 3.1). The salient difference is that the sciences of the artificial are concerned with the study of artefacts, 'things' that are constructed by human beings in order to achieve some end, goal or purpose. Strasser (1985:59) defines a practical science as a 'science which is conceived in order to make possible, to improve, and to correct a definite kind of extra-scientific praxis'. Note that the wall between the two paradigms is permeable, as there will be researchers working primarily in one paradigm who also have an interest in the other. For example, scientists in biology include plant biologists designing new strains of wheat. Conversely, researchers in the applied-science paradigm might develop artefacts that influence theorising in the science paradigm, as when newly developed computer systems were used by cognitive psychologists as a means of understanding human memory processes. The distinction drawn by Strasser between an applied science and a practical science is that in the former the science is 'accidentally' applied to a practical issue, whereas in practical sciences such as agriculture the essential aim is towards a definite kind of praxis.

---

[1] The history of the philosophy of science is worthy of close regard. The degree of emphasis on inductivism versus deductivism and empiricism versus rationalism and the degree of recognition for the need for creativity and imagination in scientific thinking have swung one way and then the other. What is of interest for this chapter are the definitive shifts in focus as to the phenomena of study. In the time of the ancient Greeks, philosophy included all branches of knowledge. The emphasis on the natural sciences and even the coining of the word 'scientist' accompanied the age of enlightenment in the eighteenth century. Another major shift can be distinguished with the distinction drawn by Dilthey (1883) between the natural and *human* sciences. The author believes another major shift has begun with the emphasis since the later part of the twentieth century on design or practical sciences, in which the phenomena of interest are artefacts (Simon 1996; Strasser 1985).

The consequences of what a study of artefacts means for theory building are discussed in detail in the following sections.

Table 3.1 The science and the artificial-science paradigms

Features	Paradigm	
	Science	Practical science/sciences of the artificial
Foci of interest	Naturally occurring phenomena, 'as is', the necessary	Designed artefacts, 'what can be', the contingent
Distinguishing feature	Observation of phenomena	Creation and observation of artefacts
Discipline examples	Astronomy, biology, chemistry geology, physics, sociology	Accounting, art, computer science, design, economics, engineering, ethics, information systems, management, marketing, medicine

After Simon (1996)

Theory building in general

Some fairly basic ideas inherited from science about theory building continue to be influential in the artificial sciences and to some extent are adopted unquestioningly. As the discussion below indicates, this uncritical attitude might not be a good thing.

A key influence has been an idealised view of the scientific process known as the 'hypothetico-deductive method' (see Godfrey-Smith 2003:70), which contains the following steps.

- Step 1: conjectures are generated, possibly as a result of observations.
- Step 2: observational predictions (hypotheses) are deduced from the conjectures.
- Step 3: if predictions match the hypotheses, the theory is supported; if not, the theory is not supported and should be rejected.

The idea of theory building itself can be interpreted in differing ways. In a narrow sense, the term could refer to Step 1—the process of arriving at hypotheses that can then be tested. This narrow sense will be referred to as 'theory generation' in the remainder of this chapter. In a wider sense, 'theory building' can be taken to refer to the overall process in which there are cycles of activities including observation, hypothesising, testing and theory refinement or extension, with the resultant theory becoming stronger in successive cycles and increasing in explanatory and predictive power.

Divergent thinking about even the simple hypothetico-deductive model can be found among philosophers of science. Karl Popper (1980) notably had little interest in where conjectures came from in the first place and was also opposed to the idea that theories became 'stronger' as they survived more and more tests, owing to the problems with inductive reasoning. That is, strictly speaking, one cannot infer by inductive reasoning from any large number of observations in the past, or any amount of theorising, that a new observation will conform to what has already occurred (the next swan might indeed be black). Although inductive scepticism has a place, in practice, the philosophy of science has moved on and there are now more varied views on how theory development can occur. There is greater recognition that theories develop and are extended in a cumulative fashion over time and that theories that have a greater weight of evidence behind them and have survived more thorough testing are to be preferred to other, less well-tried theories (Godfrey-Smith 2003).

Further, more recent work has treated inductive reasoning more favourably for theory building in the narrow sense (Step 1). Examples include the grounded theory work of Glaser and Strauss (1967). Merton (1968:47), writing about sociological theory, advocates the development of theory of the middle range and the building of theory on an adequate base of 'antecedent empirical enquiry'. Merton (1968:39) defines theories of the middle range as '[t]heories that lie between the minor but necessary working hypotheses that evolve in abundance during day-to-day research and the all-inclusive systematic efforts to develop a unified theory that will explain all the observed uniformities of social behaviour, social organization and social change'.

Merton saw the development of mid-range theories as a more achievable aim in emerging disciplines, the state of affairs in much of established science and a necessary step on the way to increasingly comprehensive theory.

The management literature also provides some discussion of the processes of theory building. Kaplan (1964) distinguishes between theory growth 'by intention', when a new theoretical explanation is given for a wide region, and theory growth 'by extension', when theory from one smallish region is extended to adjoining regions in a piece-by-piece manner. Bourgeois (1979) provides a description whereby theory of the middle range is generated in a non-linear process with seven steps: 1) the topic of investigation is identified; 2) the method of theory generation is explicated; 3) literature is reviewed; 4) theory is generated by induction from an empirical base; 5) theory is extended with deduction of propositions; 6) metaphysical elaboration; and 7) conclusions. Steps 3, 4 and 5 occur concurrently rather than sequentially. Weick (1989) sees theory construction as 'disciplined imagination'.

There has also been some work on how theory is developed when the field of inquiry is treated as a science concerned with artefacts. Van Aken (2004, 2005) calls for the distinguishing in management studies of 'management theory', a design science that has as its goal the development of 'field-tested and grounded technological rules'. The technological rule is part of a mid-range theory with a validity limited to a specified application domain. Venable (2006) proposes ideas for both the form and the details required of theory in design science and also a framework for the interaction of design science with other scientific paradigms. Goldkuhl (2004) proposes a framework for the multi-grounding of design theory empirically, theoretically and internally. These sources and others are drawn on in advancing the principles in the next section.

Principles for theory building in IT-related disciplines

This section proposes a number of principles that it is argued underlie *all* theorising in the design fields related to IT. The main thrust of the argument, however, is couched in terms that relate to IS—a field that requires some knowledge of technology, but also knowledge from the behavioural sciences. It is acknowledged that aspects of the argument could be less applicable to areas in which the human behavioural aspects of technological use are less, or not at all, salient (for example, computer engineering).

For a number of reasons, the fields of study relating to IT require their own unique examination of how theorising is carried out. In brief

- IT is *not natural science*, yet natural science is implicated in design; IT concerns designed artefacts and belongs to the artificial-sciences paradigm, as argued above; knowledge from science is implicated in that the IT artefacts constructed conform to physical laws
- IT disciplines are *not social or behavioural (human) science*, although the social sciences are implicated in design, in that their knowledge can help explain interactions between IT and individuals and groups and inform the design of artefacts; yet the social sciences are not, for the most part, design disciplines
- IT disciplines *differ from other design disciplines*. IT artefacts are different because they concern complex systems, whereas artefacts dealt with in many other design disciplines are not.

These three characteristics taken together mean that the IT discipline is unique. Other disciplines deal with complex systems—for example, biology—but the systems (mostly) are not constructed by human agency. Other design disciplines deal with complex systems—for example, management and economics—but their artefacts are not based on technologies that are based in physical science. Possibly the closest discipline that matches the characteristics of IT is medicine, in which there are designed artefacts, such as drugs, that conform to scientific analysis, but there are also interventions with human beings, and knowledge of biological and behavioural sciences is required. Perhaps a difference still occurs in that the medical artefacts are not themselves complex systems. Further, the natural sciences are relied on (biology and physiology) rather than the physical sciences (electronics).

It is argued that eight principles that arise from these three defining characteristics underlie theory building in IT disciplines. These principles were derived from consideration of the defining characteristics of IT as a design discipline above, supplemented by an analysis of the extant literature relating to theory building.

Each principle is presented with some illustrative examples of what the principle means to research practice. Table 3.2 provides an overview of the principles. These principles are meant to apply both to researchers focusing on artefact construction, in an interior mode, and to researchers theorising about artefacts from the outside in an exterior mode (see Principle 8).

Table 3.2 Principles for theory building in a design discipline

No.	Key idea	Principle
1	Artefact centrality	IT artefacts are central to theorising
2	Artefact purposefulness	Purposefulness of IT artefacts is recognised and outcomes studied
3	Artefacts are systems	IT artefacts are systems (or involved with systems)
4	Design research variants	The range of design research approaches should be recognised
5	Differing logics	Different logics are needed
6	Types of theory	Different types of theory are needed, including design theory
7	Mid-range theorising	Mid-range, well-grounded theorising is of particular value
8	Interior and exterior modes	Theorising is done in both interior and exterior modes

Principle 1: IT artefacts are central to theorising

In this chapter, by definition, IT design disciplines such as IS concern artefacts and we would expect to find an artefact playing a central role in theorising. This point has been argued by others, including Benbasat and Zmud (2003), Iivari (2003), Orlikowski and Iacono (2001) and Weber (1987).

This principle distinguishes theory that belongs to IS from *reference or kernel* theories—theories that can be useful in the study of artefacts, as explanations for artefact behaviour or for design ideas, but which do not have an IT artefact as a primary focus. An example is a theory of interpersonal trust, which belongs as a reference theory to the social sciences, whereas theory about how trust is engendered in online communications could belong to IS.

Practical application

Research work is more likely to find acceptance in IT publication outlets if it concerns theory relating to IT artefacts. In IS, the leading journal, *MIS Quarterly*, has as its objective 'the enhancement and communication of knowledge concerning the development of *IT*-based services, the management of *IT* resources, and the use, impact, and economics of *IT* with managerial, organizational, and societal implications' (MIS Quarterly 2008; emphasis added). Although professional issues affecting the IS discipline are also dealt with, the key message is that papers should relate to IT artefacts in some way. Personal experience as an editor has shown the author that papers are likely to be rejected if they relate more to a reference discipline than to IS. A paper that purports to deal with knowledge-management systems but deals only with scenarios regarding knowledge sharing and not with any features of a technology-based system is unlikely to be accepted.

Principle 2: purposefulness of IT artefacts is recognised and outcomes studied

A distinguishing feature of an artefact is that it serves some purpose, although purposes can be many and varied. For example, an ornament has ornamentation as its purpose. This concept dates back to Aristotle in his depiction of the *causa finalis*—the final cause or end of an artefact, 'what it is for', one of the four causes of any thing (Hooker 1993). The artefact's purpose relates to the context in which it is used. Heidegger (1993) gives the example of a silver chalice, of which, in order to understand its purpose, we need to understand the religious ritual in which the chalice is to be used. The purpose of the artefact might not always be that of the original designer and some of its uses and effects could be unintended. Nevertheless, in studying artefacts, it is needful to consider the goal, end or aim of the artefact as originally intended or as arising in use.

Further, given this distinguishing feature, theorising tends to be more satisfactory if some assessment is made of the outcomes of the artefact's use: whether it achieves a goal or purpose in some way. The constructor of artefacts is expected usually to give some demonstration that the artefact at least works. The observer of artefacts will often evaluate the efficacy or consequences of its use.

This idea finds varied expression across a number of fields. In medicine, the evidence-based approach uses the *PICO model*, in which P stands for patient or population, I for intervention (drug or procedure), C for comparison (against what alternatives) and O stands for *outcomes* (what you can hope to accomplish, measure, improve or affect) (University Libraries 2008). We find something of this thinking also in van Aken (2005:29) where he says in management design propositions 'the independent variable must describe something of value to the organization, like financial performance'. In IS, Jarvinen (2007) proposes that we should use a goal function for measuring the goodness of a new artefact. The goal function could cover both intended and unintended consequences of the developed artefact.

Practical application

This principle addresses the 'so what' factor. So you have invented a new database ontology or modelling method. What does that mean? Will the method work? Is it better than other existing methods? In the exterior mode, theorising can be more interesting and acceptable for publication if the phenomena studied include outcomes of IT use. Thus, the research question 'What types of knowledge intermediaries are made use of in organisations' is likely to be of less interest than an alternative question, 'What types of knowledge intermediaries lead to more effective knowledge sharing and dissemination in organisations?'

Principle 3: IT artefacts are systems

It hardly seems necessary to demonstrate that IT artefacts should be regarded as systems (or tools that are used in dealing with systems). Basic definitions of a computer or information *system* use words such as input, output, control, feedback and external environment. The first computers appeared after general systems theory had been advanced (Ashby 1956; von Bertalanffy 1968) and relied on many of its concepts. Social-science reference theories commonly talk in terms of social systems. Characteristics of systems are: they are open to and interact with their environment; they acquire new properties through emergence and continually evolve; and the parts of a system interact to form a whole that is independent of the separate constituents. Systems concepts include the system–environment boundary, input, output, processes, state, hierarchies, goal directedness and information (Heylighen and Joslyn 1992).

That systems need to be treated differently in scientific reasoning and explanation has been argued by biologists, who are also intimately concerned with systems, albeit those that are animated by life. Nagel (1979:401) gives a comprehensive treatment of this claim and concludes that there are indeed good reasons for differentiating biology from the physical sciences in an essential way: 'One is the dominant place occupied by teleological explanations. The other is the use of conceptual tools uniquely appropriate to the study of systems whose total behaviour is not the resultant of the activities of independent components.'

These considerations apply equally well to the study of computer-based information systems as they do to biology.

Simon has used systems theory concepts extensively in *The Sciences of the Artificial* (1996). He argues for modern artefacts to be viewed as complex systems and (p. 6) for an artefact as a 'meeting point—an interface' between an '"inner" environment, the substance and organization of the artifact itself, and an "outer" environment, the surroundings in which it operates. If the inner environment is appropriate to the outer environment, or vice versa, the artifact will serve its intended purpose.'

Practical application

This principle has a number of potential applications.

Systems theory itself is likely to be a strong underlying influence on theory development in IS. One example can be found in Weber's (1997) theory of representation. More recently, Braa et al. (2007) used complexity science as a support for theory concerning standard development in a healthcare environment in developing countries.

Levels of analysis issues need to be dealt with in theorising. More recent theoretical models have captured some of the complexity of multi-level influences. For example, Melville et al. (2004) present a model with influences at the level of the external environment, the industry and the firm itself on IT value generation. Burton-Jones and Gallivan (2007) dealt with the problem of the system usage construct at different levels of analysis. Further, researchers often seem to struggle with the need to specify their own level of analysis clearly in theorising and in matching their metrics appropriately to the level of analysis.

The box and arrow diagrams that are commonly used for research models in quantitative studies can capture only a small part of theories about IT artefacts. These diagrams are usually unidirectional and do not encompass any notions of time or reverse causality. Theorising could be improved if more consideration is given to the temporal aspects of problems concerning systems.

A conjecture is that theorising will more and more be concerned with longitudinal analysis and reverse causality, even in quantitative studies, as more sophisticated statistical tools become available for dealing with these issues. Recent submissions to journals indicate that this trend has begun.

Principle 4: the range of design research approaches should be recognised

IT artefacts owe their existence to human creativity and imagination coupled with knowledge of the constraints that govern an artefact's operation when it operates in an external real-world environment.

There are many ways of thinking about the design process and innovation and of how designers work in practice (see Cross 2001). Design itself can be thought of as more an art than a science. Atwood et al. (2002) give a useful overview of how the design community thinks about design in general, across many fields. Simon (1996) argues against design as a rational decision process and proposes that human designers—when confronted with myriad design choices—are likely to settle for good or satisfactory solutions rather than optimal ones.

As systems design and implementation are activities performed by IT professionals, methods exist for aiding designers in everyday routine design activity, including the many systems development methodologies. These methods tend to focus on the design of systems to meet predetermined user requirements. This developmental activity, however, is still a creative one, and in practice IT professionals can produce artefacts that are new and interesting from a research point of view. For design theory to be produced, reflecting on what has been done is required (see Schön 1983) and design principles need to be abstracted. This systemisation of knowledge gained through practice is a legitimate academic activity and one that has led to a number of influential design theories. For example, Davenport and Short (1990) abstracted ideas from case studies in 19 companies to first depict the general method of business process redesign. Van Aken (2004:232) refers to this type of activity as an *'extracting case study'* or 'best-practice' approach and notes that it has produced a number of very powerful technological rules (design theory), such as the Kanban system and just-in-time approaches.

When engaging with artefact construction as a research activity, the onus is more on the designer to produce an artefact that is new or novel in some way. In van Aken's terms, this is the *'developing case study'* approach. The design-science literature now treats this research activity in some depth. A good overview of design science in IS is provided by Kuechler and Vaishnavi (2008). Design-science research activities are often described in terms of design-build-evaluate cycles and as a problem-solving process. Hevner et al. (2004) utilise a means–end analysis conception of design activity.

Other design research activities that can lead to design knowledge include action research and collaborative clinical research (see van Aken 2005).

It should be noted that experimentation can play a large role in design activities in the sense that designers think of an idea then try it out to see if it works, make a decision then proceed on to other design decisions. This experimentation is part of the process of designing rather than being the experimental method as proposed in science to identify cause–effect relationships. In anything more than a trivial design problem, the designer will make very many design decisions and it would be infeasible to test every design decision point by conducting a formal experiment.

When studying the use of artefacts from the point of view of an observer (the exterior mode), it is well to recall that the theorising should inform subsequent design activities. To this end, one could expect that at least some of the independent variables studied are potentially manipulable by designers.

Practical application

The different ways in which design theory can be generated from design activities give researchers a number of avenues to pursue. These avenues include extracting design theory from case studies and action research in addition to artefact construction in design-science terms.

Principle 5: different logics are needed

An issue that has not been much touched on is the question of the underlying logic that is required for design theorising. Simon (1996:114–24) considers whether a special logic of imperatives is needed for design work but concludes it is unnecessary.[2] He sidesteps the issue, however, in restricting his discussion

---

[2] Standard propositions in logic are statements of fact such as 'X is the case' (that is, method X was successful). A prescriptive (hypothetical imperative) statement has the form 'To achieve Y then do X' (but X might not be the *only* way of achieving Y). An imperative (categorical imperative) statement says 'Do X'. A predictive statement says 'If X occurs then Y will follow'.

to the use of imperative logic in optimisation methods and means–end analysis, where ordinary mathematical deductive logic can be used to identify the best option from a range of identifiable alternatives.

Designers, however, are not confronted only by optimisation problems, but also by problems in which the range of potential solutions is large and not identifiable at the design point. Such problems cannot normally be solved by deductive logic. An engineer faced with the problem of building a bridge over a ravine has no clear guidance from deductive logic as to which design to implement. About the best that can be done is to think that such and such a design worked in similar situations in the past and reason *inductively* to assume that the design is likely to work again in this similar situation (engineering analysis indicating that there is no reason to believe it will not work). Thus, as has been pointed out by a number of authors, inductive logic is useful in design research. The extracting case study strategy of van Aken's (2004) is an example. Van Aken followed Bunge (1967) in proposing the development of prescriptive technological rules developed inductively for design knowledge. A technological rule is 'an instruction to perform a finite number of acts in a given order and with a given aim' (Bunge 1967:132). Inductive logic will only lead us to the conclusion, however, that a particular strategy or rule *could* be used to address a design problem and that it is expected to lead to certain outcomes.

The problem of practical as opposed to theoretical reasoning is addressed in some depth by Edgley (1969), who distinguishes between 'What is the case?' (questions of fact and science) and 'What is to be done?' (questions of action). Edgley shows that prescriptive statements about action do not necessarily follow from descriptive knowledge. To extrapolate, imperative statements about design and action cannot be deduced from scientific knowledge. For example, as a matter of science, one might know that an insecticide kills an insect pest. One cannot deduce from this knowledge that 'in order to kill the insect pest one must use insecticide'; there could be other ways of killing the pest.

The conclusion is that design prescriptions and theory cannot be deduced in any simple and direct manner from reference theories from science or social science. Inductive reasoning from prior experience can, however, be useful.

Practical application

The hypothetico-deductive method of science does not lead directly to design knowledge and theory; inductive methods can be more useful. The generation of research models in IS deductively from reference theories for quantitative studies should be done with extreme care and not without some degree of grounding in IT use in practice. Often it appears that researchers have added variables to their models with only slight attention to their importance in something like a 'shopping-basket' approach.

Reference theories can indicate that a large number of explanatory variables could have some relationship with outcome variables and the inclusion of many variables will lead to more variance being explained in statistical models. This result does not mean that key factors that designers of interventions can manipulate to bring about desired results have been identified. Recent disquiet about the rather ad hoc extensions to the Technology Acceptance Model (TAM) that occur is an illustration of this problem (see the special issue in *Journal of the AIS*, 2007, vol. 8, titled *Quo Vadis TAM?*).

Principle 6: different types of theory are needed, including design theory

The previous discussion has indicated that theory that is needed for design and action will take a different form from other types of theory and will include prescriptive statements such as the technological rules of Bunge (1967) and van Aken (2005). The case for different types of theory depending on the purpose of the theorising is made by Gregor (2006), who distinguishes five interrelated types of theory: Type 1—theory for analysing; Type II—theory for explaining; Type 3—theory for predicting; Type IV—theory for explaining and predicting; Type V—theory for design and action. Gregor and Jones (2007) show in detail the structure and components of a design theory (Type V).

An advance on the reasoning in that prior work is to argue that in a design discipline design theory (Type V) is the ultimate aim. The other types of theorising can contribute to Type V theory. In contrast, in non-design disciplines such as science, Type V theory is not needed.

The Type V knowledge might not take a form that is generally recognised as theory. For example, Davenport and Short's (1980) description of business process redesign is probably not regarded as theorising, yet it has been an extremely influential, well-cited paper and has led to much academic research. Preceding arguments, especially under Principles 4 and 5, have suggested that in many situations, best practice is the best guidance a designer might have, as scientific knowledge from reference disciplines does not necessarily lead to practical design ideas. Some research will recognise this codified best practice under labels such as 'accumulated business wisdom' (see, for example, Melville et al. 2004).

The lingering influence of conventional scientific views of theory leads to charges that papers are 'atheoretic' if they do not include reference theories of the non-design type. Novice researchers are nervous about doing work that does not have 'theory'. An illustration is the plight of a PhD candidate who was investigating project management success. In response to a question as to whether she had considered knowledge of project management methodologies, she replied 'but that's not theory'. Support for a counterargument is provided by published papers that do not contain any theory other than design theory (an example is Iversen et al. 2004, in which design theory is developed from other design theories).

Practical application

Papers are not necessarily 'atheoretic' if they do not contain reference theory. The IS disciplines will have reached a more mature stage when the theories that are presented are native to IS and concern IT artefacts and their behaviour. Supporting explanations from other disciplines for why and how artefacts lead to the outcomes that they do could be desirable, but are not strictly essential.

Principle 7: mid-range, well-grounded theorising is of particular value

The quest for high-level 'grand' theories with wide applicability in IT disciplines is a challenging one. Perhaps the most likely prospects remain general systems theory and its derivatives, which provide such general statements as the Law of Requisite Variety: only variety in a system's responses can keep down variety in outcomes when the system is subjected to a set of disturbances (Ashby 1956). Weber (1997) gives a generalised theory of representation, which aims to model the desirable properties of information systems at a deep level and be a theory native to IS. Apart from these few instances, the imprecise nature of knowledge relating to the behaviour of humans interacting with technology and the changing nature of technologies themselves suggest that highly generalised, unchanging laws as can be found in science will be rare in IT design disciplines.

On the other hand, theory by definition must not be too narrow. The solving of one specific design problem or reporting of one case does not mean a design theory has been developed. At least some degree of abstraction and generalisation must occur so that the solution can be generalised to a class of problems and have some applicability in other settings.

An intermediate position is mid-range theory—theory that has moderate coverage and can easily lead to testable hypotheses. Mid-range theory is seen as particularly important for practice disciplines (Merton 1968) such as IS. Similarly, van Aken (2005:238) sees that technological rules are not general knowledge, but rather mid-range theories of practice: 'They are only valid for a certain application domain, a range of settings that have key attributes in common with the settings in which the rules were developed and tested.'

Importantly, theory in IT needs to be grounded in practice. As argued under Principle 5, it is difficult or impossible to arrive at design knowledge deductively from a general theory outside the design discipline itself. A theory of interpersonal trust is not going to provide sufficient guidance to develop a design for trustworthy online communication. Knowledge that informs design will also be developed by learning from past designs.

Practical application

Very general high-level theory for IT is a laudable goal but instances could be rare. Research that produces mid-range theory should be regarded as valuable and publications in journals indicate that this is so. One example is the design theory of Markus et al. (2002) for systems that support emergent knowledge processes: a theory that is generalisable to a particular class of artefacts. Review articles that attempt to pull a number of studies together and advance more general theory are of course also still extremely valuable.

Principle 8: theorising is done in both interior and exterior modes

The foregoing discussion points to two general modes of research activity and theorising: the interior and exterior modes.

The interior mode is where theorising is done to produce theory for design and action (Type V), with prescriptive statements about *how* artefacts can be designed, developed and brought into being. The exterior mode, to which we loosely apply the term 'indirect design theorising', includes the other types of theory (Types I to IV), which aim primarily at analysing, describing and predicting *what* happens as artefacts exist and are used in their external environment.

This division into two modes follows Simon's (1996:7) insights into systems complexity in which the division between the inner and outer environment 'is highly convenient'. The separation of the inner from the outer allows the simplification of tasks. The detail of the inner environment can be hidden when we talk about an artefact attaining its goals and only minimal assumptions might need to be made about the inner environment, as the same end could be achieved by different mechanisms. It is this principle that underlies the mastering of complexity by decomposing hierarchically ordered systems into subsystems in which details of the subsystems' operation are 'hidden'.

These two modes of theorising are seen as two sides of a coin. Both are needed in the design disciplines of IT and they are complementary to each other. Theory in the exterior mode can include propositions such as 'A system with feature X will perform better on measure M than a system without feature X'. If empirical testing shows that this proposition is supported then the proposition can be 'turned around' to give a design proposition: 'If you want to achieve M then include feature X.'

It helps to distinguish the two modes in terms of theorising as they involve different activities and different ways of thinking about theory. Moreover, a single piece of research in a journal article or thesis is likely to include research conducted in either one mode or the other and it is well to consider what is to be regarded as acceptable theorising in each mode.

The principles expounded above have shown the different methods that can be used to produce design ideas in the interior mode (Principle 4). Indirect design theorising in the exterior mode yields ideas about phenomena that can inform design in several ways: through explaining why artefacts work as they do, whether they achieve their stated goals, whether one feature of a designed artefact leads to certain effects, and so on. Going further, however, the argument is also made that theorising on the second side of the coin requires thinking that differs from that common in the pure sciences, in terms of focusing on explanatory factors that can be manipulated and outcome variables that indicate whether artefacts are achieving purposes (Principles 1, 2 and 7). The result will be theory that can be more directly 'turned around' to yield design ideas and principles—a desirable state of affairs in an applied discipline.

Practical application

Researchers are likely to work in only one mode at a time and our community of scholars needs to recognise how much can reasonably be expected in a single article or thesis. A researcher who has devoted a great deal of effort to showing how a new artefact can work—and in showing that it is a novel artefact—might not have the time and effort to do the comprehensive evaluation that would be expected if he/she was working in the exterior mode assessing an artefact constructed by someone else. The IT design communities would do well to reflect and define their expectations in this respect.

Researchers working in the interior mode and theorising about how artefacts can be constructed should be aware of the range of approaches available to them—not just the design-science approaches of design/build/evaluate, but also the extraction of design principles from case studies.

Researchers working in the exterior mode can improve their theorising by study of a number of the principles: focusing on an IT artefact (Principle 1);

considering outcomes of use (Principle 2); using systems concepts (Principle 3); and accepting that inductive theory building and mid-range theorising native to IS are valuable (Principles 5 and 7).

Concluding remarks

This chapter addresses a complex issue—that of theory building—and it does it from the point of view of a design discipline, a perspective that has been little considered. Thus, the arguments made are advanced for discussion and to further debate, rather than being regarded as fixed and certain ideas. There are many new ideas appearing in the literature of design, which as a study of the design of complex artefacts dates back only about 50–60 years. It is expected that it will be some time before a common understanding and means of describing our problems emerge. This chapter is just one step along the path.

A limitation of the chapter is that it does not cover some of the necessary and more generally accepted features of theory-building and research methods. Thus, the advantages and limitations of different research approaches are not discussed. At heart, the chapter is about logical reasoning; the principles derived are arrived at by logical extension from the defining characteristics of IT and its nature as a design discipline.

The contribution of the chapter is that it provides a high-level framework for thinking about the different types of theorising in the paradigm of science versus that of design. Many of the ideas in the chapter stem from Simon's seminal work (1996), yet there are differences—particularly in the identification of the need for different logics. Further, Simon did not give much thought to the actual process of theorising and both he and subsequent writers have not explicated the special features of theorising in the exterior mode in a design discipline.

The ideas with regard to practical application of each principle are in part conjectures. In future work, it would be valuable to explore whether the principles appear, even implicitly, in what could be regarded as 'good' theorising or seminal work in IS.

Further work could also usefully be done to make the study of the processes of theory building more transparent. Space precludes such examination in this chapter.

References

Ashby, W. R. 1956, *An Introduction to Cybernetics*, Chapman & Hall, London.

Atwood, M., McCain, K. and Williams, J. 2002, 'How does the design community think about design?', Symposium on Designing Interactive Systems, pp. 125-132

Benbasat, I. and Zmud, R. 2003, 'The identity crisis within the IS discipline: defining and communicating the discipline's core properties', *MIS Quarterly*, vol. 27, no. 2, pp. 183–94.

Bourgeois, L. 1979, 'Toward a method of middle-range theorizing', *Academy of Management Review*, vol. 4, pp. 443–7.

Braa, J., Hanseth, O., Heywood, A., Mohamamd, W. and Shaw, V. 2007, 'Developing health information systems in developing countries: the flexible standards strategy', *MIS Quarterly*, vol. 31, no. 2, pp. 381–402.

Bunge, M. 1967, *Scientific Research II: The search for truth*, Springer Verlag, Berlin.

Burton-Jones, A. and Gallivan, M. J. 2007, 'Towards a deeper understanding of system usage in organizations: a multilevel perspective', *MIS Quarterly*, vol. 31, no. 4 (December), pp. 657–79.

CC2005 2005, *Computing Curricula 2005. The overview report*, Association of Computing Machinery, New York, and IEEE Computer Society, Washington, DC.

Cross, N. 2001, 'Designerly ways of knowing: design discipline versus design science', *Design Issues*, vol. 17, no. 3, pp. 49–55.

Davenport, T. and Short, J. 1990, 'The new industrial engineering: information technology and business process redesign', *Sloan Management Review*, vol. 31, no. 4, pp. 11–27.

Dilthey, W. 1883, 'Introduction to the human sciences', *Stanford Encyclopedia of Philosophy*, Stanford University Press, Calif., <plato.stanford.edu/entries/dilthey/>

Edgley, R. 1969, *Reason in Theory and Practice*, Hutchinson University Library, London.

Glaser, B. and Strauss, A. L. 1967, *The Discovery of Grounded Theory: Strategies for qualitative research*, Aldine Publishing Company, New York.

Godfrey-Smith, P. 2003, *Theory and Reality*, University of Chicago Press, Ill.

Goldkuhl, G. 2004, 'Design theories in information systems—a need for multi-grounding', *Journal of Information Technology Theory and Application*, vol. 6, no. 2, pp. 59–72.

Gregor, S. 2006, 'The nature of theory in information systems', *MIS Quarterly*, vol. 3, no. 30, pp. 611–42.

Gregor, S. and Jones, D. 2007, 'The anatomy of a design theory', *Journal of the Association of Information Systems*, vol. 8, no. 5, article 2, pp. 312–35.

Heidegger, M. 1993, 'The question concerning technology', *Basic Writings*, Harper, San Francisco, pp. 311–41.

Hevner, A., March, S., Park, J. and Ram, S. 2004, 'Design science in information systems research', *MIS Quarterly*, vol. 28, no. 1, pp. 75–105.

Heylighen, F. and Joslyn, C. 1992, 'Systems theory', in F. Heylighen, C. Joslyn and V. Turchin (eds), *Principia Cybernetica Web*, Principia Cybernetica, Brussels, viewed August 2008, <http://pespmc1.vub.ac.be/systheor.html>

Hooker, R. 1993, 'Aristotle: the four causes—physics II.3', viewed 15 March 2007, <http://www.wsu.edu:8080/~dee/GREECE/4CAUSES.HTM>

Iivari, J. 2003, 'Towards information systems as a science of meta-artifacts', *Communications of the AIS*, vol. 12, no. 37 (November), pp. 568–81.

Iversen, J., Mathiassen, L. and Nielsen, P. 2004, 'Managing process risk in software process improvement: an action research approach', *MIS Quarterly*, vol. 28, no. 3, pp. 395–434.

Jarvinen P. 2007, 'On reviewing results of design research', *ECIS 2007*, St Gallen, Switzerland, 7–9 June.

Kaplan, A. 1964, *The Conduct of Enquiry*, Chandler, San Francisco.

Kuechler, W. and Vaishnavi, V. 2008, 'The emergence of design science research in information systems in North America', *Journal of Design Research*, vol. 7, no. 1, pp. 1-16.

March, S. T. and Smith, G. F. 1995, 'Design and natural science research on information technology', *Decision Support Systems*, no. 15, pp. 251–66.

Markus, M., Majchrzak, L. A. and Gasser, L. 2002, 'A design theory for systems that support emergent knowledge processes', *MIS Quarterly*, vol. 26, no. 3, pp. 179–212.

Melville, N., Kraemer, K. and Gurbaxani, V. 2004, 'Review: information technology and organizational performance: an integrative model of IT business value', *MIS Quarterly*, vol. 28, no. 2, pp. 283–322.

Merton, R. 1968, *On Theoretical Sociology*, Free Press, New York.

MIS Quarterly 2008, MIS Quarterly Central Home Page, viewed August 2008, <http://www.misq.org/>

Nagel, E. 1979, *The Structure of Science*, Hackett Publishing, Indianapolis.

O'Hear, A. 1989, *Introduction to the Philosophy of Science*, Clarendon Press, Oxford.

Orlikowski, W. J. and Iacono, C. S. 2001, 'Research commentary: desperately seeking the "IT" in IT research—a call to theorizing the IT artifact', *Information Systems Research*, vol. 12, no. 2, pp. 121–34.

Parry, R. 2007, 'Episteme and techne', *Stanford Encyclopedia of Philosophy*, Stanford University Press, Calif., viewed November 2007, <http://plato.stanford.edu/entries/episteme-techne/>

Popper, K. 1980, *The Logic of Scientific Discovery*, Unwin Hyman, London.

Scharff, R. C. and Dusek, V. 2003, *Philosophy of Technology: The Technological condition. An anthology*, Blackwell Publishing, Malden, Mass.

Schön, D. 1983, *The Reflective Practitioner*, Basic Books, New York.

Simon, H. 1996, *The Sciences of the Artificial*, Third edition, MIT Press, Cambridge, Mass.

Strasser, S. 1985, *Understanding and Explaining Basic Ideas Concerning the Humanity of the Human Sciences*, Duquesne University Press, Pittsburgh.

University Libraries 2008, Real-Time EBM Program: The P I C O Model, viewed August 2008, <http://www4.umdnj.edu/camlbweb/ebm/picomodel.htm>

van Aken, J. 2004, 'Management research based on the paradigm of the design sciences: the quest for field-tested and grounded technological rules', *Journal of Management Studies*, vol. 41, no. 2, pp. 219–46.

van Aken, J. 2005, 'Management research as a design science: articulating the research products of mode 2 knowledge production in management', *British Journal of Management*, vol. 16, no. 1, pp. 19–36.

Venable, J. 2006, 'The role of theory and theorising in design science research', *First International Conference on Design Science Research in Information Systems and Technology*, Claremont, Calif., pp. 1–18.

von Bertalanffy, L. 1968, *General System Theory*, Braziller, New York.

Weber, R. 1987, 'Toward a theory of artifacts: a paradigmatic base for information systems research', *Journal of Information Systems*, vol. 1, no. 1 (Spring), pp. 3–19.

Weber, R. 1997, *Ontological Foundations of Information Systems*, Coopers & Lybrand, Melbourne.

Weick, K. 1989, 'Theory construction as disciplined imagination', *Academy of Management Review*, vol. 14, no. 4, pp. 516–31.

4. Incommensurability in design science: which comes first—theory or artefact?

MICHAEL DAVERN
ALISON PARKES
UNIVERSITY OF MELBOURNE

Abstract

There has been much debate and discussion in recent literature about the nature of information systems (IS) theory, the role of theory in design and the notions of design science and design theory. A central idea in much of this literature is the interplay between traditional theory-based research and the development of design theory through the building of information systems artefacts. In this chapter, we describe our recent experiences in the development of an artefact (a rule-based expert system called DG-In) based on a behavioural theory and the challenges we found as we attempted to reconcile it with relevant design theory. The potential for incommensurability in the research cycle between theory and artefact has significant implications for IS research—from both a design-science perspective and a behavioural-science perspective. It brings into question core ideas such as the development of a cumulative research tradition and notions of theory-based design and design theory more generally.

Introduction

The objective of design science is to create artefacts (broadly defined, including processes and methodologies) that are useful (Hevner et al. 2004). Design science, however, is more than building something useful. Good design science 'is the synergy between relevance and rigor' (Hevner 2007:91). Good design science should thus draw on the existing knowledge base of theories, frameworks and the like (see Hevner et al. 2004) and it must also contribute back to that knowledge base. It is in this regard that design science is more than simply good engineering. Iivari (2007) and Hevner (2007) are both quick to note, however, that good design science can be overly constrained creatively if it must be grounded only in theory. Rather a mix of sources (both theory and artefact) is preferred. Indeed, the mark of good design science lies in its rigorous evaluation of the artefacts developed (Iivari 2007; March and Smith 1995) and in its clear contribution to the 'knowledge base' (Hevner et al. 2004).

These premises for design science in the creative process (Hevner 2007) of design do, however, beg the question: *which comes first—theory or artefact?*

It is not our contention that either is more 'privileged' but rather, as we seek to demonstrate in this chapter, the difference in order can be non-trivial for the continuing development of theory, the advancement of artefact design and more broadly for the development of a cumulative research tradition (the 'knowledge base' in Hevner et al's [2004] terms).

The structure of the remainder of the chapter is as follows. In section two, we clarify our use of the terms 'theory' and 'artefact' and describe the cyclical relationship between the two. Using a context of explanation facilities and decisional guidance in intelligent systems, in section three, we contrast the artefact with theory and theory with artefact approaches. In section four, we document the relevant aspects of the artefact development that reveal to us the challenges and conflicts between the two approaches. We then describe the resulting incommensurability we observe in section five, and conclude in section six with the implications and questions for the future that are raised by the potential for incommensurability in IS research.

Cycles and theories

In practice, design science progresses not simply from theory to artefact or from artefact to theory, but cycles between the two (Hevner 2007; Hevner et al. 2004). In this cycle, theory can provide design guidance (prescriptions) and the artefact can inform theory. As Hevner et al. (2004:80) note, 'An artifact may have utility because of some as yet undiscovered truth', where truth is seen as the goal of behavioural science and utility is the goal of design science.

Theory and artefact are inseparable, as truth and utility are inseparable (Hevner et al. 2004). Indeed, drawing on Walls et al.'s (1992) concept of 'kernel theories' (theories from the natural and social sciences that inform design), Iivari (2007) claims that such kernel theories are a 'defining characteristic' of a 'design theory'. Consider Gregor's (2006) taxonomy of theories in IS. Gregor's taxonomy comprises five types—most notably: Type IV, explanation and prediction, and Type V, design and action. Type IV is found to be the most common in IS research and sits squarely in the domain of the natural and social sciences. It is the common notion of a theory. Type V theories prescribe how to do 'something'—providing, for example, a justified approach to developing an IS artefact. Notably, both Type IV and Type V theories are mutually interrelated; they inform each other. Artefact (an instantiation of a Type V theory) informs theory (Type IV) and theory informs artefact. For simplicity, we use the generic term 'Theory' to refer to a Type IV theory and the generic term 'Artefact' to refer to a Type V theory as it is instantiated in a design creation.[1]

The theory-to-artefact or artefact-to-theory issue in IS is paradigmatic. Both perspectives recognise the importance of the other—for example, from the design-science side Gregor (2006; Gregor and Jones 2007) emphasises the importance of theory, whereas Orlikowski and Iacono (2001), from the 'theory' side, emphasise the centrality of the IT artefact. If, however, we take as a premise that these are different paradigms for research then by definition they will be incommensurable (Kuhn 1970). Thus, it is not simply an issue of which comes first—theory or artefact—but rather from which direction one is coming at any particular stage in the cycle between theory and artefact. Despite efforts to make the IT artefact more central in theory-driven research—and comparable efforts to build a 'design theory' from artefacts—the potential for incommensurability exists. It is this incommensurability that we seek to exemplify in this chapter. Importantly, our goal here is not to render the two incompatible, but rather through exposing the challenges of incommensurability we seek to enhance the quality of the exchange between these two world views. Initially, we focus our discussion on the broad distinction between Theory and Artefact; subsequently, we delve into the components of a design theory as articulated by Gregor and Jones (2007) to formalise our analysis of incommensurability.

Directions matter: artefact to theory and theory to artefact

Our perspective on the issue of incommensurability arose in the context of a program of research in decision support systems. The program of research was inspired by an artefact—an expert system called INSOLVE (Arnold et al. 2004a)—and research on the concept of decisional guidance (Silver 1988, 1990, 1991). The program of research entailed the development of a new artefact, (DG-

---

[1] Notwithstanding there could be some debate about our use of these labels, and by no means do we seek to imply that either has a more privileged status in scientific endeavour.

In),[2] to test a behavioural theory about improving reliance on decision support systems through the provision of decisional guidance. Thus, at the outset, our research offered the potential to be informed by elements of artefact and elements of theory. Originally, we thought this would be a strength, but we had not anticipated the potential for incommensurability around central concepts and design features. Although we did not initially realise it, we were being driven more by theory than by artefact.

Critical to our behavioural theory was the concept of decisional guidance. Decisional guidance is defined as *'how a decision support system enlightens or sways its users'* (Silver 1991). Decisional guidance has been operationalised in a number of ways, including manipulating data display formats (Wilson and Zigurs 1999), providing differing types of explanations (Limayem and Desanctis 2000), prompting decision makers to consider causally related information cues (Montazemi et al. 1996), providing feedback on decision accuracy (Montazemi et al. 1996) and providing information relating to available decision models (Parikh et al. 2001).

Two important issues are immediately evident here. First, we see that theoretical concepts such as decisional guidance can underdetermine design, as evidenced by the sizeable diversity of ways in which it has been operationalised. This is an issue we will return to when we reflect more broadly on matters of incommensurability. Second, and more specifically, in the context of expert systems, explanation facilities appear to be one form of the broader concept of decisional guidance (Limayem and Desanctis 2000). This suggests mapping is possible between the two concepts. To explore this mapping, we looked at established taxonomies of explanation facilities and decisional guidance.

An artefact-based taxonomy of explanation facilities

Gregor and Benbasat (1999) provide a review of research pertaining to explanation facilities in expert systems and present a taxonomy of explanation types. Notably, the research from which the taxonomy is derived is largely without 'theory'. Specifically, Gregor and Benbasat (1999:500) identify two streams of research—'design' and 'empirical': the former has 'few or no theoretical bases' and the latter employs 'designs mostly based on considered

---

2 DG-In (pronounced 'dig in') is a completely new and independent artefact from INSOLVE. Substantively, its commonality with INSOLVE lies only in the domain of application (insolvency decision making) and in the use of a common model of insolvency practitioner decision making (gathered through knowledge acquisition processes in the development of INSOLVE). There is no common code; indeed, the platforms are entirely different, as DG-In is web based.

opinion and wisdom, rather than on the basis of theory'. The taxonomy is thus largely, in present language, artefact based (that is, the taxonomy is essentially a Type V theory).

The taxonomy proposed by Gregor and Benbasat (1999) comprises four types of explanation facilities

- trace or line of reasoning (which draws on data or rules to explain why decisions are or are not made)
- justification or support (which links back to underlying deep knowledge to justify the reasoning process)
- control or strategic (which explains the behaviour and/or decision strategy)
- terminological (which supplies definitional information).

The taxonomy is applied to a set of empirical papers to improve understanding of issues such as whether and why users need explanations, whether and how use of an explanation facility is beneficial and what type of explanations should be provided. It is a Type V Theory in Gregor's (2006) terms.

The existing INSOLVE artefact that partially inspired our work was an expert system that was specifically designed to provide explanations in a manner conformant with the Gregor and Benbasat (1999) taxonomy (see Arnold et al. 2004a for details). Indeed, Arnold et al. (2004a:6) specifically note that the design of the explanation facilities in INSOLVE are 'heavily grounded in the extant literature on optimal explanation facility design' and 'follow a theory synthesised by…Gregor and Benbasat (1999) to motivate our explanation types' (p. 9). Our 'Artefact' perspective was thus informed by the Gregor and Benbasat taxonomy—both in terms of the theory and in terms of its instantiation into INSOLVE. Mapping this taxonomy to the decisional guidance literature was thus an obvious requirement for advancing the development of our new artefact, DG-In.

A theory-based taxonomy of decisional guidance

While the roots of Gregor and Benbasat's explanation taxonomy were in artefacts, Silver's notion of decisional guidance was more about human behaviour. Indeed, Silver's (1990, 2008) own view is that understanding decisional guidance is about understanding a system as an agent of change. Unlike the Gregor and Benbasat taxonomy (a Type V theory), which seeks to say 'how to' design explanation facilities, Silver's development of decisional guidance is about 'the effects of system design features on the processes through which managers make decisions' (Silver 2008). Philosophically, decisional guidance would thus appear to be more rooted in the behavioural sciences (Silver's PhD is in decision sciences). While the decisional guidance taxonomy can inform design, it appears more commonly in literature grounded in theory (that is, Type IV theory) than artefact (Type V theory). It thus provides a contrasting perspective to the Gregor and Benbasat taxonomy. Nonetheless, it can and does inform design, although a design theory of decisional guidance has yet to fully emerge (not all the components of a design theory required by Gregor and Jones [2007] are yet present; see below for further discussion).

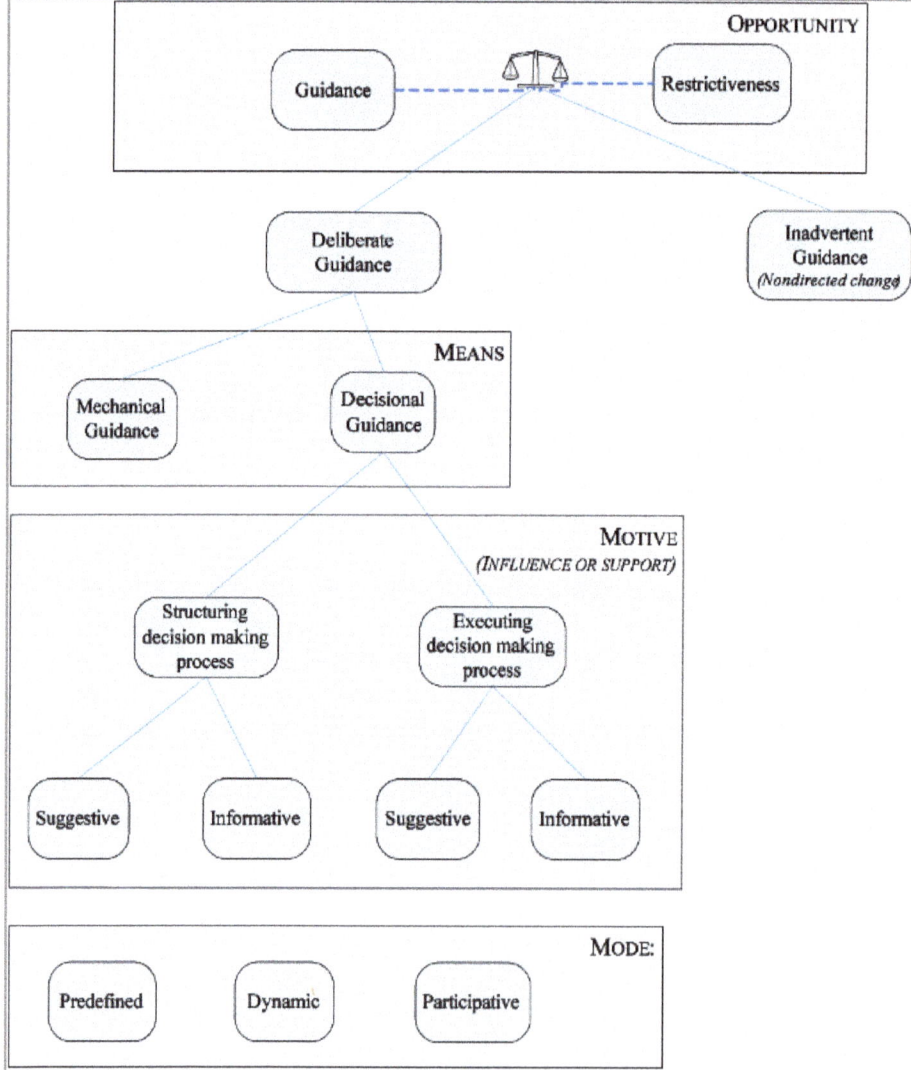

Figure 4.1 Decisional guidance overview

Adapted from Silver (1990:Figure 4, Forms of guidance)

Decisional guidance can provide support for decision makers executing a given decision process in differing ways. Silver (1990) suggests that there is a choice to be made between suggestive guidance (swaying a decision maker by making recommendations) and informative guidance (enlightening decision makers by providing them with unbiased, pertinent information). A single decision aid can contain both forms of decisional guidance and either, or both, can be offered at any judgment point (Silver 1990). Empirically, it is unclear which of these forms of guidance is superior, particularly as existing empirical studies have not explicitly considered support for differing types of decision makers and decision tasks. Montazemi et al. (1996) find that informative guidance produces better decision outcomes when a task is complex, but a later study (Parikh et al. 2001) does not directly consider task complexity and finds that suggestive guidance produces better decision quality and user satisfaction in less time. It was these mixed findings that theoretically motivated our program of behavioural research that led to the development of DG-In.

Figure 4.1 synthesises decisional guidance concepts (Silver 1988, 1990, 1991) and visually depicts the taxonomy of decisional guidance. It is beyond the scope of the present work to fully describe this taxonomy. For the present purposes, our interests are primarily in the execution of decision processes and the role of informative versus suggestive guidance.

In seeking to develop and justify the design of the new DG-In, drawing primarily on the decisional guidance taxonomy, we were confronted with how it related to the taxonomy of explanations. It was here that the incommensurability became evident, so now we turn to a discussion of our development of DG-In.

A theory-based artefact: the development of DG-In

DG-In is a rule-based expert system purpose-built for a program of behavioural research about the effects of decisional guidance on user reliance on a knowledge-based system. DG-In supports users in an insolvency-based judgment task requiring a decision about the future of a company that has recently entered into voluntary administration. DG-In focuses on the initial impression that insolvency practitioners must form to decide at the outset whether to liquidate the distressed business or attempt to trade out of difficulty. It employs an underlying decision model and materials gathered in an extensive knowledge acquisition effort that led to the original INSOLVE system (Arnold et al. 2004a, 2004b; Collier et al. 1999; Leech et al. 1999), but in all other respects is an independent and distinct artefact. The decision model in DG-In has been independently validated by expert insolvency practitioners and employed in empirical research with practitioners—a majority of whom indicated they would find the tool useful in their practice.

For experimental purposes, several versions of DG-In were created, depending on the particular forms of decisional guidance that were desired. The underlying decision model was identical in all cases. Suggestive guidance was operationalised by leveraging the inherent hierarchical structure of the decision model. Specifically, where multiple underlying factors contributed to an interim judgment within the decision model, the opportunity existed to both ask users directly for the interim judgment and provide suggestive guidance as to the interim judgment. After extensive modelling exercises, an additive model was found to be the most effective way of generating the suggestive guidance. Figure 4.2 shows the relevant underlying factors and then the resulting suggestive guidance.

Example underlying factors: Question 3. Will the practitioner be paid?

3.1   Will there be sufficient funds to pay the practitioner's fees and continuing expenses?

3.2   Is a challenge to the practitioner's priority to receive payment of their fees and expenses unlikely?

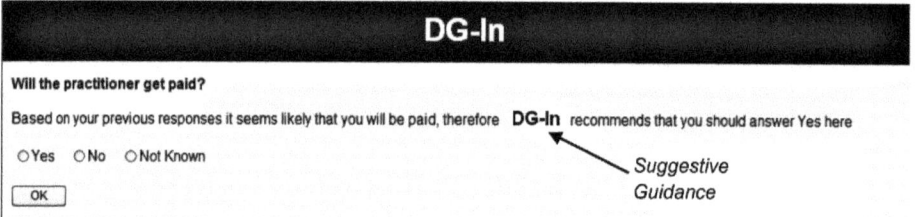

Figure 4.2 Suggestive guidance operationalisation

Informative guidance in the form of definitional text was also embedded into appropriate questions.

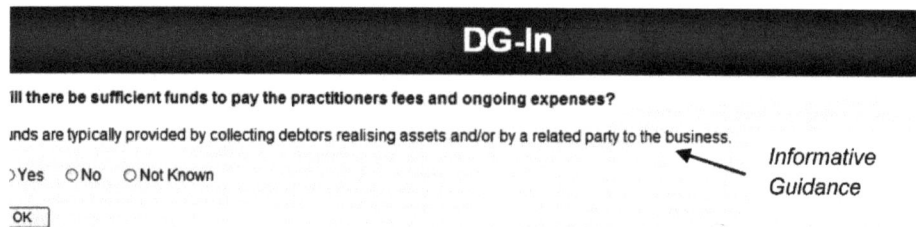

Figure 4.3 Example screenshot displaying informative guidance treatment

As noted earlier, decisional guidance has been operationalised in many ways. Thus, there was some interpretation used here since the theoretical concept, as an abstraction, underdetermined the design. This design interpretation was guided by immersion in the decisional guidance literature, discussions with Silver (the originator of the concept) and a guiding principle of 'would Silver recognise this as the form of decisional guidance intended'. This principle became quite important in the face of pressure from colleagues to align the design more closely with the Gregor and Benbasat (1999) taxonomy.

Demonstrating incommensurability

Mapping between the two taxonomies.

Attempts to map from the two forms of decisional guidance (informative versus suggestive) to Gregor and Benbasat's (1999) four types of explanation (trace, justification, strategic, terminological) proved to be less than straightforward and were a source of much debate among the research team and colleagues more broadly. Interestingly, in consulting with colleagues during the development of DG-In there was substantial negative feedback about the decisional guidance concept from colleagues who had been involved in the development of the original INSOLVE artefact. Having developed INSOLVE with explanation facilities as per Gregor and Benbasat (1999), they repeatedly challenged us to reconcile the explanation facilities taxonomy with the decisional guidance taxonomy. Importantly, they did not reject the concepts and theory of decisional guidance; rather they wanted them reconciled with their artefact perspective.

As the above example of informative guidance suggests (see Figure 4.3), informative guidance mapped quite clearly to the terminological category in Gregor and Benbasat's taxonomy. Suggestive guidance, however, did not seem to fit easily with any of the other categories. This was perplexing in both directions. A priori, decisional guidance appeared to be a broader concept than explanation facilities, so we were surprised we could not map suggestive guidance to the other elements in the Gregor and Benbasat taxonomy, no matter from which direction we approached the issue.

When considering these possible mappings, we could see that suggestive guidance (recommending what to do) was somewhat similar to explaining a problem-solving strategy (a control or strategic explanation in Gregor and Benbasat's [1999] taxonomy). Providing a recommendation does not, however, necessarily involve explaining how that recommendation was arrived at, leading us to conclude that suggestive guidance is not synonymous with a control or strategic explanation. Similarly, providing a recommendation does not necessarily include explaining why that recommendation is being made (ruling out a mapping to trace or line of reasoning explanations)—nor is it necessary to justify why the action is being recommended (ruling out a mapping to justification or support explanations). The remaining explanation type—terminological—is clearly unlike suggestive guidance and in fact maps directly to informative guidance (providing additional unbiased information). Thus, despite our a priori expectations, the expectations of colleagues and indeed the premise of a cycle between theory and artefact, we found the two taxonomies to be largely incommensurable (importantly, both taxonomies have been presumed in the literature to be comprehensive).

Comparing two theories or two artefacts

To formalise our arguments regarding incommensurability, we turn to Gregor and Jones's (2007) specification of the components of a 'Design Theory'. More specifically, we seek to compare the design theory specified by Gregor and Benbasat (1999) with a design theory based on the decisional guidance literature. Gregor and Jones identify eight components to a design theory: purpose and scope; constructs; principles of form and function; artefact mutability; testable propositions; justificatory knowledge; principles of implementation; and expository instantiation. Notably, the current decisional guidance literature does not yet adequately address all eight components of a design theory—reflecting its origins as a Type IV theory rather than a Type V theory. Table 4.1 details exemplars in Gregor and Benbasat (1999) of each of the eight components of a design theory. In Table 4.1, we also present potential exemplars of a design theory for decisional guidance derived from prior literature.

Table 4.1 Design theory components for explanations and decisional guidance

Type	Exemplars in Gregor and Benbasat (1999)	A 'design theory' for decisional guidance
Purpose and scope Goals and boundaries of the artefact/design theory	To present a unifying framework that integrates existing empirical work on explanations on intelligent systems. To improve performance and learning and improve user perceptions of intelligent systems. In essence, to guide design choices to achieve more effective and appropriate explanation facilities.	To build a knowledge base to better understand decisional guidance and be able to provide more effective support for decision makers.
Constructs 'Entities of interest'	Relevant examples: explanation types, format, provision mechanism and content; trace, justification or support, control or strategic, terminological.	Relevant examples: inadvertent guidance, deliberate guidance, suggestive guidance, informative guidance.

Principles of form and function Abstract plan of the artefact	Suitably designed explanations improve performance, learning and user perceptions of the system (per Gregor and Benbasat 1999; Figure 4.1).	Deliberately (as opposed to inadvertently) incorporating guidance in a system offers potential for more supportive systems.
Artefact mutability Scope for change or variability in artefact design under the theory	Explanations can be case/context specific rather than generic. Reasoning trace, justification and control explanations are typically specific; terminological explanations are usually generic.	Different guidance mechanisms can be instantiated in a variety of ways and the appropriate type of guidance is dependent on the nature of the support that is required.
Testable propositions Statements that can be empirically tested	See Propositions 1–9 in Gregor and Benbasat (1999) — for example: explanation use improves performance; explanations that require less effort will be more effective; novices and experts use explanations differently.	Different types of guidance influence decision makers differently.
Justificatory knowledge 'Kernel theories' that support the design	Theories from cognitive psychology on human reasoning, such as cognitive learning theory and Toulmin's theory of argumentation.	Synthesises a broad base of decision-making judgment and choice literatures and prior DSS literature.
Principles of implementation Processes for instantiating the theory into an artefact in a given context	Explanations should be provided 'automatically, if this can be done relatively unobtrusively, or by hypertext links' (Gregor and Benbasat 1999:517).	Decisional guidance has been operationalised in a variety of ways; specific principles of implementation are the subject of continuing empirical investigation.
Expository instantiation An artefact that is a physical and testable manifestation of the theory	INSOLVE	DG-In

Table 4.2 details on a component-by-component basis the differences between the design theory of Gregor and Benbasat (1999) and a design theory of decisional guidance based on our interpretation of the literature and as instantiated in DG-In.

Table 4.2 Comparing 'design theories'

Type	Comparison between Gregor and Benbasat (1999) (G&B) and a 'design theory' for decisional guidance
Purpose and scope	G&B's 'classification of explanations...reflects...the historical development of explanation facilities'. It seeks to integrate prior artefact-based research. In contrast, the decisional guidance taxonomy was established as theory to guide DSS research into the future.
Constructs	G&B describe components and types of explanations based on observations from artefacts and theories. The decisional guidance literature starts from theory and provides a taxonomy centred on the intentions of the designer and the nature of support intended.
Principles of form and function	While there are some overlaps here, G&B emphasise that better design results in better outcomes, whereas Silver emphasises that better designs provide more support for users. Both consider process and outcomes, but the emphasis is different (reflecting their intellectual heritage and stage of development).
Artefact mutability	Both G&B's and Silver's decisional guidance concepts allow for variability in contextualising or instantiating constructs. Notably, this variability only enhances the potential for incommensurability.
Testable propositions	G&B are able to be much more specific about design-relevant testable propositions as they synthesise and taxonomise existing artefact-based research. In contrast, the testable propositions evident in the decisional guidance literature reflect the potential variability for instantiating abstract concepts into design implementations.
Justificatory knowledge	G&B use existing theory to explain/justify the theory and taxonomy. In contrast, the decisional guidance literature begins with existing theory and creatively synthesises it to develop a taxonomy to guide designs that post date the creation of the taxonomy.
Principles of implementation	While there have been several behavioural studies of decisional guidance, principles of implementation have not yet coalesced. In contrast, the G&B taxonomy is heavily derived from artefacts so the principles of implementation are more clearly established.
Expository instantiation	INSOLVE versus DG-In

The analyses in Tables 4.1 and 4.2 provide some clues as to the source of incommensurability we observed. While there is a not insubstantial body of literature on decisional guidance it is still not adequate to specify fully all the necessary components of a design theory. The principles of implementation, in particular, are still open to interpretation. In short, the design of an artefact based on the theory and literature surrounding decisional guidance under-specifies the artefact; multiple interpretations are possible. Similarly, we see that Gregor and Benbasat (1999) use multiple theoretical perspectives as justificatory knowledge. It is thus difficult to connect the artefact elements described by Gregor and Benbasat's taxonomy to a single or unified coherent Type IV theory. The cycle between theory and artefact is problematic in both directions—the essence of incommensurability.

Reflections and implications of incommensurability

One interpretation of our experience here is simply that we have two incompatible 'theories': decisional guidance and explanations. Yet both are intended to feed design through the iterative cycle between theory and artefact. This is obvious in Gregor and Benbasat's work, which constitutes a Type V theory. While Silver's (1988) original research is behavioural and comes from a Type IV theory background, Silver (2008) himself now describes his research focus as being on 'design'. The problem is thus much broader. It illustrates that despite the best of intentions (ours and, arguably, Silver's and Gregor and Benbasat's), the literature that develops from the theory (Type IV) side can result in designs incommensurable with the developments in the literature on the Artefact side (Type V). The conceptualisation (Gregor 2006; Hevner 2007; Hevner et al. 2004; Iivari 2007) of design feeding from both advances in design theory and more traditional theory-based research becomes a little more challenging to realise in practice.

Fundamentally, the concern is not whether we have incommensurable approaches or simply incompatible theories; rather the issue is: are our experiences of the challenges in the development of DG-In an outlier event or a common occurrence? We believe it to be the latter and that this presents a great challenge for design-science and behavioural-science researchers in IS. The underlying problem is that theory underdetermines design and artefact design can generalise to multiple theoretical abstractions. Theory as an abstraction underdetermines reality. The implication for design science—with no disrespect intended—is that you can potentially build multiple theories from an artefact. The implication for behavioural science is that a given theory can be instantiated into multiple different artefact designs (because of the lack of detailed implementation principles), with potentially different consequences.

At issue is whether, in terms of design principles, we have different levels of granularity—specifically, whether Type IV theories could be less design specific than Type V theories. Indeed, we would argue that in practice the distinction between Type IV and Type V becomes less of a dichotomy and more of a continuum of varying degrees of design specificity (or, to put it another way, the extent to which all the components of a design theory required by Gregor and Jones [2007] are present). Thus, we can face incommensurability in design and incommensurability in theory when we cycle between Type IV and Type V theories in the effort to advance design.

We recognise there could be debate about some of the issues we have observed, described and reflected on in this chapter. Our purpose has not been to make a definitive argument here, but rather to describe an experience that led us to ask some challenging—and currently largely unanswered—questions for IS research. In short, if there is a broader potential for incommensurability akin to what we have observed, we are left with several burning questions.

- What does it mean to conduct theory-driven/grounded design-science research?
- What does it mean when the two approaches to design agree theoretically (for example, as in our experiences with informative guidance)?
- Does this mean we have the theory right?
- Does this mean we have the design right?
- What does it mean when the two approaches to design are theoretically incommensurable (for example, as in our experiences with suggestive guidance)?
- Does this mean we do not yet have adequate theory?
- Does this mean we need to consider more carefully the difference in granularity of theories with respect to design specificity?
- How can the field at large meaningfully create a cumulative research tradition in IS with the IT artefact at the centre?
- What are the implications of incommensurability for how we evaluate research—both in the design-science tradition and in the behavioural-science tradition?

At the very least, we hope we have sensitised the research community to the potential for incommensurability—a problem likely only to be exacerbated by the rapid technological advancement we face in IS and the relatively slow pace of progress in traditional theory-based research.

References

Arnold, V., Clark, N., Collier, P. A., Leech, S. A. and Sutton, S. G. 2004a, 'Explanation provision and use in an intelligent decision aid', *International Journal of Intelligent Systems in Accounting, Finance & Management*, vol. 12, no. 1, pp. 5–28.

Arnold, V., Collier, P. A., Leech, S. A. and Sutton, S. G. 2004b, 'Impact of intelligent decision aids on experienced and novice decision-makers' judgments', *Accounting & Finance*, vol. 44, no. 1, pp. 1–26.

Collier, P. A., Leech, S. A. and Clark, N. 1999, 'A validated expert system for decision making in corporate recovery', *International Journal of Intelligent Systems in Accounting, Finance & Management*, vol. 8, pp. 75–88.

Gregor, S. 2006, 'The nature of theory in information systems', *MIS Quarterly*, vol. 30, no. 3, pp. 611–42.

Gregor, S. and Benbasat, I. 1999, 'Explanations from intelligent systems: theoretical foundations and implications for practice', *MIS Quarterly*, vol. 23, no. 4, pp. 497–530.

Gregor, S. and Jones, D. 2007, 'The anatomy of a design theory', *Journal of the Association for Information Systems*, vol. 8, no. 5, pp. 312–35.

Hevner, A. R. 2007, 'A three cycle view of design science research', *Scandinavian Journal of Information Systems*, vol. 19, no. 2, pp. 87–92.

Hevner, A. R., March, S. T. and Park, J. 2004, 'Design science in information systems research', *MIS Quarterly*, vol. 28, no. 1, pp. 75–105.

Iivari, J. 2007, 'A paradigmatic analysis of information systems as a design science', *Scandinavian Journal of Information Systems*, vol. 19, no. 2, pp. 39–64.

Kuhn, T. 1970, *The Structure of Scientific Revolutions*, Second edition, University of Chicago Press, Ill.

Leech, S. A., Collier, P. A. and Clark, N. 1999, 'A generalized model of decision-making processes for companies in financial distress', *Accounting Forum*, vol. 23, no. 2, pp. 155–74.

Limayem, M. and Desanctis, G. 2000, 'Providing decisional guidance for multicriteria decision making in groups', *Information Systems Research*, vol. 11, no. 4, pp. 386–401.

March, S. T. and Smith, G. F. 1995, 'Design and natural science research on information technology', *Decision Support Systems*, vol. 15, pp. 251–66.

Montazemi, A. R., Wang, F., Nainar, S. M. K. and Bart, C. K. 1996, 'On the effectiveness of decisional guidance', *Decision Support Systems*, vol. 19, pp. 181–98.

Orlikowski, W. J. and Iacono, C. S. 2001, 'Desperately seeking the "IT" in IT research—a call to theorizing the IT artifact', *Information Systems Research*, vol. 12, no. 2, pp. 121–34.

Parikh, M., Fazlollahi, B. and Verma, S. 2001, 'The effectiveness of decisional guidance: an empirical evaluation', *Decision Sciences*, vol. 32, no. 2, pp. 303–31.

Silver, M. S. 1988, 'Descriptive analysis for computer-based decision support', *Operations Research*, vol. 36, no. 6, pp. 904–16.

Silver, M. S. 1990, 'Decision support systems: directed and nondirected change', *Information Systems Research*, vol. 1, no. 1, pp. 47–70.

Silver, M. S. 1991, 'Decisional guidance for computer-based decision support', *MIS Quarterly*, vol. 15, no. 1, pp. 105–22.

Silver, M. S. 2008, Fordham University web site, New York, <http://www.bnet.fordham.edu/public/ics/msilver/msilver.html>

Walls, J. G., Widmeyer, G. R. and El Sawy, O. A. 1992, 'Building an information systems design theory for vigilant EIS', *Information Systems Research*, vol. 3, no. 1, pp. 36–59.

Wilson, E. V. and Zigurs, I. 1999, 'Decisional guidance and end-user display choices', *Accounting, Management & Information Technology*, vol. 9, pp. 49–75.

5. An exploration of the concept of design in information systems

JUDY MCKAY
SWINBURNE UNIVERSITY OF TECHNOLOGY

PETER MARSHALL
UNIVERSITY OF TASMANIA

GREG HEATH
SWINBURNE UNIVERSITY OF TECHNOLOGY

Abstract

This chapter explores the concepts of design and design science in a number of disciplines, including information systems (IS). The authors identify and explore various viewpoints or perspectives on design in a number of disciplines including management, engineering, architecture and product development. These perspectives include design as product, design as process or action, design as intention, design as planning including modelling, representation and method, design as communication, design as user experience, design as a value, design as professional practice and design as service. This broad and diverse set of perspectives is contrasted with what is identified and characterised by the authors as a limiting technological perspective of design adopted by the current extant papers in the mainstream IS journals. The chapter concludes with a call to broaden and further develop the concept of design, and hence design science, into an integrated holistic socio-technical view that includes the human social and organisational factors alongside the technical factors.

Introduction

There has been rapid growth in interest in the notion of design—and hence in the building of a design science—in information systems (IS) in the past decade. Many seminal papers have been published that have proved very influential in the field, and thus have inevitably begun to shape the discourses that take place (essentially through publications) and the practices around design science that emerge over time. Notable among these seminal papers is that of Hevner et al. (2004) entitled 'Design science in information systems research', published in *MIS Quarterly*. It needs to be acknowledged, however, that this work was itself informed by some work of earlier writers, particularly Walls et al. (1992), March and Smith (1995) and Markus et al. (2002).

While the position of these authors and others has formed, to an extent at least, somewhat of an orthodoxy or mainstream on design science in IS at the current time, there are other views emerging (see, for example, Carlsson 2006, 2007; McKay and Marshall 2005, 2007; Niehaves 2007a, 2007b; Niehaves and Becker 2006). These papers question some of the perspectives adopted and promoted by the mainstream and put forward alternative perspectives on design and design science. Given this, the argument that will be articulated and explored in this chapter is that some of these differences could stem from differences in how information systems themselves are conceptualised and in how the construct 'design' is conceptualised. Indeed it will be argued—based on arguments articulated by Campbell (1979) in writing about the concept of organisational effectiveness—that no single, all-encompassing definition of either IS or design in IS can be established. Rather it will be asserted that a particular conceptualisation of design in IS could be useful only in certain circumstances, and thus to be made sense of it must be located within a theoretical framework or context of what IS is perceived to be. This builds on the notions articulated by El Sawy (2003), who noted, in comparing different positions put forward in the 'What is the core of IS?' debate, that any single perspective is just that: a single view among many possible views of 'reality'. El Sawy (2003) notes that each perspective both highlights and backgrounds different elements: different perspectives are not right or wrong, but offer differing views and insights. In applying this thinking to design in IS, we can conclude that the differing positions emerging are helpful to build knowledge about the perspective of design adopted and that multiple perspectives could be useful in building a broader-based design science in IS. Thus, depending on the circumstances, different conceptualisations of design, of IS and of design in IS could be necessary and helpful in building an overarching IS design science. From this perspective, it would be limiting to take too parochial a view in defining such terms, as in doing so we could limit the applicability of our research findings in these important areas.

This chapter will thus argue for multiple conceptualisations of design to be accepted as applicable within the field of IS, and thus the production of new knowledge of design in IS—the very basis of building a science of design in IS—can progress along a much broader front. Further, the chapter will argue that in addition to the important work already undertaken by Hevner et al. (2004), Walls et al. (1992), Markus et al. (2002), and others, in starting to articulate what we here label as a technology-centred design science in IS, knowledge needs also to be built in a human-centred design science (Roth 1999:24) in IS. Together, the technology-centred design science and the human-centred design science will offer greater insights and account for more contexts than either will on their own, and should thus serve to progress the understanding of design in the IS discipline.

The chapter is structured as follows. In the sections that follow, Hevner et al.'s position on design science will be discussed and from that we will deduce and argue that their views on design science stem from a particular view of IS—akin to what El Sawy (2003) describes as a connection view of IS. The chapter will then consider the domains of design and use this to consider the ways in which design is conceptualised in many non-IS disciplines—among them management, organisational development, architecture, engineering, industrial design and education. Such conceptualisation will then be compared with the ways in which design would appear to be conceptualised in the current IS design-science literature, and it will be shown that in IS design science currently, there is a much narrower view of design. If we accept Campbell's (1979) argument, this would suggest that the science of design that is being built will be constrained by the conceptualisations we have of design. The chapter will then discuss a number of issues associated with this conceptualisation and will suggest other ways of thinking about, and hence conducting research into, design and IS. The chapter concludes with an argument that both technology-centred design science and human-centred design science are needed to together advance our understanding of design in IS along a broader front and to thus build an overarching theory of design in IS.

An exploration of Hevner et al.'s position

Hevner et al. (2004) delineate IS knowledge as falling within two paradigms: the behavioural science and the design-science paradigms. Essentially, they argue that design science in IS is about the design of 'new and innovative artifacts' (Hevner et al. 2004:75)—IT artefacts—which are then implemented or instantiated in particular situations to solve problems identified within organisational contexts. In contrast, it is argued that the behavioural paradigm seeks to explain and predict 'organizational and human phenomena *surrounding* the analysis, design, implementation, management, and the use of information systems' (Hevner et al. 2004:76; emphasis added). In Figure 5.1, from Hevner et al. (2004:79), the relationships between business and IT strategies and infrastructures are depicted, and it is noted that the interplay between these four elements is seen as rightly falling within the interests of IS researchers. While Hevner et al. (2004) recognise that there are many design activities involved in realising alignment between IS and the organisational strategies—thus effectively exploiting the capabilities of IT to enable the organisation (and its members) to achieve its goals and objectives—their interest in design science in IS is, however, limited to the design activities associated with the building of an IS infrastructure (circled in Figure 5.1). Hevner et al. (2004:78) write that '[o]ur subsequent discussion of design science will be limited to the activities of building the IS infrastructure within the business organization. Issues of strategy, alignment, and organizational infrastructure are outside the scope of this paper.' This and subsequent statements in their paper—'we do not include people or elements of organization in our definition [of the IT artefact], nor do we explicitly include the process by which such artifacts evolve' (Hevner et al. 2004:82) and 'artifacts constructed in design science research are rarely full-grown information systems that are used in practice' (p. 83)—would seem to reveal world views (perspectives) on both 'design' within an information systems context and 'information systems', which serve to delimit their subsequent argumentation.

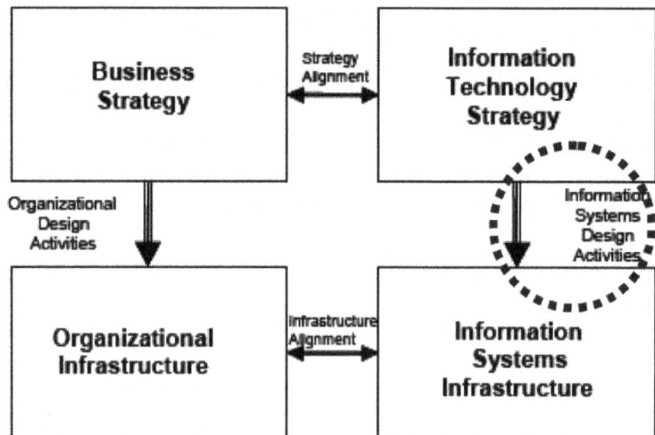

Figure 5.1 The focus of design interest in IS according to Hevner et al. (2004)

Carlsson (2007) argues that in the writings of Hevner et al. (2004) and other key authors such as Walls et al. (1992), March and Smith (1995) and Cao et al. (2006), design and the design-science paradigm in IS are arguably presented as being about the IT artefact—that is, elements of the innovative combination of hardware and software and the means by which these can be realised (specific instantiations or models, representations, constructs, vocabulary and the like surrounding the technical artefact). Hevner et al. (2004:78) note the dichotomy that design is about product (the artefact itself and attendant methods and models, for example) and the process, the set of activities by which such innovative products are produced. Another important distinction is drawn between what they describe as routine design and design-science research. Routine design is characterised by applying existing knowledge and IT artefacts to organisational problems, whereas design-science research focuses on finding innovative, new solutions to important unsolved organisational problems and, from this, new knowledge can be added to the existing knowledge base around design in IS (Hevner et al. 2004:81). In addition, they argue that other interests—the social, cultural, political and human dimensions associated with the implementation, use, acceptance and exploitation of the technical artefact in an organisational context—all fall within the behavioural-science paradigm in IS. This, then, suggests a particular view of design and IS, which is illustrated in Figure 5.2.

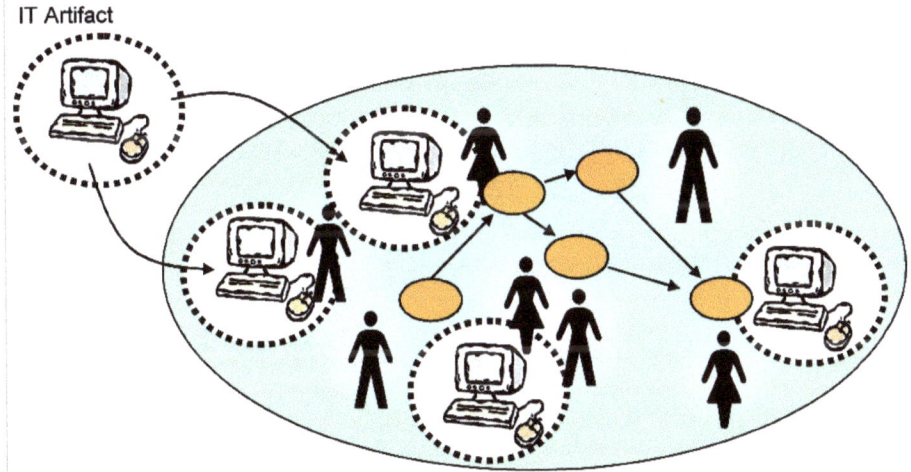

Figure 5.2 The IT artefact 'surrounded' by the organisational context.

The IT artefact in Figure 5.2 is viewed as consisting of the new innovations described by Hevner et al. (2004), which could be combinations of innovative software and hardware (instantiations) or constructs, models and methods, and the like. This IT artefact is of interest to the design-science researcher who, through building and evaluating such artefacts, builds knowledge in the design-science paradigm. The knowledge, insights and skills revealed by a design-science researcher collectively build a science of design. For the purposes of this chapter, we will refer to this as a *technology-centred design science*. The IT artefact can then be implemented into an organisational (socio-technical) context, and hence the 'things' in the organisation can become of interest to the IS researcher working in the behavioural-science paradigm. Note that such artefacts are seen as being 'surrounded' by human and organisational phenomena or arguably as being able to be split out from the organisational context in which they are implemented. Thus, the Hevner et al. (2004) conception of IS would seem to embrace a bounding of the IT artefact from other constituent elements of an organisational context. There would appear to be similarities between this and what El Sawy (2003:591) describes as the connection view of IS, in which IT is 'a separate artifact that can be connected to people's work actions and behaviors'.

Hevner et al. (2004:78) note that other design activities of interest to IS researchers are evident in organisations (labelled 'Organizational design activities' in Figure 5.1), but argue that research into these aspects of design falls within the behavioural-science paradigm. Thus, within IS, knowledge built about design is seen as falling across two paradigms: the design-science paradigm for technology-centred design science and the behavioural-science paradigm. This causes some discomfort; the recognition of the building of a science of design in IS is shared broadly across the IS academic community, but the position adopted by Hevner et al. (2004) would appear to result in a split between two different spheres of design knowledge. It is the authors' contention that such a view is not held in other, non-IS disciplines in which design is of considerable interest. Further, it will be discussed whether the connection view of IS (El Sawy 2003) leads to a narrow conceptualisation of design in IS. The question to be considered is whether a different and broader conceptualisation of design in IS might be helpful in building new and insightful knowledge and practices about design as it impacts on IS.

Design in different contexts and disciplines

Design is not an activity or phenomenon that is solely the province of IS researchers and practitioners. Indeed, it is a very broad concept and has developed a very substantial literature in a variety of disciplines and fields. In this section, we consider the conceptualisation of design in disciplines other than IS to see if there are insights to be gained from the way others construct, and thus understand and research, design.

Buchanan (1989) argues that design is impacted and shaped by essentially three 'domains of knowledge' (see Figure 5.3): the need to make things work properly (engineering-type knowledge), the need for the form and appearance of designed artefacts to meet appropriate aesthetic requirements (knowledge from art and aesthetics) and knowledge of the human sciences, of how people communicate and relate to artefacts within particular contexts.

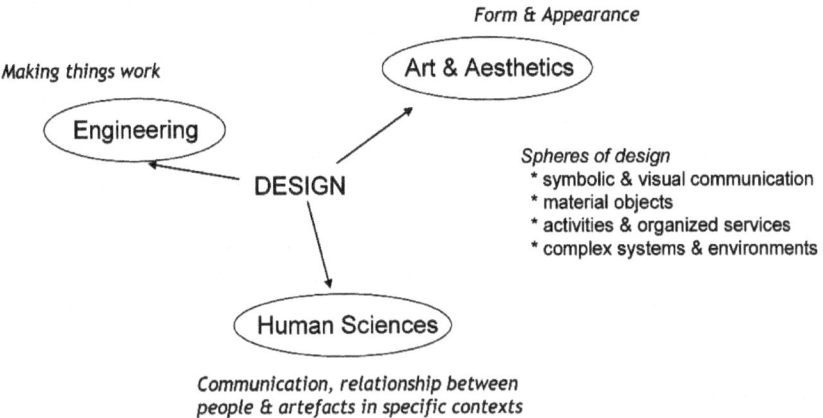

Figure 5.3 The three domains of knowledge impacting on design spheres of activity

Buchanan (1992) argues that there are few aspects of contemporary life that are untouched by design and suggests that there are four broad spheres of design activity, which are not discipline specific, but rather that characterise the application of design ideas to very different problem types and different subject matters. These will be described briefly as they serve a useful starting point for a consideration of how design is conceptualised in different contexts and disciplines. The first of these Buchanan (1992) labels as *design of symbolic and visual communication*, which includes traditional graphic design and illustration, but now includes film and television, photography and computer display. The second area he describes as the *design of material objects*, which embraces a wide range of everyday items, including tools, machines, vehicles, apparel and domestic objects. Buchanan (1992:9) notes a trend in the literature to move from thinking purely of the object itself to a broader interest 'and diverse interpretation of the physical, psychological, social and cultural relationships between products and human beings'. The third area is the *design of activities and organised services*, which embraces the organisation of various resources in efficient sequences and schedules so that particular objectives can be achieved. This area is concerned particularly with logistics and logical decision making, but Buchanan (1992:9–10) also notes a recent shift to a broader consideration of 'how better design thinking can contribute to achieving an organic flow of experience in concrete situations, making such experiences more intelligent, meaningful and satisfying'. The final area is the *design of complex systems or environments for living, working, playing and learning.* This clearly includes town planning and architecture, but Buchanan (1992:10) again notes a shift in emphasis to embrace 'the central idea, thought, or value that expresses the unity of any balanced and functioning whole'. Against this very broad backdrop, it is now possible to consider the ways in which design is conceptualised in a range of non-IS disciplines.

Design as problem solving

Across many disciplines, design is commonly referred to as problem solving, a way of defining problems (Boland et al. 2008; Buchanan 1992), and it is argued that this rational problem-solving view of design has become dominant and normalised in conceptualising design in many disciplines (Dorst 2006). When viewed as problem solving, design is often characterised as a 'means of ordering the world' (Dilnot 1982:144), of meeting needs and making desired improvements, of transforming and improving the material environment (Friedman 2003; Willem 1990). Emphasis is often placed on design involving careful analysis and definition of the problem and on gathering adequate information about the problem before seeking solutions (Kruger and Cross 2006). In some conceptualisations of design as problem solving, however, the emphasis is placed not so much on the notion of there being a problem, but rather on design as being the solution to the problem. In this way, the conceptualisation of design shifts slightly to generating solutions and, at times, redefining the problem in light of these emerging solutions (Kruger and Cross 2006). It is thus argued that design solves problems by being solution oriented, as involving designing or developing solutions to situations regarded as problematic by stakeholders (Keys 2007; van Aken 2007). These design problems are of certain types, however, with van Aken (2007) distinguishing between knowledge problems (which arise through limitations in knowledge) and field problems (which arise from a recognition or desire to realise a better social reality). Design is seen as solving field problems and the problem-solving activity involves not only designing a solution but also realising or implementing that solution in some material or social reality.

Design as product

Many writers note the distinction between 'design' as a noun (an object or product) and 'design' as a verb (an action or process). In conceptualising design as a product, writers generally refer to objects, entities or artefacts that arise within particular social and historical contexts and are imbued with meaning within those contexts (Dilnot 1982). This type of definition—in which the focus is clearly on the designed artefact—has been called the 'product view of design' (Marxt and Hacklin 2005:414), and there is often reference to the importance of design's involvement in giving material form to a problem solution, of the artefact meeting some perceived need or solving some sort of organisational, technical or human problem (Willem 1990). The concept of design as product thus sometimes is linked into discourse about consumption and the economics of production (Teymur 1996). The role of the designer is often mentioned and always assumed, in the sense that the designer is seen as adding characteristics of desirability and/or utility to the object of interest (Dilnot 1984a), which serves to emphasise that the design of products is an outcome of human creativity and industry. The designer is thus inextricably linked to and involved with the product of design; design is thus not viewed as a mechanistic replicable activity, for whereas replication in the physical sciences is seen as possible and quite independent of the scientist, the designer working within a particular context gives rise to the shape and form of the artefact produced.

Design as process, action

The limitations of the product view of design arguably stem from the fact that the activity or process involved in materialising a problem solution is marginalised, and thus definitions of the product view of design cause angst in some circles, where there is a tension perceived between the *product* of creation and the *activity* of creation. For example, Miller (2004) asserts that the product or result of creation is an entity, an output of design, but is not design itself. Thus, from this perspective, a chair is a chair, an output of designing a chair, but a chair is not itself a design. In contradistinction to the product view of design, there is what could be called the *process view of design*: design is a process, a series of thoughts and activities by which an artefact is created and realised (Andreasen et al. 2002; Miller 2004). The concept of problem solving is often retained in definitions of these types, in which design is seen as the activity involved in moving from a vague, possibly ill-defined problem to a clear and creative response, and in these activities shaped by context lies the essence of design (Ryan 1997). The goal of design from this perspective is thus to take action and to produce change in human contexts (Willem 1990). Galle (1999) takes this notion a little further and calls for an expansion of the notion of design such that it embraces all human activities dedicated to both realising an artefact and embedding that artefact in a context of use in which it is met with approval and use (or not).

Design as intention

In some literature, the aspect of design that is emphasised is generally its utility and the fact that it results from intentional activity (Dipert 1995; Hilpinen 1995). Thus, an extension of the notion of design as activity is the view of design as intention or intentional activity. Miller (2004) emphasises the importance of intentional thought processes in design activity, including insight by which a designer is able to see connections between problem (challenge) and possibilities, intuition and hunches and reasoned problem solving, which are synthesised throughout the design process. Willem (1990:45) argues that 'design occurs when the intention to design is present', suggesting that it is an intentional creative response to external events. Galle (1999) notes the potential complexity when, from this perspective of design, not only the designer's intentions but those of the problem owners and solution users become enmeshed in the design activity. This view of design puts the focus clearly onto the internal thought processes of the designer and how they can be guided by the intentions of the user of a design, and the context of use.

Design as planning (modelling, representation, method)

Furthering the view of design as intention, Buchanan (1992:8) argues that design can be regarded as a plan or 'working hypothesis', which constitutes or formalises the designer's intention. Along similar lines, Dilnot (1984b, drawing from the work of Papanek 1974) suggests that design can be thought of as a conscious attempt to plan and build patterns that will then shape the emergence of an artefact from a conceptualisation of the designer. Wieringa and Heerkens (2007) broadly agree with such viewpoints, arguing that design involves specifying what you intend to do before you in fact do it, and thus is fundamentally concerned with conceiving and planning something in one's mind. Galle (1999:65) refers to this as the problem of the 'absent artifact', the challenge of conceptualising, planning and realising something that does not currently exist. Dilnot (1984a) notes that before the Industrial Revolution, designing, planning and making artefacts were conceived of as one construct. Typically, since the onset of the Industrial Revolution, however, the planning and designing of artefacts have been separated from the making of artefacts. The perspective of Galle (1999) is sympathetic to this view, as he argues that in the process of realising an artefact and embedding it in its context of use, there are several stages of planning involved. Thus, in moving from conception of a solution to realised artefact, there are stages of design representation or plans, including conceptual, logical and physical plans and models. Van Aken (2005a) argues that such plans are themselves designs—the plans and sketches of a house, for example, are the design of the house. According to the conceptualisation of van Aken (2005a), following the design is another stage of planning, the plans of action and activities involved in the realisation of the physical artefact, in which the design representations are transformed into an artefact of utility. As in many disciplines, conceiving designs and making artefacts now involves significant complexity and knowledge intensity; another form of design as planning emerges—that of design of the design process itself. In other words, in large, complex projects, the processes involved in design representation and the processes involved in realising the design can be of such complexity that these processes could themselves need designing. This van Aken (2004) has called design-process design.

Design as communication

Buchanan (1989:105) asserts that 'some kind of communication exists in designed objects'. This argument is justified in asserting that designers either knowingly or unknowingly enshrine human values and opinions in their designs, based on their own world view and on their understanding of either a specific or a general audience for which the design is intended. A design resonates with an audience when it appeals to their interests, values and attitudes, for example, and in this way communicates with its audience (Lunenfeld 2003). Kazmierczak (2003) argues that design is the process by which the meanings intended by the designer are communicated to an audience and received either as intended or as reconstructed by the audience given their context, values and the like. Thus, Kazmierczak (2003:45) defines designs as 'cognitive interfaces that enable reconstruction of intended meanings'. This perspective of design is thus quite different from many of those presented above. It moves from notions around objects or artefacts, and the processes by which the artefact is realised, and rather focuses on the conceptual characteristics embodied in objects that serve to communicate with their audience or users. Kazmierczak (2003:45) writes that '[i]t redefines designs from finite, fixed objects of aesthetic and practical consideration to semiotic interfaces enabling the reconstruction of meaning by receivers'. Defined in this way, design becomes associated with form and content, with emphasis placed not just on the role of the designer in shaping form, but also on an essential role of the designer in shaping communicative content that is evidenced through the meaning, interpretations or thoughts a design induces in an audience. Design, thus conceived, becomes linked to a designer using the 'right' language to express his/her intentions in a way that can be accurately comprehended and responded to by the audience (Krippendorff 1996; Redstrom 2006). Kazmierczak (2003:48–9) argues that 'designs are not designs unless there is a receiver' and suggests that the success of a design is dependent on the successful comprehension of the design by its intended audience.

Design as user experience

The notion of design as communication is extended by Redstrom (2006), who suggests that design is best conceived as the user's experience of an object. Thus, it is not just the communicative element of design that is important, but the experiences that design creates and enables for its recipient audience. In this way, the user or audience becomes the subject of design, through their 'dynamic and multisensory' experiences of an artefact (Redstrom 2006:126). This represents a substantial shift away from the object or artefact and the processes surrounding the conceptualisation of the object and its physical realisation. Design thus becomes concerned with how one designs user experiences, not just in terms of utility or usability, but in terms of communication, interpretation, understanding and experience (Boztepe 2007; Kazmierczak 2003; Redstrom 2006).

Design as value

Some writers note that design itself has become associated with value—often not an intrinsic part of the artefact itself, but as some sort of iconic status that becomes associated with a particular object. In this sense, we get expressions such as 'good design', 'designer jeans' or 'designer labels', in which value becomes associated with the significance attached to an object rather than the object itself (Dilnot 1984a, 1984b). The designer involved in the value-association view of design is often conceived as the loner-hero-artist—often an iconic and easily recognisable figure to a certain subculture. Their audience or users value the objects they design by what they communicate or mean to a wider audience, and thus value becomes associated with what the object comes to symbolise (Lundgren 1978).

Design as professional practice

Many definitions of design include close consideration of the designer and some come to argue that design is 'what designers do' (Dilnot 1984b). Thus, design starts to be conceptualised more as professional practice, with identified responsibilities to clients, fellow designers, the public and broader social and environmental responsibilities (<www.aiga.org>). Design as a professional practice can be viewed as a way of thinking and an attitude towards a design task (Wangelin 2007), as a practice delimited by the design task (Hooker 2004) or as engagement directly in a specific design activity (Fallman 2003). This view of design emphasises the situatedness of the designer in a real-world context involving uncertainty, ambiguity and value conflict (Fallman 2003, citing Schon 1983), and inevitably links design to the personal experiences, capabilities, knowledge and intuition of the designer. In this way, Louridas (1999) and Wangelin (2007) argue that design is bricolage—an attitude towards a problem in which previous knowledge and experiences, tools and resources can be intuitively adapted and applied to a current challenge. This view of design serves to emphasise the subjective nature of interpretation and value judgments made about the problem at hand, the intended audience, and so on. Considering design as a professional practice implies a need to think much more closely about the knowledge, skills and attributes required of designers as they conceptualise and realise artefacts intended to improve problem situations

(Friedman 2003; Keys 2007), and hence, a need to retain a 'sense of design as a pluralistic and multiple activity, a synthesis of heterogeneous activities defined not by the separate activities, but by their integration' (Dilnot 1982:141).

Design as service

When thinking about design, often the vision that tends to emerge is that of a lone designer, a hero figure, who is highly creative, innovative and bold and who manages to turn the design of a product with various aesthetic values into an outlet for personal expression (Dilnot 1984b). Lundgren (1978) shies away from this, arguing that in post-industrial societies, most design activity is centred on service provision rather than heroism or what Dilnot (1984b:4) describes as 'non-esthetically motivated service…or problem solving design'. Lundgren (1978:20) writes that 'design activity…has so much more to do with sustained service, an anonymously methodical day-in, day-out solving of problems, than with the constant ferment of creative choices exercised by the loner hero-artist'. In this view, designers function to effectively solve problems presented to them by others. The design-as-a-service view encapsulates the ability to understand the problem as experienced by these problem owners and their objectives in seeking a resolution of that problem. The context in which the problem is embedded is thus critical to successful design. The designer must, in addition to the skill requirements for designing in a particular field, have insights into and appreciation of the cultural, political and moral aspects of social forces that shape individual perspectives of the problem and that of possible solutions (Keys 2007).

This list of differing conceptualisations of, and nuances associated with, the construct design from non-IS fields is not intended to be exhaustive—nor are these mutually exclusive. There are clearly overlaps and close relationships between the differing perspectives of design discussed here. It illustrates, however, some of the ways in which design is understood, taught and researched in a range of non-IS fields. Willem (1990) notes that it could be 'disconcerting' to take such a broad view of a range of possible activities and entities that are considered under the rubric of design. To not do so, however, is to arbitrarily assign the label of design to a subset of these activities, which Willem (1990) argues could seem somewhat capricious. Willem (1990:45) goes on to note that 'the recognition of a large host of coherent activities as design may provide a richness of experience that is presently missing'. He notes that science accommodates a large range of disciplines and activities within its fold without having a detrimental effect on any of them. Design can do likewise. Further, this broader conceptualisation of design, we argue, helps make sense of a statement made in the introduction—based on the arguments of Campbell (1979)—in which it is argued that no single, all-encompassing definition of design can be established. Rather, any particular definition of design delimits a world view of design and thus locates design within a particular frame or context. Knowledge production is then also located within that context and, while it could offer important insights about that particular world view, it is also limited in not offering insights into the many other possible world views that could be entertained.

Design in IS

Table 5.1 offers a comparison of the ways in which design is conceptualised in non-IS areas as opposed to its conceptualisation in IS journals. To construct Table 5.1, the authors independently read the papers listed, identifying the ways in which design was conceptualised. These independent assessments were then discussed and consolidated. The table is presented here for noting, as indicative of what we believe to be a tendency that is of interest in this chapter.

In disciplines other than IS, we see a very broad understanding of design and this arguably shapes the ways in which researchers consider suitable topics for research within design and how such knowledge can best be produced. When compared with IS publications, the contrast is quite stark. In the small sample of papers examined for illustrative purposes, currently there are four predominant conceptualisations: design as problem solving, design as product or artefact, design as process—often referred to as building and evaluating—and design as planning, modelling and representing (see Table 5.1).

The concepts of design as product and design as process or activity are well represented in the current IS design-science literature (see Table 5.1). Design as problem solving is also represented, but less so. A key reference in this context is Hevner et al. (2004), who mention that the design-science paradigm is a problem-solving paradigm in the sense that information systems are often, or at least should be, designed to solve an identified organisational problem. Other authors, such as Niehaves (2007b), follow Hevner et al. (2004). In Niehaves' (2007b) paper, the notion of problem is broadened to include social constructionist formulations and an increased focus on organisational context.

Table 5.1 Conceptualisations of design in IS and non-IS literature

Non-IS papers

Author(s)	Year	Problem solving	Product, artefact	Process, action	Intention	Planning (modelling, representation, method)	Communication	User experience	Value	Professional practice	Service
Andreasen et al.	2002			x							
Boland et al.	2008	x									
Boztepe	2007							x			
Buchanan	1989						x				
Buchanan	1992	x				x					
Dilnot	1982	x	x							x	
Dilnot	1984a		x			x			x		
Dilnot	1984b					x			x	x	x
Dipert	1995				x						
Dorst	2006	x									
Fallman	2003									x	
Friedman	2003	x								x	
Galle	1999			x	x	x					
Hilpinen	1995				x						
Hooker	2004									x	
Kazmierczak	2003						x	x			
Keys	2007	x								x	x
Krippendorff	1996						x				
Kruger and Cross	2006	x									
Louridas	1999									x	

5. An exploration of the concept of design in information systems

Non-IS papers	Conceptualisation of design										
Author(s)	Year	Problem solving	Product, artefact	Process, action	Intention	Planning (modelling, representation, method)	Communication	User experience	Value	Professional practice	Service
Lundgren	1978								x		x
Lunenfeld	2003						x				
Marxt and Hacklin	2005		x								
Miller	2004			x				x			
Redstrom	2005						x				
Ryan	1997			x							
Teymur	1996		x								
van Aken	2004					x					
van Aken	2005a					x					
van Aken	2007	x									
Wangelin	2007									x	
Wieringa and Heerkens	2007					x					
Willem	1990	x	x	x	x						
Selected IS papers											
Arnott	2006		x	x							
Au	2001		x	x							
Cao et al.	2006	x	x	x							
Hevner et al.	2004	x	x	x							
Iivari	2007		x	x	x						
March and Smith	1995		x	x							
Markus et al.	2002		x	x							
Niehaves	2007b	x	x	x							
Walls et al.	1992		x	x							
Walls et al.	2004		x	x							

In terms of design as product, the literature clearly discusses the design of software, modelling approaches and innovative combinations of software, hardware and networks, for example. The focus is clearly on the technical artefact, however, and there is seldom consideration of a designed organisational space, context or environment as being a product of design. For example, Hevner et al. (2004) mention distributed database designs that include network latency considerations but would be unlikely to view such artefacts situated in an organisational context with attendant process change, work and information flow changes, job design changes and so on all holistically viewed as a design product. Thinking about and researching such phenomena could add important knowledge to a design science in IS. There is, however, almost no attention paid to the concepts discussed by Teymur (1996) of consumption and the economics of production in IS design science. For example, there is no research into the move from bespoke to packaged software or what this means from a design perspective. Largely absent too in the IS design-science literature is the explicit role of the designer in shaping designs, in embedding values, beliefs and an ethical position within software, in understanding the creativity and creative processes by which thought becomes artefact, and so on. Both Markus et al. (2002) and Arnott (2006) explicitly concern themselves with design as process, and in other IS design-science literature, notions such as approaches to modelling and systems development are featured. There appears to be little research, however, into the processes involved in advancing from fuzzy, ill-defined problem to creative response to instantiation or artefact. McKay and Marshall (2007) discuss this process, but do not conduct any empirical research into such processes. While there is undoubtedly IS literature surrounding taking action and producing change when implementing IS in organisations, this is rarely—with the possible exception of Markus et al. (2002)—framed as design. Arguably, there is great opportunity to think of IS implementation in terms of designing organisational contexts and spaces and much that can be learned from considering the design-science literature that has developed in the field of organisational development (see Romme 2003; Trullen and Bartunek 2007; van Aken 2007).

Thinking of design as intention obviously overlaps with both problem solving and process (activity), but note that in the non-IS literature, this conceptualisation involves linking the designer's intention and creativity to action and also to the intentions of problem owners and those of solution users. These all seem fertile ground for design-science research in IS, but are notably absent from much of the current IS design-science literature. Design as modelling, representation and method or planning has historically been well represented in the IS literature and is also featured in the more recent IS design-science literature. There seems, however, to be scope to research the impacts of models and methods—for example, on the creativity and intentions of the designer, the problem owner and the solution user—on how these models and methods contribute to shaping solutions. Further, there is little discussion in IS design science of Galle's (1999) idea of the absent artefact, the intrigue that surrounds how one effectively models, plans and represents something that does not yet have material form, but that could have conceptual 'realness' for stakeholders in the IS artefact.

Whereas in other disciplines areas of research have emerged on product semantics (Krippendorff 1996) and the semiotics of interfaces (Kazmierczak 2003), it seems that this whole area of design as communication is absent from current IS design-science literature, although it could feature in some of the HCI literature (Fallman 2003) and the earlier studies in IS (see, for example, Galliers 1987; Stamper 1973). Research into how and why IS designs resonate and communicate with their intended audiences (Lunenfeld 2003) in both intended and unintended ways seems under-done in IS design science—as is a range of topics associated with the ways in which the communicative properties of IS artefacts influence user adoption and appropriation (or lack thereof) of such systems. Design as user experience brings the concept of design in context to the fore, which challenges some of the conceptualisations of Hevner et al. (2004) and others. Thus, users in context as the subject of IS design and how to design IS user experience can become potentially important topics of concern to a holistic, broadly focused and organisationally aware IS design science. The notion of design as value is connected to notions of the semantics and symbol, which likewise seem absent from current IS design-science research. Arguably, many people can associate symbols and values associated with SAP or IBM, for example, but researching these from a design perspective and understanding the impacts and influence ascribing such values to IT artefacts seem not to have been well articulated in IS design science. Thinking of design as professional practice and service poses interesting questions about how IS practitioners really work, how they design and shape organisational spaces and contexts and how as designers they influence the success or failure of IT artefacts, which also seem fertile, but underdeveloped areas for research.

While a much narrower conceptualisation of design in IS design science than that which has emerged in many other design-oriented disciplines might not be of concern per se, the perspective adopted here is that currently IS is far too limited in what is legitimised as a researchable conception of design, thus also limiting what might fall under the rubric of design research and hence what might constitute design knowledge or a science of design. Some of these perspectives discussed above could have been present in IS literature (often dating back 20–30 years—see, for example, the collection of readings in Galliers 1987) but have been underrepresented in the recent swell of interest in design in IS, and opportunity exists to revisit these from an IS design perspective. The problem, we assert, is that the current conceptualisation of design in IS design science is too limited to embrace the rich possibilities discussed above. It is our view that the narrow conceptualisation raises a number of important issues, and these will be explored more fully in the next section.

Issues in current conceptualisations of design science in IS

Thinking about the notion of design in IS requires us to be mindful of the reasons why we design. There are obviously economic imperatives—for greater efficiency and remaining competitive in a global marketplace that is complex, uncertain and turbulent. A design imperative in IS must surely be to help organisations manage these forces and to achieve sustainability in such environments. There are also cultural, social and ethical imperatives that would revolve around thinking about designing information systems that utilise IT to help humans enrich their experience of organisation, of work, of society and of education, to add meaning and value to what they do (Buchanan 1996:79). If we accept both these, it could be argued that we need to build a design science in IS that—in addition to the technology-centred design knowledge—builds knowledge in our designers (and hence creates knowledge, capabilities and a culture among our IS professionals) so that they know how to achieve both these things (economic and socio-cultural imperatives) through their range of design activities in organisations. What they know will limit and shape what they can do—thus, a technology-centred conceptualisation of design will potentially perpetuate technology-centred solutions being proffered as solutions to design problems.

The world view that would apparently underpin Hevner et al.'s conceptualisation of IS (see Figure 5.2 and related discussion) is well suited to the articulation of design knowledge relating to the IT artefact as they define it. It is not, however, sufficient to support the breadth of research activity that could take place under the rubric of design within an IS context if some of the conceptualisations of design from non-IS disciplines were adopted within IS. Opponents of this stance could assert that in the Hevner et al. (2004) view, many of the broader conceptualisations of design and the associated research problems would certainly remain within the interests of IS research, but would be seen as belonging to the behavioural-science paradigm. That is certainly one way of dealing with this problem. We know of no other discipline, however, in which such a separation has been made. In the other disciplines that were included in our reading of the design literature, there had been no such attempt to split design interest and the knowledge that accrued from research into such interests into design science and behavioural science. Thus, in engineering (Marxt and Hacklin 2005), in management (Boland 2004; Boland et al. 2008; Friedman 2003), in organisational development (van Aken 2004, 2005a, 2005b), in industrial design (Cross 2001), in education (Brown 1992; Edelson 2002) and in the arts and humanities (Lunenfeld 2003), for example, design and design knowledge are not viewed as being split across two paradigms, but multiple conceptualisations are embraced within a design science. Thus, other world views are possible and important and need to be considered in gaining a new perspective of what the construct design might mean in IS. Figure 5.4 depicts one other possibility.

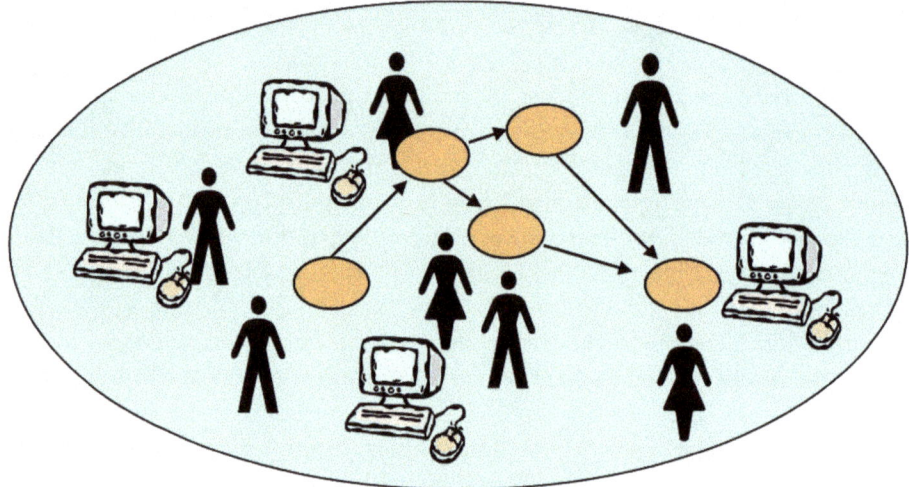

Figure 5.4 A socio-technical view of IS situated in context

The world view captured in Figure 5.4 takes a socio-technical view of IS and thus views IS as fundamentally different from the IT artefact in the 'situatedness' of the technology within an organisational context. An IS emerges from the relationships and behaviours that results in organisational contexts that involve people, activities, information, technology, culture, politics, history and the like. It is not divisible. Viewed in this way, IS is not *surrounded* by organisational and human phenomena but is part of those phenomena, is socially constructed by designers (IS practitioners) and society shaping (Hughes 1987) and hence shapes and is shaped by the context of use. IT artefacts are components of IS, as are people, activities and so on. But the *IS artefact* emerges from the interactions and interdependencies that result from looking at the whole, rather than constituent elements. This view seems more in harmony with the fusion view defined by El Sawy (2003). Design in IS in this fusion view occurs in shaping organisational contexts by changing the way information is communicated, stored, created, shared, used, and so on, in shaping the way work is done, in shaping the way people interact, in shaping the way organisations are structured and in shaping the way in which cultural and power relationships are played out (Boland et al. 2008). Such design activity must be cognisant of the culture, politics, sociology and history of that context. Thus, the IS artefact and its situated utilisation in a particular wider socio-technical context become the objects of research interest. Indeed, this argument parallels that of Simon (1996) with regard to organisations and management: managers, in creating structures, writing plans, developing processes, policies and procedures and the like, are designing—they are creating organisations or organisational environments as designed artefacts (Boland et al. 2008). We can describe the task of management, then, as responsibly construing and shaping problem spaces and designing artefacts in response to that problem construction (Boland 2004). These designed artefacts, when implemented in the target organisation, form part of the improvement of the problem space or situation. For IS researchers and practitioners, this emphasises the need for broad conceptualisation and interest in design and the need also to recognise, understand and elucidate practices with respect to transforming situations (by the responsible application of IT artefacts) into more desired states, taking account of context and the uses for which people could appropriate such systems. For the purposes of further discussion, we will call this the *human-centred view of design*. Human-centred design knowledge and technology-centred design knowledge should both be recognised as falling legitimately within a design science in IS.

Hevner et al. (2004) differentiate between routine and innovative design. Innovative design—the fundamental breakthroughs that build knowledge that previously did not exist—is seen as being in the province of technology-centred design science, whereas routine design, applying knowledge of design in organisational contexts, falls outside the bounds of design science and thus presumably within behavioural science. Other authors, however, offer different insights in this regard. For example, Hughes (1987) also draws a distinction between conservative and radical design, which closely parallels the sorts of distinctions made by Hevner et al. (2004). Hughes (1987), however, regards both as design—as would be the case in the human-centred design world view. Willem (1990:45) takes the distinction slightly further in suggesting that design occurs when 'the intention to design is present and when the action taken is derived at least in part from a creative sense rather than instinct or imitation'. Thus, routine (conservative) and innovative (radical) design are both forms of design—possibly in different contexts—and knowledge accumulated about both should legitimately fall within a science of design; instinctive responses, and imitation, such as mass production are not design. Thus, once again, it is argued that the concept of design has to be made sense of within a world view of design and then it is useful only for a certain purpose shaped by the context. Distinctions between routine and innovative design are highly contingent on world view, and within the human-centred view of design, research into both is essential to build our disciplinary knowledge of design.

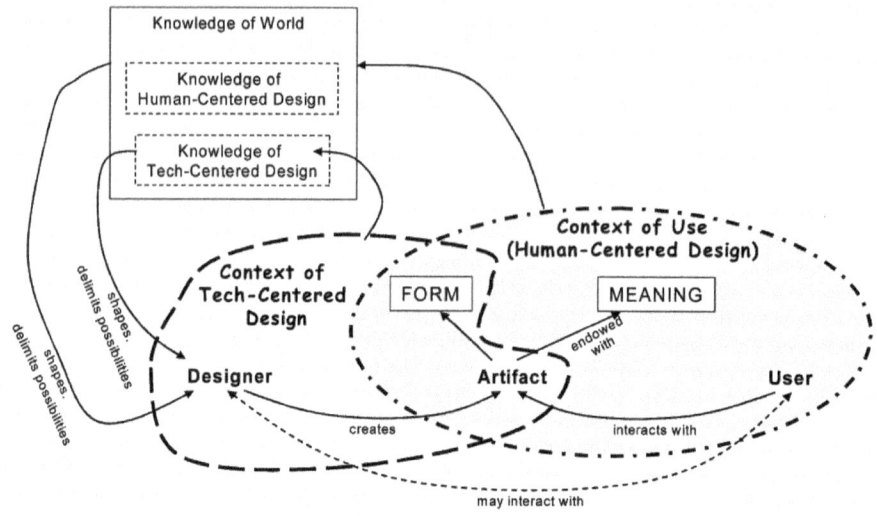

Figure 5.5 Components of IS design science

From Galle (1999); Krippendorff (1996).

From considering the differences between world views, a much more complex view of design starts to emerge (see Figure 5.5). Taking the technology-centred view of design, the focus is on the IT artefact (Carlsson 2007)—specific instantiations or models, representations, constructs, vocabulary and the like surrounding the technical artefact—and the resultant form that it is given as a result of design activity within a context of design. Through research and reflection, the body of knowledge about technology-centred design is built and accumulates over time. When that artefact is implemented within an organisational context, a user interacts with that artefact and endows it with meaning within that particular context of use. Through research and reflection, knowledge of design within organisational contexts (human-centred design knowledge) is likewise built and accumulates over time. Such knowledge bases form part of our knowledge of the world. Designers are inevitably shaped and limited by their knowledge of design in both senses (technology centred and human centred). The world view of Hevner et al. (2004) focuses primarily on technology-centred design and building a design science based on the knowledge accrued in this context of interest; the alternative world view articulated in this chapter focuses primarily on human-centred design and argues that a design science can be built from knowledge accumulated in the context of use. The various perspectives of design can also be interpreted against this diagram and an argument will be put forward to suggest that broadening our current conceptualisation of design can lead to a much richer and broader understanding of design in IS, and hence of the types of research into design that can, and indeed should, be pursued. It is also the contention of this chapter that IS as a discipline is better served and greater coherence in the discipline is achieved if these potentially two design sciences are seen as one. If this is to be accomplished, a way must be found to avoid splitting out these interests into design science and behavioural science.

Implications and discussion

A way forward in the design science–behavioural science dichotomy could be offered by van Aken (2004, 2005a, 2005b, 2007), who suggests that a distinction can be drawn between the explanatory sciences and the design sciences. From van Aken's perspective, explanatory science (physics, chemistry, biology and sociology) attempts to build valid knowledge about the world (both natural and social). It attempts to describe, explain and sometimes to predict natural and social phenomena—hence is concerned with explanation and 'truth'. The outcomes of explanatory research can be a causal model as in the physical sciences, for example, or in the social sciences—an understanding of causal patterns shared between the researcher and an informed audience (van Aken 2005b, citing Peirce 1960). In contrast, van Aken (2007:68–70) suggests that design sciences (such as engineering, medicine and law) are geared towards improving the human condition through finding solutions to 'field problems'—problems involving how we design and realise a better reality. Thus, design is seen as solution oriented, involving the design of a solution and the realisation and implementation of a solution in 'material or social reality'. Design science is thus geared more towards making improvements and ensuring that change works well. It is aimed at intervening in contexts to make improvements and is thus oriented towards the future—not just describing and understanding what is. Design science aims to develop knowledge that can be used by practitioners in their field to design solutions to problems. It also aims to develop knowledge of how to implement and particularise the solution in the relevant context (Carlsson 2007; Trullen and Bartunek 2007; van Aken 2007).

Research in design science is thus interventionist and solution oriented, in which the ultimate aim is to produce theories and actionable knowledge (Argyris 1996) that can be used for designing solutions to real-world problems and their implementation and integration in such contexts. Carlsson (2007) echoes similar sentiments to van Aken (2004, 2005b, 2007) in suggesting that the outcomes of design-science research would take the form of technological rules, algorithmic or heuristic design exemplars for knowledgeable professionals (practitioners), which would enable them to apply the general knowledge gained from their discipline to specific solutions for specific problem contexts. Whereas in technology-centred design science, algorithmic technological rules might be one outcome, it is anticipated that in human-centred design science, heuristic technological rules—often qualitative in nature—might be the norm. Such heuristic rules would mean that practitioners do not start from a blank slate for each designed organisational intervention, but rather they recognise the right solution concept and then design a specific variant that suits a particular context (Carlsson 2007; van Aken 2007). Thus, Hevner's routine design (which was not regarded as design science) would be encapsulated in human-centred design science and if subject to rigorous sound research could result in heuristic technological rules.

Taking a broader view of what design science in IS could be also requires thinking more broadly about the types of knowledge that might form such a science of design. From Keys (2007) and Carlsson (2007), it would be argued that IS design knowledge could include the following in addition to the types of knowledge described by Hevner et al. (2004) and other researchers in the technology-centred design-science area

- meta-knowledge about context (organisational, social, political, historical and cultural setting of the problem of interest)
- tacit and explicit knowledge gained from design experiences in previous projects (problem-solving activities)
- knowledge of how to apply heuristic technological rules and design exemplars, and of how to particularise a heuristic technological rule or design exemplar to suit a specific context
- contingent knowledge of a specific situation (able to recognise the complexity and uncertainty)
- relational knowledge—knowledge of interpersonal relationships, the ability to 'see' what social interactions mean in a particular context
- knowledge of methods, tools and techniques.

The standpoint of the authors of this chapter is that a design science that incorporates the human-centred perspective—and hence expands its perspective and vision to include the types of knowledge above—would be richer and more generally applicable than one that is restricted to the technology-centred perspective of the mainstream or dominant view in the extant IS literature.

Conclusion

This chapter has assessed the design literature in fields outside IS, such as management, engineering, architecture, organisation development, education and the like, and has concluded that a broad, holistic view of design—and hence of design science—is emerging in these fields. This is leading to a richer and more broadly applicable design science in those fields. We have argued that the IS field would also benefit from broadening its current technical perspective of design and design science. Indeed, the importance of a broad viewpoint incorporating considerations of—and emphasising the significance of—psychological, social and organisational factors has been present in much of the IS research of the past 20 years, but these insights seem to have been forgotten in the recent surge of interest in design and design science in IS. Further, it is not sufficient to characterise the psychological, social and organisational factors as somehow belonging to a different discipline or 'paradigm', as has been done in some of the mainstream IS design and design-science literature. Such an approach leads to a disconnect between the technical and human factors in IS, when all the experience of previous research is that a holistic, integrated view of the human and technical factors is much preferred for generating relevant and practical advice for practitioners and other consumers of research outputs. Thus, it is argued that a holistic and integrated stream of design-science research needs to emerge in IS, embracing both the technology-centred and the human-centred design-research activities and knowledge.

References

Andreasen, M. M., Wognum, N. and McAloone, T. 2002, 'Design typology and design organisation', in D. Marjanovic (ed.), *Design 2002. Volume 1*, The Design Society, Dubrovnik, pp. 1–6.

Argyris, C. 1996, 'Actionable knowledge: design causality in the service of consequential theory', *Journal of Applied Behavioral Science*, vol. 32, pp. 390–406.

Arnott, D. 2006, 'Cognitive biases and decision support systems development: a design science approach', *Information Systems Journal*, vol. 16, pp. 55–78.

Au, Y. A. 2001, 'Design science I: the role of design science in electronic commerce research', *Communications of the Association for Information Systems*, vol. 7, no. 1 (July).

Boland, D. 2004, 'Design in the punctuation of management action', in R. J. Boland and F. Collopy (eds), *Managing as Designing*, Stanford Business Books, Calif.

Boland, R. J., Collopy, F., Lyytinen, K. and Yoo, Y. 2008, 'Managing as designing: lessons for organizational leaders from the design practice of Frank O. Gehry', *Design Issues*, vol. 24, no. 1, pp. 10–25.

Boztepe, S. 2007, 'User value: competing theories and models', *International Journal of Design*, vol. 1, no. 2, pp. 55–63.

Brown, A. L. 1992, 'Design experiments: theoretical and methodological challenges in creating complex interventions in classroom settings', *Journal of the Learning Sciences*, vol. 2, pp. 141–78.

Buchanan, R. 1989, 'Declaration by design: rhetoric, argument and demonstration in design practice', in V. Margolin (ed.), *Design Discourse*, University of Chicago Press, Ill.

Buchanan, R. 1992, 'Wicked problems in design thinking', *Design Issues*, vol. 8, no. 2, pp. 5–21.

Buchanan, R. 1996, 'Myth and maturity: towards a new order in the decade of design', in V. Margolin and R. Buchanan (eds), *The Idea of Design*, MIT Press, Cambridge, Mass.

Campbell, J. P. 1979, 'On the nature of organizational effectiveness', in P. S. Goodman, J. M. Pennings and Associates (eds), *New Perspectives in Organizational Effectiveness*, Jossey-Bass, San Francisco.

Cao, J., Crews, J. M., Lin, M., Deokar, A., Burgoon, J. K. and Nunamaker, J. F. Jr. 2006, 'Interactions between system evaluation and theory testing: a demonstration of the power of a multifaceted approach to information systems research', *Journal of Management Information Systems*, vol. 22, no. 4, pp. 207–35.

Carlsson, S. A. 2006, Design science in information systems: a critical realist perspective, Seventeenth Australasian Conference on Information Systems, Adelaide, 6–8 December 2006.

Carlsson, S. A. 2007, 'Developing knowledge through IS design science research: for whom, what type of knowledge and how', *Scandinavian Journal of Information Systems*, vol. 19, no. 2, pp. 75–86.

Cross, N. 2001, 'Designerly ways of knowing: design discipline versus design science', *Design Issues*, vol. 17, pp. 49–55.

Dilnot, C. 1982, 'Design as a socially significant activity: an introduction', *Design Studies*, vol. 3, no. 3, pp. 139–46.

Dilnot, C. 1984a, 'The state of design history, part I: mapping the field', *Design Issues*, vol. 1, no. 1, pp. 4–23.

Dilnot, C. 1984b, 'The state of design history, part II: problems and possibilities', *Design Issues*, vol. 1, no. 2, pp. 3–20.

Dipert, R. R. 1995, 'Some issues in the theory of artifacts: defining "artifact" and related notions', *The Monist*, vol. 78, no. 2, pp. 119–35.

Dorst, K. 2006, 'Design problems and design paradoxes', *Design Issues*, vol. 22, pp. 4–17.

Edelson, D. C. 2002, 'Design research: what we learn when we engage in design', *Journal of the Learning Sciences*, vol. 11, pp. 105–21.

El Sawy, O. A. 2003, 'The IS core—IX: the 3 faces of IS identity: connection, immersion and fusion', *Communications of the Association of Information Systems*, vol. 12, pp. 588–98.

Fallman, D. 2003, 'Design-oriented human–computer interaction', *CHI Letters*, vol. 5, no. 1, pp. 225–32.

Friedman, K. 2003, 'Theory construction in design research: criteria, approaches and methods', *Design Studies*, vol. 24, pp. 507–22.

Galle, P. 1999, 'Design as intentional analysis: a conceptual analysis', *Design Studies*, vol. 20, pp. 57–81.

Galliers, R. 1987, *Information Analysis: Selected readings*, Addison-Wesley, Sydney.

Hevner, A. R., March, S. T., Park, J. and Ram, S. 2004, 'Design science in information systems research', *MIS Quarterly*, vol. 28, no. 1, pp. 75–105.

Hilpinen, R. 1995, 'Belief systems as artifacts', *The Monist*, vol. 78, pp. 136–55.

Hooker, J. N. 2004, 'Is design theory possible?', *Journal of Information Technology Theory and Application*, vol. 6, pp. 63–72.

Hughes, T. P. 1987, 'The evolution of large technological systems', in W. E. Bijker, T. P. Hughes and T. F. Pinch (eds), *The Social Constructions of Technological Systems: New directions in the sociology and history of technology*, MIT Press, Cambridge, Mass., and London, UK.

Iivari, J. 2007, 'A paradigmatic analysis of information systems as a design science', *Scandinavian Journal of Information Systems*, vol. 19, no. 2, pp. 39–64.

Jenkins, M. A. 1985, 'Research methodologies and MIS research', in E. Mumford, R. Hirschheim, G. Fitzgerald and T. WoodHarper (eds), *Research Methodologies in Information Systems*, Elsevier Science Publishers, Amsterdam, pp. 103–17.

Kazmierczak, E. 2003, 'Design as meaning making: from making things to the design of thinking', *Design Issues*, vol. 19, no. 2, pp. 45–59.

Keys, P. 2007, 'Developing a design science for the use of problem structuring methods', *Systems Practice and Action Research*, vol. 20, pp. 333–49.

Krippendorff, K. 1996, 'On the essential contests of artifacts or on the proposition that "design is making sense (of things)"', in V. Margolin and R. Buchanan (eds), *The Idea of Design*, MIT Press, Cambridge, Mass.

Kruger, C. and Cross, N. 2006, 'Solution driven versus problem driven design: strategies and outcomes', *Design Studies*, vol. 27, pp. 527–48.

Louridas, P. 1999, 'Design as bricolage: anthropology meets design thinking', *Design Studies*, vol. 20, pp. 517–35.

Lundgren, N. 1978, 'Transportation and personal mobility', *Leisure in the Twentieth Century*, Design Council, London, pp. 20–3.

Lunenfeld, P. 2003, 'The design cluster', in B. Laurel (ed.), *Design Research: Methods and perspectives*, MIT Press, Cambridge, Mass.

McKay, J. and Marshall, P. 2005, 'A review of design science in information systems', in B. Campbell, J. Underwood and D. Bunker (eds), *Socialising IT: Thinking about the people. Proceedings of the Australasian Conference on Information Systems (ACIS 2005)*, Sydney, pp. 1–11.

McKay, J. and Marshall, P. 2007, 'Science, design, and design science: seeking clarity to move design science research forward in information systems', in M. Toleman, A. Cater-Steel and D. Roberts (eds), *ACIS2007 Proceedings of the Eighteenth Australasian Conference on Information Systems*, Toowoomba, Qld, pp. 604–14.

March, S. T. and Smith, G. 1995, 'Design and natural science research on information technology', *Decision Support Systems*, vol. 15, no. 4 (December), pp. 251–66.

Markus, M. L., Majchrzak, A. and Gasser, L. 2002, 'A design theory for systems that support emergent knowledge processes', *MIS Quarterly*, vol. 26, no. 3 (September), pp. 179–212.

Marxt, C. and Hacklin, F. 2005, 'Design, product development, innovation: all the same in the end? A short discussion on terminology', *Journal of Engineering Design*, vol. 16, no. 4 (August), pp. 413–21.

Mason, R. O. and Mitroff, I. I. 1973, 'A program for research on management information systems', *Management Science*, vol. 19, no. 5, pp. 475–87.

Miller, W. R. 2004, Definition of design, viewed 9 June 2007, <http://static.userland.com/rack4/gems/wrmdesign/DefinitionOfDesign1.doc>

Niehaves, B. 2007a, 'On epistemological pluralism in design science', *Scandinavian Journal of Information Systems*, vol. 19, no. 2, pp. 99–110.

Niehaves, B. 2007b, On epistemological diversity in design science—new vistas for a design-oriented IS research?, Twenty-Eighth International Conference on Information Systems, Montreal.

Niehaves, B. and Becker, J. 2006, 'Epistemological perspectives on design science in IS research', *Proceedings of the Twelfth Americas Conference on Information Systems*, Acapulco, Mexico, 4–6 August 2006.

Redstrom, J. 2006, 'Towards user design? On the shift from object to user as the subject of design', *Design Studies*, vol. 27, pp. 123–39.

Romme, A. G. L. 2003, 'Making a difference: organization as design', *Organization Science*, vol. 14, no. 5 (September–October), pp. 558–73.

Roth, S. 1999, 'The state of design research', *Design Issues*, vol. 15, pp. 18–26.

Ryan, D. 1997, 'Enzo Mari and the process of design', *Design Issues*, vol. 13, no. 3, pp. 29–36.

Simon, H. 1996, *The Sciences of the Artificial*, Third edition, MIT Press, Cambridge, Mass.

Stamper, R. 1973, *Information in Business and Administrative Systems*, B. T. Batsford, London.

Teymur, N. 1996, 'The materiality of design', *The Block Reader in Visual Culture*, Routledge, London.

Trullen, J. and Bartunek, J. M. 2007, 'What a design approach offers to organization development', *Journal of Applied Behavioral Science*, vol. 43, pp. 23–40.

van Aken, J. E. 2004, 'Management research based on the paradigm of the design sciences: the quest for field-tested and grounded technological rules', *Journal of Management Studies*, vol. 41, no. 5 (March), Blackwell Publishing, Oxford, pp. 219–46.

van Aken, J. E. 2005a, 'Valid knowledge for the professional design of large and complex processes', *Design Studies*, vol. 26, pp. 379–404.

van Aken, J. E. 2005b, 'Management research as design science: articulating the research products of mode 2 knowledge production in management', *British Journal of Management*, vol. 16, pp. 19–36.

van Aken, J. E. 2007, 'Design science and organization development interventions: aligning business and humanistic values', *Journal of Applied Behavioral Science*, vol. 43, pp. 67–88.

Walls, J. G., Widmeyer, G. R. and El Sawy, O. A. 1992, 'Building an information system design theory for vigilant EIS', *Information Systems Research*, vol. 3, no. 1 (March), pp. 36–59.

Walls, J. G., Widmeyer, G. R. and El Sawy, O. A. 2004, 'Assessing information system design theory in perspective: how useful was our 1992 initial rendition?', *Journal of Information Technology Theory and Application*, vol. 6, no. 2, pp. 43–58.

Wangelin, E. 2007, Matching bricolage and hermeneutics: a theoretical patchwork in progress, Design Semiotics in Use, SeFun International Seminar, Helsinki, Finland, 6–8 June 2007.

Wieringa, R. and Heerkens, H. 2007, 'Designing requirements engineering research', *Proceedings of the Comparative Evaluation in Requirements Engineering Conference (CERE 07)*, New Delhi.

Willem, R. A. 1990, 'Design and science', *Design Studies*, vol. 11, no. 1, pp. 43–7.

6. Evaluating information systems: an appropriation perspective

JUSTIN FIDOCK
RMIT UNIVERSITY, AND DEFENCE SCIENCE AND TECHNOLOGY ORGANISATION

JENNIE CARROLL
RMIT UNIVERSITY

ANITA RYNNE
LAND WARFARE DEVELOPMENT CENTRE,
DEPARTMENT OF DEFENCE

Abstract

This chapter describes the application of an appropriation perspective to support the evaluation, development and design of a knowledge management system—the Army Knowledge Domain (AKD) prototype—in the Australian Army. The AKD prototype was developed using an iterative approach informed by a modified form of the technology appropriation cycle (TAC). The TAC is a model that represents the process of appropriation through which technology is adopted, adapted and incorporated with personal, social and organisational practices, and describes how an understanding of users' appropriation choices can inform the design of future iterations of the system and supporting context. Results from the evaluation presented in this chapter have informed the next iterative development step for the AKD prototype. The utility of employing the modified TAC to support the evaluation, development and design of systems is then explored, including the support that the model provides to an expanded view of technology design.

Introduction

Evaluation is central to human experience (Hirschheim and Smithson 1999). We evaluate the outcomes of our own and others' endeavours—from a meal prepared by the chef at a local restaurant through to the performance of our elected Member of Parliament. Such evaluations guide and shape our attitudes, beliefs and expectations and hence our future actions—to recommend the restaurant to our friends or to shun the elected member at the next election. These evaluations are primarily informal; however, a variety of frameworks, methods, tools and techniques has been developed to formalise the evaluation process (Farbey et al. 1993; Owen and Rogers 1999; Symons 1991).

In the information systems (IS) domain, formal evaluations of projects are not often undertaken (Klecun and Cornford 2005). When undertaken, such evaluations have tended to focus on technical and tangible aspects of system development and implementation: reliability, performance, usability and cost–benefits (Klecun and Cornford 2005). The social dimension has largely been ignored in preference to providing rational, objective and quantitative explanations (Hirschheim and Smithson 1999). There appears to have been a shift, however, towards giving greater attention to the social and organisational context—including history, work practices, infrastructure, organisational norms and values, information flows and stakeholder perspectives—in recognition that IS projects are an organisational intervention, not just a technical intervention (Farbey et al. 1993; Hallikainen and Chen 2006; Huang 2003; Symons 1991). There is also recognition that the process of evaluation plays an important role in supporting the design and development of systems (Hevner et al. 2004; Symons 1991).

Information systems development (ISD) researchers and practitioners have similarly embraced the importance of attending to the 'soft' aspects of development, by adopting user-centred design approaches such as prototyping and agile systems development in order to reduce usability problems and capture emerging user requirements (Hall 2001; Surendra 2008). This has occurred in response to the recognised constraints of the more orthodox and mechanistic ISD approaches, which construe requirements as relatively predictable and therefore limit their capture from customers to the requirements elicitation phase (Hirschheim and Klein 1989; Surendra 2008). An underpinning assumption of all of the above approaches, however, appears to be that the design is fixed once development work ceases—that design and implementation are discrete steps. Furthermore, emphasis is placed on how the designed system shapes the user's behaviour. There is, however, a body of thought that argues that technology not only shapes the behaviour of users, but users in turn shape how the system comes to be instantiated through use (Chae and Poole 2005; DeSanctis and Poole

1994; Orlikowski 1992). From this interactionist perspective, system designs are not fixed at the end of the formal design process (Carroll 2004). Instead, designs are completed once 'realized in action…[and once] integrated into the everyday practices of human actors for whom the designs are a means to an end' (Orlikowski 2002:3). The designs are completed through a process of enactment or appropriation whereby the use or performance of the design unfolds over time. There are two important implications of this perspective: first, a focus on appropriation draws attention to the context of use and the consequent need to employ evaluation methods that are well suited to such phenomena; second, the unfolding of use over time that is associated with appropriation suggests that evaluations conducted to support system design should continue beyond the completion of the formal design process. Evaluations conducted in this way can yield insights and requirements that can shape subsequent formal system designs in a way that is complementary to extant ISD approaches, as well as better support the unfolding of design through use, via modification of the use context (Fidock and Carroll 2006).

Models and theories surrounding appropriation and enactment have been developed and applied to supporting the evaluation of IS (Carroll et al. 2003a; Nandhakumar et al. 2005), but not in a way that has informed subsequent formal designs. The technology appropriation cycle (TAC) model (Carroll 2004) represents an initial attempt to capture the process of appropriation and the implications an understanding of appropriation might have for shaping the formal design of future systems. The proposed link between appropriation and subsequent system design has, however, not been explored.

The TAC is intended to be a generic model that can be tailored to assist with understanding particular technologies and user cohorts (Carroll 2004). The model describes the process of appropriation through which technology is evaluated by people over time and adopted, adapted and incorporated into their practices, and through which the design of technology is stabilised through use. In describing people's evaluations of technology, the model is referring to their everyday responses and reactions, not formal evaluations. The formation of these evaluations is shaped by a variety of influences that are posited to change over time. An understanding of what these influences are for a particular technology, sample of users and context therefore has the potential to inform the formal design process, leading to a redesigned or new system (Carroll 2004). The model has not, however, been applied or modified to explicitly support the conduct of a formal IS evaluation as part of a system's development.

The TAC shows promise in guiding the formal evaluation, development and design of a system; it captures the process and phases through which people's evaluations of technology change over time; it provides an explicit representation of the link between appropriation and formal design; and it starts to address the context of use by emphasising the adaptation and incorporation of technologies with practices. For the preceding reasons, the research question in this study is: 'What is the utility of applying an appropriation perspective, encapsulated within a modified form of the TAC, to support IS evaluation, development and design?'

This chapter describes the evaluation, development and design of a knowledge management system (KMS) from the perspective of the TAC, which has been modified to support the conduct of a formal IS evaluation in an organisational context. The modified TAC (mTAC) is first described, followed by the KMS evaluation and system development context and approach. Some results are then presented in order to illustrate how they informed the next iterative development step for the KMS. The utility of employing the mTAC to support the evaluation, development and design of systems will then be explored.

The technology appropriation cycle

The TAC was developed by Carroll (2004) to assist with understanding the process of appropriation through which users adopt, adapt and incorporate a technology with their personal, social and work practices (top half of Figure 6.1). Such understanding has implications for evaluating the success of a technology since it is only once technology is used in the context of particular practices that the realisation of any anticipated benefits can be assessed (Marchand 2004; Peppard et al. 2007). The model also captures how an understanding of the appropriation process can inform the formal design process, leading to a redesigned or new system (bottom half of Figure 6.1) (Carroll 2004).

There is a variety of influences that shapes the evaluations and subsequent appropriation choices of people engaged in the process of appropriating a particular technology. Of particular significance are the nature of the technology itself and the attributes of people—their knowledge, skills, experiences, beliefs and attitudes. The generic TAC model was modified by adding three other categories of contextual influences to capture issues of importance in the conduct of a formal IS evaluations in organisational contexts (represented by the triangles at the perimeter of Figure 6.1)

- the technological context: the infrastructure within which the particular technology is embedded, the ways in which the technology is developed, implemented, managed or supported, as well as the goals, objectives and aspirations of stakeholders responsible for developing or supporting the particular technology

- the organisational context: its size, structure, culture, politics, processes (formal and informal), leadership, history and the degree of institutional inertia
- the environmental context: the resources available, extent of dynamism, complexity, competition and government regulation (Fidock and Carroll 2006; Mintzberg 1979; Owen and Rogers 1999; Scott Morton 1991; Symons 1991).

These additions were made because research associated with the development of the generic TAC model has to date explored organisational contexts to only a limited extent and focuses largely on technological and individual-level influences (Carroll et al. 2003b; Herszfeld et al. 2003; Mendoza et al. 2007). Furthermore, these studies built inductively on the model, rather than modifying it by drawing on organisational and evaluation literatures, as was done in the present study.

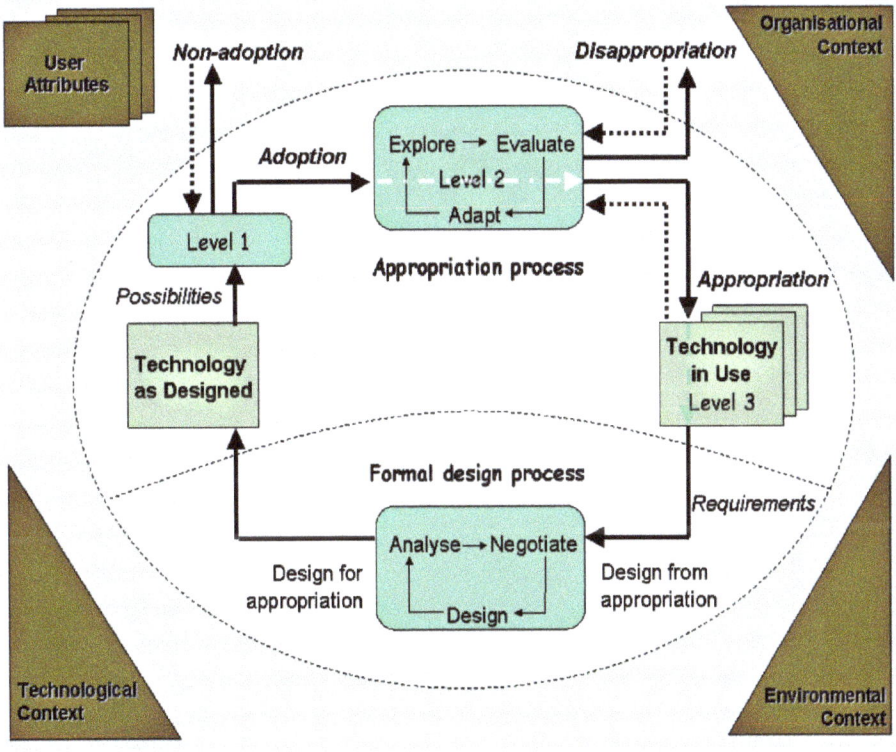

Figure 6.1 The modified technology appropriation cycle

Adapted from Carroll (2004)

The top half of the TAC describes three stages of the appropriation process: adoption, adaptation and incorporation (Carroll et al. 2003a). At each of these stages there is an associated level of evaluation. When first exposed to a technology, potential users are presented with an artefact constructed by its designer(s) to provide certain functionality—referred to as *technology as designed*. From the perspective of potential users, the technology suggests certain possibilities for addressing their wants or needs or those of their organisation. A number of influences affect the evaluations that people make during their initial exposure to a technology, such as ease of use, aesthetics, marketing and system performance. As a result of this level-one evaluation, certain expectations about the capacity of the technology to deliver are formed. These expectations in turn lead to a decision by people to persist with exploring the technology and thereby continuing the process of appropriation. Alternatively, users' expectations are not met, leading to non-adoption of the technology—although circumstances might cause them to change their views of the technology at a later time, potentially leading to adoption (represented by the dashed arrow from non-adoption to Level 1 in Figure 6.1).

The process of appropriation is continued as users evaluate the technology more deeply through using the technology and exploring its capabilities (level-two evaluation). As people explore the technology, they learn the ways in which it can support their practices. Carroll (2004) argues that at this stage mutual adaptation occurs, with people adapting practices associated with use of the technology and also adapting the technology itself. During this adaptation stage, people's evaluations are again shaped by various influences—for example, the extent to which the technology enhances their ability to perform. The result of these level–two evaluations is a decision to either appropriate or disappropriate the technology.

After a period, mutual adaptation ceases, with the design of the technology and practices around use of the technology stabilising (Mendoza et al. 2005; Tyre and Orlikowski 1994). It is at this stage that the design can be thought of as being fixed. A state of appropriation is reached whereby the technology becomes just another part of users' taken-for-granted experience of work—referred to as *technology in use* (Carroll et al. 2003a). This state is maintained as long as users' continuing evaluations of the technology continue to encourage persistent use. Influences that operate on these level–three evaluations might include the performance of the technology or the attitudes of one's peer group towards the technology. Use can, however, be destabilised if users' evaluations of the technology change, leading them to re-evaluate the technology with the potential for it to be disappropriated or rejected (Carroll et al. 2003a).

It is proposed that reflection on the influences that shape people's evaluations and subsequent appropriation choices can be used to guide the formal design process (see bottom half of Figure 6.1). People's unmet expectations or requirements surface as they engage in the process of appropriating a technology to support their personal, social and organisational practices (Carroll 2004). These requirements can serve as an input into the redesign of the existing system or the design of a new system—referred to as *designing from appropriation*. The formal design process is a generic representation; the process does not prescribe a particular ISD approach. The requirements that emerge throughout the process of appropriation—reflected by the dashed arrows passing through the Level 2 and 3 boxes in Figure 6.1—therefore can be drawn on to support a variety of approaches. The focus on mutual adaptation suggests, however, the mTAC is particularly well suited to approaches that address the emergent nature of requirements, such as prototyping and agile systems development (Hall 2001; Surendra 2008). The tendency for people to adapt technologies to suit their needs also suggests that technologies should be *designed for appropriation* by making them more tailorable, malleable and flexible in order to better support technology adaptation (Carroll 2004; Hevner et al. 2004; MacLean et al. 1990). Furthermore, the insights gained from reflecting on the process of appropriation for a particular user cohort and use context can potentially guide changes to contextual influences, leading to appropriation behaviours that are more productive and persistent. Such changes might include improving competence in using the technology, developing a tailoring culture to better exploit the functionality offered or providing continuing access to training to encourage more productive use (Fidock 2004; MacLean et al. 1990; Mendoza et al. 2005).

Reflecting on the process of appropriation requires access to evaluation findings that are able to reveal the context-dependent and heterogeneous nature of appropriation, the influences on users' appropriation choices and unfolding of appropriation over time. The multiple methods employed at multiple data points in the research associated with the TAC's development—which included focus groups, interviews, participant observation, questionnaires and scrap books (Carroll et al. 2003a; Mendoza et al. 2005)—are suggestive of the sorts of methods needed to generate findings of sufficient richness and validity.

The mTAC shows promise as a heuristic or framework for designing formal evaluations that can support the development and implementation of systems. It clearly conveys how deriving an understanding of people's evaluations of technology and subsequent appropriation choices can be used to generate requirements and encourage the design of systems that are more amenable to being adapted and appropriated. For these reasons, the mTAC was selected to support the evaluation and development of the AKD prototype.

AKD prototype evaluation and development

Since the end of the Cold War, many armies around the world have been confronted with dramatically altered strategic contexts and priorities. Up to this point, military forces were structured primarily for conventional state-on-state warfare in a relatively stable strategic context. With the end of the Cold War, however, the war-fighting environment has increased in complexity and uncertainty, driven to a large extent by an enemy—terrorists and militia—who are not readily identifiable and who do not employ conventional weapons and tactics. As in the commercial world, such a shift in the environmental context places pressure on organisations to reconfigure to respond to the new circumstances (Aylwin-Foster 2005). This is achieved through organisations investing in technology and in people and through structural and cultural reforms (Groth 1999; Nadler and Tushman 1997). Armies are, however, strongly hierarchical organisations, with cultures imbued with tradition, and as a consequence changes can be difficult to implement (Macredie and Sandom 1999). The Australian Army has embraced the need for such reforms by investing in new technologies, introducing substantial structural reforms, endeavouring to change its culture and further developing its people (The Australian Army 2005). Army personnel need to have appropriate technical proficiency and understanding of context, as well as the moral, physical and intellectual capacities to operate in complex and uncertain environments. Collectively, these attributes are referred to as professional mastery (The Australian Army 2002). There is recognition that the development of such mastery is underpinned by the Army's culture, knowledge, training and education. It is as part of efforts to enhance professional mastery that a trial to develop the Army Knowledge Domain (AKD) prototype was established. The development of an AKD is seen as providing a means of improving access to and sharing of current and relevant knowledge within the Army (The Australian Army 2007). The Army's efforts in this regard parallel similar efforts in the business world (Al-Alawi et al. 2007).

The initial prototype was a portal developed to bring together some of the Army's disparate range of knowledge sources into one domain. The knowledge to which it provided access is codified and organisationally sanctioned and is drawn on primarily by personnel to support their training and education. From the start of the trial, it was decided that a user-centred prototype development approach, supported by an evaluation guided by the mTAC, would be employed. This decision was taken so as to reduce the risks associated with full-scale implementation, to help refine requirements, systems and concepts, and to support a more gradual change process. The requirements were developed in the context of extant KMS that provided stovepiped access to Army's codified knowledge.

The AKD prototype portal was developed using a combination of open source software (AJAX) and commercial off-the-shelf technology. An in-house team developed a web portal that would accept feeds from various repositories. The interface they developed provided access to this knowledge via a series of tabs along the top of the interface, as well as via a tree structure in the left frame (Figure 6.2). In addition, an XML viewer to support user access to selected content was included in the centre frame. The prototype also allowed users to click on words highlighted in italics to see the definition, presented in the right frame. The bottom frame was reserved for listing the 10 most related information sources as identified by enterprise search technology developed by Autonomy. This functionality was, however, not enabled. In addition, the interface provided access to this search technology via a dialogue box at the top of the page, but due to licensing constraints access to the search technology was provided via a commercial search interface called Retina (Figure 6.3), developed by Autonomy. The AKD prototype therefore comprised two distinct components accessed via a web browser: the prototype portal and Retina. The prototype portal and Retina both provided evaluation participants with the capacity to access different knowledge sources via a single point of entry. This was achieved either via presentation in a structured form (the prototype portal) or via search returns (Retina). The knowledge sources accessible via these two prototype components are currently accessed via two separate KMS available via the defence intranet, the Army Doctrine Electronic Library (ADEL) and Army Knowledge Online (AKO). ADEL provides access to formalised army knowledge—particularly strategy and tactics—and the AKO to less formalised content.

It was recognised before the start of the trial that an evaluation would need to be undertaken in order to determine its success. The first author—in his role as an organisational analyst employed by the Department of Defence—was approached to lead this evaluation and held some preliminary discussions with key personnel associated with the trial. The mTAC was selected as the conceptual basis of the evaluation because it highlighted how the influences that shaped users' evaluations and subsequent appropriation choices changed over time as they engaged in the process of appropriating a technology to support their practices. An understanding of these influences has implications for the formal design of systems through uncovering people's unmet expectations and requirements, which can be used to support the iterative development of systems in a way that is complementary to ISD approaches such as prototyping (*designing from appropriation*). By focusing on the context of use, the mTAC could also assist in understanding contextual constraints and enablers, as well as uncovering requirements for designing the system support context. These features of the mTAC were conveyed to senior project stakeholders, which assisted them in appreciating the importance of capturing influences on users' evaluations of the prototype over time in order to support the refinement and elicitation of requirements. The mTAC, therefore, served as a heuristic or tool that assisted in communicating ideas about evaluation and design to people who did not have technical expertise or experience in technology development.

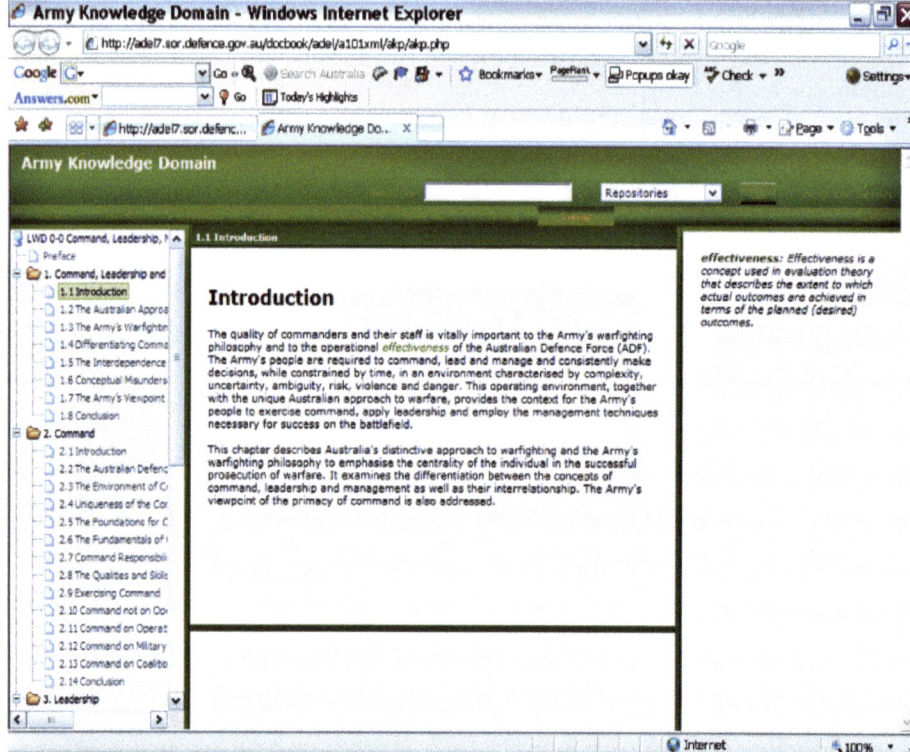

Figure 6.2 The prototype portal

The mTAC was drawn on to assist with developing the evaluation plan for the trial, including the selection of appropriate methods. In the first instance, three foci for the evaluation were identified, with each corresponding to a particular aspect of the mTAC. First, attention was given to understanding the technology *as designed*—the AKD prototype—in order to determine how well it met the requirements in terms of its functionality, usability and usefulness. Second, thought was given to how best to draw out appropriation of the prototype to support learning practices and work practices. The aim here was to identify the extent to which the prototype might enhance the capacity of personnel to learn or to undertake aspects of their role that relied on formalised knowledge. Third, the broader context and influences that shaped users' evaluations and subsequent appropriation choices were considered—the technological, organisational and environmental context, as well as users' attributes (see section two for details).

In addition, the plan identified the need to capture changes in users' evaluations and appropriation choices over time, and the influences on their evaluations, so as to inform subsequent iterations of the prototype's development.

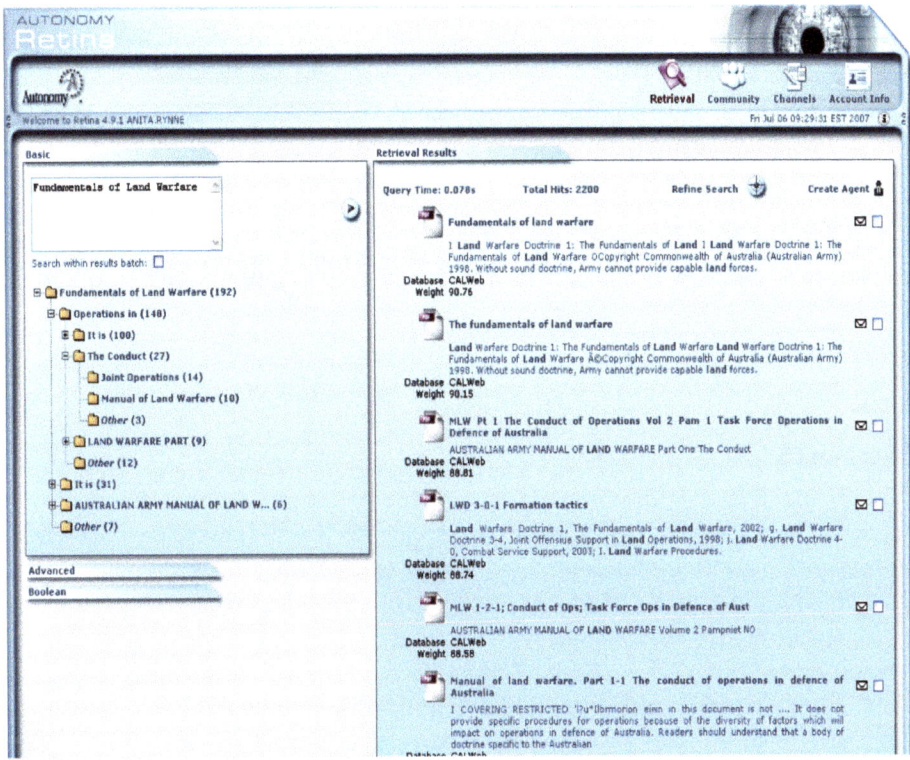

Figure 6.3 The Retina interface

The nature of these three foci and the concern to reveal changing influences on users' evaluation of technology over time led to a data-collection approach focused on generating findings of sufficient richness and validity to inform the next iteration of the prototype. A multi-method approach was therefore employed, which included contextual interviews, group discussions, questionnaires, workshops, lab experiments, observations, video screen capture of system usage, notes from discussions and documentary evidence (Carroll et al. 2003a; Holtzblatt and Beyer 1993; Mendoza et al. 2005). In addition, data-collection activities were structured in such a way as to identify the unfolding of people's appropriation choices over time; workshop participants' impressions or evaluations of the AKD prototype were captured after a short presentation, which also entailed the presentation of other KMS to serve as points of comparison (level-one evaluation; refer to mTAC, Figure 6.1), as well as during and after having an opportunity to explore and use the technology to support various tasks (level-two evaluation). The above activities were designed to support the elicitation of requirements.

An important influence on the development of the mTAC was the evaluation approach developed by Owen and Rogers (1999), which highlighted the value of collecting information from a wide variety of different stakeholders and sources. This was done so as to increase confidence in the findings of the evaluation, to better understand the agendas, goals and aspirations of key stakeholders and to develop a clearer picture of the broader context within which the AKD would be situated.

In the next section, a portion of the results is presented. These served to inform the next iterative development step for the prototype (*designing from appropriation*).

Results

In 2007, two evaluation workshops were held—each lasting for two days. A total of 15 participants took part. These workshops were designed to give participants an opportunity to explore the usability and functionality offered by the prototype in comparison with existing systems—primarily ADEL and to a lesser extent the AKO—via completion of a series of tasks analogous with what they might undertake as part of learning and work-related activities. ADEL was used as the main point of comparison since it was used extensively by army personnel to support their learning needs and because the initial requirements for the AKD had been influenced by this KMS. Before putting the systems to use, participants were first given an overview of six different systems—including Retina, the prototype portal, an alternative screen design for the prototype portal, an American system, ADEL and the AKO—so as to capture their initial impressions (level-one evaluation of the mTAC). Participants were asked to rank in order the different interfaces and provide comments relating to use of colour, layout, use of space, and so on. The aggregated results presented in Table 6.1 show that Retina was the highest ranked interface and ADEL the lowest ranked. Most participants commented favourably on Retina's search capability. They liked the way the search results were presented and grouped into thematic folders (see left frame of Figure 6.3, below the search query box). For the prototype portal, there were minimal concerns raised, other than a couple of comments about the colour scheme and difficulties in differentiating tab buttons (see Figure 6.2).

Table 6.1. Rank ordering of interfaces

Interface	A sample of participants' comments	Average rank	Overall rank order
Retina	Simple interface; good design and colour; like the folder hierarchy; nice layout; front page boring	2.29	1
AKD prototype portal	Simple layout; easy to use; more cluttered; text too small; colour poor; different colour options; no borders on buttons	3.27	3
Mock-up for AKD prototype portal	Looks professional; uncluttered; better colours; good layout; don't like colour scheme, font [too] small	3.54	4
ADEL	Very busy; cluttered, slow; simple layout, easy to use; good use of tabs at top; no abstracts with search results	4.11	6
AKO	Too busy, info hard to read; cluttered; logical grouping; hard to search; good colour	4.10	5
US system	Access to email and other info sources; one central portal; cluttered; nice, crisp; good colour	3.18	2

One of the tasks undertaken by participants involved answering two sets of 22 questions that required access to codified army knowledge. The purpose of these questions was to get people to actively engage with the technology to support a task that was analogous to what they might do as part of pre-course preparation before attending a formal training course. The participants were divided into two subgroups. One subgroup used extant systems or resources—particularly ADEL and the AKO—to answer the first question set, then used the AKD prototype (Retina and/or the prototype portal) to answer the second question set. The second subgroup used the AKD prototype on question set one and extant systems on question set two. This comparative experimental activity was undertaken to increase the validity of findings in relation to system performance issues, but also to elicit requirements based on an exploration of users' level-two evaluations and appropriations of the systems—which in the case of the AKD prototype were only preliminary—in a quasi-realistic use context. The results of the activity suggested that the AKD prototype (primarily Retina) was a more responsive KMS than extant systems (primarily ADEL), with an average of 7.79 questions completed correctly compared with 4.71 ($F = 4.02$, $p = 0.066$). Additional information about how the systems were being employed to support the task was collected to help build an understanding of participants' appropriation choices and associated influences. Retina was preferred not just because it was much faster in returning search results, but because it was perceived to provide superior search results through the presentation of summary information associated with each search return that supported participants in making judgments of relevance.

During the activity, participants made a range of other appropriation choices—a selection of which is now described. Surface-level adaptations were made to the prototype portal by changing the default colour scheme. Features used by participants also varied. With Retina, some participants used both the thematic folders (left side of Figure 6.2) and the search return list (right side), while others showed a preference for using one or the other. In addition, the systems used by participants also varied, with participants showing a preference for ADEL over the AKO and Retina over the prototype portal in completing the activity. In the latter case, participants could access structured information via the prototype portal or employ Retina to run a search query in order to answer the questions. Participants' appropriation choices and associated comments provided strong evidence that participants appropriated Retina more readily than the prototype portal. Associated with system variations were differences in the approaches taken to complete the same task, which provided evidence of practices being adapted in response to technology. Both ADEL and Retina had search functionality, but with ADEL participants had to wait seconds or even minutes for returns to be provided. As a result, some participants opened up additional windows and entered search terms associated with another question or they gave up in frustration and tried a new search term. With Retina, no such behaviour was observed.

Discussion

The findings in relation to Retina were significant for the trial since up to this point the intention was to proceed down the path of developing an in-house web-based client for the AKD prototype (the portal, Figure 6.2), including the provision of search results via this interface rather than via Retina. There was significant inertia associated with pursuing the path of transitioning the in-house solution to the next stage of the AKD's implementation. This was in part being driven by a strong preference for open-source solutions among the staff charged with developing the prototype portal—an approach they had also employed in developing and supporting ADEL. The combination of standard usability and user interface data, as well as the comparative exploration of the impacts of systems on task performance and practices, which was a data-collection approach shaped by the mTAC, provided a weight of evidence that was hard to ignore. As a result, the decision was made to continue to evaluate the in-house prototype portal *and* Retina, but also include other commercial applications in additional evaluation activities (for example, comparing the portal's XML viewer with PDF viewers). This decision represented an acknowledgment that the trial's purpose was not necessarily to develop a bespoke prototype. Instead, the trial presented participants with an opportunity to explore a range of functionality from a variety of different systems, in order to support the refinement and identification of requirements for the next stage in the implementation of the AKD.

The findings in relation to ADEL were also important since they highlighted some of the negative consequences for participants' knowledge search practices associated with system latency issues and reinforced the requirement for a more responsive and effective system. One of the consequences of participants using the prototype was to put into sharp relief the functionality and performance of ADEL. The workshops encouraged people to re-evaluate a technology—ADEL—which most of them had appropriated and, if given a choice, would now reject in favour of the prototype. While ADEL was widely used by participants to support training and work needs, this appeared to be driven by it being the corporately sanctioned source for an important class of the Army's codified knowledge. Its lack of responsiveness and poor search functionality meant, however, that as soon as a viable alternative was presented participants were eager to explore and use the technology.

IS evaluation approaches have traditionally paid limited attention to what happens to the designed and developed system after its deployment or initial implementation (Davis and Venkatesh 2004; Davis et al. 1989; Marchand 2004). These approaches have therefore constrained the window within which users' attitudes and responses to the technology are captured to the period just before or after limited exposure to the system (Davis and Venkatesh 2004; Davis et al. 1989; Marchand 2004). Limiting the window for capturing people's evaluations and requirements in this way is seen as minimising the costs that would otherwise be incurred by changing the system design later in the development process (Davis and Venkatesh 2004). Such an approach affords more flexibility to designers in changing core system functionality earlier in the system development process and appears to be based on the assumption that people's evaluations of technology and patterns of use become stable quite quickly. This view is, however, inconsistent with evidence in support of the TAC, suggesting that users' evaluations of technology and associated appropriation choices unfold over time and that the influences on people's evaluations also vary over time as people adopt, adapt and then incorporate a technology with their practices (Carroll et al. 2003; Mendoza et al. 2005). Data-collection activities were therefore deliberately structured so as to bring to the surface the influences on users' evaluations before, during and after exploring the system in various use scenarios. Additional evaluation activities are scheduled to occur this year to support the next phase of the AKD project. This will involve evaluating the AKD prototype in real-world use contexts so as to identify influences on appropriation specific to various use contexts.

Adopting an evaluation approach informed by an appropriation perspective appeared to complement and support the application of the prototyping approach. The evaluation of the AKD prototype and extant systems provided insights into participants' initial impressions (level-one evaluation), but also uncovered a range of different appropriation choices and associated influences as users engaged with the technology to support various learning-related activities (level-two evaluation). From these findings, requirements were refined and new requirements identified. In addition, the evaluation helped to clarify the purpose of the prototype development approach, as described above, and shaped decisions about the next steps to take in developing and evaluating the AKD. The mTAC helped to reinforce the importance of continuing the evaluation beyond the trial period so as to keep on identifying requirements to inform subsequent iterations in the design and development of the AKD and also ways in which the use context could be modified to better support users' appropriations of the system.

The evaluation approach adopted also confirmed the long-observed phenomena of users being shaped by and shaping technology over time, encapsulated in such terms as technology adaptation, reinvention or customisation (Johnson and Rice 1984; Trigg and Bødker 1994; Tyre and Orlikowski 1994). These phenomena are here viewed as part of realising the design of the system through a process of appropriating the technology. Participants did not simply adopt a technology and employ its features in a way that was readily predictable given the material and functional constraints of the technology—the *technology as designed*. Instead, they were observed to make active choices about how best to employ a particular technology to meet their needs, shaped by the functional and performance characteristics of the technology, as well as modifying the technology and their patterns of feature use to suit their aesthetic and work style preferences. While not considered in detail here, this mutual adaptation of practices and technology highlights the need to consider where the boundaries of IS design should be drawn. Rather than holding to the method-driven and analytical distinction between design and implementation, it is here proposed that a designed system continues to be designed as it is implemented—as users appropriate it over time. The mTAC provides a model and theory of this process of technology appropriation and serves as a framework to help guide evaluation practice that embraces a broader view of IS design.

The adoption of a broader view of IS design afforded by drawing on the mTAC also has implications for the conduct of design-science research. Such research is concerned with the development of innovative and new artefacts to enhance human and organisational capabilities (Hevner et al. 2004). These artefacts are created through an iterative process of 'build' and 'evaluate', thereby positioning evaluation as core to design science (Hevner et al. 2004). Given the centrality of evaluation to design science, the research reported on here suggests that the remit of the design-science researcher need not be limited to the formal design and development stage. Instead, the design principles associated with design science can be applied as systems are appropriated by users over time in the context of use. Design science therefore can have application not just to new and innovative artefacts; it can support the redesign of mature and old artefacts.

There are a number of limitations in this study. This represents the first application of the mTAC to support IS evaluation, development and design, therefore only tentative conclusions can be drawn about the utility of the approach. The evaluation did not extend beyond use of the system in various use scenarios. There was no opportunity to explore real-world use. This would have limited the identification of some influences that were unique to particular use contexts, such as performance issues associated with particular nodes in the Defence Department's wide area network. It also constrained the identification of changes to the supporting context that could enhance the quality of users' appropriations. Finally, conducting evaluations that explore use in context and over time is resource intensive, which is likely to limit the application of such an approach.

Conclusion

This chapter has described the evaluation, development and design of the AKD prototype. The development of the AKD prototype was informed by the mTAC. It initially served as a heuristic for communicating ideas about the role of evaluation in supporting system development. The model was then drawn on to help develop the evaluation plan for the trial in a way that shaped the identification of appropriate methods and focused attention on both technical and contextual factors, as well as uncovering the influences that act on people's evaluations of technology as they appropriate technology over time, thereby realising the design through use. The appropriation perspective and associated evaluation approach adopted here therefore draw on an expanded view of what constitutes design—a view in which the boundaries of IS design are extended beyond formal design. The understanding derived from the evaluation activities was used to shape the design and development path of the prototype. This study therefore provides preliminary evidence of the utility of applying an appropriation perspective, as encapsulated within the mTAC, to support the practice of IS evaluation, development and design.

References

Al-Alawi, A. I., Al-Marzooqi, N. Y. and Mohammed, Y. F. 2007, 'Organizational culture and knowledge sharing: critical success factors', *Journal of Knowledge Management*, vol. 11, no. 2, pp. 22–42.

Aylwin-Foster, N. 2005, 'Changing the army for counterinsurgency operations', *Military Review*, November–December, pp. 2–15.

Carroll, J. 2004, 'Completing design in use: closing the appropriation cycle', *Proceedings of the 12th European Conference on Information Systems (ECIS 2004)*, Turku, Finland, [CD-ROM].

Carroll, J., Howard, S., Peck, J. and Murphy, J. 2003a, 'From adoption to use: the process of appropriating a mobile phone', *Australian Journal of Information Systems*, vol. 10, no. 2, pp. 38–48.

Carroll, J., Kriss, S. and Murphy, J. 2003b, 'Developing CRM systems that encourage user uptake', *Proceedings of the 7th Customer Contact World Conference*, Sydney.

Chae, B. and Poole, M. S. 2005, 'The surface of emergence in systems development: agency, institutions, and large-scale information systems', *European Journal of Information Systems*, vol. 14, no. 1, pp. 19–36.

Davis, F. D. and Venkatesh, V. 2004, 'Toward preprototype user acceptance testing of new information systems: implications for software project management', *IEEE Transactions on Engineering Management*, vol. 51, no. 1, pp. 31–46.

Davis, F. D., Bagozzi, R. P. and Warshaw, P. R. 1989, 'User acceptance of computer technology: a comparison of two theoretical models', *Management Science*, vol. 35, no. 8, pp. 982-1003.

DeSanctis, G. and Poole, M. S. 1994, 'Capturing the complexity in advanced technology use: adaptive structuration theory', *Organization Science*, vol. 5, no. 2, pp. 121–47.

Farbey, B., Land, F. and Targett, D. 1993, *How to Assess Your IT Investment: A study of methods and practice*, Butterworth-Heinemann, Oxford.

Fidock, J. 2004, 'Factors influencing user acceptance of a mature and embedded computer system', *Proceedings of the 15th Australasian Conference on Information Systems*, Hobart, pp. 1–10.

Fidock, J. and Carroll, J. 2006, 'The model of technology appropriation: a lens for understanding systems integration in a defence context', in S. Spencer and A. Jenkins (eds), *Proceedings of the 17th Australasian Conference on Information Systems*, Australasian Association for Information Systems, Adelaide, Paper 88.

Groth, L. 1999, *Future Organisational Design: The scope for the IT-based enterprise*, John Wiley & Sons, Chichester, UK.

Hall, R. R. 2001, 'Prototyping for usability of new technology', *International Journal of Human–Computer Studies*, vol. 55, no. 4, pp. 485–501.

Hallikainen, P. and Chen, L. 2006, 'A holistic framework on information systems evaluation with a case analysis', *Electronic Journal of Information Systems Evaluation*, vol. 9, no. 2, viewed 24 June 2008, <http://www.ejise.com/volume-9/v9-iss-2/hallikainen_and_chen.pdf>

Herszfeld, S., Carroll, J. and Howard, S. 2003, 'Job allocation by SMS: technology appropriation in the construction industry', *Proceedings of the 14th Australasian Conference on Information Systems (ACIS 2003)*, Perth.

Hevner, A. R., March, S. T., Park, J. and Ram, S. 2004, 'Design science in information systems research', *MIS Quarterly*, vol. 28, no. 1, pp. 75–105.

Hirschheim, R. and Klein, H. 1989, 'Four paradigms of information systems development', *Communications of the ACM*, vol. 32, no. 10, pp. 1199–216.

Hirschheim, R. and Smithson, S. 1999, 'Evaluation of information systems: a critical assessment', in L. Willcocks and S. Lester (eds), *Beyond the IT Productivity Paradox*, John Wiley & Sons, Chichester, UK, pp. 381–409.

Holtzblatt, K. and Beyer, H. 1993, 'Making customer-centered design work for teams', *Communications of the ACM*, vol. 36, no. 10, pp. 93–103.

Huang, J. P. H. 2003, 'An evaluation framework to support development of virtual enterprises', *Electronic Journal of Information Systems Evaluation*, vol. 6, no. 2, paper 13, viewed 24 June 2008, <http://www.ejise.com/volume6-issue2/issue2-art13.htm>

Johnson, B. M. and Rice, R. E. 1984, 'Reinvention in the innovation process: the case of word processing', in R. E. Rice (ed.), *The New Media: Communication, research, and technology*, Sage, Thousand Oaks, Calif., pp. 157-184.

Klecun, E. and Cornford, T. 2005, 'A critical approach to evaluation', *European Journal of Information Systems*, vol. 14, no. 3, pp. 229–43.

MacLean, A., Carter, K., Lovstrand, L. and Moran, T. 1990, 'User-tailorable systems: pressing the issues with buttons', *Proceedings of the SIGCHI Conference on Human factors in Computing Systems: Empowering people*, ACM Press, Seattle, pp. 175–82, <http://doi.acm.org/10.1145/97243.97271>

Macredie, R. D. and Sandom, C. 1999, 'IT-enabled change: evaluating an improvisational perspective', *European Journal of Information Systems*, vol. 8, no. 4, pp. 247–59.

Marchand, D. A. 2004, 'Reaping the business value of IT: focus on usage, not just deployment, to optimize payback', *IMD Perspectives for Managers*, no. 114, pp. 1–4.

Mendoza, A., Carroll, J. and Stern, L. 2005, 'Adoption, adaptation, stabilization and stagnation: software appropriation over time', in B. Campbell, J. Underwood and D. Bunker (eds), *Proceedings of the 16th Australasian Conference on Information Systems (ACIS 2005)*, Australasian Chapter of the Association for Information Systems, Sydney, pp. 1–10 (CD-ROM).

Mendoza, A., Stern, L. and Carroll, J. 2007, 'Plateaus in long-term appropriation of an information system', *Proceedings of the 18th Australasian Conference on Information Systems (ACIS 2007)*, Australasian Chapter of the Association for Information Systems, Toowoomba, Qld, pp. 189–98.

Mintzberg, H. 1979, *The Structuring of Organizations*, Prentice-Hall, Upper Saddle River, NJ.

Nadler, D. A. and Tushman, M. 1997, *Competing by Design: The power of organizational architecture*, Oxford University Press, UK.

Nandhakumar, J., Rossi, M. and Talvinen, J. 2005, 'The dynamics of contextual forces of ERP implementation', *The Journal of Strategic Information Systems*, vol. 14, no. 2, pp. 221–42.

Orlikowski, W. 1992, 'The duality of technology: rethinking the concept of technology in organizations', *Organization Science*, vol. 3, no. 3, pp. 398–427.

Orlikowski, W. 2002, 'Design in the punctuation of management action', *Proceedings of the Workshop on Managing as Designing: Creating a vocabulary for management education and research*, Case Western Reserve University, Cleveland, Ohio, <http://design.case.edu/2002workshop/Positions/orlikowski.doc>

Owen, J. and Rogers, P. 1999, *Program Evaluation: Forms and approaches*, Second edition, Sage, Thousand Oaks, Calif.

Peppard, J., Ward, J. and Daniel, E. 2007, 'Managing the realization of business benefits from IT investments', *MIS Quarterly Executive*, vol. 6, no. 1, pp. 1–11.

Scott Morton, M. (ed.) 1991, *The Corporation of the 1990s: Information, technology and organizational transformation*, Oxford University Press, UK.

Surendra, N. 2008, 'Using an ethnographic process to conduct requirements analysis for agile systems development', *Information Technology and Management*, vol. 9, no. 1, pp. 55–69.

Symons, V. J. 1991, 'A review of information systems evaluation: content, context and process', *European Journal of Information Systems*, vol. 1, no. 3, pp. 205–12.

The Australian Army 2002, *The Fundamentals of Land Warfare*, Department of Defence, Canberra, viewed 14 August 2008, <http://www.defence.gov.au/army/LWD1/index.htm>

The Australian Army 2005, *The Hardened and Networked Army*, Department of Defence, Canberra, viewed 14 August 2008, <http://www.defence.gov.au/update2005/defence_update_factsheet.pdf>

The Australian Army 2007, 'Centre for army lessons enhancing war fighting capability', *Defence: The official magazine of the Australian Department of Defence*, no. 2, viewed 14 August 2008, <http://www.defence.gov.au/defencemagazine/editions/200708_02/groups/army01.htm#top>

Trigg, R. H. and Bødker, S. 1994, 'From implementation to design: tailoring and the emergence of systematization in CSCW', in R. Furuta and C. Neuwirth (eds), *Proceedings of the Conference on Computer Supported Cooperative Work (CSCW'94)*, ACM Press, New York, pp. 45–54.

Tyre, M. J. and Orlikowski, W. J. 1994, 'Windows of opportunity: temporal patterns of technological adaptation in organizations', *Organization Science*, vol. 5, no. 1, p. 98.

Applications

7. On using materiality in information systems development: a research brief

ANDREA CARUGATI
UNIVERSITY OF AARHUS

Abstract

This research brief presents a discussion on the use of the concept of materiality and material knowing in information systems development (ISD). The discussion addresses some of the practical problems still plaguing ISD, augmenting existing ISD methodologies with contributions from systems theory and in particular the idea of inquiring systems. The discussion builds on different contemporary concepts that are rooted in the inquiring systems idea: the notion of stakeholders (designer, client, user and their interchanging roles), the notions of a boundary object and boundary spanners and the notion of materiality as a scaffold of knowledge. Through the example taken from a case study of a complex and innovative systems development, we outline two design principles to be embedded in modular fashion in ISD processes: 1) whenever possible, start ISD efforts by developing a graphical simulator of the material environment of the users; and 2) embed and use the simulator as a proper boundary object.

Introduction

The development of proprietary information systems has been and continues to be a very complex activity marked by few successes and clamorous failures (Beck 1999; Remenyi et al. 1997). Despite a continuous search for better techniques, as Avison et al. (1995) point out, the problem is not in the tools used but in the lack of attention to organisational and individual issues and their interaction with technology. Responding to this situation, research and practice have begun to consider the information system development (ISD) process as a social rather than a technical problem (Gibson and Singer 1982; Winter et al. 1995). A social constructivist approach to ISD, in which systems and requirements emerge from the interaction of multiple stakeholders, has begun to be preferred to an objectivist approach that considers requirements as exogenous factors, existing outside the interaction of individuals. Hence, the attention has shifted on to user participation, which has risen to become one of the most important components of system success (Avison et al. 1995; Barki and Hartwick 1989, 1994; McKeen and Guimaraes 1997; Winter et al 1995). This interaction between users and other different groups (for example, developers, managers and analysts) can be considered as the minimal activity to bring about just enough knowledge exchange to make the system requirements emerge. Within this view, it has become very important to address the issue of how to facilitate the process of knowledge creation and exchange among the stakeholders involved in ISD projects. Starting from these premises, knowledge issues in ISD have also been addressed and treated both explicitly (for example, Beck 1999) and implicitly (Avison and Fitzgerald 1995). This is because the successful development of information systems depends on the assimilation and combination of knowledge coming from different domains and on the intangible, cognitive and social nature of some ISD goals.

Yet, despite the advances in research and practice in ISD, the situation does not seem to improve. Informal discussions with programmers in leading Danish software houses (most of them using SCRUM) have pointed out that they still have problems engaging the customers in the discussions and therefore can use agile methods in only a sub-optimal way:

> Sure there are tons of methods out there and why do you think that is? Because they have not found the answer yet. Take SCRUM, for example, the one we use. The basic idea is good but no customer wants to waste time in talking with us and they expect you to be the professional with the answers. (Programmer, software house, Denmark, 2008)

So, while it is widely accepted nowadays that the pursuit of knowledge exchange in ISD is the way to go, apparently the way it is done in practice is too cumbersome to be practical. Knowing about the inquiring cycle (Carugati 2008), about the boundaries (Levina 2005; Levina and Vaast 2005) and about the iterations (Lindstrom and Jeffries 2004) provides invaluable elements but something more needs to be done. This something has to decrease the involvement of the customer while favouring the knowledge exchange.

It is the belief of the author that this missing element can be found only in what is under the eyes of the programmers: the material environment of the customer. The missing element in the ISD discourse is the role of the environment of the users in the development process. Most research focuses on office applications (Kellogg et al. 2002; Levina 2005; Levina and Vaast 2005) and these settings represent only a small part of the field of uses of information systems. In industrial settings (for example, manufacturing versus services), the physical layout where the information system has to be used plays a key role in how the system has to be and how the users can capitalise on their knowledge to interact with the developers. According to Orlikowski (2006), human action depends on physical artefacts such as buildings, machines, vehicles, and so on. In other words, what we do depends on the material world that surrounds us. What we do and how we do it are related to what we know (Churchman 1971) and also to how we learn (Cohen and Levinthal 1990). These three events are not, however, sequential but rather happen in a synchronous fashion. Orlikowski defines this situation as 'material knowing', indicating that knowledge is intimately connected with the materiality that surrounds us. While the work on boundary objects (Carlile 2002) focuses the attention on (material) objects created on the boundaries to facilitate the passage of knowledge, the way in which we read Orlikowski (2006) here refers mostly to the materiality of the environment existing around the users.

A way to improve the ISD process is therefore to take into account not only the creation process and the object created but also the materiality of the situation that, to quote Orlikowski, scaffolds the problem definition. The goal of this research brief is therefore to present a way to introduce the notion of materiality and boundary objects to ISD.

The chapter briefly introduces the notions of materiality and boundary objects and, using a case to anchor the discussion, presents the concept of material software objects. Throughout the chapter, we refer to experiences gained from the development of an inventory-control system for a shipyard (SteelCo). The SteelCo case will be described in the next section to provide the basic elements for the discussion.

The SteelCo case

SteelCo, a multinational shipyard located in Denmark, is known worldwide for producing very sophisticated vessels with designs at the forefront of the market. During the period 1999–2002, it earned about €1 billion per annum, employing about 3000 people. SteelCo builds vessels that are among the largest container carriers in the world. Building a container ship of the maximum size entails the cutting and welding of more than 150 000 steel elements, 30 000 larger components and 11 000 pipes. Consequently, this production process places heavy demands on planning and logistics. One of the key departments in SteelCo is the steel-plates inventory since the near totality of steel elements comprises parts cut out of these large plates. The inventory is the centre of reception and distribution of steel plates and therefore a key element in the internal logistics of SteelCo.

Figure 7.1a shows the layout of the inventory (1). Starting from the bottom, we have the sea with the ship from the supplier (11) that delivers the steel plates. The plates (Figure 7.1b) are stacked in 256 piles organised like a chessboard (8–32). Each pile could have up to 200 plates. Each plate is unique and identified by a product number written on it. There are two yellow cranes that move the plates (Figure 7.1b). The cranes move on the same rail and therefore cannot pass each other. On the bottom left (Figure 7.1b) is shown the beginning of the preparation line where the plates are cleaned and painted and prepared for the plasma cutters.

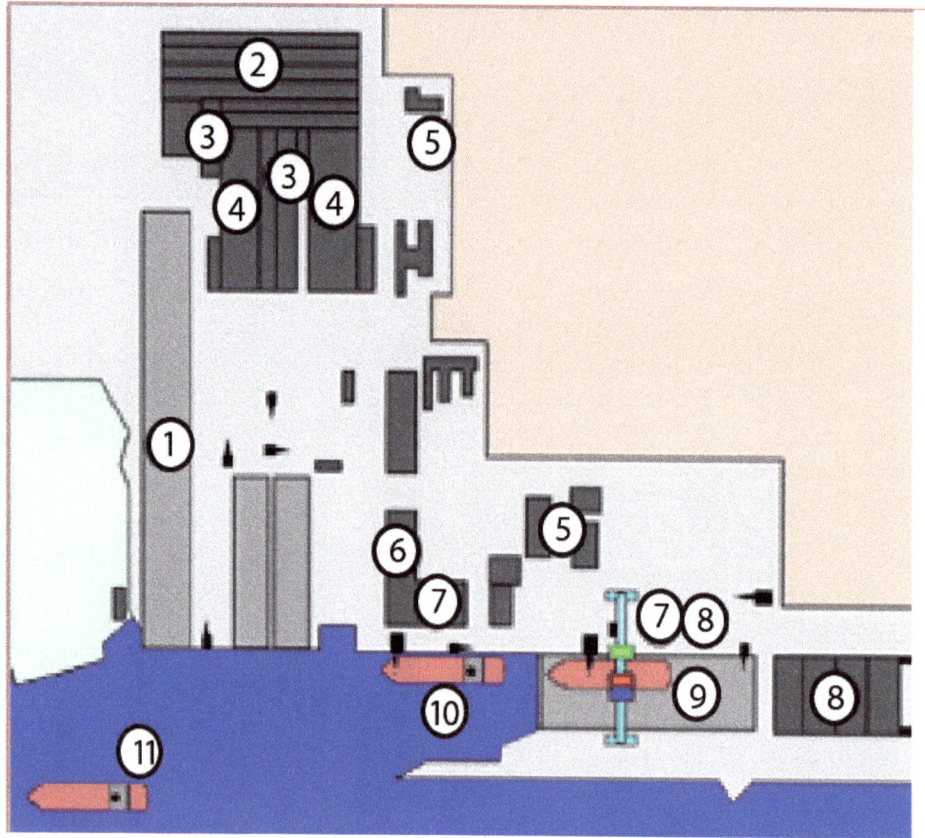

Figure 7.1a Aerial map of SteelCo

Figure 7.1b Inventory

The crane operator does not know exactly in which pile a specific plate is located; he or she only knows that it can be found in one of four to six different piles. It is left to the experience and memory of the crane operators to know and find where a specific plate is. Given the production needs of the plasma cutters, the job of the crane operators is to find the right plates in the piles by moving the ones above to other piles. The main problem of the inventory is therefore the location of the plates and their movements so as to ensure a continuous flow of work for the plasma cutters of the right plates at the right time and to facilitate future work in the inventory.

The inventory is hierarchically organised. Those responsible for the inventory tour the plasma cutters in the morning and prepare the delivery lists based on the needs of the plasma cutters and the actual production plan. This list (a sheet of paper) is given to the crane operators, who move the plates around in the inventory, dig up the delivery plates and place them on the preparation line. The plates' delivery sequence and the movements of the other plates are completely up to the crane operator.

SteelCo has, over the years, experimented with information technology (IT) to find and exploit many possible ways to augment the efficiency and effectiveness of the inventory management. The characteristics of the setting have, however, defied all attempts. Among these characteristics, the most commonly mentioned were the weather, the bending of the plates, the errors in reading the plates' identification numbers, cranes picking up multiple plates in one lift, plates becoming wedged in the conveyor belt and even cranes' wheels becoming 'square' over time. Among the many solutions (automated plate reception, plate position monitoring, a crane-positioning system, and so on), the one that most concerned the management of SteelCo was the implementation of a software tool that could guide the crane operators in deciding the sequence and destination of the plates' movements. The goal was to minimise the number of movements, minimise the hours worked, minimise work in relation to changes in the production plan and minimise reaction time in response to orders while at the same time respecting the physical constraints of the layout. For this problem, there did not exist (at least to the knowledge of the actors) ready software solutions acquirable on the market or solutions to be customised.

For this reason, it was decided to try to solve the problem with tailor-made software. The idea was to include in the software an algorithm based on the combinatorial optimisation technique. This technique promised to deliver a solution that could fit multiple and changing goals. Combinatorial optimisation is a very complex technique for which there are no known development methods for industrial use. The main difficulty with its use is that—as far as the actors are concerned—the algorithm has to be developed from scratch to completion before the system can be tested. Furthermore, since the work on the inventory was completely manual, the problem of using software to guide the crane operators was a completely new problem for the different actors. Thus, the situation was that there was an unsolved problem, the approach requested of the developers was innovative and the development activities were unstructured and not predictable in advance. At the outset, it was considered that the inventory project would take one year to complete.

Materiality, boundary objects and ISD

In her 2006 article on material knowing, Wanda Orlikowski makes an argument for taking materiality seriously in IS research. To stress the importance of the argument in the article she quotes Latour: 'There exists no relation whatsoever between the material and the social world, because it is the division that is first of all a complete artifact. To abandon this division is to rethink the whole assemblage from top to bottom and from beginning to end' (Latour 2004:227).

In Orlikowski's view, the material characteristics of the world surrounding us are an integral part of what we do and what we know. In this view, material forms, artefacts, spaces and infrastructure play critical roles in everyday practices and the knowledge embedded in the practices. As Latour points out, however, researching in the integration of materiality and practices in fact means going back to the basis of human sciences.

The view of Orlikowski (2006) is in line with that of this chapter, because she states that her arguments fit a performative view of knowledge—a knowledge that is not static but a dynamic and continuing social accomplishment. This view fits perfectly in the ISD landscape, where developers and users engage continuously in activities that have knowledge creation as output (Carugati 2008). What Orlikowski so well articulates and adds to the discussion about knowledge is that knowing is not only *emergent, embodied and embedded* (three concepts that are now slowly being integrated in ISD efforts), it is also *material*.

By knowledge being material, Orlikowski means that everyday practices and therefore the knowing attached are 'deeply bound up in the material forms, artifacts, spaces, and infrastructures through which humans act' (p. 460).

In the SteelCo case, for example, the actions of the crane operators are highly dependent on readily apparent objects such as cranes, plates and ships as well as by less conspicuous ones such as the production plan or the information infrastructure of the shipyard. As Orlikowski points out, at the 'level of conceptualising and theorising, we tend to disregard this knowing, and render our accounts of knowledge in organisations without attention to material matters' (p. 460). This influences all aspects of IS research and therefore also ISD. This is especially true since the majority of recent cases on ISD that take knowledge issues into account are grounded in 'office' cases (for example, Levina 2005) where the materiality issue is much less visible (but by no means irrelevant).

Forgetting materiality seems to be quite widespread nowadays since the dominating paradigm in ISD is human centric, focusing largely on human interpretation of actions while technology tends to take a backstage role (Orlikowski and Iacono 2001). This problem leads us back to Latour's statement about the lack of attention to materiality as an inseparable part of human action.

As one of the main problems in ISD is the exchange of knowledge across different parties—typically users and developers (Carugati 2008; Levina 2005)—we can look at how the idea of bringing materiality into the discussion helps to solve or to improve the problem. Orlikowski offers the concept of a 'scaffold' as the mechanism by which materiality can sustain knowledge. Scaffoldings have the following characteristics (Orlikowski 2006:461–2).

- Scaffolds are *temporary*: they are erected on a building site to support the construction of particular elements. They typically exist for the duration of

the project (or less) and are dismantled once the elements are completed or self-supporting.
- Scaffolds are *flexible*: they are constructed in situ and adapted to fit the particular local conditions. As such, they can be erected in many different situations.
- Scaffolds are *portable*: they are relatively quickly and easily assembled, modified and disassembled, as needed, on different building sites.
- Scaffolds are *diverse*: there are many different kinds of scaffolds—for example, scaffolds that allow people to walk along the outside of buildings, scaffolds that suspend workers from above, scaffolds that serve as structural columns to hold up slabs until the poured concrete is cured and scaffolds that serve as reinforcing formwork that then becomes integrated into the final element being built.
- Scaffolds are *heterogeneous*: they comprise multiple different components, reflecting both the requirements of the element(s) to be supported and the materials at hand.
- Scaffolds are *emergent*: they are erected over time, changing in form and function as needed to continue supporting the changing scale and scope of the element(s) being built. While in place, scaffolds afford a certain temporary *stability* to the disparate assembly of people, materials and space bound together.
- Scaffolds are *dangerous*: as temporary, emergent and rapidly constructed assemblages, they are vulnerable to breakdown and failure.
- Scaffolds are *generative*: they serve as the basis for other (creative) work, facilitating the performance of activities that would have been impractical without material augmentation.
- Scaffolds are *constitutive* of both human activity and outcomes, shaping the kind of construction work that is possible and the construction outcomes that emerge (for example, scaffolds afford the building of skyscrapers).

In situations in which knowledge has to be exchanged at a boundary—such as the one existing between developers and users—the main mechanisms facilitating the passage that could function as a scaffold are the boundary objects (Carlile 2002; Star and Griesemer 1989). Boundary objects are artefacts especially designed to ease the passage of knowledge. Boundary objects in ISD can be models, documents, diagrams, prototypes or software releases. During meetings, these boundary objects become the focal point around which discussion revolves.

The design of an effective boundary object is not as straightforward as it might seem. If badly designed, a boundary object can in fact impede the passage of knowledge. This is a known phenomenon in which the inappropriate use of a boundary object strengthens the power position of one group or the other and reinforces the boundary rather than bridges it (Wenger 2000). Let us consider the characteristics of a boundary object applied, for example, to a possible prototype created for the SteelCo case.

The boundary object must be visual (Brooks 1985; Carlile 2002). Visual artefacts are easy to inspect and are quickly understood. The software prototype has to replicate the environment of the users such that they can verify whether the developer's understanding of it is accurate enough. Visualisation responds to the need for making knowledge explicit.

The boundary object must be usable/functional (Brown and Diguid 2001). Not all knowledge can be made explicit by visualisation. Some knowledge that remains tacit can be demonstrated only through action. By working with the prototype, the users enact their daily routines and can immediately identify the misunderstandings of the developers. Visual and functional boundary objects will also facilitate the establishment of a common language (Wenger 2000).

A boundary object must be up-to-date (Carlile 2002). The prototype has to be the newest product of the developers. The main function of the prototype is that the developers can take home the comments of the users, change their understanding of the problem and create more accurate solutions. If the developers present to the users an obsolete prototype while they are already working on newer versions two problems might happen. First, the developers will be focused on newer problems and will miss the importance of the users' feedback. Second, invested knowledge will create inertia against the doing of rework.

The boundary object must work both ways (Boland and Tenkasi 1995). Prototypes are built for the users to learn about the system's possibilities but also for the developers to collect feedback. Mechanisms must be built in the prototypes to facilitate the collection of the feedback. For example, the prototype can be made with a 'recording' mechanism built in so that everything done with the prototype and everything said can be recorded and replayed at will. This feature will give the developers a chance for retrospective sense making and facilitate the improvement of the software.

Perhaps one other key characteristic boundary objects need to function, as such, is that they have to be *incomplete*. Incompleteness generates the need for concerted action.

We can imagine designing a special type of boundary object that supports knowledge transfer by functioning as an imitator of the material world. Such a boundary object should at the same time be temporary, flexible, portable, diverse, heterogeneous, emergent, dangerous, generative, constitutive and visual, usable, up-to-date, bi-directional and…incomplete.

As can be imagined, a boundary object lends itself very well to representing a material setting. For example, physical scale models or three-dimensional computer-aided design (CAD) drawings are normally used in construction (Gal et al. 2008). In the inventory case, there was so much 'materiality' defining the setting that the problem was not what to represent but rather comprehending the importance of this representation.

Example of use of materiality to scaffold knowledge exchange in the SteelCo case

In the initial phases of the SteelCo case, the developers began their investigation of the setting with the business problem, focusing on both the material and the conceptual sides of it. In this initial phase, the definition of the business problem was detailed, resulting in a material model of the system: a drawing of the inventory on paper and a conceptual software model. These models acted as boundary objects, at an early stage facilitating knowledge exchange from the users to the developers and enhancing the developers' understanding of the domain.

The models became the basis for the design even though they were not directly related to how the software system was built (see more on this issue in Carugati 2008). The first version of the software—what was called the proto-prototype—presented to the users only a table of white numbers on a black DOS screen. From the lack of feedback from the users about this proto-prototype, it quickly became clear that these black-box prototypes would not further knowledge exchange, so a discussion was initiated to find a better way to do it. The discussion revolved around whether or not to include a visual simulator as an additional module in the inventory software. Supporters maintained that a visual simulator would improve understanding and feedback while their opponents replied that it was useless (the DOS screen respected the requirements) and too complex and time-consuming to develop. The two factions fought lengthy battles on the issue until a developer took out his computer and showed a visual simulator of a welding robot used at the shipyard. The visual simulator was showing on the screen the actual robot on the production floor. While the programmer was focusing on the numbers, the users in the background (they were literally standing behind the programmer) were commenting on their actual understanding of the situation:

> Hey, look there, that's the turn where it always gets stuck…
>
> Yesterday in that corner they programmed it wrong so it welded a hole…
>
> Wow…programming it like that you could make it go much faster…

The visualisation had such an impact on the users that after the demonstration there was complete agreement that the visual simulator had to be done even though why it had to be done had different reasons for different roles. The materially grounded boundary object, used in a participative setting, had played a key role in bringing the different actors to agreement.

As a direct result of this discussion, the first real prototype integrated the DOS screen in a graphical user interface (GUI) that resembled the inventory seen from above. For this case, the discussion about the prototype was very limited whereas the second prototype received much more attention. The screen of the second prototype is shown in Figure 7.2. This GUI resembles the inventory seen from the top: the sea on the upper side, the two cranes with the same appellation as used in SteelCo and the grey plates. The left side of Figure 7.2 is what could be called a material software model. On the right side, we find instead the list of plates that have to be delivered on the day. This list comes from the database of the production plan.

On presentation of the first material prototype, the users were more relaxed than before in the discussion. They were smiling and definitely interacting in pointing out problems in the crane movements.

Unfortunately, the programmers presented this prototype after the planning algorithm was ready—as is evident from the central part of Figure 7.2 that specifies the executions for the cranes. As became clear later in the case, the material model should have been used before the planning algorithm was done. The time and knowledge invested in the creation of the algorithm caused the developers to resist the feedback of the users instead of welcoming it.

In the SteelCo case, the prototypes like the one in Figure 7.2 were good material models because they furthered understanding, but poor boundary objects because they impeded feedback and positive reconstruction of the work done. A characteristic that the prototype had lacked, as a boundary object, was usability. It was too complete and therefore not bi-directional because one group—the developers—was not interested in changing it.

Despite its poor result as a boundary object, the prototype as visualised in Figure 7.2 represented a turning point in the SteelCo case. It showed to all parties that progress had been made; it showed that there was a common point of understanding of the problems; and it showed this in a concrete and discussable way. As the project manager of SteelCo said, 'It was as if the program was brought to life for us. It was not that the DOS version was wrong, maybe it was…I cannot judge that, but this one was different; we just got it.'

Information Systems Foundations: The Role of Design Science

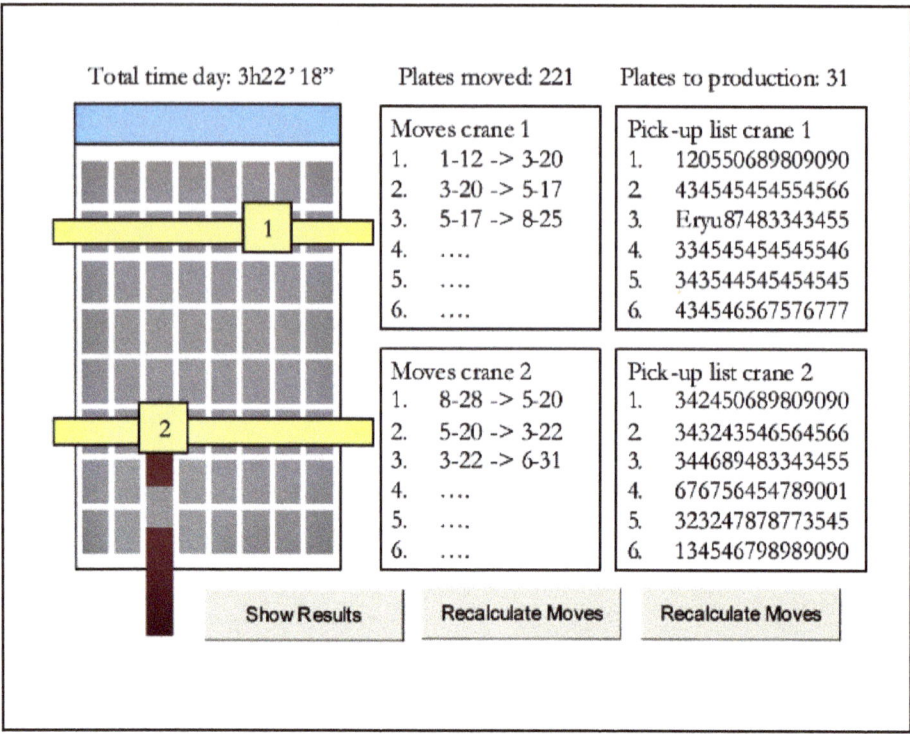

Figure 7.2 Material model in the inventory software

The programmers saw it in a similar way: 'The big change happened when we introduced the simulator; it was there that the discussion really started. We should have handled it differently...for the feedback...It would have been different if we had done it at the beginning but nobody had told us.'

These last two comments point back to Latour's quote of rethinking the way we operate. The project manager and the programmers had considerable experience with software projects, yet for them the results of introducing the material model were surprising. In the discussion about the introduction of the simulator they were in fact against it. Given the results, the professionals' attitude and their reactions, we can begin to delineate two design principles for IS development in complex settings

- whenever possible, start ISD efforts by developing a graphical simulator of the material environment of the users
- embed and use the simulator as a proper boundary object.

Use of materiality in ISD

In this section, we present some ideas on how to include the two design principles in ISD. Over the years, many strategies and techniques have been described that have improved greatly the chances of creating successful information systems. The difficulty in determining the business problem leads to the design of *iterative processes* that allow for *frequent revisions*. The need for *knowledge exchange* requires the creation of *boundary objects* as focus points in discussions. To reduce the negative effects of *invested knowledge, short iterations and simple prototypes* are required. This in turn reflects the need for splitting the software into *smaller development tasks* that can be tackled within one iteration. The combination of these techniques in different situations has given birth to the concept of agile methodology. To this we would add—responding to the practitioners' call for light customer involvement and riding the wave of material knowledge proposed by Orlikowski—that *starting a development effort with the creation of a simulator that mimics the material setting of the customer* increases the amount of knowledge exchange while limiting the need for customer involvement.

A methodology that includes the design principles could involve the following steps

1. business problem definition
2. material modelling and usage modelling
3. iteration and release planning
4. design and implementation
5. evaluation
6. integration.

These steps can be viewed as the steps of an agile development or as a sequential process. It is, however, only through the iterative process and the integration of practice-based feedback that it can be used. If the agile paradigm is chosen then the methodology focuses on a process that facilitates frequent and constructive encounters between developers and users while at the same time trying to minimise the amount of time used for discussion without the support of the proper boundary object. The process involves repeating the phases of the methodology many times in an iterative fashion in order for the knowledge exchange to take place. The idea is to use the knowledge of the material setting as much as possible to minimise the impact of the development on the customer and instead to put effort in the activities of evaluation and validation, redefinition of use cases and iteration and release planning that are more meaningful when based on a materiality-based software prototype.

Figure 7.3 shows an example of how the methodology phases might unfold over a series of three iterations. For reasons of space, the stages of the methodology are indicated by numbers 1–6 in Figure 7.3. In the figure, the methodology stages are mapped against the system life-cycle activities proposed by the ISO 15704 to show which activities are involved in each stage. The figure shows that in the first iteration, when the material setting is discovered and modelled, few resources are used to define the business problem and then in the second iteration the business problem is revised as a result of learning from the first cycle. In stage four, the developers design, implement and test the system. In stage five, the users evaluate and test the system. In accordance with the characteristics of boundary objects, the prototype should be functional and therefore evaluation is a stage that involves operation of the system. The barred box in stage six represents the integrated system only for evaluation and testing purposes by the users. In the third iteration, stage six represents the introduction of the system in use. Integrating software whenever possible is not only a source of immediate value for the users; software releases are the best boundary objects since the users can provide feedback to the developers from real usage.

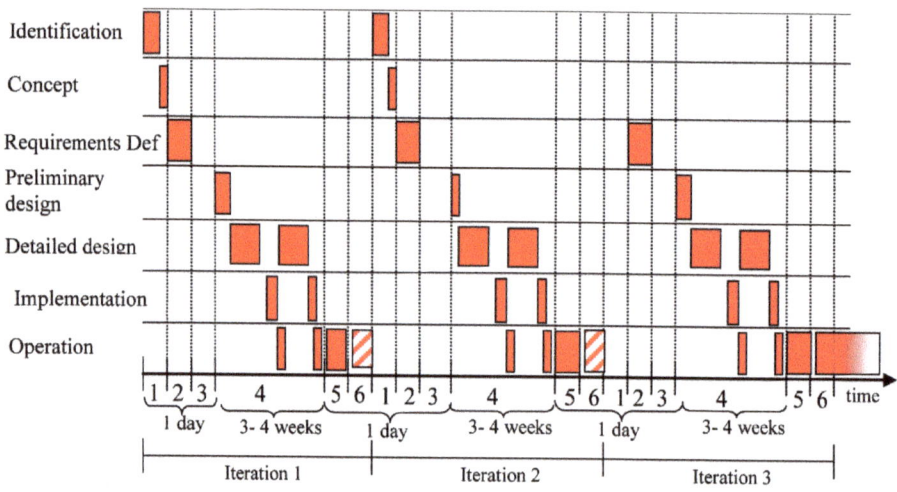

Figure 7.3 An example of iterations over time

The situation is explained further in Figure 7.4. This figure refers to the evolving nature of goals and objectives and shows a representation of the goals and objectives of the developers. At the beginning of the first iteration, the developers receive an initial understanding of the setting and they proceed to develop the materiality-based prototype (square one in the figure) as a boundary object. When they show the prototype to the users, they (together) achieve a new understanding of the goals. They will easily find out if a part of the first prototype was out of scope because of its visible and familiar

7. On using materiality in information systems development

characteristics. In the second iteration, the developers proceed to develop the second prototype and correct the first, represented by the area of overlap of the squares marked with 1 and 2. In the following presentation, the situation is repeated. Parts of the second prototype are out of scope and parts have to be corrected. The process continues in this fashion until the work done during the entire development effort covers all the needs for the final version of the goals and objectives. Obviously, the shape of goals and objectives changes not only because the software prototypes help the users to understand what they want from the IS, but because something in the environment has changed.

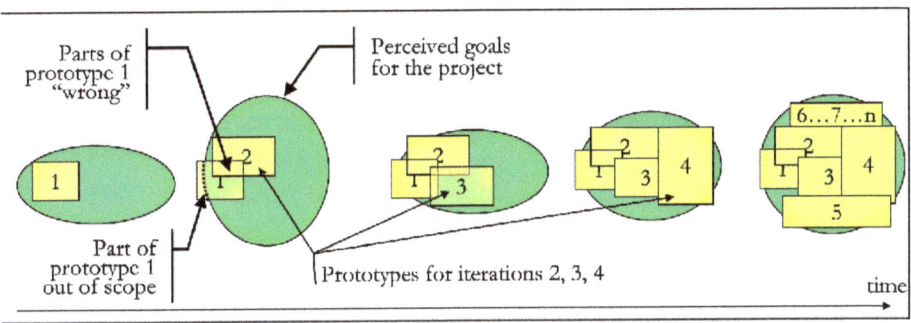

Figure 7.4 Evolving goals, objectives and development efforts

Figure 7.5 depicts what this methodology could look like in a case similar to the SteelCo case in which the scope is to develop planning software. The figure shows an example of six iterations. In the beginning, a first version of the requirements for the IS is formulated based on the initial definition of the business goals. In the first iteration, the focus is on creating the simulator of the material setting that must be used as a boundary object to focus the discussion between developers and users. The setting is the first indicator of what the client needs to do. As a surrogate of complex and time-consuming interaction with the customer, the setting can be observed, studied, photographed, and so on, and it can be used as the basis for creating the material model. The final system might lose the graphical characteristics, but the initial attempt has to be grounded in materiality as much as possible. In the first iteration, a GUI representing the setting is created along with a database connection (DB). This is to prepare, at the very beginning, a visual and usable prototype. In this phase, there is no intelligence in the system and all the operations are left to the user (the boundary object has to be incomplete and the scaffold emergent). In the following iterations, more core elements are added as a result of agreement between users and developers.

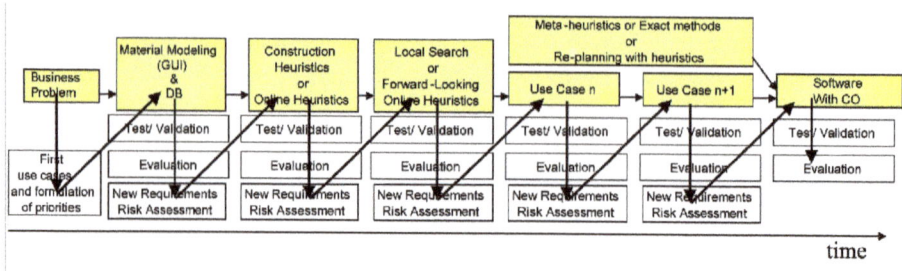

Figure 7.5 ISD process for information systems (for planning)

Generic system architecture and material model

Regarding the question of how the material model has to be embedded in the system, Figure 7.6 depicts a generalised version of the system architecture used in the SteelCo case. The material model, scaffolded by the materiality of the setting (reality in Figure 7.6), was the visible part of the software and, while interacting with the users on the human side, it provided the required data to the data model instead of the reality. This was particularly convenient in the SteelCo case because the system was for planning so the material model in fact worked as a simulator for the system core to test new plans. This could be useful in many settings where, for example, there is the need to test new routines. This could be done conveniently without disrupting the work environment. Figure 7.6 summarises the characteristics of reality as a scaffold of the material model as well as stating the characteristics of the material model if we want it to work as a boundary object. By paying attention to both sides of the figure, and recalling that they are by no means stable, we can create software architectures that are fit to support emerging knowledge in an emergent and changing world.

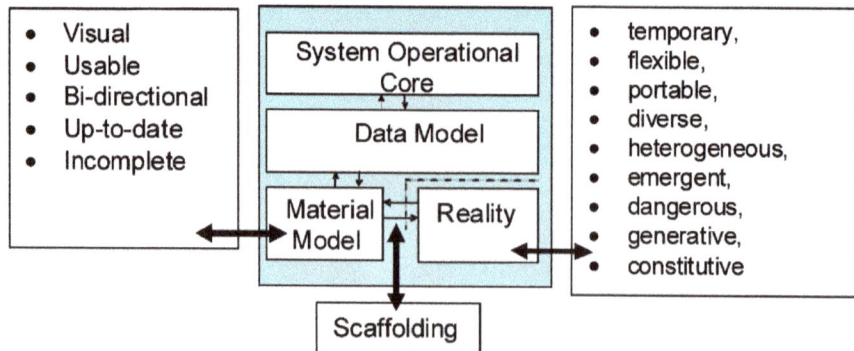

Figure 7.6 Generic system architecture and material model

Conclusions

In this chapter, we have proposed two design principles to account for and take advantage of material knowing in ISD. The principles are

- whenever possible, start ISD efforts by developing a graphical simulator of the material environment of the users
- embed and use the simulator as a proper boundary object.

These design principles help the ISD process in different ways: helping to make software tangible—a problem not felt as much in other fields but very important in ISD; enhancing knowledge exchange and quality of feedback; and decreasing the need for user participation in ISD.

The point of departure of our chapter is that, still today, ISD methodologies fail to meet the requirements of software houses either because the customer cannot be involved as much as they should or because the technology is too complex to allow for rapid solutions.

We have, therefore, proposed a design principle that uses the environment instead of people to aid the process. It starts from the materiality of the users' setting to achieve the knowledge exchange necessary without the continuous involvement of the customer.

Materiality of the setting presents high potential for improving the practice of ISD because of its nature as a boundary object and because of its connection to what we know and how we learn. On the other side of the coin, it also represents a highly underdeveloped element in ISD and as such it needs more exploration. This study presents an attempt at taking materiality seriously in ISD and also represents a call for more studies into this field.

References

Avison, D. E. and Fitzgerald G. 1988, *Information Systems Development: Methodologies, techniques and tools*, Blackwell Scientific, Oxford.

Avison, D. E., Wood-Harper, A. T., Vidgen, R. T. and Wood, J. R. G. 1998, 'A further exploration into information systems development: the evolution of Multiview2', *Information Technology & People*, vol. 11, no. 2, pp. 124-139.

Barki, H. and Hartwick, J. 1989, 'Rethinking the concept of user involvement', *MIS Quarterly*, March, vol. 13, no. 1, pp. 53–63.

Barki, H. and Hartwick, J. 1994, 'Measuring user participation, user involvement, and user attitude', *MIS Quarterly*, March, vol. 18, no. 1, pp. 59–82.

Beck, K. 1999, *Extreme Programming Explained: Embrace change*, First edition, Addison-Wesley, Reading, Mass.

Bhoem, B. 1988, *A Spiral Model of Software Development and Enhancement*, IEEE Computer Society, Washington, DC.

Boland, R. J. and Tenkasi, R. V. 1995, 'Perspective making and perspective taking in communities of knowing', *Organization Science*, vol. 7, no. 4.

Brooks, F. P. 1995, *The Mythical Man-Month*, Addison-Wesley, Reading, Mass.

Brown, J. S. and Diguid, P. 2001, 'Knowledge and organization: a social-practice perspective', *Organization Science*, vol. 12, no. 2, pp. 198-213.

Carlile, P. R. 2002, 'A pragmatic view of knowledge and boundaries: boundary objects in new product development', *Organization Science*, July/August, vol. 13, no. 4, pp. 442-455,

Carugati, A. 2008, 'Information system development activities and inquiring systems: an integrating framework', *European Journal of Information Systems*, vol. 17, no. 2, pp. 143-155..

Checkland, P. and Scholes, J. 1999, *Soft Systems Methodology in Action*, Wiley, Chichester, UK.

Churchman, C. W. 1971, *The Design of Inquiring Systems*, Basic Books, New York and London.

Cohen, W. and Levinthal, D. 1990, 'Absorptive capacity: a new perspective on learning and innovation', *Administrative Science Quarterly*, vol. 35, no. 1, pp. 128–52.

Collins, C. and Miller, R. 2001, XP distilled, <http://www.rolemodelsoftware.com>

Fowler, M. and Scott, K. 1999, *UML Distilled: A brief guide to the standard object modeling language*, Second edition, Addison-Wesley, Reading, Mass.

Gal, U., Lyttinen, K. and Yoo, Y. 2008, 'The dynamics of IT boundary objects, information infrastructures, and organizational identities: the introduction of 3D modelling technologies into the architecture, engineering, and construction industry', *European Journal of Information Systems*, vol. 17, no. 144 (June), pp. 290–304.

Gibson, C. F. and Singer, C.J. 1982, 'New risks for MIS managers', *Computerworld*, April.

Hert, S., Kettner, L., Polzin, T. and Schäfer, G. 2002, *ExpLab—A tool set for computational experiments. Version 0.6*, Max-Planck-Institut für Informatik, Saarbrücken, Germany, <http://explab.sourceforge.net/>

Hughes, J. and Wood-Harper, T. 2000, *An Empirical Model of the Information Systems Development Process: A case study of an automotive manufacturer*, Blackwell, Oxford.

Kellogg, K., Orlikowsky, W. and Yates, J. 2002, 'Enacting new ways of organizing: exploring the activities and consequences of post-industrial work', *Academy of Management Conference Proceedings*, Denver, Colo.

Latour, B. 2004, 'Nonhumans', in S. Harrison, S. Pile and N. Thrift (eds), *Patterned Ground: Entanglements of nature and culture*, Reaktion Books, London, pp. 224–7.

Levina, N. 2005, 'Collaborating on multiparty information systems development projects: a collective reflection in action view', *Information Systems Research*, vol. 16, no. 2, pp. 109–30.

Levina, N. and Vaast, E. 2005, 'The emergence of boundary spanning competence in practice: implications for information systems implementation and use', *MIS Quarterly*, vol. 29, no. 2 (June), pp. 335–63.

Lindstrom, L. and Jeffries, R. 2004, 'Extreme programming and agile software development methodologies', *Information Systems Management*, vol. 21, no. 3, pp. 41–52.

McKeen, J. D. and Guimaraes, T. 1997, 'Successful strategies for user participation in system development', *Journal of Management Information Systems*, vol. 14, no. 2, pp. 133-150.

Markus, M. L. and Keil, M. 1994, 'If we build it, they will come: designing information systems that users want to use', *Sloan Management Review*, vol. 35 (Summer), pp. 11–25.

Nonaka, I. and Takeuchi, H. 1995, *The Knowledge Creating Company: How the Japanese companies create the dynamics of innovation*, Oxford University Press, New York.

Orlikowski, W. J. 2006, 'Material knowing: the scaffolding of human knowledgeability', *European Journal of Information Systems*, vol. 15, no. 5 (October), pp. 460–6.

Orlikowski, W. J. 2007, 'Sociomaterial practices: exploring technology at work', *Organization Studies*, vol. 28, no. 9, pp. 1435–48.

Orlikowski, W. J. and Iacono, C. S. 2001, 'Research commentary: desperately seeking the "IT" in IT research—a call to theorizing the IT artifact', *Information Systems Research*, vol. 12, no. 2, pp. 121–34.

Pidd, M. 1998, *Computer Simulation in Management Science*, Fourth edition, John Wiley & Sons, New York.

Pirlot, M. 1992, 'General local search heuristics in combinatorial optimization: a tutorial', *Belgian Journal of Operations Research, Statistics and Computer Science*, vol. 32, no. 1-2, pp. 7-69.

Pries-Heje, J. 1995–96, 'Nyere systemudviklingsmetoder: Hvad følger efter vandfaldsmodellen og strukturerede metoder', *Økonomistyring og Informatik*, vol. 11, no. 2.

Remenyi, D., White, T. and Sherwood-Smith, M. 1997, 'Information systems management: the need for a post-modern approach', *International Journal of Information Management*, vol. 17, no. 6, 421-435.

Star, S. L. and Griesemer, J. R. 1989, 'Institutional ecology, "translations" and boundary objects: amateurs and professionals in Berkeley's Museum of Vertebrate Zoology, 1907–39', *Social Studies of Science*, vol. 19, no. 4, pp. 387–420.

Valacich, J. S., George, J. F. and Hoffer, J. A. 2001, *Systems Analysis & Design*, Prentice-Hall, Upper Saddle River, NJ.

Weick, K. 1979, *The Social Psychology of Organizing*, Second edition, McGraw-Hill, New York.

Wenger, E. 2000, 'Communities of practice and social learning systems', *Organization*, vol. 7, no. 2, 225-246..

Winter, M. C., Brown, D. H. and Checkland, P. B. 1995, 'A role for soft systems methodology in information systems development', *European Journal of Information Systems*, vol. 4, 130-142.

8. How IS design can contribute to a major climate change mitigation project

WALTER FERNÁNDEZ
AUSTRALIAN NATIONAL UNIVERSITY

BIRGITTA BERGVALL-KÅREBORN
LULEÅ UNIVERSITY OF TECHNOLOGY

MICHAEL DJORDJEVIC

KEITH LOVEGROVE

JAVIER FERNÁNDEZ-VELASCO

MISHKA TALENT
AUSTRALIAN NATIONAL UNIVERSITY

Abstract

Around the planet, numerous research initiatives are taking place to mitigate the effects of climate change. These activities—emerging from diverse research projects from basic and applied science—often suffer from lack of an overall design strategy that would allow capitalising on cross-specialised knowledge by having an integrative, holistic and synergistic approach to innovation design and implementation. This chapter discusses a particular research project and describes how a design methodology could help to address issues such as equality, empowerment, autonomy, creativity, performance and cycle times and provide for the necessary balance between control, speed and flexibility.

Introduction

The societal awakening to the problems caused by climate change seems to be sudden, yet scientists have been working in their labs for years on different ways to alleviate this problem. At The Australian National University, for example, we are working on a program to establish new and sustainable carbon-neutral energy sources that capitalises on Australia's natural advantages and know-how. Our project's ultimate objective is to develop a new oil industry to significantly reduce our dependency on fossil fuels. This aim will be achieved by producing a range of products, such as bio-fuels, without using food crops, destroying rainforests or arable land or competing with traditional agriculture for fresh water.[1] This project could have national and international importance, yet we have struggled to define a project approach that is sensible, efficient and effective and also easy to communicate to decision makers and potential partners.

In this chapter, we describe some of the general aspects of this initiative and suggest a way in which potential synergies can be achieved. The chapter presents our problem and current state of ideas with the aim of generating discussion that could result in more substantial research and practical outcomes. We are interested not so much in *being right* as in developing useful and enabling knowledge from a given starting point. To attain the chapter's goal, we will depart from the traditional form of presenting the literature review at the beginning of the chapter. Rather, we will address the literature *after* describing the problem domain and the knowledge emerging from our project. The following description of the project is critical to situate this chapter's central discussion.

The BioSolar project

The embryonic idea for this project was born out of research work on oil-extraction methods from micro-algae conducted at The Australian National University by Mishka Talent under the supervision of Keith Lovegrove and Javier Fernández-Velasco (Talent 2006). This section provides an overview of the problem domain and explains the basic concepts behind the project.

---

1 The term 'bio-fuel' refers to liquid, gas and solid fuels predominantly produced from biomass—such as: bio-ethanol, bio-methanol, vegetable oils, bio-diesel, biogas, bio-synthetic gas (bio-syngas), bio-oil, Fischer-Tropsch liquids and bio-hydrogen (Demirbas 2008).

The problem domain

We depend on petroleum products to fuel our cars, to warm our homes and to provide petroleum-based components for plastics, medicines, food items and a host of other products. The continued use of fossil fuels as an energy source is, however, having adverse effects on the environment and alternative sources are urgently required (Witze 2007). Simultaneously, worldwide concerns about global warming, climate change and pollution have sharpened public demand for sustainable energy solutions. Thus, a considerable effort is required to find and deploy sustainable solutions without derailing economies or sacrificing modern lifestyles. One of these potential solutions can be found in the innovative use of solar energy.

Several technologies have been developed to capture solar energy, including the harvesting of sunlight as plant biomass in a variety of 'energy' crops. The International Energy Agency (IEA 2004) raises doubts, however, over the economic viability of current bio-fuels. Furthermore, feedstocks such as corn, sugar, soya beans and wheat are perceived as critical food sources for an increasing world population. Arable land is required for growing food crops that can be utilised for oil production (Demirbas 2008) and the diversion of food crops to energy production is one of the alleged reasons for spikes in food prices.

In contrast, marine micro-algae can be grown *without* competing for fresh water or arable land used in classical agriculture. Research shows that selected micro-algae (single-celled plants and bacteria) can photosynthetically generate biomass, protein, oil and other feedstocks potentially with productivities much higher than the best traditional crops (Chisti 2008).

Micro-algae can grow in seawater or wastewater that is unsuitable for other purposes (Chisti 2007). Micro-algae can utilise carbon dioxide (CO_2) and other greenhouse gases generated by fossil-fuel combustion and, through biotechnology, we can manipulate micro-algae to generate new feedstock sources for pharmaceutical and chemical industries.

We are currently at the problem definition phase and are trying to plan the activities required and the resources needed to develop sustainable industries based on combining micro-algal cultivation and solar-thermal technologies. Sub-projects that combine these two technologies can result in the production of bio-fuels such as bio-diesel, hydrogen, ethanol, methane and also new feedstock sources for other industries. Recognising that the scope of the project goes beyond the technical and scientific components, the project is receiving contributions from the fields of project management and information systems (IS), making it a cross-campus initiative. We call this broad and evolving initiative *the BioSolar project*.

Basic concepts behind the BioSolar project

The BioSolar project aims to provide a blueprint for sustainable, carbon-neutral and efficient production of fluid fuels for Australian and international markets. To achieve this objective, we need to combine best-of-breed micro-algal and solar-thermal technologies while remaining open to complementary technologies that could be coupled to the system.

Micro-algae represent an untapped and versatile cropping system. Selected micro-algae can photosynthetically generate biomass, oil, protein and other industrial feedstocks and, with effective carbon dioxide supplementation and non-limiting growth conditions, they can achieve this with productivities up to 10 times higher than the best traditional crops and forestry systems (Chisti 2007, 2008).

These micro-algae can industrially transform sunlight energy into bio-diesel or hydrogen—both sustainable sources of energy—and into other industrial feedstock. In addition, micro-algae can contribute to atmospheric carbon dioxide abatement—indirectly, by minimising the need for fossil fuels, and directly, by acting as net carbon sequesters. Net carbon sequestration can occur by converting the biomass to char through a process called pyrolysis (Lehmann 2007). The carbon captured in the char is stable for long periods and the application of char to crops is reported to lead to increases in crop biomass.

Solar-thermal technology collects sunlight energy as heat for industrial use, including the generation of electricity and superheated water (Lovegrove et al. 2004). The BioSolar production plants could utilise highly efficient solar-thermal technologies to provide all the energy required for the industrial processing of the micro-algae. Because the selected solar-thermal technology can provide all the electrical and heat power needed to operate the full industrial plant, it is possible to efficiently generate carbon-neutral sustainable energy and a set of products for agriculture and other industries.

Marine micro-algae offer the simplicity of biological production systems common to all plants but with a number of significant advantages over traditional crops. During early discussions, we articulated a number of reasons why micro-algae could become the preferred new crop for most purposes where biomass is required; this initial set included adaptability, productivity, industrialisation and ecological impact.

The science involved in solar-thermal and micro-algae technologies is well advanced and offers great potential for further improvement. By coupling biomass generation via micro-algal photosynthesis to solar-thermal technologies, a variety of products can be obtained, ranging from human and animal foods to substances of energetic or medical importance. These include: aviation fuel, biodiesel, plastics, biogas, ethanol, pharmaceuticals, neutraceuticals, antibiotics, bioremediation, sewage treatment, animal feed, soil conditioner and net carbon dioxide sequestration. Solar-thermal concentrators such as The Australian National University's Big Dish system can produce temperatures high enough to drive thermo-chemical reactions. In particular, biomass and water mixtures can be processed to produce carbon monoxide and hydrogen mixtures that are the basic feedstocks for processes producing a range of liquid fuels. In doing so, the solar concentrator is adding to the energy stored in the biomass and simultaneously processing it into a more useful form. A key hypothesis behind the BioSolar project is that combining algae with solar-thermal technology into an integrated and optimised system will give a result that is better economically than either technology on its own. The BioSolar project aims to successfully combine these technologies, producing a market-ready solution to a unique and pressing problem. To deploy an effective commercial solution, however, far more needs to be accomplished, and this is discussed next.

The blank slate and the green field

With the 1970s and 1980s oil crises over, research funds into algal-based biofuels practically disappeared. The scientific knowledge is, however, available and ready to be reactivated. In terms of biological science, we are starting from a solid base and with proven technology. The key challenge, however, remains in the industrialisation and commercialisation aspects of this technology. We need to take the production of oil from the controlled environment of the laboratory's bench to the industrial and commercial environment, and this task is too complex and too urgent to be left to chance.

To achieve the transformation from laboratory bench to product delivery, we have to confront a number of important issues—including, but not limited to: scalability; automation; business process analysis and design; management of development activities; integration and coordination of multiple concurrent projects; skill development for scientists, engineers and technical personnel; design and development of information systems, information technology (IT) and special equipment; automation and remote management systems; identification of complementary algal technologies; environmental accounting assessments; development of replicable and adaptable production protocols; and implementing effective supply chains.

We have a *green field* in front of us. This is a significant challenge, as many minds, from many fields, with different world views and agendas, will need to work in a coordinated manner, addressing priorities and developing a long-term plan of action that is efficient, effective and flexible enough to accommodate the uncertainties of innovative endeavours. Without planning, the many activities will grow organically—some to success, others to failure. Yet we are facing a problem that forces us to respond in a short time and with the minimum of waste. Thus, the option for unplanned or isolated evolution seems, at best, risky.

The overall planning for this major project is, however, a difficult and complex task because our knowledge of the problem domain is far from perfect and its context is plagued with uncertainties. Consequently, the planning tools need to be flexible and evolutionary, adopting a performing view of project knowledge in which knowledge is regarded 'not as static or given, but as a capability produced and reproduced in recurrent social practices' (Orlikovski 2006:460).

We need an effective way of designing a new industry in a manner that is incremental in nature and facilitates the end-to-end efficient and effective management of the project—from conceptual design to prototype design and to product and services design. The elements to be designed and implemented in this project are many, including, among others, engineering, biotechnology, commerce, manufacturing, training, regulatory frameworks, partnerships and information systems. Further, the techno-centric approach seems to be limited, as we need to develop the technology in a social and political context, taking into consideration demands from business, government and academic stakeholders, among others.

To successfully design and implement the socio-technical innovation, a suitable methodology must include human and technical aspects and work across complementary fields. This approach needs to act as a scaffold for the generation of knowledge and physical artefacts. Orlikovski (2006) describes the notion of scaffolding as a useful metaphor for studies of performative knowledge. Certain elements of scaffolding, with regard to human agency, can be useful to our project. We are attracted to the notion that scaffolding can *extend, complement, link, stabilise, reconfigure* and *transform* human agency (Orlikovski 2006). The next section describes a method that has been successfully used in Europe to manage innovative projects and that appears *promising* in addressing our significant challenges.

FormIT: designing complex and innovative systems

During the initial planning stage of the BioSolar project, we understood that to succeed we needed to produce a system that considered the human aspect of the technology in order to enhance the effectiveness and implementation of the technology. Some guidance for this kind of design can be found in the ISO 13407:1999 human-centred design process for interactive systems. This international standard describes aspects of software and hardware systems so project managers can understand the basic issues involved when including human-centred activities throughout a development life cycle, but it does not cover all aspects of project management. It also does not cover in detail the practical issues of conducting human-centred design or the necessary methods and techniques.

The starting point to manage projects such as BioSolar can be found in FormIT (Bergvall-Kåreborn et al. 2007; Ståhlbröst and Bergvall-Kåreborn 2007a)—an approach originally created for developing IT-based artefacts and services that takes a 'human-centred' (Kling and Star 1998) approach to design. FormIT aims to guide and facilitate the development of innovative services that are based on a holistic understanding of people and their behaviour, grounded in *needs* and *wants* that stakeholders experience as relevant. FormIT takes seriously issues such as equality, empowerment, autonomy and control in relation to real *use situations*—that is, including the whole system in development and in operation. These issues are critical to achieve the collaboration necessary for the project to work in a synergistic manner, having the necessary flexibility to enhance creativity and innovation and the critical controls to ensure that we advance in a coordinated and planned manner.

FormIT is inspired by three theoretical streams: soft systems thinking (SST), appreciative inquiry and need finding. From SST (Checkland and Holwell 1998; Checkland and Scholes 1999), FormIT borrows the assumption that changes can occur only through changes in mental models. This implies that we need to understand our own as well as other stakeholders' world views and we need to be clear about our interpretations and the base on which they are made (Bergvall-Kåreborn and Ståhlbröst 2007; Ståhlbröst and Bergvall-Kåreborn 2007b). Hence, we aim to *interpret and understand situations through an iterative and interactive process with stakeholders*. This concept fits well with the principles stated in the BioSolar project since we strongly believe that complex systems with multiple stakeholders cannot be successfully developed in the isolation of the laboratory's bench. We also need to define what success means to the project; this definition is a social construction that facilitates the project's outcome (Thomas and Fernández 2008).

Appreciative inquiry (Cooperrider and Avital 2004; Cooperrider and Whitney 2005; Cooperrider et al. 2005; Norum 2001) has encouraged the Swedish author(s) to start the development cycle by identifying different stakeholders' dreams and visions of how technology can improve and support the lives of people. This includes a focus on opportunities related to specific trends, contexts or stakeholder groups and on the positive and life-generating experiences of people. This way of thinking is closely aligned with the philosophy behind SST since it also highlights the importance of people's thoughts about themselves and the world around them in design situations. Hence, *instead of starting the process by searching for problems to solve in a situation, we identify what works well and use this as a basis for design.* In the BioSolar project, we have identified technologies that work well (algal technologies and solar thermal) as the starting point for our design.

Need finding (Bergvall-Kåreborn et al. 2007) is about focusing on stakeholders' needs throughout the development process and using these as a foundation for requirement specification. Patnaik and Becker (1999) state that the main motivator for the need-finding approach is that needs are not highly influenced by trends—hence, they are more long lasting. Therefore, the project must include and provide adequate resources for the needs-elicitation process (Kankainen and Oulasvirta 2003; Kankainen et al. 2003; Tiitta 2003). In our perspective, identifying opportunities is the basis for appreciating needs since needs are opportunities waiting to be exploited.

FormIT also strongly emphasises the importance of the first phase in the development cycle—usually referred to as analysis or requirements engineering. Since this phase creates the foundation for the rest of the process, errors here become very hard and expensive to correct in later stages. Following the human-centric approach, this is also the phase where stakeholders make the strongest contribution by really setting the direction for the design, rather than responding to half-finished prototypes. Since stakeholder needs and requirements can change as they gain more knowledge and insight into possible solutions, it is important, however, to continually reassess these needs and to ensure that needs correlate to given requirements.

In conclusion, FormIT is an iterative method in which continuous interaction with stakeholders is an understood prerequisite. The basic idea is that knowledge increases through iterative interactions between phases and people with diverse competencies and perspectives. In this way, knowledge increases through dialogue between participants (Ståhlbröst and Holst 2006). The cross-functional interaction enables the processes of taking knowledge from one field to another to gain fresh insights, which then facilitates innovative ideas. The shared understanding of the situation informs and enriches the learning processes and thus facilitates changes in perspective and leads towards innovative design

8. How IS design can contribute to a major climate change mitigation project

processes (Holst and Mirijamdotter 2006). This, in turn, increases our ability to design systems that answer to stakeholder needs. A more detailed description of the method follows.

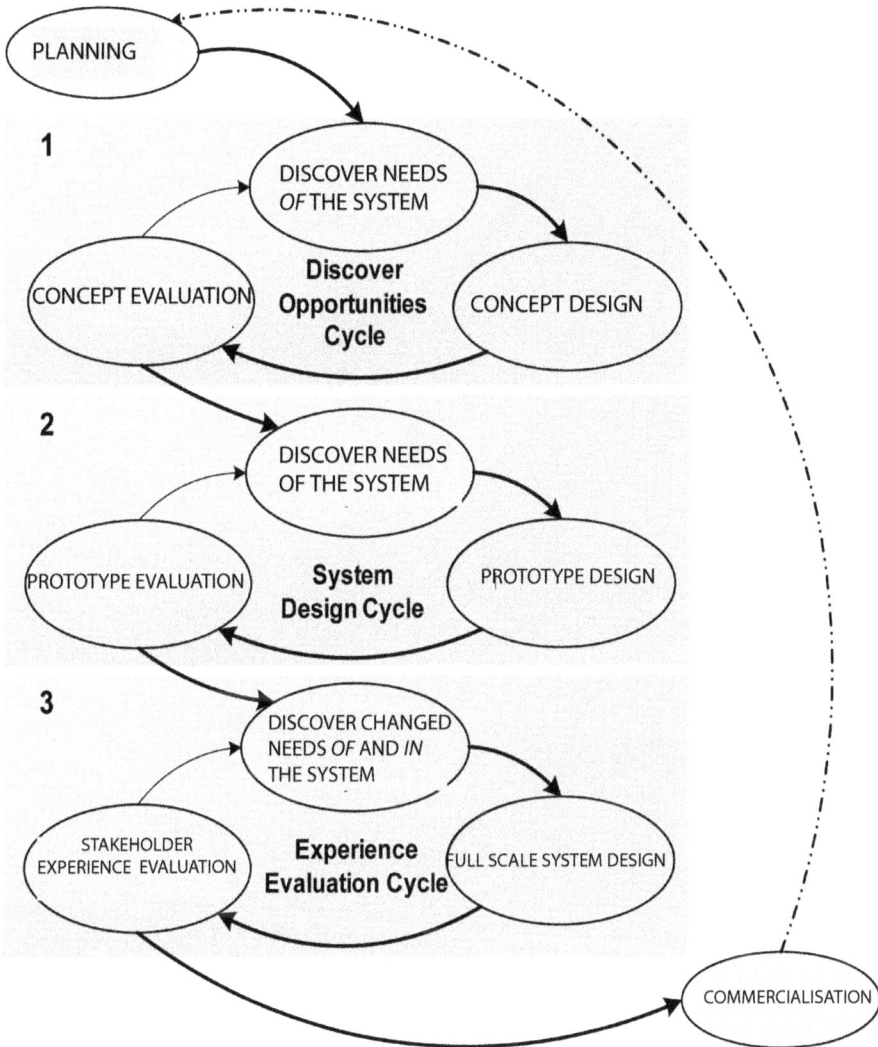

Figure 8.1 The FormIT process for innovation development

The FormIT method

FormIT can be seen as three interconnected evolutionary cycles (discover opportunities, system design and experience evaluation) in which the design becomes increasingly clear, while the attention of the evaluation broadens from a focus on concepts and prototype to a holistic view of the use of the system.

Within each of the cycles three basic phases are repeated (discover needs, design and evaluate). The full methodology includes two additional phases (planning and commercialisation), as seen in Figure 8.1.

Planning stands for planning the intervention as a whole and here it is important to gain as much information as possible about the underlying circumstances for the project: its aim and scope, different perspectives on the project and constraints and boundaries that need to be accepted. Three important perspectives that need to be considered and combined are the human, technological and business perspectives of a project. It is common that different stakeholders assign different priorities to each of these perspectives. There is nothing wrong with this as long as everyone understands the importance of all three perspectives and how they contribute to, and interact with, each other.

While planning the intervention can be seen as the start-up phase of the project as a whole, many of the guidelines and lessons learned in relation to this phase can also be applicable in the planning of the subsequent phases. In a large, complex and multidisciplinary project such as the one described in this chapter, the planning phase is extremely important since divergent views on the aim and scope of the project—as well as on roles, responsibilities and authority—can put the whole project at risk. Hence, before leaving this phase, a sense of 'accommodation' (Checkland and Scholes 1999) concerning these issues needs to be reached between key stakeholders.

The commercialisation work needs to be integrated into the development work but is often treated as a separate project in which the aim is to implement the system and to introduce it to the market. While the commercialisation effort and focus are greater nearing project completion, this phase is definitely not a passive sink collecting the results of previous cycles. We acknowledge that system design cycles inform commercialisation and are also informed by commercialisation issues. This is critical to facilitate effective end-to-end alignment. Also, lessons learned from commercialisation experiences inform the planning of future systems. As this chapter focuses on the planning phase and the subsequent design cycles, the commercialisation phase is mentioned here for completeness purposes only.

Before discussing the steps required for the BioSolar project, the following subsections provide a short description of the character and main activities of each one of the three cycles.

The first cycle: needs of

The first cycle focuses on discovering the basic needs that different stakeholders have *of* the system. These are the needs that motivate them to buy and use a particular product or service. Following the language of soft systems methodology, these needs are part of the *'weltanschauung'* (Checkland and Davies 1986)—the world view that makes the service meaningful to use. The needs of the system can vary and take different forms depending on stakeholder, context and situation. The challenge in the *discovery phase* of the first cycle is thus to identify the key needs of the system and the different expressions they might take. This is done by obtaining a rich picture of different stakeholders, their behaviour, attitudes and values. When this is achieved, the needs are translated into design concepts in the form of scenarios or mock-ups. By doing this, the focus shifts from the discovery phase to the design phase. The aim of the *design phase* is to develop new and innovative concepts based on the data from the discovery phase. The concepts need to be detailed enough for the stakeholders to understand the basic objective and functions of the system. From here, the focus shifts again—this time from the design phase to the *evaluation phase*. The aim of the evaluation of the first cycle is to make sure that the stakeholders agree with the basic objectives of the developed concepts. This means relating the basic objectives and functions of the system to the identified needs of the system, making sure that these are consistent. If they are not, this cycle needs to be repeated until such coherence is achieved.

The second cycle: needs in

The second cycle starts with the process of identifying stakeholders' needs *in* the system. That is, what needs in the finished system are important for stakeholders. As in the first cycle, this is done through a variety of data-gathering methods such as interviews and observations. The challenge in this second cycle is to separate needs *of* the system (visions and motivations) and needs *in* the system (goals, processes and functions). One way of doing this is to keep the concept design—with key needs related to it—visible for the stakeholders during the data-collection activities so it is possible to relate to these during the discussions. When the data collection no longer generates new insights and findings, we consider that we have reached saturation and the focus again shifts to the design phase. In the second cycle, however, the design of the system broadens to include basic functions, workflows and interfaces. The prototype or design needs to be detailed enough for the stakeholders to understand and be able to experience how the final system will look and feel. This leads us to the evaluation, which is centred on structure, processes, activities and information flows in the second cycle. It includes questions and analyses concerning how different subsystems need to be integrated and how they affect each other and the system as a whole. The evaluation is focused on the interaction between the parts and the whole.

The third cycle: needs of and in

The third cycle starts by analysing the results from the prototype evaluation in order to discover changes in the needs *of* and *in* the system. Small changes and adjustments in the needs are quite common, especially in relation to the needs *in* the system, as the system develops and stakeholders' understanding of structure, content, workflow and interface deepens. Based on these changes, alterations in the design of the system also take place, as well as in the general development work to finalise the system as a whole. When this is done, the last evaluation phase takes place and now the evaluation is focused on the relation between the system and its users. Stakeholder experiences and goals are primarily subjective qualities and concern how a system feels to a stakeholder. They differ from more objective performance goals in that they are concerned with how stakeholders experience the system and its performance and how useful they consider the system to be, rather than assessing how efficient or productive a system is.

Using FormIT in the BioSolar project

As discussed above, each critical cycle is divided into three phases that iterate until the cycle is successfully completed. This section briefly describes a number of recommended actions and the state of our knowledge regarding potential activities to be conducted in future interventions in the BioSolar project.

Initial planning of the BioSolar project

We have found that, as in every project, it is highly important to gain a common perspective of the main purpose of the project (Ståhlbröst et al. 2005). This can be difficult to accomplish since project participants usually want to make contributions to many different areas. In large, complex and multidisciplinary projects, as with the BioSolar project, this is particularly challenging since it can be hard for participants to grasp the project as a whole, as well as to fully understand the more detailed work tasks of stakeholders from other disciplines. It is therefore important to support a communicative approach that builds trust and confidence between the stakeholders (Ståhlbröst 2006) and to find ways of illustrating how the different parts of the project relate to each other. For this, we could adopt PAWDAC (Bergvall-Kåreborn et al. 2004) or critical systems heuristic's boundary questions (Bergvall-Kåreborn 2006; Ulrich 1987, 1998). For example, using PAWDAC would involve discussing and reaching consensus related to the following questions.

- *Process*: what is the key process to be carried out in the project? What are the main sub-processes and their relationships? What is the time frame of the project and critical milestones?
- *Affectees*: who are the beneficiaries and victims of the project?
- *Weltanschauung*: what is the motivation of the project, as well as its purposes and goals? What is the problem or opportunity that the project aims to contribute to and the background and needs that formed the project idea?
- *Decision maker*: identify those with authority and responsibility over the project and with prime concern for its performance. Any power relations that are of importance to the project should also be considered, along with consideration of how these could have influence on the intervention.
- *Actors and other resources needed*: what competencies and resources are important to the process? What technology does the project require? Does this technology exist today or will it be developed within the project?
- *Boundaries and constraints*: what in the context might influence the intervention and what in the intervention might influence the context?

When these questions have been discussed and agreed on, the first phase of the FormIT process—the discover needs phase—can start.

Phase one in each cycle: discovering the needs of the BioSolar system

This phase is repeated in all three cycles. In the first cycle, it is called *discover needs of*; in the second cycle, it is called *discover needs in*; and in the third cycle, it is called *discover needs of and in* (as in Figure 8.1)—but the focus is slightly different in the different cycles. In the first cycle, the aim is to gain insight into the different basic needs that different stakeholders have *of* the BioSolar system.

To do this, we plan to use a mixture of data-collection methods, including focus-group interviews, individual interviews, storytelling, observations and formal documents. In both focus-group interviews and the individual interviews, we will ask the participants to tell stories that reveal their views on their present and future situations and how the BioSolar system will help them to make this transformation. These stories will include stories based on their positive experiences related to their everyday situation and technology usage. Focusing on past, present and future situations instead of present problems and existing technological solutions is important to generate a positive and creative atmosphere in the group. This atmosphere, combined with the focus-group interview technique, stimulates the stakeholders to generate innovative ideas and visions together in a conversational mode. In these conversations, users become inspired—hence, they stimulate each other to go beyond their own frame of mind by developing ideas generated by others. This produces a fruitful and interesting snowball effect, which helps all group members to participate actively during the discussion. In the first cycle, we plan to have more heterogeneous and non-established groups since this creates understanding and knowledge sharing between existing groups and subjects within the project. It also allows for different views and ideas to cross-fertilise and creates new and innovative ideas. In the second cycle, we will use more homogenous and established groups since this facilitates the discussion of in-depth questions within a field or subject.

Since it sometimes can be complicated to encourage participants to tell rich stories in the mode and depth that are needed for eliciting needs in group discussion, we will also use individual interviews in order to focus on and excavate specific issues or stories expressed by single participants in the group interviews. To focus on one single participant in a group interview might lead to the feeling among the other participants of not being fully included. In addition, focusing on one person's story and digging into that can result in a feeling of being singled out in front of the other participants. Individual interviews will also be used when the area of concern is of sensitive character, such as confidential information that might be of value for the project.

Our experience is that appreciating strengths and dreaming of the future are difficult for most people because they are stuck in present problems and in their picture of currently existing technological possibilities. To stimulate this 'shift to the future', we will use scenarios as stimuli in two different ways: we will present scenarios for the stakeholders in order to help participants get started in their process and we will ask them to describe a scenario to us.

The usage of stimulus material, such as scenarios or mock-ups, needs to be considered in depth. We have found that stimulus material can have a noticeable impact on the topics being addressed in the groups. The stimulus material can smooth the progress of the discussions and we have also used it to fuel discussions when they have started to diminish. In these situations, the material can boost the discussions and the focus-group participants' imaginations. Hence, the respondents become aware of new needs and more possible solutions than they had been aware of previously. The usage of stimulus material is, however, not risk free. It can also steer the discussion away from revealing the critical needs of the stakeholders. Thus, to carefully consider and try to imagine the impact of the stimuli are of utmost importance if a high level of validity is desired in the study.

In addition, our experience in Sweden shows that it is necessary to have a blend of competence among the moderators facilitating the interviews since respondents sometimes ask important questions about a certain technology that need to be understood for the discussion to develop.

Phase two in each iteration/cycle: design the BioSolar system

The aim of this phase is to design and develop innovative concepts on the basis of the identified needs from the earlier phase. The design phase is also carried out in all three iterations. In the first iteration, it is called *concept design*; in the second, *prototype design*; and in the third, it is called *full-scale system design* (as in Figure 8.1). So far, we have focused on the conceptual design that is part of the first cycle of the FormIT process and the cooperation between different stakeholders to ensure that knowledge is shared both across and within competence areas.

Based on our research, we have found that to ensure that the final solution answers stakeholders' needs, and does not merely reflect what is technically possible, a close interaction between stakeholders representing the human, technical and business perspectives is needed. This does not mean, however, that all stakeholders need to be involved in all the stages of development; rather cooperation should build on mutual communication around these perspectives when designing the system. The objective is to ensure that the knowledge gained from earlier stages is guaranteed to be included and considered in the final design.

In this phase, the known needs as well as identified strengths and dreams form the basis for the vision of the system that takes shape here. Usually a basic idea of the future solution has started to take form—hence, the idea will be elaborated on and expressed textually, in the form of key concepts, and pictorially, in the form of user stories, scenarios or mock-ups of the system. Broadly speaking, there are two types of design: conceptual and physical. Conceptual design is concerned with developing models that capture what the product will do and how it will behave, while physical design is concerned with details of design such as chemical processes, innovative use of solar-thermal energy, work flows or security systems.

In the BioSolar project, many different concepts need to be designed, representing everything from methods of growing the micro-algae and developing it into different products to information systems that facilitate and control these processes, as well as managing the project as a whole and the production site once the project is implemented. All these concepts then need to be clustered and discussed in order to generate new, innovative solutions by relating diverse concepts together, but also to understand how the different key concepts fit together into a meta-model. From the selected concepts, requirements are generated and from the requirements the first prototypes are designed and refined. Through the design phases, it will be important to continuously assess the design outcomes against the needs representations from the previous phase.

We have found in previous projects that in order to communicate the idea of a product or service, different types of visualisations are very powerful. In the BioSolar project, we will therefore use a number of methods, including

- storyboarding—a series of drawings that shows how the user might progress through a task using the intended design
- scenarios—an informal story description that describes the tasks the user will undertake when s/he uses the design; these stories will be closely related to the stakeholder's contexts and expected behaviours; further, they will be related to the goal, or needs, that the stakeholder has expressed
- use cases—a representation that focuses on the interaction between the stakeholder and the system rather than specific user tasks; the use case scenario represents one possible path of behaviour
- essential use cases—a combination of use cases and scenarios; this is a structured story consisting of user action and a step-by-step description of the responsibility of the system
- paper prototypes, mock-ups and card-based prototypes—ways to design the system and present it in sketches in which each sketch can represent a screen or a view of the system.

As the process iterates through the model, the key concepts and pictorial expressions of the system will be developed into prototypes and, later, a finished system. The challenge here is to convince the system developers and technical engineers to consider the list of prioritised needs as a starting point for the vision and then the functional requirements and technical specifications. Since many developers and engineers are unfamiliar with this way of working, they often want to skip this part and go directly to the requirements and specifications.

Phase three in each cycle: evaluation of the BioSolar system

As with the previously described phases, this phase is carried out in all three cycles. It is called *concept evaluation* in the first cycle, *prototype evaluation* in the second and in the third it is called stakeholder *experience evaluation* (see Figure 8.1). The goal of this phase is to produce a thorough evaluation of the system to determine if further iterations are required within a particular cycle before proceeding to the next cycle (or to commercialisation in the case of the third cycle).

In this phase, stakeholders are encouraged to give their impressions of the system that has been developed, based on stated needs. At this point, the system can have different forms depending on where in the development process the system is. In the first cycle, the initial evaluation process completes the first iteration of the cycle by evaluating system concepts, or ideas, in relation to the discovered needs. Yet this is not just a simple verification exercise; the evaluation also aims to identify new and unexplored needs or modifications of needs. When these evaluations and investigations do not give any new insights regarding stakeholders' needs *of* the service, the next cycle can start.

In the second cycle, the focus is on evaluating a prototype of the system related to stakeholder needs *in* the system. Hence, the focus is on relationships between parts of the system and the system as a whole, concerning aspects such as processes, structures, activities and information flows. Also in this phase, the process is iterated until no new insights are identified.

The third cycle focuses on combining users' needs *of* and *in* the system and then it is developed into a full-scale system. Here the focus is on how the system really works and fits its context of use. For the development project to be successful, ownership of the system must be handed over to and accepted by the involved stakeholders. In this process, the participants might need to change their traditional way of working and acting because long-lasting and substantial change could have occurred. Thus, we need to consider process change management requirements as one of the deliverables of the design process.

Based on our experiences from working in IT innovation projects, we have found that determining what methods to use when evaluating innovative systems can be complicated. One aspect to consider here is the characteristics of the system or subsystem. Since the BioSolar system consists of many different subsystems of chemical, technological, ecological, economic, business and social natures, the system needs to be evaluated both on an overall level, covering all aspects, and on a subsystem level, with particular focus on the aspects governing a specific subsystem. Also, aspects such as whether the system or subsystem under consideration is a product or a service will affect the evaluation and its criteria.

The evaluation process enables discussion among stakeholders as to how the concepts, prototypes or final solution can be related and refined to answer the needs identified in the earlier phases. Hence, the issues that need to be dealt with are

- what is the approach and purpose for the evaluation
- what is the main question that needs to be answered
- should the evaluation be of summative, formative or interactive character
- what kind of data are expected from the evaluation—qualitative or quantitative
- define what methods to use in the evaluation—interviews, logs, surveys, observations in relation to the purpose
- study the context to determine what, in the context, can influence the evaluation results
- create questions, observation schemas or other preconditions for the evaluation; at this stage, develop questions on the basis of the identified needs and requirements
- define the number of stakeholders and stakeholder groups and selection criteria such as age, gender, occupation, and so forth
- define what the characteristics of the innovation are; identify important 'has to' in the evaluation—such as when the test has to be done, the duration of the test, the character of the interaction, what a natural behaviour around the innovation is, degree of participation and so forth.

To sum up, the focus for this stage varies depending on where the innovation is in the development process. In the first cycle, the focus is on elaborating, with stakeholder needs *of* the system, while in the second cycle the focus is on the prototype and stakeholders' needs *in* the system. In the last cycle, we focus on user experiences and here the main aspect is to hand over the system to the various stakeholders and to ensure that all important roles, responsibilities and authorities needed to run the system have been defined and handed out. The objective here is to gain insight into stakeholders' needs *of* the system combined with their needs *in* the system.

Conclusion

In this chapter, we have presented a continuing project, providing a glimpse of the complexity involved. We propose that collaborative projects with multiple stakeholders and different world views require careful management. We have also argued that in managing projects in which significant collaborative innovations must be deployed, managers must pay special heed to the human aspects of the project in addition to the technical aspects. In this way, we do not perceive a dichotomy between technical and social considerations, but rather a natural integration of these aspects.

Hence, we need a methodology that allows for flexibility and that fosters creativity and understanding among stakeholders. We believe that a successful design methodology must provide the basic elements and processes necessary to produce the system in an efficient and effective manner. We believe that FormIT—a methodology used successfully to develop IT innovations—appears suitable for the BioSolar project. FormIT seems able to handle some of the identified problems and to provide the basis for further development of the innovation.

We have described the cycles in the process and given an example of potential techniques to elicit requirements, to facilitate and to verify the design. Furthermore, because the design method has a strong and coherent philosophical approach, we suggest that it can act as a guide to the overall project strategy, providing a system of belief appropriate for complex projects concerned with the development of innovative greenfield industries. The methodology is based on a holistic understanding of the problem domain and allows for evolution and flexibility while keeping the project grounded in the needs and wants of key stakeholders.

Our chapter is limited, however, in that it does not include a discussion of competing design approaches or a review of the innovation literature; it does not address the lack of a defined research question or problem or provide a discussion of academic politics and its role in the development of science and industry. In addition, we have taken a different approach to present our argument—a risky strategy not advisable for more formal research outlets but one that we believe is necessary at this stage. Perhaps the least clear aspect of this chapter is its contribution to knowledge. A reviewer suggested that possible contributions might be in the areas of complex systems development, project and program management, design science or alternative energy. These contributions are, however, speculative, so we can only offer this chapter as an attempt to bring to the discussion table some of the challenges we are currently facing in this project. The chapter itself is a boundary object devised to focus the development of a shared vision of problems and solutions (Gasson 2006).

Finally, the adopted design method provides the general strategy for managing the project, but, as with any complex project, both the method and the project evolve *in action* (Fitzgerald et al. 2002; Latour 1987). We need to apply the method as a scaffold to build project knowledge and to allow for the efficient and effective progress of the project. FormIT was developed from a human-centric viewpoint that, taken to extremes, could negate the importance of the technology. How much we are going to be able to address this bias to reach a middle ground that takes into account both the technical and the human is debatable. We must insist, however, that our intention is not to stress the formality of the approach but rather its potential for flexibility and adaptablity in use. We agree with Berg (1997:406) that

> the idea of an intelligent or self-sufficient formal tool within the complexity of the informal/empirical is an anathema. By themselves, formal tools are utterly powerless…[and t]he formal is symbolic, clean, abstract, homogeneous; the empirical is messy, heterogeneous, concrete, and not [to be] ordered within one single scheme. The formal is the representation, the map; the empirical is the represented, the terrain.

Thus, we do not claim a perfect match nor do we claim that the work in methodology design has been completed. It will remain a work-in-progress as more ideas emerge and new activities need to be conducted to let the terrain shape the map that will in turn shape the terrain. Certainly, integrating FormIT into a general project management framework requires more empirical work. The conceptualisation of design cycles, however, the simplicity and consistency of the phases and our perceived compatibility with the philosophical approach offered by FormIT provide a good starting point for our project.

References

Berg, M. 1997, 'Of forms, containers, and the electronic medical record: some tools for a sociology of the formal', *Science, Technology, & Human Values*, vol. 22, no. 4, pp. 403-433.

Bergvall-Kåreborn, B. 2006, 'Diversity is in the air—it is time to challenge our *weltanscauung*', *Systemist*, vol. 28, no. 2, pp. 13–25.

Bergvall-Kåreborn, B. and Ståhlbröst, A. 2007, 'The elusive nature of user needs in existing information systems literature', *Proceedings of the 8th IBIMA Conference: Information management in the networked economy*, Dublin, pp. 479–87.

Bergvall-Kåreborn, B., Holst, M. and Ståhlbröst, A. 2007, 'Creating a new leverage point for information systems development', in M. Avital, R. Boland and D. Cooperrider (eds), *Advances in Appreciative Inquiry—Designing information and organisations with a positive lens*, Elsevier, Amsterdam, pp. 75–95.

Bergvall-Kåreborn, B., Mirijamdotter, A. and Basden, A. 2004, 'Basic principles of SSM modelling: an examination of CATWOE from a soft perspective', *Systemic Practice and Action Research*, vol. 17, no. 2, pp. 55–73.

Checkland, P. B. and Davies, L. 1986, 'The use of the term "weltanschauung" in soft systems methodology', *Journal of Applied Systems Analysis*, vol. 13, pp. 109–15.

Checkland, P. and Holwell, S. 1998, *Information, Systems, and Information Systems: Making Sense of the Field,* John Wiley & Sons, Chichester, UK.

Checkland, P. B. and Scholes, J. 1999, *Soft Systems Methodology in Action: A 30-year retrospective*, John Wiley & Sons, Chichester, UK.

Chisti, Y. 2007, 'Biodiesel from microalgae', *Biotechnology Advances*, vol. 25, no. 3, pp. 294–306.

Chisti, Y. 2008, 'Biodiesel from microalgae beats bioethanol', *Trends in Biotechnology*, vol. 26, no. 3, pp. 126–31.

Cooperrider, D. L. and Avital, M. (eds) 2004, *Advances in Appreciative Inquiry, Constructive Discourse and Human Organisation*, Elsevier, Oxford.

Cooperrider, D. L. and Whitney, D. 2005, *Appreciative Inquiry—A positive revolution in change*, Berrett-Koehler Publishers, San Francisco.

Cooperrider, D. L., Whitney, D. and Stavros, J. M. 2005, *Appreciative Inquiry Handbook*, Berrett-Koehler Publishers, San Francisco.

Demirbas, A. 2008, 'Biofuels sources, biofuel policy, biofuel economy and global biofuel projections', *Energy Conversion and Management*, vol. 49, no. 8 (August), pp. 2106–16.

Fitzgerald, G. B., Russo, N. L. and Stoltermane, E. 2002, *Information Systems Development: Methods-in-action*, McGraw-Hill, Maidenhead, UK.

Gasson, S. 2006, 'A genealogical study of boundary-spanning IS design', *European Journal of Information Systems: Special issue: action in language and organisations*, vol. 15, no. 26, p. 1.

Holst, M. and Mirijamdotter, A. 2006, 'Interaction in cross-functional team work: making sense through the POM model', *Systems Research and Behavioural Science,* vol. 18, pp. 323-333.

International Energy Agency (IEA) 2004, *Biofuels for Transport: An international perspective*, International Energy Agency, Paris.

Kankainen, A. and Oulasvirta, A. 2003, 'Design ideas for everyday mobile and ubiquitous computing based on qualitative user data', in N. Carbonell and C. Stephanidis (eds), *User Interfaces For All*, Springer-Verlag, Berlin, pp. 458–64.

Kankainen, A., Tiitta, S. and Rantanen, M. 2003, 'Exploring everyday needs of teenagers related to context and presence aware mobile services', *Proceedings of Human Factors in Telecommunications*, pp. 19–26.

Kling, R. and Star, S. L. 1998, 'Human centered systems in the perspective of organizational and social informatics', *Computers and Society*, March, vol. 28, no. 1, pp. 22–29.

Latour, B. 1987, *Science in Action: How to follow scientists and engineers through society*, Harvard University Press, Cambridge, Mass.

Lehmann, J. 2007, 'A handful of carbon', *Nature*, vol. 447, pp. 143–4.

Lovegrove, K., Luzzi, A., Soldiani, I. and Kreetz, H. 2004, 'Developing ammonia based thermochemical energy storage for dish power plants', *Solar Energy*, vol. 76, nos 1–3 (January–March), pp. 331–7.

Norum, K. E. 2001, 'Appreciative design', *Systems Research and Behavioral Science*, vol. 18, pp. 323–33.

Orlikovski, W. J. 2006, 'Material knowing: the scaffolding of human knowledgeability', *European Journal of Information Systems*, vol. 15, pp. 460–6.

Patnaik, D. and Becker, R. 1999, 'Needfinding: the why and how of uncovering people's needs', *Design Management Journal*, vol. 10, no. 2, pp. 37–43.

Ståhlbröst, A. 2006, *Human-Centric Evaluation of Innovation*, Department of Business Administration and Social Sciences, Luleå University of Technology, Sweden.

Ståhlbröst, A. and Bergvall-Kåreborn, B. 2007a, 'FormIT—an approach to user involvement', in J. Schumacher and V.-P. Niitamo (eds), *European Living Labs—A new approach for human centric regional innovation*, Wissenschaftlicher Verlag Berlin Olaf Gaudig and Peter Veit GbR, Berlin, pp. 63–76.

Ståhlbröst, A. and Bergvall-Kåreborn, B. 2007b, Unveiling the mysterious needs of users, 30th Information Systems Research Seminar in Scandinavia, IRIS30, Department of Computer Sciences, University of Tampere, Finland.

Ståhlbröst, A. and Holst, M. 2006, 'Appreciating needs for innovative IT design', *International Journal of Knowledge, Culture and Change Management*, vol. 6, no. 4, pp. 37–46.

Ståhlbröst, A., Mirijamdotter, A. and Bergvall-Kåreborn, B. 2005, 'Needs and accommodation in evaluation design', *12th European Conference on Information Technology Evaluation (ECITE 2005)*, Turku, Finland, pp. 457–64.

Talent, M. 2006, 'A sustainable photosynthetically derived liquid fuel for developing countries: a simple method of extracting oil from microalgae', *Engineering*, The Australian National University, Canberra.

Thomas, G. and Fernández, W. 2008, 'Success in IT projects: a matter of definition?', *International Journal of Project Management*, vol. 27, no. 7, pp. 733-742.

Tiitta, S. 2003, 'Identifying elderly people's needs for communication and mobility', *Include 2003*, vol. 7 (March), pp. 266–71.

Ulrich, W. 1987, 'Critical heuristics of social systems design', *European Journal of Operational Research*, no. 31, pp. 276–83.

Ulrich, W. 1998, *Systems thinking as if people mattered*, Working Paper No. 23, Centre for Systems Research, Lincoln School of Management, University of Lincolnshire and Humberside, UK.

Witze, A. 2007, 'That's oil, folks…', *Nature*, vol. 445, pp. 14–17.

9. An intelligent agent-assisted logistics exception management decision support system: a design-science approach

SHIJIA GAO
DONGMING XU
UNIVERSITY OF QUEENSLAND

Abstract

With the increased complexity and uncertainty in business operations, adaptive and collaborative business processes and exception management (EM) are gaining growing attention. In the logistics industry, the current logistics exceptions are managed using human resources together with the traditional workflow technology-based supply-chain management or other logistics tools. The traditional workflow technology models and manages business processes and anticipated exceptions based on predefined logical procedures of activities from a centralised perspective that offers inadequate decision support for flexibility and adaptability in EM. These procedures are limited when monitoring logistics activities in real time in order to detect and resolve the exceptions in a timely manner. In order to mitigate these problems, a design-science research approach—specifically an intelligent-agent decision support approach in logistics EM—has been proposed and investigated in this research. It contains three interrelated research phases. The first research phase focuses on the conceptualisation of the logistics EM. It consists of two parts. The first part is logistics exception classification, in order to enable more efficient decision support practices for logistics EM. The second part focuses on the development of the conceptual framework (an artefact) for design and development of logistics EM systems for decision making. The second research phase focuses on the formalisation of the conceptual framework. A multi-agent-based logistics EM system is designed based on the conceptual framework. The third research phase will focus on the development of the designed logistics EM artefact. It will include two stages. First, a prototype will be developed. To provide more adaptive, flexible and collaborative decision support, the intelligent agent technology will be used for implementation. Second, the prototype will be evaluated via social-science research methods: semi-structured interviews and laboratory experiment. It is proposed that this theory-driven agent-based logistics EM system will provide more efficient and timely decision-making support for managers in relation to logistics EM. The designed artefacts and the research design are the major contributions of this research, which add knowledge to design-science research theory and practice. The conceptualisation-formalisation-development research approach can be applied in other similar IS design-science research.

Introduction

Businesses today around the world are facing the challenges of a rapidly changing environment due to the development of new business markets and technology. The business climate is changing from centralised and closed to distributed and open (Wang and Wang 2006). Today's changing and distributed environment is full of complex and dynamic business processes. Moreover, the unpredictability of business processes requires that business applications support exception management (EM) with the ability to adapt dynamically to the changing environment. An *exception* is any phenomenon that prevents the successful completion of normal business processes (Klein et al. 2000). Traditional approaches dealing with EM are based on workflow technology and business process redesign. Traditional approaches provide inadequate support for flexibility and collaboration in EM (Jennings et al. 2000; Klein and Dellarocas 2000) and they can cost a lot in business process redesign or reconstruction.

Logistics is one example of this situation. According to Becker (2000), companies can lose between 9 per cent and 20 per cent of their share value over a six-month period due to logistics exceptions. The logistics exceptions have various consequences such as delayed production, increases in costs or decreases in customer satisfaction (Huhns et al. 2002). In order to minimise the exception consequences, it is crucial to detect and handle exceptions appropriately. In current practice, most exceptions are managed using the knowledge and skills of working professionals together with traditional workflow technology-based supply-chain management or logistics tools (Dellarocas and Klein 2000; Dellarocas et al. 2000; Huhns et al. 2002). Workflow technology, however, offers inadequate flexibility and adaptability in EM (Wang and Wang 2006). Moreover, it is limited when monitoring business activities in real time in order to detect and resolve the exceptions in a timely manner.

EM in logistics is a complex, dynamic and distributed process. To provide decision support for logistics EM in real time, business activity monitoring (BAM) is deployed in a three-layered architecture (Dresner 2003). BAM is the real-time reporting, analysing and alerting of significant business events (that is, exceptions) accomplished by gathering data, key performance indicators (KPIs) and business events from multiple applications (Dresner 2003). In addition, a system designed for real-time distributed logistics EM requires a high degree of cooperative problem-solving capability. Thus, it is very important to start from a decision-making/problem-solving perspective when analysing and representing logistics EM domain knowledge. In this study, to inform the design of a logistics EM system, we have adopted Simon's (1977) decision-making/problem-solving process theory and the Cynefin sense-making framework (Snowden 2002) to classify the logistics exceptions and use different decision-making strategies to tackle them. Then, in order to overcome the limitations of the traditional workflow technology solutions, we will apply intelligent agent (IA) technology to logistics EM by taking advantage of the agent's autonomy, reactivity, proactivity and social ability. System development is fundamentally a process of design (Hevner et al. 2004). This chapter reports a design-science research study that attempts to provide a real-time decision-support mechanism to monitor and handle logistics exceptions in a more effective and efficient way.

The organisation of this chapter is as follows. First, the design-science research approach employed in this study is presented. Next, the relevant literature is briefly reviewed. Section four identifies and classifies logistics exceptions. Based on a logistics EM conceptual framework presented in section five, the design of a multi-agent-assisted decision-support system for EM in the logistics domain is proposed in section six. Section seven describes the planned evaluation for the designed artefacts. Section eight concludes the chapter.

Design science as a research method

As mentioned in the introduction, this research has created and will evaluate a logistics EM conceptual framework and a decision-support system. The research uses a design-science approach. Design science 'is an alternative, or complement, to the natural science approach that is dominant in information systems (IS) research' (Arnott 2006:57). In design science, the researcher 'creates and evaluates IT artefacts intended to solve identified organizational problems' (Hevner et al. 2004:77). March and Smith (1995:253) clearly draw the distinction between natural and design science: 'Whereas natural science tries to understand reality, design science attempts to create things that serve human purposes.'

Information Systems Foundations: The Role of Design Science

Design science is particularly relevant to IS research (Arnott 2006). Figure 9.1 presents the research approach used in this chapter. On the left-hand side of the figure are five distinct research processes. These are adapted from Nunamaker et al. (1991), who propose an IS development process model. This process model is consistent with aspects of other frameworks and models for conducting design-science research in IS. For example, this process model can be seen to map onto Gregg et al.'s (2001) IS design-science software engineering research methodology (SERM) framework. SERM comprises three interrelated phases: conceptualisation, formalisation and development. Gregg et al. (2001) argue that rigorous design research must address at least two of the three phases. In Figure 9.1, 'conceptualisation' is the *construct a conceptual framework* step, 'formalisation' is covered by *develop a system architecture* and *analyse and design the system* steps, and 'development' is addressed by *building* and *evaluating the system*. In addition, March and Smith (1995) propose build and evaluate as the two fundamental design research processes. *Build* effectively covers the first four processes in Figure 9.1. Teasing out build into four sub-processes makes the research design much clearer and the execution much easier.

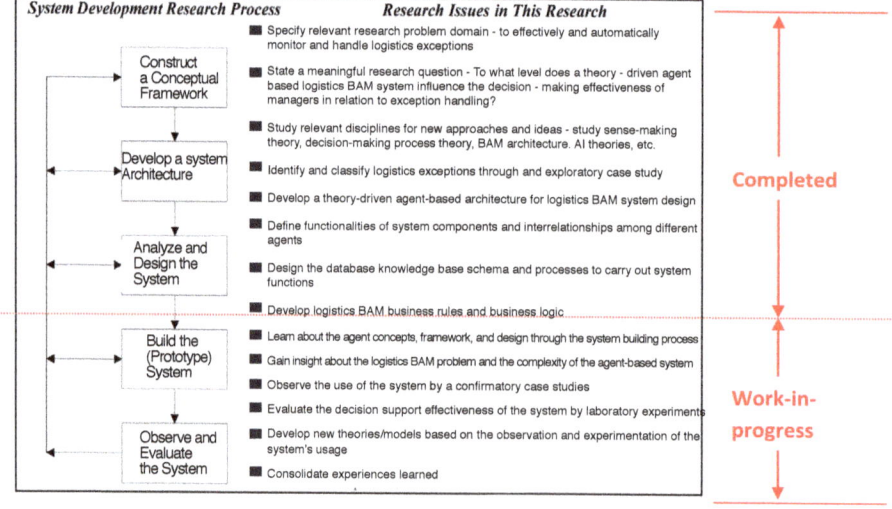

Figure 9.1 Issues in the system development research process in this research

Adapted from Nunamaker et al. (1991)

The right-hand side of Figure 9.1 shows how the current research uses the design-science methodology based on Nunamaker et al.'s (1991) IS development process model. Research issues that should be addressed in each stage in this research are identified. Currently, the first three steps have been completed while the last two steps are still in progress. The details of each process step are presented in the rest of this chapter. The next section is the literature review of the theoretical foundations for constructing the conceptual framework.

Literature review

Exception management in logistics business processes

The occurrence of exceptions is a fundamental part of business activities. In order for business management systems to support such unpredictability they must support exception handling with the ability to adapt to today's dynamic, uncertain and error-prone environment (Kammer et al. 2000). Because business exceptions are related mostly to business activities or business processes, most efforts to handle exceptions have utilised workflow technology to include conditional branches in the workflow model or redesign business systems to deal with anticipated exceptions. Such approaches, however, offer limited support for flexibility and collaboration during process management (Jennings et al. 2000; Klein and Dellarocas 2000) and they can cost a lot in business process redesign or reconstruction. Several techniques have been suggested for supporting exception handling in workflow systems and to dynamically adapt to the changing environment—for example: knowledge-based approaches, run-time dynamism, configurable execution, reflexivity, evolving models from workflow instances, and the like (Klein et al. 2000). While providing mechanisms for the seamless integration of exception handling into workflow descriptions, such approaches lack the consideration of practical aspects that become important in workflow systems such as the participation of autonomous, heterogeneous legacy systems and the strong impact of human intervention. EM is a complex and dynamic process and collaborations between logistics partners are usually required in such activities. If a system has to cope with undefined errors or failures, or there is a need for real-time collaboration, more flexible and robust approaches are needed (Moitra and Ganesh 2005).

Gartner Inc. (McCoy 2002) defines business activity monitoring (BAM) as providing real-time access to critical business performance indicators to improve the speed and effectiveness of business operations. BAM encompasses the real-time reporting, analysis and alerting of significant business events, accomplished by gathering data, KPIs and business events from multiple applications (Dresner 2003). Unlike traditional real-time monitoring, BAM draws its information from multiple application systems and other internal and external (inter-enterprise) sources (Nesamoney 2004), enabling a broader and richer view of business activities (McCoy 2002).

Manufacturing and logistics companies are among the most open-minded and willing to be early adopters of BAM (McKeefrey 2002). According to Parameswaran (2004), the benefits of a BAM solution to the logistics industry are that it

- enables operational managers to receive alerts from the existing IT applications when a snag occurs
- informs on-duty personnel about last-minute shipment changes
- alerts truck drivers when the perishable goods they are carrying will waste if they are stopped
- plans deliveries
- manages containers
- checks profit and loss
- performs maintenance and repairs
- tracks perishable goods
- identifies underutilised space.

It is clear that there are many benefits for the logistics industry in deploying BAM solutions, but what functionality is required to deliver a BAM architecture or a BAM solution? Gartner provides a layered BAM logical architecture (Dresner 2003), shown in Figure 9.2. Business events are fed into an event absorption layer and filtered, then processed against rules that, when met, generate exceptions. The exceptions are delivered: an action is triggered or a display is fed. This architecture provides the base to develop the logistics EM conceptual framework and system architecture.

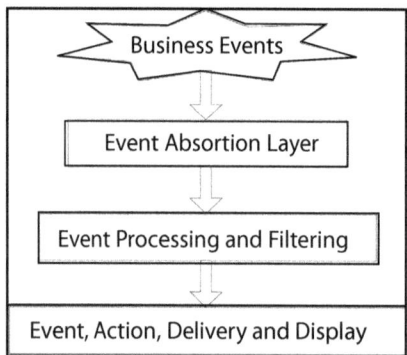

Figure 9.2 Gartner's BAM architecture

Source: Dresner (2003:8)

Intelligent agents technology and its business application

According to Dresner (2003), one technology that can be used to design and develop the logistics BAM/EM system is that of intelligent agents (IA), which can overcome the limitations of the traditional workflow technology solutions. In the past decade, the study and use of IAs have gained popularity among IS researchers (Jennings 2000). IA is a software-based computer system that is capable of flexible action in order to meet its design objectives, where flexibility includes properties such as autonomy, social capability, reactivity and proactivity (Wooldridge 2002; Wooldridge and Jennings 1995). A *multi-agent system* consists of a group of agents that interact with one another to collectively achieve their goals (Jennings and Wooldridge 1998). By absorbing other agents' knowledge and capabilities, agents can overcome their inherent bounds of intelligence.

In recent years, there has been considerable growth of interest in the design of a distributed, intelligent society of agents capable of collaboratively dealing with complex problems and vast amounts of information (Kuo and Lin 2000). Because agent technology provides flexible, distributed and intelligent solutions for business applications, researchers have proposed numerous IA-based business systems (Gao et al. 2005, 2007; Vahidov and Fazlollahi 2004; Wang et al. 2002). The benefits of an IA approach are its flexibility, adaptability and decentralisation.

Agent-based systems are well suited for EM (Liu et al. 2001; Wang et al. 2002). IAs can be deployed with specific EM domain knowledge and they can intermediate on behalf of business EM analysts by being able to perform numerous, error-free calculations. IAs can also aid rapid interpretation of the precise requirements of business managers regarding EM (Wang et al. 2002).

Decision-making mechanisms

Real-time EM in logistics is a complex, dynamic and distributed process. Therefore, a system designed to support logistics EM decision making requires a high degree of cooperative problem-solving capability. Accordingly, one problem-solving/decision-making process and one sense-making framework are reviewed and they form the theoretical foundations that inform the design in this research.

Herbert Simon's decision-making/problem-solving process theory

According to Vahidov (2005), productive human decision support system collaboration can be achieved if the system is organised to fit human decision-making processes. Simon's (1977) model of the decision-making/problem-solving process fits human decision-making processes very well. Simon's (1977) model comprises four distinct phases—intelligence, design, choice and review—shown in Table 9.1. Although generic and simple in nature, Simon's model has been applied and validated in a wide array of situations, such as optimisation models (Dutta 1996), crisis problem finding (Gallupe et al. 1988) and investment optimisation (Gao et al. 2007; Vahidov and Fazlollahi 2004).

Table 9.1 Simon's decision-making/problem-solving phases

Phase	Description
Intelligence	The decision maker gathers information about the situation and recognises the problem at hand.
Design	The decision maker structures the problematic situation, develops criteria and identifies the various alternatives through which the problem can be solved.
Choice	The decision maker chooses the best alternative that meets the criteria and makes the final decision.
Review	The decision maker uses the feedback from the results of the decision to review how well the process was executed. Such reflection on past processes can form a basis of the intelligence phase for future decisions.

The Cynefin sense-making framework

The Cynefin framework is a sense-making device originating in the practice of knowledge management (Snowden 2002). It has been applied extensively in consultancy and action research in management (Stewart 2002), strategy (Snowden 2004), health care (Mark 2006), policymaking (O'Neill 2004), product development, branding, customer relationship management and supply-chain management (Kurtz and Snowden 2003).

The Cynefin sense-making framework helps people make sense of complexities. It has five domains, four of which are named, and a fifth central area that is the domain of disorder—occupied by those who have no awareness of their context. The details of the four named domains are shown in Table 9.2 (Kurtz and Snowden 2003; Snowden 2002).

Table 9.2 The Cynefin sense-making framework domains

Domain name	Explanation	Decision model
Known	Known causes and effects. Cause and effect relationships are generally linear. It is the only legitimate domain of best practice. Within known limits, we can both predict and prescribe behaviour.	To *sense* incoming data, *categorise* that data and then *respond* in accordance with predetermined practice.

Knowable	Knowable causes and effects. While stable (that is, complicated but linear) cause and effect relationships exist in this domain, they might not be fully known or they might be known only by a limited group of people.	To *sense* incoming data, *analyse* that data and then *respond* in accordance with expert advice or interpretation of that analysis.
Complex	Complex relationships. There are cause and effect relationships between the agents, but both the number of agents and the number of relationships defies categorisation or analytical techniques. Emergent patterns can be perceived but not predicted.	To create *probes* to make the patterns or potential patterns more visible (*sense*) before we take any action (*respond*).
Chaos	There are no perceivable relationships. The system is turbulent. There is nothing to analyse, and waiting for patterns to emerge is a waste of time.	To *act*, quickly and decisively, to reduce the turbulence, and then to *sense* immediately the reaction to that intervention so that we can *respond* accordingly.

Logistics exceptions classification

Based on the above reviewed Cynefin sense-making framework, in this section, logistics exceptions are examined, identified and classified.

Exception analysis

In this research, exception analysis was conducted in two ways. First, the logistics exceptions were reviewed through the literature. Second, a single exploratory case study in a major logistics company in Australia was conducted to investigate how the exceptions happened in daily business process/operations. The logistics company was chosen because it was an internationally recognised and leading logistics provider and the single case study design was chosen because this logistics company was representative (Yin 2003:41). The data were collected from June to September 2007, in the electronic team of the logistics company, and following Yin's (2003) case study methodology rigorously. All eight team members (six female; two male), including one team manager, were interviewed. The interviews were semi-structured (semi-structured interviews are considered most appropriate as they are often used in exploratory research [Yin 2003]) and lasted from one to two hours each. All interviews were audio recorded and notes were also taken. Key interviews were fully transcribed, thematically coded by two researchers by using QSR NVivo Version 7.0 software and analysed manually. In synthesising the literature review with the findings from the case study, six exceptions in logistics operations were identified. Based on the results of the case study, for each logistics exception, related causes were identified and current handling methods summarised. In addition, the problems of the current exception handling methods were identified and they will be addressed subsequently. The corresponding literature references that indicate the same logistics exceptions were also summarised. Two example exceptions are shown in Table 9.3.[1]

Table 9.3 Analysis of logistics exceptions, related causes and handling methods

Exception description	Logistics company examples		Problems of current exception handling methods	References
	Causes of the exception	Current exception handling methods		
Delayed delivery or no delivery	Weather factor—for example, storm Traffic Change to routes, which take longer to the destination Space-allocation problem Human factor—for example, driver is sick The customs not cleared	Use alternative routes to get to the destination quicker Use different transport mode for delivery Reschedule the delivery	Delivery exceptions monitoring and handling are human based, which is inefficient (not real time and time-consuming to handle) and error prone (human errors)	Grosof and Poon 2004 Hall and Potts 2003 Helo et al. 2006 Özkohen and Yolum 2006 Zimmer 2002
Poor system data quality (incorrect data or missing data)	Human error People are lazy, sometimes just copy and paste System not updated System error	Check the data to find out the correct information and fix everything Overwrite the data	System data exceptions monitoring and handling are human based, which is inefficient and error prone	Dejonckheere et al. 2002 Lee et al. 1997 Piramuthu 2004

Logistics exceptions classification by the Cynefin sense-making framework

Based on the literature review and the case study results, no particular complex or chaotic logistics exceptions were identified.[2] Therefore, in this study, only the known and knowable logistics exceptions are studied. Based on the review in Table 9.2 and the descriptions in Table 9.3, the six identified logistics exceptions are classified into known and knowable—shown in Table 9.4 with some justifications. In addition, based on the 'Cause of the exception' in Table 9.3, the 'Monitoring factors for logistics EM' are identified in Table 9.4. These factors

---

1   For the full logistics exceptions analysis, please contact the authors.
2   The interviewees did not identify any complex or chaotic exceptions in their business operations. There is also no literature alluding to such situations in the logistics domain. There might be two explanations: 1) people will not treat the exceptions they have already resolved as complex or chaotic exceptions. They will put them into either known or knowable categories. The complex exceptions might still exist, but people either are not aware of them or treat them as something other than exceptions. 2) Logistics is a mature industry. All operations or business processes are well modelled. There might be no unknown events to disturb the normal business operations.

will be used to monitor the logistics exceptions in the EM system. Similarly, based on the 'Current exception handling method' in Table 9.3, the 'Business rules for logistics EM' are formulated in Table 9.4. These business rules are used as the guidance to define the business rules and logic in the logistics EM system. How our approach addresses the problems of current handling methods is also summarised. Following the previous two logistics exception examples, the classification, factors and business rules for logistics EM are shown in Table 9.4.

Table 9.4 Exceptions classification, factors and business rules for logistics EM

Exception	Exception classification	Monitoring factors for logistics EM	Business rules for logistics EM	How to address the problems
Delayed delivery or no delivery	**Knowable** *Justification*: Multiple indicators to monitor When exception occurs, it requires additional information to re-estimate the delivery time When handling the delayed delivery, extra information and analysis are required	Weather condition Traffic status Delivery milestones Space availability Driver status Customs clearance status	If exception occurs, gather more information, recalculate the estimated time for delivery and alert the EM personnel If there is going to be delay, gather more information, recalculate the delivery routes, use alternative transport or reschedule the delivery with the clients	By using the logistics EM system, the delivery exceptions monitoring and handling will be automated, in real time, more efficient and more accurate
Poor system data quality (incorrect data or missing data)	**Known to knowable** *Justification*: If the system data are incomplete, it is a known exception; follow the routine to alert the EM personnel It could require the acquisition of additional information to analyse whether the system data are accurate, which makes it a possible knowable exception	System data completeness System data accuracy System status	If anything goes wrong (that is, exception occurs), alert the EM personnel and provide them with evidence of the correct data	By using the logistics EM system, the system exceptions monitoring and handling will be automated in real time, more efficient and more accurate

Information Systems Foundations: The Role of Design Science

Logistics exception management conceptual framework development

Based on the basic BAM logical layered architecture (see Figure 9.2), in order to provide a more efficient and effective decision support framework for logistics EM and inform the logistics EM system design, the classification of logistics problems/exceptions (see section four, 'Logistics exceptions classification') is added to this BAM architecture. According to the logistics exceptions classification, the appropriate courses of action can be determined to speed up the logistics EM process for decision making. The logistics EM conceptual framework is shown in Figure 9.3.

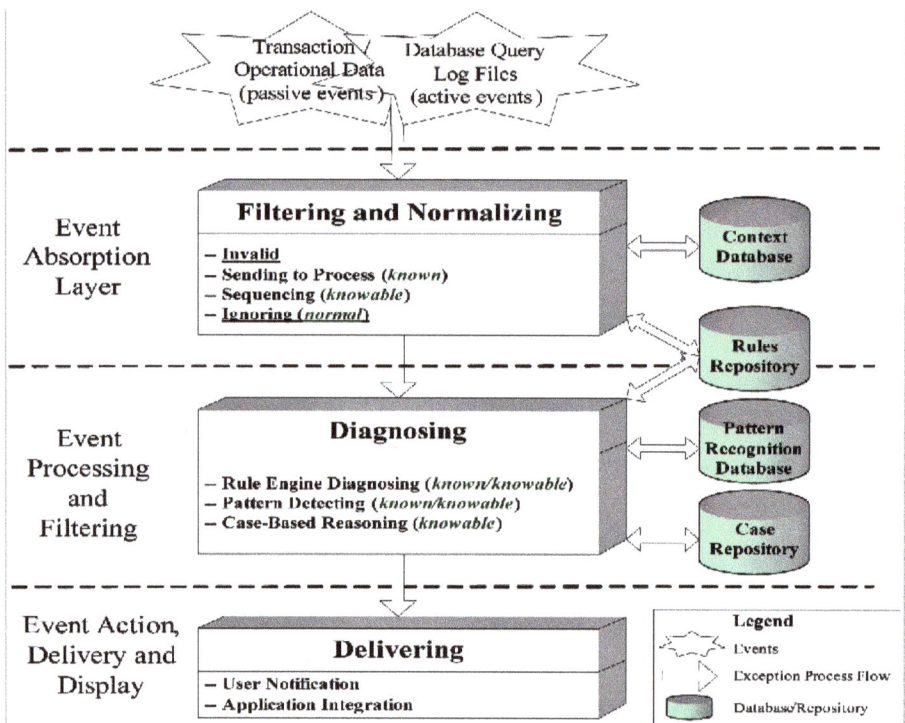

Figure 9.3 Logistics EM conceptual framework

Event absorption layer

In this layer, the logistics EM system first collects logistics events and prepares them to be analysed. Logistics events can be obtained through active or passive means. Passive events are those that are subscribed to. Active events are created by an agent or adapter who might poll applications and databases for changes and threshold crossings. Once the logistics event has been received, it needs to be validated first; an invalid event will not be processed further. The logistics event is then filtered for relevancy. The majority of events are normal events that require no action. The EM system will ignore these events; they are not for processing. Some logistics events are problematic or exceptional events, which are the activities that need to be monitored. They are further categorised into: 1) sending to next layer for diagnosing, which are *known* exceptions. The system knows how to handle them by applying rules or matching them with known patterns. 2) Sequencing, which are *knowable* exceptions. As long as more information is obtained, they will be sent for further diagnosis.

Event processing and filtering layer

The event processing and filtering layer is the most important layer of a logistics EM system. The scope of this research is on monitoring the *known* and *knowable* problems/exceptions. In Figure 9.3, however, there are not many details to show the different diagnostic processes for *known* and *knowable* exceptions. Informed by Simon's (1977) problem-solving/decision-making process and the Cynefin (Snowden 2002) decision model, the detailed diagnostic processes for *known* and *knowable* logistics exceptions are described below.

When a *known* logistics exception is detected, according to the Cynefin decision model (Snowden 2002), it will be categorised based on the relevant rules and patterns. As the *known* logistics exceptions have been fully understood and well modelled, a corresponding resolution report (containing one resolution) based on a priori established procedures will be issued to the handling personnel for execution. This process is portrayed in the top half of Figure 9.4. As a decision-making process, referring to Simon's (1977) process theory, the categorisation belongs to the *design* phase, as the exceptions are structured and the criteria are developed, while the release of the resolution report and execution represent the *choice* phase, as the decision has been made and executed. After the personnel have handled the *known* logistics exception, the rules and patterns are accumulated and organised in the rule repository and pattern recognition database.

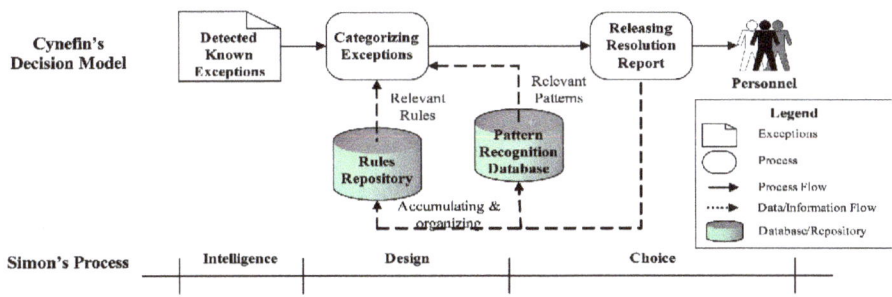

Figure 9.4 Diagnostic process for known logistics exceptions

When a *knowable* logistics exception is detected, additional information is retrieved and the search and navigation process in the case repository is initiated. The case repository will provide the relevant past logistics cases that are useful references for evaluating the detected *known* or *knowable* logistics exception. According to the Cynefin decision model (Snowden 2002), the *knowable* logistics exception will be analysed based on past similar cases, relevant rules and patterns. Because of the complicated nature of the event and insufficient information, no single solid solution will be provided after the analysis. Instead, a number of possible alternatives will be generated. The handling personnel will be the final decision makers determining which alternative to choose as the best solution to handle the exception. In such a decision-making process, referring to Simon's (1977) process theory, the analysis and alternative generation are in the *design* phase, as the problems/exceptions are structured, the criteria are developed and the alternatives are identified. The human decision making is the *choice* phase, as the human decision maker chooses the best alternative that meets the criteria, and makes the final decision. After the personnel have handled the *knowable* logistics exception, the case is accumulated and organised in the case repository along with the associated rules and patterns. The diagnostic process for *knowable* logistics exceptions is portrayed in Figure 9.5.

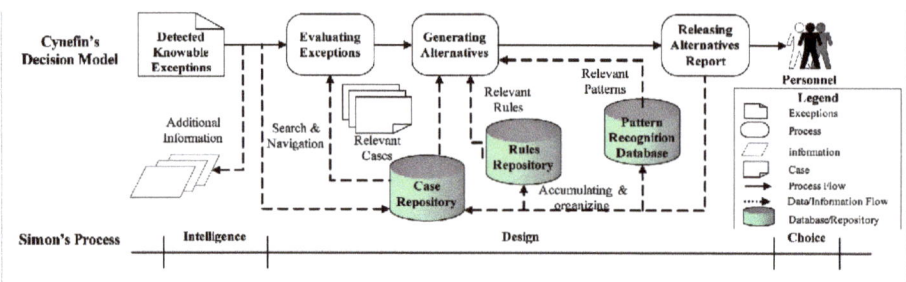

Figure 9.5 Diagnostic process for knowable logistics exceptions

Event action, delivery and display layer

In this last layer, the output of a logistics EM system is an alert or notification. It can be sent to a person or linked with another process.

Logistics exception management multi-agent system architecture development

To illustrate the proposed logistics EM conceptual framework, the design of a multi-agent-based logistics EM system is presented in this section. This design architecture aims to automate the monitoring, diagnosis and reporting of logistics exceptions so as to assist a logistics operator to gain quicker results. The logistics EM conceptual framework is applied by delegating logistics EM tasks to a collection of agents. Each agent plays a role in logistics EM and is in charge of specific tasks. The logistics EM system architecture is portrayed in Figure 9.6, which describes the internal interactions among agents and the external relationships between the logistics EM system and legacy logistics operation systems. Based on the logistics EM conceptual framework (Figure 9.3), Figure 9.6 is also classified into three layers. According to the detailed diagnostic process (Figures 9.4 and 9.5), intelligent agents in Figure 9.6 are deployed by Simon's (1977) problem-solving/decision-making process, in which the *design* group agents and their processes are derived from the Cynefin sense-making framework (Snowden 2002).

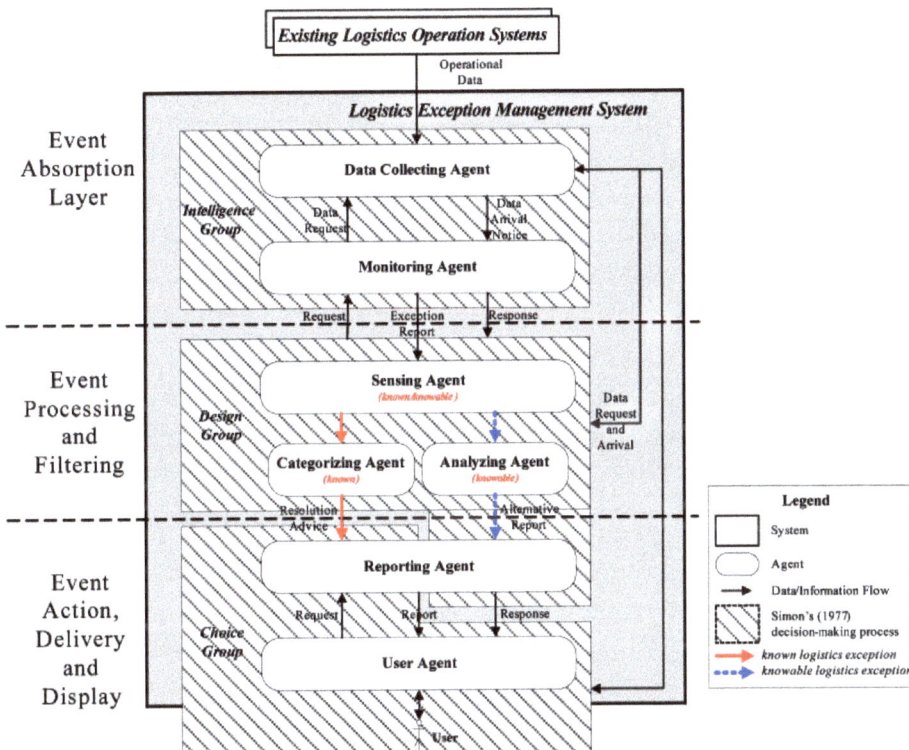

Figure 9.6 Logistics EM system architecture

The agents are distributed in the organisations or departments involved in logistics. All these agents work autonomously and collaboratively in the multi-agent environment. The *user agent* acts as an effective bridge between the user and the computer. It can make the human–computer interface more intuitive and encourage types of interactions that might be difficult to evoke with a conventional interface. In the system, this agent enables users to view the current state of the operations and exception monitoring, diagnostic and reporting processes and allows them to convey their own judgments, opinions and arguments relative to logistics EM to the rest of the organisation. The agent also enables the corresponding users to issue requests to the other agents in the system.

The *intelligence group* contains two agents: the *data-collecting agent* enables the system to collect data. The subsequent *design* and *choice groups* may request information relating to their task from the *data-collecting agent*, if required. The *monitoring agent* monitors the logistics operations. When the *monitoring agent* captures a possible exception, it will classify the exception into *known* or *knowable*, based on predefined business rules and logic (see Table 9.4). The output of the *monitoring agent* is an *exception report*, which will be sent to the *sensing agent* for diagnosis.

- *Known* exceptions will be categorised by applying the rules and existing patterns by the *categorising agent*. Then it will issue a *resolution advice* with a priori established procedures.
- *Knowable* exceptions will be analysed by the *analysing agent* based on: 1) *exception reports* from the *monitoring agent*; and 2) any additional information, if necessary, to examine the case. The *analysing agent* adopts a case-based reasoning and rule-based approach. After the analysis, an *alternative report* will be generated.

Different agents will process different types of exceptions, which are indicated by different colours and types of arrows in Figure 9.6. Different kinds of reports will be sent to the *reporting agent* as deliverables. The *reporting agent* will present and communicate the report to the appropriate personnel through the *user agent* for EM investigation and action. Alternatively, the *reporting agent* will automate or take a specific action. Complicated exceptions for investigation are filtered and prioritised based on the severity of the exceptions to the business. The *reporting agent* is able to support the business process to assist with exception investigation by providing all relevant past cases and information, ensuring the exception handling personnel have all of the relevant information at hand for decision making.

Evaluation

As the designed system is purposeful, it should yield value for logistics EM users in making decisions for solving logistics exceptions more effectively. In the later stage of this research, a prototype system based on the system architecture will be implemented. Hevner et al. (2004) identify five classes of methods for evaluating designed artefacts. To evaluate the performance of exception handling decision making, this research uses the first class of evaluation, observational (comprising case studies and field studies), and the third class, experimental (comprising controlled experiments and simulation), as follows.

1. We will conduct a confirmatory case study with the same logistics staff in the same logistics company to investigate whether they are satisfied with the prototype system. Semi-structured interviews with all previous interviewed logistics staff (seven to nine people) will be conducted. Each interview will last for one to two hours. During the interview, the conceptual framework and system architecture will be explained and the prototype system will be tested by the interviewees. Semi-structured questions will be designed based on the prior literature. Feedback on the artefacts, regarding the system design and decision support effectiveness of the prototype, will be obtained, coded (by using QSR Nvivo) and analysed in order to refine them.

2. A laboratory experiment will be conducted to evaluate the system EM decision support effectiveness. The decision-making effectiveness of people supported by the proposed agent-based logistics EM system will be compared with people without the system support. The subjects will be recruited from the same logistics company, but will be from different teams. A total of at least 60 subjects will be recruited. The subjects will be randomly assigned to one of the two groups: treatment group—with logistics EM system support; and control group—without logistics EM system support. Sprague and Carlson (Sprague 1982) describe four major categories—productivity, process, perception and product measures—which have proven to be valid evaluation models of decision support system effectiveness in research (Gao et al. 2007; Sainfort et al. 1990; Sharda et al. 1988; Vahidov and Fazlollahi 2004). Based on this logistics EM decision-making research domain—and following on from this successful approach—the proposed agent-based logistics EM system will be examined in the sense that it improves (or does not improve) the process, outcomes and user perceptions regarding decision making. A set of logistics exception handling tasks will be designed based on the existing business cases (collected from the exploratory case study described in the 'Exception analysis' subsection). Before the laboratory experiment, a pilot study will be conducted with a small group of logistics experts to test the experimental protocol. The feedback from the pilot study will be used to refine the experimental protocol. During the laboratory experiment, two groups will do the same tasks, followed by the completion of a questionnaire that tests their perceptions. Both groups will see the same logistics exception case simulation. When a logistics exception occurs, however, the control-group participants will need to resolve the exception by themselves while the treatment-group participants will receive the exception report, which includes the nature of the exception, the cause of the exception and the

resolution/alternatives for resolution of the exceptions. Both groups need to make a decision regarding how to resolve the exception. The decision-making process will be measured by the time used to make the decision and the number and quality of the alternatives generated. The decision outcome will be measured for the final decision quality. The user perceptions will be measured by the quantitative analysis of the questionnaire data. The general expectation is that the decision-making effectiveness of the people who are supported by the theory-driven agent-based logistics EM system will be higher than that of the people without the system support.

Research summary

With the increased complexity, uncertainty and risks in business operations, adaptive and collaborative business process and EM are gaining growing attention in business applications. This chapter has presented design-science research that aims to understand logistics exceptions, provide a real-time decision-making mechanism to monitor and handle the logistics exceptions in an efficient way and has proposed a comprehensive decision-support system architecture for logistics EM. This research creates and will evaluate two IT-designed artefacts (conceptual framework and prototype) intended to efficiently and automatically monitor and handle logistics exceptions, which is design-science research according to Hevner et al. (2004). Two designed artefacts are strictly informed by, and incorporated with, three different theories: Simon's (1977) decision-making/problem-solving process, the Cynefin sense-making framework and decision models (Snowden 2002) and Gartner's BAM architecture (Dresner 2003). The exploratory case study (the 'Exception analysis' subsection) and the later design evaluation (the 'Evaluation' section) follow Yin's (2003) case study methodology and experimental design methodology. The results of the evaluation will be used to refine the designed artefacts. Such a build-and-evaluate loop will iterate several times before the final design artefact is generated. The research includes technical presentation and practical framing in terms of application in the logistics exception monitoring and handling domain.

There are three research phases, each focusing on a different research perspective and forming the prerequisite foundation for the next research phase.

The first research phase focuses on the conceptualisation of the logistics EM. It consists of two parts. The first part is logistics exceptions classification, in order to enable more efficient decision-support practices for logistics EM. The second part focuses on the development of the conceptual framework (an artefact) for design and development of a logistics EM system for decision making. This is informed by sense-making theory (Snowden 2002), decision-making process theory (Simon 1977) and BAM architecture (Dresner 2003). In this research phase, the research problem is recognised, relevant theories are studied and the conceptual framework is constructed.

The second research phase focuses on the formalisation of the conceptual framework. A multi-agent-based logistics EM system is designed based on the conceptual framework, whereby system users can be notified and provided with decision support for handling logistics exceptions in real time.

The third research phase will focus on the development of the designed logistics EM artefact. It will include two stages. First, a prototype will be developed. To provide a more adaptive, flexible and collaborative decision support, intelligent agent technology will be used for implementation. Second, the prototype will be evaluated via social-science research methods: semi-structured interviews and laboratory experiment. It is proposed that this theory-driven agent-based logistics EM system will provide more efficient and timely decision-making support for the managers in relation to logistics EM.

The designed artefacts and the research design are the major contribution of this research. The artefacts are the real-time extension of Simon's (1977) classic decision-making/problem-solving process model in logistics EM by incorporating BAM (Dresner 2003). In addition, by adding the Cynefin sense-making framework, the artefacts provide a more efficient decision-making routine for logistics EM. The three theory-driven artefacts are believed to enable efficient real-time decision making in the logistics EM domain. In addition, the logistics EM conceptual framework can be applied to other EM situations, such as fraud detection, compliance with regulations, anomalies detection, and the like. In this chapter, we apply the conceptualisation-formalisation-development research approach in the logistics EM decision support domain. We argue that the same research approach can be applied in other similar IS design-science research. In practice, the logistics exceptions classification, logistics EM conceptual framework and incorporation of agent technologies into logistics EM will assist logistics companies to develop their logistics exception handling decision-making strategies and solutions.

References

Arnott, D. 2006, 'Cognitive biases and decision support systems development: a design science approach', *Information Systems Journal*, vol. 16, pp. 55–78.

Becker, T. J. 2000, 'Putting a price on supply chain problems: study links supply chain glitches with falling stock price', *Georgia Tech Research News*, <http://gtresearchnews.gatech.edu/newsrelease/CHAINR.html>

Dejonckheere, J., Disney, S. M., Lambrecht, M. R. and Towill, D. R. 2002, 'The impact of information enrichment on the bullwhip effect in supply chains: a control engineering perspective', *European Journal of Operational Research*, vol. 153, no. 3, pp. 727–50.

Dellarocas, C. and Klein, M. 2000, 'A knowledge-based approach for designing robust business processes', in W. van der Aalst, J. Desel and A. Oberweis (eds), *Business Process Management, Models, Techniques, and Empirical Studies*, Springer, Berlin, pp. 60–5.

Dellarocas, C., Klein, M. and Rodriguez-Aguilar, J. A. 2000, 'An exception handling architecture for open electronic marketplaces of contract net software agents', *Proceedings of the ACM Conference on Electronic Commerce*, pp. 225–32.

Dresner, H. 2003, 'Business activity monitoring: BAM architecture', *Gartner*, <http://www.pikos.net/documents/german/Gartner.pdf>

Dutta, A. 1996, 'Integrating AI and optimization for decision support: a survey', *Decision Support Systems*, vol. 18, nos 3–4, pp. 217–26.

Gallupe, R. B., Desanctis, G. and Dickson, G. W. 1988, 'Computer-based support for group problem-finding: an experimental investigation', *MIS Quarterly*, vol. 12, no. 2, pp. 277–96.

Gao, S., Wang, H., Wang, Y., Shen, W. and Yeung, S. 2005, 'Web-service-agents-based family wealth management system', *Expert Systems with Application*, vol. 29, no. 1, pp. 219–28.

Gao, S., Wang, H., Xu, D. and Wang, Y. 2007, 'An intelligent agent-assisted decision support system for family financial planning', *Decision Support Systems*, vol. 44, no. 1, pp. 60–78.

Gregg, D. G., Kulkarni, U. R. and Vinze, A. S. 2001, 'Understanding the philosophical underpinnings of software engineering research in information systems', *Information Systems Frontiers*, vol. 3, pp. 169–83.

Grosof, B. N. and Poon, T. C. 2004, 'SweetDeal: representing agent contracts with exceptions using semantic web rules, ontologies, and process descriptions', *International Journal of Electronic Commerce*, vol. 8, no. 4, pp. 61–97.

Hall, N. G. and Potts, C. N. 2003, 'Supply chain scheduling: batching and delivery', *Operations Research*, vol. 51, no. 4, pp. 566–84.

Helo, P., Xiao, Y. and Jiao, J. R. 2006, 'A web-based logistics management system for agile supply demand network design', *Journal of Manufacturing Technology Management*, vol. 17, no. 8, pp. 1058–77.

Hevner, A. R., March, S. T., Park, J. and Ram, S. 2004, 'Design science in information systems research', *MIS Quarterly*, vol. 28, no. 1, pp. 75–105.

Huhns, M. N., Stephens, L. M. and Ivezic, N. 2002, 'Automating supply-chain management', *Proceedings of the 1st International Joint Conference on Autonomous Agents and MultiAgent Systems (AAMAS)*, ACM Press, pp. 1017–24.

Jennings, N. 2000, 'On agent-based software engineering', *Artificial Intelligence*, vol. 117, no. 2, pp. 227–96.

Jennings, N. and Wooldridge, M. 1998, *Agent Technology: Foundations, applications, and markets*, Springer-Verlag, Berlin.

Jennings, N., Faratin, P., Norman, T., O'Brien, P. and Odgers, B. 2000, 'Autonomous agents for business process management', *International Journal of Applied AI*, vol. 14, no. 2, pp. 145–89.

Kammer, P., Bolcer, G., Taylor, R., Hitomi, A. and Bergman, M. 2000, 'Techniques for supporting dynamic and adaptive workflow', *Computer Supported Cooperative Work*, vol. 9, nos 3–4, pp. 269–92.

Klein, M. and Dellarocas, C. 2000, 'A knowledge-based approach to handling exceptions in workflow systems', *Computer Supported Cooperative Work*, vol. 9, nos 3–4, pp. 399–412.

Klein, M., Dellarocas, C. and Bernstein, A. 2000, 'Introduction to the special issue on adaptive workflow systems', *Computer Supported Cooperative Work*, vol. 9, nos 3–4, pp. 265–7.

Kuo, M. H. and Lin, M. J. 2000, 'Using software agents to retrieve information from WWW', *SCI'2000*, Orlando, Fla, pp. 400–5.

Kurtz, C. F. and Snowden, D. 2003, 'The new dynamics of strategy: sense-making in a complex and complicated world', *IBM Systems Journal*, vol. 42, no. 3, pp. 462–83.

Lee, H. L., Padmanabhan, V. and Whang, S. 1997, 'Information distortion in a supply chain: the bullwhip effect', *Management Science*, vol. 43, no. 4, pp. 546–58.

Liu, K., Sun, L., Dix, A. and Narasipuram, M. 2001, 'Norm based agency for designing collaborative information systems', *Info Systems Journal*, vol. 11, no. 3, pp. 229–47.

McCoy, D. W. 2002, 'Business activity monitoring: calm before the storm', *Gartner*, <http://www.gartner.com/resources/105500/105562/105562.pdf>

McKeefrey, H. L. 2002, 'Business intelligence goes real-time', *VARBusiness*, <http://www.crn.com/it-channel/18828781>

March, S. and Smith, G. F. 1995, 'Design and natural science research on information technology',*Decision Support Systems*, vol. 15, pp. 251–66.

Mark, A. L. 2006, 'Notes from a small island: researching organizational behavior in healthcare from a UK perspective', *Journal of Organizational Behavior*, vol. 27, no. 7, pp. 851–67.

Moitra, D. and Ganesh, J. 2005, 'Web services and flexible business processes: towards the adaptive enterprise', *Information & Management*, vol. 42, no. 7, pp. 921–33.

Nesamoney, D. 2004, 'BAM: event-driven business intelligence for the real-time enterprise', *DM Review*, vol. 14, no. 3, pp. 38–40.

Nunamaker, J. F. jr, Chen, M. and Purdin, T. D. M. 1991, 'Systems development in information systems research', *Journal of Management Information Systems*, vol. 7, no. 3, pp. 89–106.

O'Neill, L. 2004, 'Faith and decision-making in the Bush presidency: the god elephant in the middle of America's living-room', *E: CO*, vol. 6, no. 1, pp. 149–56.

Özkohen, A. and Yolum, P. 2006, 'Predicting exceptions in agent based supply chains', *Engineering Societies in the Agents World VI Lecture Notes in AI*, vol. 3963, pp. 168–83.

Parameswaran, P. 2004, 'Business activity monitoring (BAM)—the future of business intelligence', *DM Direct*, <http://www.dmreview.com/dmdirect/20041008/1011668-1.html>

Piramuthu, S. 2004, 'Knowledge-based framework for automated dynamic supply chain configuration—production, manufacturing and logistics', *European Journal of Operational Research*, vol. 165, no. 1, pp. 219–30.

Sainfort, F. C., Gustafson, D. H., Bosworth, K. and Hawkins, R. P. 1990, 'Decision support systems effectiveness: conceptual framework and empirical evaluation', *Organizational Behavior and Human Decision Processes*, vol. 45, no. 2, pp. 232–52.

Sharda, R., Barr, S. H. and McDonnell, J. C. 1988, 'Decision support system effectiveness: a review and an empirical test', *Management Science*, vol. 34, no. 2, pp. 139–59.

Simon, H. A. 1977, *The New Science of Management Decision*, Prentice-Hall, Upper Saddle River, NJ.

Snowden, D. 2002, 'Complex acts of knowing: paradox and descriptive self-awareness', *Journal of Knowledge Management*, vol. 6, no. 2, pp. 100–11.

Snowden, D. 2004, 'Facilitating innovation within the organization', *Finance & Management*, pp. 5–7.

Sprague, R. and Carlson, E. D. 1982, *Building Effective Decision Support Systems*, Prentice-Hall, Upper Saddle River, NJ.

Stewart, T. A. 2002, 'How to think with your gut', *Business 2.0*, <http://www.cognitive-edge.com/ceresources/articles/49_Thinking_with_your_Gut(T_Stewart_article_in_Bus_2).pdf>

Vahidov, R. 2005, 'Intermediating user-DSS interaction with autonomous agents', *IEEE Transaction on System, Man, and Cybernetics—Part A: System and humans*, vol. 35, no. 6, pp. 964–70.

Vahidov, R. and Fazlollahi, B. 2004, 'Pluralistic multi-agent decision support system: a framework and an empirical test', *Information & Management*, vol. 41, no. 7, pp. 883–98.

Wang, H., Mylopoulos, J. and Liao, S. 2002, 'Intelligent agents and financial risk monitoring systems', *Communications of the ACM*, vol. 45, no. 3, pp. 83–8.

Wang, M. and Wang, H. 2006, 'From process logic to business logic—a cognitive approach to business process management', *Information & Management*, vol. 43, no. 2, pp. 179–93.

Wooldridge, M. 2002, *An Introduction to Multiagent Systems*, J. Wiley, New York.

Wooldridge, M. and Jennings, N. R. 1995, 'Intelligent agents: theory and practice', *Knowledge Engineering Review*, vol. 10, no. 2, pp. 115–52.

Yin, R. 2003, *Case Study Research: Design and methods*, Third edition, Sage, Thousand Oaks, Calif.

Zimmer, K. 2002, 'Supply chain coordination with uncertain just-in-time delivery', *International Journal of Production Economics*, vol. 77, no. 1, pp. 1–15.

10. Thinking beyond means–ends analysis: the role of impulse-driven human creativity in the design of artificially intelligent systems

DONGMING XU
YONGGUI WANG
SUKANTO BHATTACHARYA
UNIVERSITY OF QUEENSLAND

Abstract

While goal-directed problem solving as advocated by Herbert Simon's means–ends analysis model has primarily shaped the course of design research on artificially intelligent systems, we contend that there is a definite disregard of a key phase within the overall design process that in fact logically precedes the problem-solving phase. While the systems designers have been obsessed with goal-directed problem solving, the basic determinants of the desired goal state remain to be fully understood or categorically defined. We propose an argumentative framework built on a set of logically interlinked conjectures that seeks to specifically highlight the importance of this hitherto neglected phase in the overall design process of intelligent systems.

Introduction

There are at least two distinct forms of human creativity that motivate design research: one that is primarily goal driven and is essentially concerned with 'problem solving'; and one that is impulse driven and is essentially concerned with 'problem creation' (Michalos 1970). Michalos opines that while there could be some common factors that underlie both forms, there are critical cognitive distinctions in terms of the intellectual as well as emotional drivers that are involved in problem-creating as opposed to problem-solving design research. Herbert Simon's (1969) initial attempt at collating the creative activity engaged in by 'every liberally educated man' (including scientists, artists and engineers), by exhorting them to share their professional experiences thus enhancing the cumulative outcome of the creative design process, stopped short of fully recognising these distinctions. So we contend that Simon's *means–ends analysis* (MEA) framework can be appropriately applied only to design research that has a definite problem-solving goal.

In this context, the design activity of 'problem creation' that we refer to is entirely separate from the task of 'problem recognition', which usually forms the beginning step in a problem-solving design activity. The outcome of a 'problem-creation' activity is a concept or idea (and not necessarily a *thing*) that has the characteristic of *'absolute newness'*—a term we shall encounter and elucidate later on.

Design research in a few fields (including information and knowledge engineering) is synonymous with *improvement research*—a designation that evidently emphasises the goal-driven nature of the involved problem-solving and/or performance-enhancing activities. This is perhaps attributable to a rather mechanistic view of systems design with origins in some of the early *artificial intelligence* (AI) programs of Simon—for example, the General Problem Solver (GPS) developed in 1957, which was simply an algorithmic execution of the MEA model for heuristic problem solving (Frantz 2003).

In this chapter, we will first critically examine the role played by the MEA framework in shaping the course of *artificially intelligent systems* (AIS) design over its fairly recent history and then go on to propose a systematic framework to help understand the equally vital (but hitherto largely neglected) role of impulse-driven creativity and resulting implications.

Influence of MEA on AIS design

When Newell and Simon first programmed the GPS (Newell et al. 1959), there was no clear distinguishing line, so to speak, between digital computer and machine intelligence. In fact, Simon posited his science of the artificial with *digital computer* being the artefact of interest. So the design of the GPS could have been stimulated partly by parallel developments in other design sciences—especially in mechanical and construction engineering, which were looking for increasingly efficient ways to numerically solve complex applied mathematical problems pertaining to those fields. While GPS was the first formal computer program that successfully separated the domain of 'problem knowledge' from that of 'solution strategy', there was, however, very little 'problem-creation' activity involved in designing GPS, as well as later variants such as the STRIPS (Stanford Research Institute Problem Solver). This was quite obvious given that these programs were nothing more than algorithmic implementations of the classical MEA model whereby an existing problem was first visualised in the form of a 'current' (that is, problem) state and a 'goal' (that is, solution) state. Once any given problem has been so visualised, the heuristic solution technique proceeds by choosing an *action* from a set of available alternatives (often mutually exclusive) so as to reduce the gap between the two states. An action leads to a new (often intermediate) state, which is somewhat better than the original state but somewhat worse than the desired goal state. This new state then becomes the current state and the process is applied recursively until the features of the current and the goal states become virtually indistinguishable (Fikes and Nilsson 1971).

An important aspect of goal-directed problem solving as applied in MEA-based intelligent systems such as GPS and STRIPS is a logical (often sequential) framework in which actions need to be taken in order to attain a particular goal (Simon 1996). Such a goal-directed problem-solving system is required to be connected to the external environment by *sensory* connectivities through which it can collate environmental information and *motor* connectivities through which it can transmit the collated information to some kind of a *central processor* and then react to the external stimuli in accordance with the outcome of such information processing. In addition, such a system has to have some means of storing pre-processed as well as post-processed information—that is, some sort of *internal memory* (Stuart and Norvig 2003). In other words, such a system is required not only to emulate the behaviour of the human designer, but in order for it to be able to do so, it has to have a rather similar internal physical organisation. This had led to a belief among a number of pioneering AI researchers that both the power and the performance of intelligent systems could be improved without bounds by simply improving their structural design so as to continually approximate the internal structure of more and more complex biological organisms, ultimately creating an 'artificial human' that could think, behave and communicate exactly like a real person. So AIS design researchers have been largely engrossed within a utopian comfort zone, believing that biological evolution has already done the hard work for them via the Darwinian process of *natural selection* in coming up with what is the most optimal design for an intelligent system, and all they need to do is simply follow. So, creativity in the context of machine intelligence has become nearly synonymous with targeted problem solving, thereby limiting intelligent system design research to the designing of artefacts that are more effective in physically emulating natural intelligence.

Such a general belief among pioneering AIS designers was clearly evident in the burgeoning of interest in the design of expert systems that were 'taught' via a supervised learning process to gain expert knowledge in a particular problem domain and then take decisions or render advice much like a human expert. *Dendral* is a well-known case of such an expert system whose main goal was to assist chemists to identify unknown organic molecules by analysing their mass spectra and utilising a chemical knowledge base (Lindsay et al. 1980). As an example of emulating human thinking within a less sombre but nevertheless problem-solving domain, chess-playing computer programs have been designed with the goal of first learning from and then beating their human masters at their own game (Levy and Newborn 1991). A parallel growth has also been observed, alongside human behaviour, in the design of AIS that attempt better emulation of human communication by means of *natural language processing*. An example of one of the earliest of such an expert system is Siklossy's ZBIE program (Siklossy 1972).

What about creativity? Can creativity be artificially generated? This is a really tough question. Never-say-die AI researchers have tended to tackle the problem of creativity by essentially transforming the question itself so that answers can be sought within some sort of MEA framework. To that effect, software programs have been written that it is claimed are 'creative' to the extent that they have demonstrated a rudimentary capability in replicating some form of creative human behaviour—for example, being able to compose a story, such as MINSTREL (Turner 1994), or paint a picture, such as 'AARON' (McCorduck 1991). The pertinent question, however, is: can one say that a piece of software is creative just by observing its output in the same sense that one can say a human child is creative just by observing the behaviour of the child at play? The fact is that while much of primordial human creativity is impulse driven, that of machine-generated creativity is goal driven and, while sometimes the distinguishing line between the two can appear very thin, that line can never completely fade out.

Where the problem lies

While the goal of natural-science research is *truth*, that of design-science research is *utility*. Pursuits of truth and utility are, however, ontologically inseparable since one informs the other—'an artefact may have utility because of some yet undiscovered truth while a theory may yet to be developed to the point where its truth can be incorporated into design' (Hevner et al. 2004). For example, the initial designs of flying machines were inspired largely by simply observing the flight of birds, but those rudimentary designs did make a contribution towards the subsequent birth and enrichment of the theory underlying modern aviation science. And although modern aircraft operate very differently to how birds fly, as Brooks points out, they did not lose their utility as an artefact even when the governing design deviated over time from the biological inspiration that motivated the original (Hearst and Hirsh 2000).

According to Aaron Sloman, any intelligent systems design process has two guiding themes: *science*, which is concerned with investigating natural intelligence and what alternative types of intelligence are possible and how they might be artificially embodied, and *engineering*, which is concerned with the building of useful things (Hearst and Hirsh 2000).

While the *engineering* theme of intelligent systems design has to do with problem solving-type tasks principally associated with the MEA framework of design science (the part of the flow chart that is enclosed within a dashed box in Figure 10.1), the *science* theme has to do more with the impulse-driven creativity aspect of design science since it is concerned with problem-creation and problem-identification tasks as distinct from problem solving.

So, while the *engineering* theme deals with the 'how' questions, the *science* theme has to tackle the 'why' ones. While it is obvious that both the 'why' and the 'how' questions need to be systematically answered in the overall design process to ensure a fruitful outcome, there is an implied natural order of precedence: the 'why' questions need to be tackled before the 'how' ones.

The successful dovetailing of aviation science into aeronautical engineering shows that only after a problem has been properly 'created' by adequately answering a basic 'why' question can the *science* theme of design meaningfully give way to the *engineering* one, which subsequently tries to answer all the ensuing 'how' questions of design.

What, however, has happened rather well in the case of flying-machine design has not happened quite so successfully in the case of intelligent machine design. The primary reason for this has been the ineffective dovetailing of information science into systems engineering. Historically, designers of AIS have tended to be more concerned with answering the 'how' questions first and have not bothered too much with the 'why' one—as a result of which the temporal growth path of AIS design has become somewhat lopsided. As Donald Mitchie has very correctly noted, there is a consistent disregard of Alan Turing's (1950) classical paper on AI in which a two-stage approach was proposed: first, to construct a teachable machine, and second, to subject the constructed machine to a course of education. As a result of this disregard towards a classical study that hinted at a basic 'why' question, the design process of intelligent machines in general and AIS in particular has become back-to-front: researchers are trying to improve the system design for obtaining solutions to a problem that still remains to be adequately created and understood (Hearst and Hirsh 2000). So, while not denying the importance of the problem-solving approach based on MEA in initiating research on AIS design, it has now become quite necessary to also explore the crucial role that impulse-driven creativity has to play in this matter.

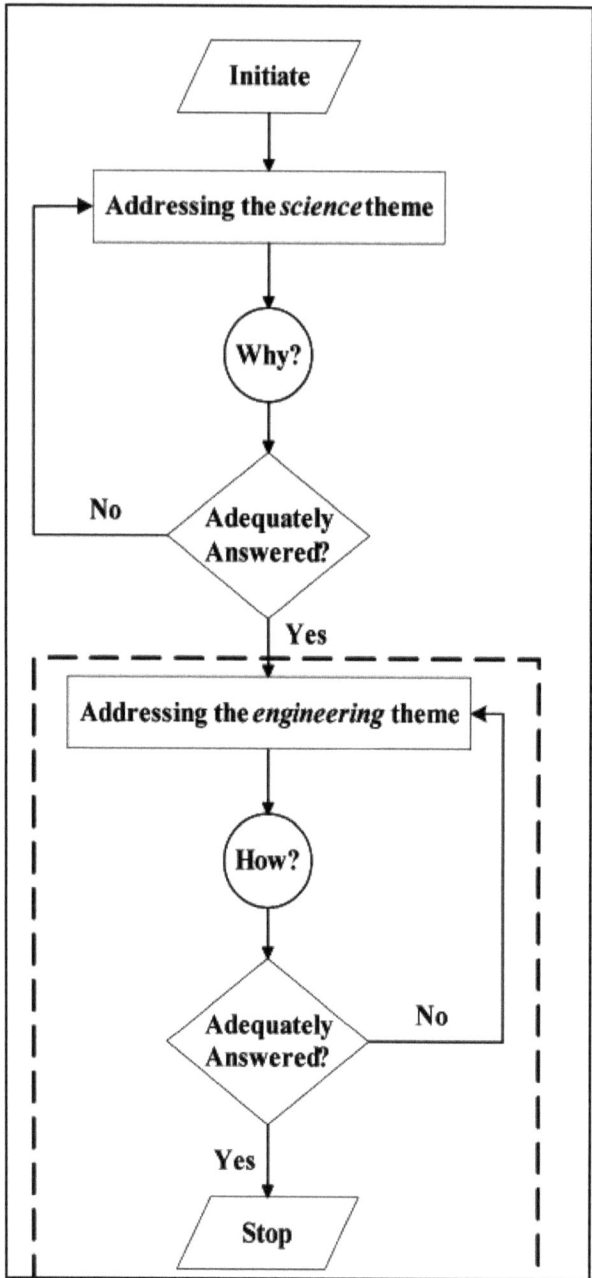

Figure 10.1 Flow chart depicting a sequential ordering of Sloman's suggested intelligent systems design themes

A systematic framework for highlighting the role of impulse-driven creativity

Subrata Dasgupta (1992) posits two qualitative laws, which he claims are valid throughout any science of design. He argues that since a major aim of design theory is 'to construct explanatory models that further enhance our understanding of design as a cognitive act', there ought to be certain fundamental *laws of design* that are valid across all the sciences of the artificial just as there are certain fundamental physical laws that always hold true across all the natural sciences.

The two design laws proposed by Dasgupta are: the *Hypothesis Law*, which states that 'a design process that reaches termination does so through one or more cycles of hypothesis creation, testing and (if necessary) modification'; and the *Impermanence Law*, which states that 'a design in any given state is never guaranteed to remain in that state'. While the first of Dasgupta's laws applies to design as a systematic process, the second applies to design as an outcome of such a systematic process. Even without going into any extended debate concerning the validity of these laws, it is not too difficult to see that these laws apply exclusively to design motivated by creativity that is primarily goal driven and concerns a problem-solving activity. In coming up with his design laws, Dasgupta draws heavily from two of the pioneers of the MEA framework as applied to AIS design: Newell's (1982) *knowledge-level* paradigm and Simon's (1979) *bounded rationality*. Dasgupta, however—possibly for the first time—presents a formal argument in support of 'newness' being an essential prerequisite for a design process to be initiated. He, however, constrains his definition of 'newness' so as to agree with MEA by considering it in relative terms: newness is considered *relative to the designer's knowledge*. This essentially brings the concept as defined by Dasgupta within the bounds of the dashed box in Figure 10.1.

It has also been argued that the creativity behind some original design inspirations can be explained via a mechanism of 'analogical transfer' (Bhatta and Goel 1997). The concept of *'absolute newness'* that we touched on in the introductory section is not, however, fully explained by this line of argument, as many significant inventions in human history have had very few if any clear analogical connections with a pre-existing artefact. Indeed, in many instances, analogical connections were drawn only after a rudimentary design of the artefact of interest had already been conceived through an act of purely impulse-driven creativity. In an apparent realisation of the uniqueness of impulse-driven human creativity, Dasgupta (2008) has recently posited that *'computational models of the creative process are fundamentally flawed as theories of human creativity*' and the power of computational models lies elsewhere. We contend that 'absolute newness'—as the hallmark of impulse-driven creativity—must possess two essential characteristics.

- To be considered 'absolutely new', *the design of an artefact should not draw from any a priori body of knowledge or repository of ideas*. For example, although there is no historical evidence to suggest that he in fact tried to physically build a flying machine (Gray 2006), Leonardo da Vinci's fifteenth-century drawings did initiate a design process with the flying machine as the artefact of interest with no known a priori body of scientific knowledge to inspire or guide his drawings of such a machine. Following Boden (1990), creativity associated with 'absolute newness' does not arise from explorations restrained within the boundaries of a pre-specified conceptual space, rather 'from a deliberate transformation or transcendence of this space'. This also corresponds to 'H-creativity' (creativity recognised as *novel* by the society at large) rather than 'P-creativity' (novel only to the agent producing it) (Boden 1999).

- 'Absolute newness' *is not to be associated with innovation*. Although they are sometimes used interchangeably, 'creativity' and 'innovation' are two distinct concepts. Innovation in design results from the successful implementation of a created concept or idea (Cooper et al. 1995). *While all innovation involves some creativity, not all creativity, however, is innovative*. In that sense, da Vinci was certainly a creator but not an innovator. The Wright brothers, however, were innovative to the extent that they in fact tried to give a physical form to their creativity. Subsequent aircraft designers were mostly innovators who primarily engaged in problem solving to improve on the existing states of design (in line with Dasgupta's second law), exhibiting goal-driven creativity.

Once a problem has been adequately created, it can be tackled effectively so that a solution can be found; a desired goal state can be achieved. Goal-driven creativity then takes over from impulse-driven creativity as acts of innovation start to improve an 'absolutely new' artefact.

So, collating the concepts discussed, we state our Conjecture 10.1 as follows.

Conjecture 10.1

As the nature of the primary activity constituting a design process shifts from problem creation towards problem resolution, the form of human creativity motivating such a process shifts from being impulse driven towards being goal driven.

This is depicted in Figure 10.2, building on the flow chart in Figure 10.1.

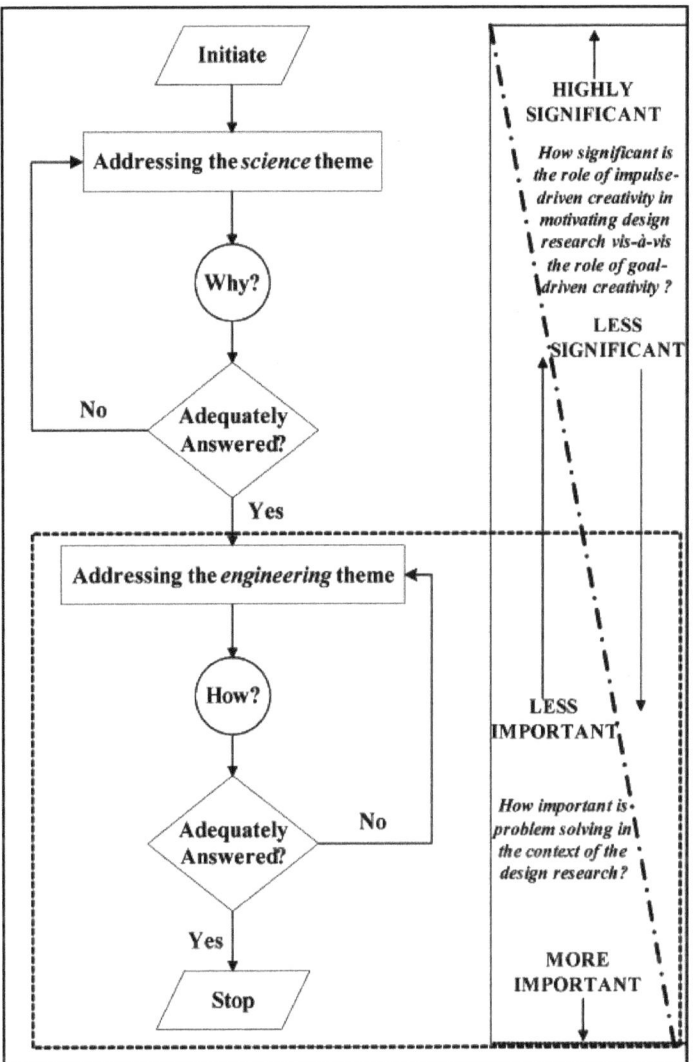

Figure 10.2 Flow chart depicting the relation between forms of creativity and the associated design activities

So goal-driven creativity should play an increasingly significant role as the design process begins to address the 'how' questions. This conceptualisation is fairly intuitive given that much of the *engineering* theme of a design process is concerned with *improvement research*—that is, how an artefact of interest should ideally shape up. In other words, it is concerned with attaining a more and more refined state of design. *Defining* logically precedes *refining*, however, and this is recognised even in the MEA framework itself in that it does put 'problem recognition' as the initiating step. Within the MEA framework, however, problem recognition is indistinguishable from goal setting. Problem creation is, however, something quite different; it initiates the design process underlying the *science* theme as shown in Figures 10.1 and 10.2.

Any artificially intelligent system—at its most refined state of design—would be expected to pass the *Turing test* (or a comparable testing process) on a *global* scale, not just within the constraining bounds of a specific problem domain (Turing 1950). Although ELIZA and PARRY are two of the earliest rule-based programs that were acclaimed to have 'passed' this test (Weizenbaum 1966; Colby 1975), it has since been argued that such rule-based systems have been able to fool a human examiner into mistaking them for human only within a rather restricted problem domain.

Moreover, it has been argued that passing the Turing test is *a necessary but not a sufficient proof* of a machine's ability to think (Searle 1980). So, even if one remains entirely within the MEA framework, it is still not very clear what is the ultimate goal state of AIS design since the determinants of that state are still disputed. The early designers of flying machines did thoroughly study and were able to broadly understand the physiological mechanisms that enabled birds to fly, identifying the exact mechanisms that were lacking in human beings making them incapable of flight. They answered the 'why' question and thereby determined the basic determinants of the desired goal state. Pioneers of intelligent systems design have, however, neglected the need to first understand the mechanisms that determine intelligent thought—to satisfactorily answer a very basic 'why' question: *'why cannot machines think like human beings?'*

Thus, AIS designers do not know and cannot say at this time what should ideally replace the question mark in Figure 10.1; is it *human thought* (mind) or *human brain* (matter)? The current AIS design state does not have a *unique* answer.

Figure 10.3 A conceptual representation of the missing 'why' in AIS design

So, again collating the concepts discussed, we state our Conjecture 10.2 as follows.

Conjecture 10.2

All the determinants of a desired goal state have to be fully understood and categorically defined before a design process can be productively motivated by human creativity of a purely goal-driven form.

This is depicted in Figure 10.4, building on the flow chart in Figure 10.2.

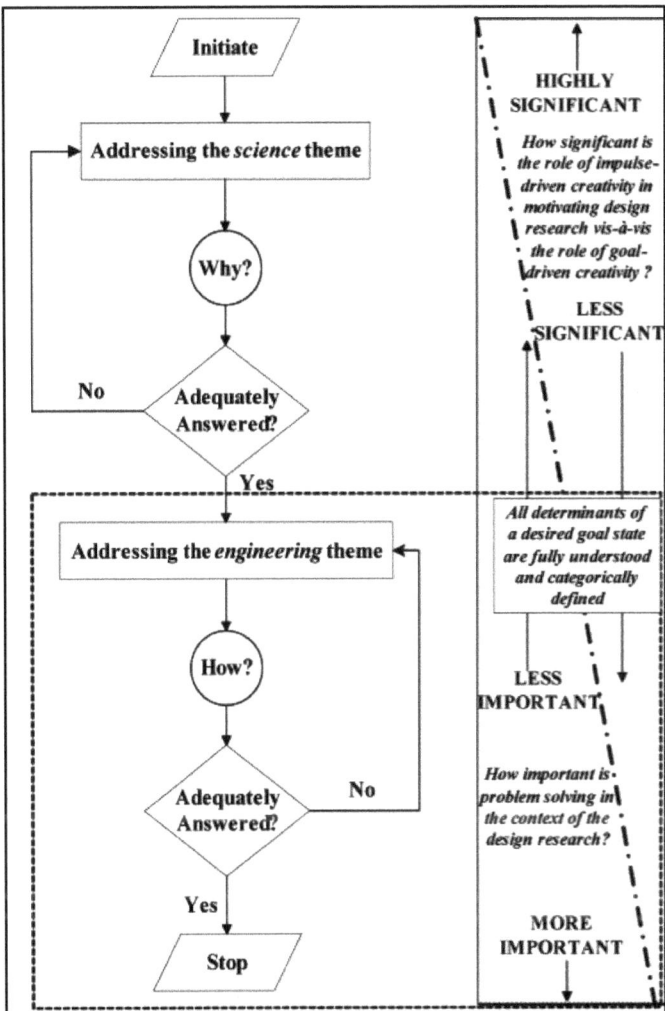

Figure 10.4 Flow chart depicting the need for understanding and defining all goal-state determinants before problem-solving design research can productively ensue

Our third conjecture arises out of the intersection of Conjectures 10.1 and 10.2 and is stated as follows.

Conjecture 10.3: → {C1 ∩ C2}

For a design process to progress productively towards successful culmination, the real shift of the form driving human creativity from impulse driven to goal driven must necessarily occur only after the determinants of a desired goal state have been completely understood and categorically defined.

This is depicted in Figure 10.5, building on the flow chart in Figure 10.4.

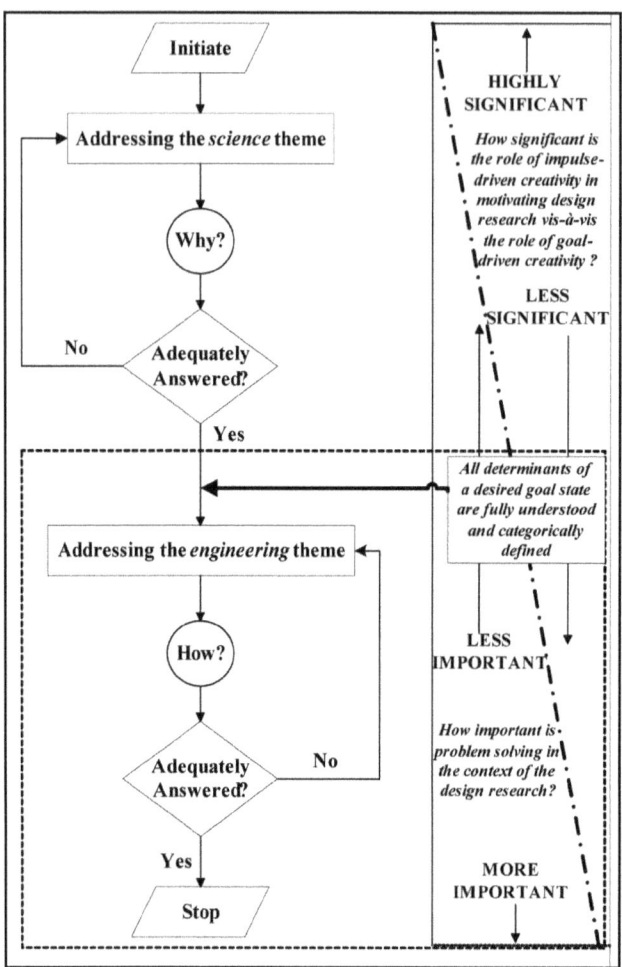

Figure 10.5 Flow chart depicting the precedence of understanding and defining determinants of the goal state over the onset of the problem-solving phase by goal-driven creativity

Given that the desired goal state of the intelligent system design process is artificial production of intelligent thought, until and unless all the determinants of intelligent thought are thoroughly understood, such a design process is very unlikely to culminate in the desired goal state if it is motivated purely by goal-driven human creativity. Thus, we state Conjecture 10.4 as follows.

Conjecture 10.4

Only after the 'why' question relating to the science theme of the design process is adequately resolved can all the determinants of a desired goal state be completely understood and categorically defined.

This is depicted in Figure 10.6, building on the flow chart in Figure 10.5.

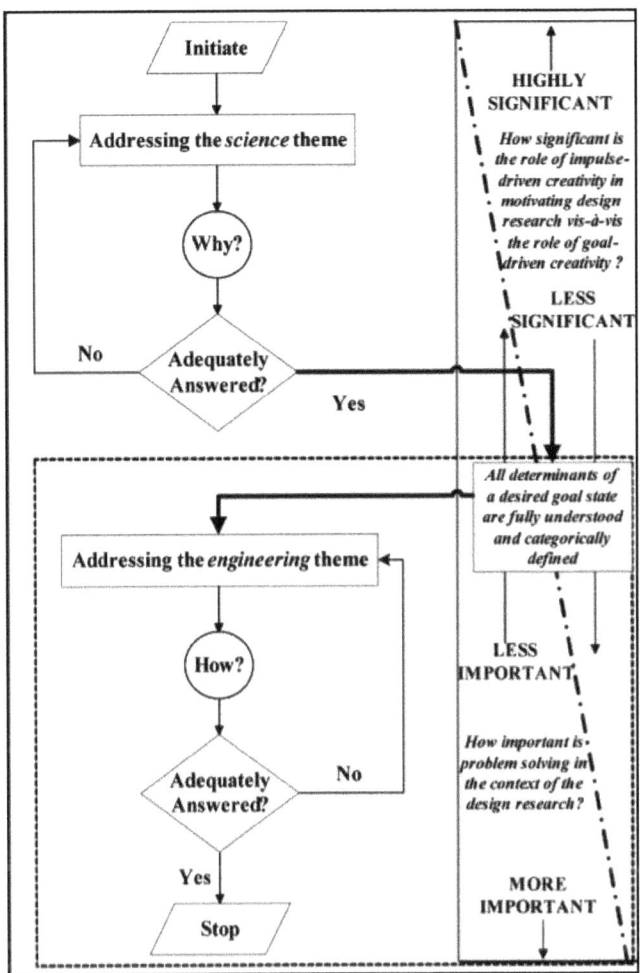

Figure 10.6 Flow chart depicting that the successful tackling of the 'why' question allows the determinants of the goal state to be fully understood and categorically defined

As we have stated previously, however, *all innovation involves creativity but not all creativity is innovative*. Innovation is indispensable for a design process to culminate successfully, to attain the desired goal state. It is essential to innovate in order to transform a creative idea into an artefact of interest. So, innovation might essentially be what jump-starts the problem-solving phase of a design process by bringing about some sort of practical implementation of the creative idea on which later designers can then improve. This brings us to our Conjecture 10.5, which we state as follows.

Information Systems Foundations: The Role of Design Science

Conjecture 10.5

Occurrence of innovation triggers the end of the problem-creating phase and the onset of the problem-solving phase in the overall design process.

This is depicted in Figure 10.7, building on the flow chart in Figure 10.6.

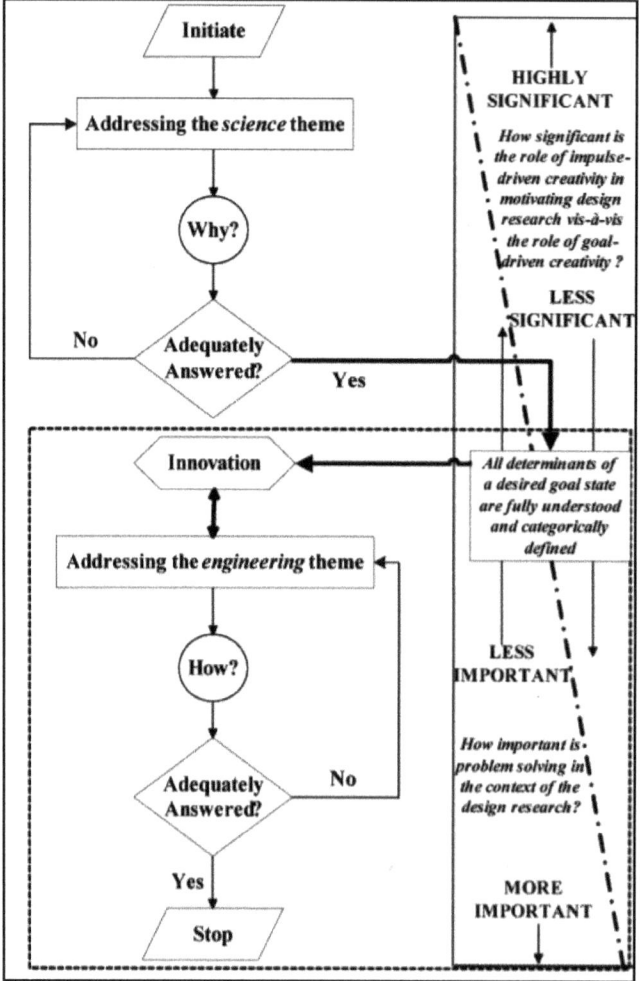

Figure 10.7 Flow chart depicting the onset of innovation as a trigger for the start of the problem-solving phase and the end of the problem-creation phase

The first time innovation occurs in a design process, it effectively *prepares the ground* for the engineering theme to be addressed. The double-headed arrow in Figure 10.7 indicates, however, that the process of addressing the engineering theme can also contribute to subsequent innovation (that is, re-innovation) as long as a current design state can be improved on and as long as all issues contributing to the 'how' bit have not been adequately addressed.

Our sixth conjecture arises out of the intersection of Conjectures 10.4 and 10.5 and is stated as follows.

Conjecture 10.6: → {C4 ∩ C5}

Innovation can start to effectively occur only after the 'why' question of the science theme of design has been adequately answered.

This is depicted in Figure 10.8, building on the flow chart in Figure 10.7.

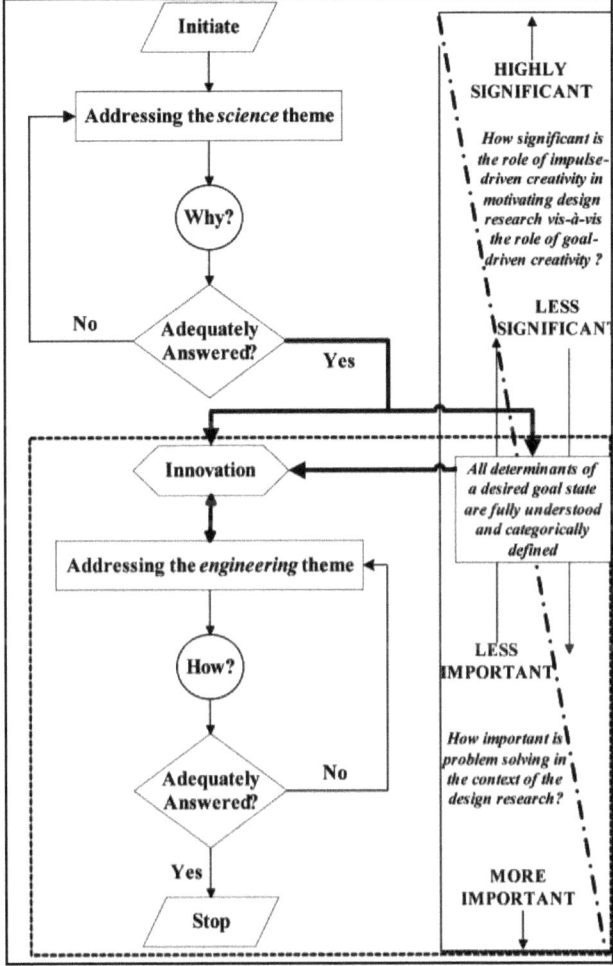

Figure 10.8 Flow chart depicting the precedence of answering the 'why' question pertaining to the science theme over the effective onset of innovation

Combining our six conjectures, our final and all-enveloping conjecture is a union of Conjectures 10.3 and 10.6 and is thus stated as follows.

Conjecture 10.7: → {C3 ∪ C6}: → [{C1 ∩ C2} ∪ {C4 ∩ C5}]

A sufficient condition for a design process to progress productively towards successful culmination is the occurrence of innovation following adequate answering of the 'why' question, which in turn necessarily implies that all the determinants of a desired goal state have already been completely understood and categorically defined.

Conjecture 10.7 essentially captures the argument that we have been making in favour of a need to shift the emphasis back on the problem-creation phase of design research for intelligent systems.

Although our framework consists merely of conjectures and not formal *proofs*, there is a certain amount of intuitive logic in what we have proposed. Going back to our comparative model of aircraft design, we do know a lot more at this stage about the determinants of the desired goal state for flying machines than we do for intelligent machines. While there has been a proliferation of computational technologies attempting to emulate human thought and behaviour, our knowledge base of what *in fact determines* intelligent thought is rather inadequate. While our proposed framework might not be the best or even the only means to highlight this gap in our current state of knowledge, it does highlight a need to appropriately refocus our attention.

How can impulse-driven creativity help in finding what determines intelligent thought? It is expected that this particular science of the artificial still requires some degree of hand-holding by at least one (likely more) of the sciences of the natural as AI researchers grapple with concepts such as intelligence and consciousness and the precise physical/biological/mental processes underlying them. So the initial breakthrough (something 'absolutely new') could originate from within a contributing natural-science field such as physics or neurophysiology, which would then re-initiate the AIS design process and put it back on course towards a definite goal. We cannot, however, and do not rule out other possibilities.

Discussion

A design is something more than just a symbolic representation of an artefact for an implementer's benefit; 'it is also a small piece of *theory* about a part of the observable world; a *micro theory*, in fact, that predicts behaviour or properties that an artefact (that does not yet exist) will exhibit' (Dasgupta 1992). Dasgupta realises that design research in information and knowledge engineering suffers from the lack of a solid repertoire of mathematical theory such as is found in design research in mechanical or civil engineering fields.

Matters are not helped by the fact that AI researchers and systems designers seem to be confused between what we prefer to call the *soft problem*, that of *producing* some workable form of synthetic intelligence, and the primordial *hard problem*, that of *defining* the very determinants of intelligent thought. The soft problems are those that relate to specific psycho-physiological processes that go on within the brain of an intelligent biological organism. Borrowing from the natural sciences, these processes can be satisfactorily explained by applying *reductionist principles* (Chalmers 1995). The *hard problem*, however, is something intrinsically different as it does not relate to any specific neural process but rather concerns issues such as *subjective experience* thereby being more a question of 'why' than of 'how'. The design objective of AIS is to make it 'learn' from a given pool of knowledge by formulating a rule-based or some other form of logic architecture. While there are ways to evaluate the efficacy or otherwise of a design process in terms of how well the AIS learns and then applies this learned knowledge to accomplish a particular problem-solving task, there is, however, no way to test whether it also does acquire some subjective experience, whether it develops its own *thoughts* about the particular process. This limitation in the current state of design stems not from an inability to address the technological issues, which we have grouped under 'how', but rather from the unanswered 'why' question. Unlike some other engineering disciplines, information and knowledge engineering has not yet been able to fully understand the determinants of its desired goal state. Until and unless the pressing issue concerning the determinants of intelligent thought is adequately addressed, our view is that a successful culmination of the overall AIS design process is not going to happen just by continuing to pursue goal-directed design research.

We wish to be very clear, however, that by taking this stand we are *not* debunking or even challenging the veracity or utility of the burgeoning research in AIS and robotics and the plethora of AIS applications that seems to be touching almost all aspects of our daily lives, ranging from cars and washing machines to security systems and even to detection of dangerous diseases such as cancer. In fact, most of the state-of-the art design research that is taking place in AIS has immediate and important implications for improving the quality of our lives. That, however, simply is not the point that we have sought to raise in this chapter. We are not saying that all of the 'outputs' produced by AIS research suffer from a serious design flaw that robs them of their utility. They might be very effective in achieving their goal states. Our point is that even the most sophisticated AIS—perhaps incorporating the most powerful neural network or genetic algorithm or some other form of biologically inspired computational feature—is, at the end of the day, just a problem-solving device. It is in creating and defining a problem that is 'absolutely new' that the true test of AI lies—and we contend that no AIS can pass this test without fully answering the 'why'.

Conclusion

In this chapter, we have proposed a formal framework to argue in favour of the role of impulse-driven vis-a-vis goal-driven human creativity in ensuring success of the AIS design process. Our position is that the current state of design of AIS stems from a constant disregard of a key phase in the overall design process that has to ideally precede the problem-solving phase, at which, ironically, almost all current design research appears to be targeted.

Our recommended way of going about it is for AI researchers and AIS designers to think outside the MEA-inspired paradigms and look for flashes of impulse-driven creativity to first get around the perplexing 'why' question. We perceive that strong dependence on one or more established natural sciences is needed at this stage and that AI has perhaps not yet reached a state of maturity to stand on its own as an independent science. A deeper ontological inquiry into the nature of the true determinants of intelligent thought is needed before we can seek to further improve on the current state of design for artificially producing or replicating such thought.

References

Bhatta, S. R. and Goel, A. K. 1997, 'A functional theory of design patterns', *Proceedings of the Fifteenth International Joint Conference on Artificial Intelligence*, pp. 294–300.

Boden, M. 1990, *The Creative Mind: Myths and mechanisms*, Weidenfeld and Nicholson, London.

Boden, M. 1999, 'Computational models of creativity', in R. J. Sternberg (ed.), *Handbook of Creativity*, Cambridge University Press, UK, pp. 351–73.

Chalmers, D. J. 1995, 'Facing up to the problem of consciousness', *Journal of Consciousness Studies*, vol. 2, no. 3, pp. 200–19.

Colby, K. M. 1975, *Artificial Paranoia: A computer simulation of paranoid processes*, Pergamon Press, San Francisco.

Cooper, R. G. and Kleinschmidt, E. J. 1995, 'Benchmarking the firm's critical success factors in new product development', *Journal of Product Innovation Management*, vol. 12, no. 5, pp. 374–91.

Dasgupta, S. 1992, 'Two laws of design', *Intelligent Systems Engineering*, vol. 1, no. 2, pp. 146–56.

Dasgupta, S. 2008, 'Shedding computational light on human creativity', *Perspectives on Science*, vol. 16, no. 2, pp. 121–36.

Fikes, R. E. and Nilsson, N. J. 1971, 'STRIPS: a new approach to the application of theorem proving to problem solving', *Artificial Intelligence*, vol. 5, no. 2, pp. 189–208.

Frantz, R. 2003, 'Artificial intelligence as a framework for understanding intuition', *Journal of Economic Psychology*, vol. 24, no. 2, pp. 265–77.

Gray, C. 2006, 'Flying machines', *Important Thoughts About & Experiments With Flying Machines 1485 to 1903*, The Pioneer Aviation Group, Encino, Calif., viewed 25 June 2008, <http://www.flyingmachines.org>

Hearst, M. and Hirsh, H. 2000, 'AI's greatest trends and controversies', *IEEE Intelligent Systems*, vol. 15, no. 1, pp. 8–17.

Hevner, A. R., March, S. T., Park, J. and Ram, S. 2004, 'Design science in information systems research', *MIS Quarterly*, vol. 28, no. 1, pp. 75–105.

Levy, D. and Newborn, M. 1991, *How Computers Play Chess*, Computer Science Press, New York.

Lindsay, R., Buchanan, B. G., Feigenbaum, E. A. and Lederberg, J. 1980, *Application of Artificial Intelligence for Organic Chemistry: The DENDRAL project*, McGraw-Hill, New York.

McCorduck, P. 1991, *Aaron's Code*, W. H. Freeman & Company, New York.

Michalos, A. C. 1970, 'Book review: The Sciences of the Artificial by Herbert A. Simon, Cambridge Mass. MIT Press 1969', Technology and Culture, vol. 11, no. 1, pp. 118–20.

Newell, A. 1982, 'The knowledge level', *Artificial Intelligence*, vol. 18, no. 1, pp. 87–127.

Newell, A., Shaw, J. C. and Simon, H. A. 1959, 'Report on a general problem-solving program', *Proceedings of International Conference on Information Processing*, pp. 256–64.

Searle, J. R. 1980, 'Minds, brains, and programs', *The Behavioral and Brain Sciences*, vol. 3, pp. 417–57.

Siklossy, L. 1972, 'Natural language learning by computer', in H. A. Simon and L. Siklossy (eds), *Representation and Meaning: Experiments with information processing systems*, Prentice-Hall, NJ.

Simon, H. A. 1969, *The Sciences of the Artificial*, First edition, MIT Press, Cambridge, Mass.

Simon, H. A. 1979, 'Rational decision-making in business organizations', *American Economic Review*, vol. 69, pp. 495–501.

Simon, H. A. 1996, *The Sciences of the Artificial*, Third edition, MIT Press, Cambridge, Mass.

Stuart, R. J. and Norvig, P. 2003, *Artificial Intelligence: A modern approach*, Second edition, Prentice-Hall, NJ.

Turing, A. M. 1950, 'Computing machinery and intelligence', *Mind*, vol. 59, no. 236, pp. 433–60.

Turner, S. R. 1994, *The Creative Process: A computer model of storytelling and creativity*, Lawrence Erlbaum, Hillsdale, NJ.

Weizenbaum, J. 1966, 'A computer program for the study of natural language communication between man and machine', *Communications of the Association of Computing Machinery*, vol. 9, no. 1, pp. 36–45.

11. An information systems design theory for an RFID university-based laboratory

SAMUEL FOSSO WAMBA
ÉCOLE POLYTECHNIQUE DE MONTRÉAL, AND
UNIVERSITY OF WOLLONGONG

KATINA MICHAEL
UNIVERSITY OF WOLLONGONG

Abstract

Radio frequency identification (RFID) technology is defined as a wireless automatic identification and data capture (AIDC) technology and is considered 'the next big thing' and 'the next revolution' in the management of the supply chain. Recently, the topic has attracted the interest of the industrial community as well as the scientific community. Following this tendency, this chapter applies an information systems design theory (ISDT) to an RFID-based university laboratory. For practitioners, the chapter provides some insights into the set-up and use of an RFID laboratory in university settings and, at the same time, offers a set of hypotheses that can be empirically tested.

Introduction

It has been stated that radio frequency identification (RFID) technology is one of the 'most pervasive computing technologies in history' (Roberts 2006:18). In the context of management, the technology has been viewed as 'the next big thing' (Wyld 2006:154) and 'the next revolution in the supply chain' (Srivastava 2004:1) since it allows 'any tagged entity to become a mobile, intelligent, communicating component of the organization's overall information infrastructure' (Curtin et al. 2007:88). The concept behind RFID is, however, not new. Indeed, it was used for the first time during World War II by the British Air Force to differentiate Allied from enemy aircraft.

Though the high potential of RFID technology in terms of operational performance optimisation is obvious, some key questions remain. For example: how should an appropriate business case be constructed? What is the impact on the firm when RFID is used with only a portion of one's trading partners? Will RFID have similar impacts inside and outside an organisation? In the same light, it is worth knowing what considerations are to be taken into account at the industry level, what factors are conducive to the adoption of RFID by a firm and whether in an inter-organisational context or internationally. Other issues are whether traditional IT adoption research paradigms are appropriate and if new performance measurement approaches are required to realise value from RFID; how a firm can make efficient use of real-time item/operator entity RFID tag placement, as well as real-time systems-based decision making. Moreover, one can ask how RFID and real-time decision making will change managerial capabilities, who does the tagging, who owns the technology and the data, who gets the value, who pays for readers that benefit multiple parties and who drives the effort to build standards, and so on (Curtin et al. 2007). Contributing to this debate, many RFID university-based laboratories are emerging around the world. The complex nature of RFID systems, however, turns the set-up of any RFID university-based laboratory into a very challenging exercise, as it is time-consuming and requires an appropriate choice of the various components of the system and support from various actors within the RFID industry. The process is even more challenging as there is no theoretical basis to provide assistance for universities in setting up such facilities. The objective of this chapter is to partially fill this gap by: 1) applying an information systems design theory (ISDT) to an RFID university-based laboratory; and 2) providing validation of our proposals.

The next section presents an overview of information systems design theories. Following this a literature review of RFID technology and a review of an RFID university-based laboratory are presented. In section four, an ISDT for an RFID university-based laboratory is proposed. Hypothesis testing appears in section five while the conclusion and future research feature are in section six.

Information systems design theories

ISDT is defined as 'a field of research concerned with the effective design, delivery, use and impact of information technology in organizations and society' (Jones et al. 2003:1). ISDT is concerned with the design of artefacts and their use in human–machine systems and involves theory and practice to achieve these goals (Gregor 2002; Markus et al. 2002; Martin 2004). The goal-oriented perspective of ISDT has created a rising interest in designing theories within the IS community (Goldkuhl 2004) as it enables them to draw theory from best practices at operational, management or strategic levels (Martin 2004).

As shown in Table 11.1, we can distinguish five types of theory: 1) analytical and descriptive theory; 2) theory for understanding; 3) prediction theory; 4) explanatory and predictive theory; and 5) theory for design and action (Gregor 2006; Jones et. al. 2003).

Table 11.1 Types of theory

Type	Question	Example of study
Analysing and describing	What is?	Bapna et al. (2004)
Understanding	How and why?	Levina and Ross (2003)
Predicting	What will be?	Bapna et al. (2003)
Explaining and predicting	What? How? Why? What will be?	Subramani (2004)
Design and action	How to do something?	Fan et al. (2003)

Sources: Gregor (2006); Jones et al. (2003).

ISDT, which is the one used in this chapter, is considered part of the theory for design and action (Gregor 2002; Jones et. al. 2003). It is concerned with how to design the artefact and the design process (Kourouthanassis 2006; Walls et al. 2004), which are components of ISDT (Table 11.2). The design product comprises: 1) the meta-requirements used to deal with a class of problems or goals to which the theory applies (Siponen et al. 2006); 2) meta-design principles, which describe a class of artefacts hypothesised to meet the meta-requirements; 3) kernel theories, which are relevant theories derived from natural or social sciences governing design requirements; and 4) testable design product hypotheses, which are used to validate the match between the artefact outcome and the meta-design. The other aspect of an ISDT is the design process and it involves: 1) a design method, which describes all procedures used for artefact construction; 2) kernel theories similar to, or different from, those being used in designing the product; and 3) testable design process hypotheses that can be used to ascertain that the design method results match the meta-design (Siponen et al. 2006; Walls et al. 2004).

Table 11.2 Components of an information system design theory

Design product	
1. Meta-requirements	Describes the class of goals to which the theory applies
2. Meta-design	Describes a class of artefacts hypothesised to meet the meta-requirements
3. Kernel theories	Theories from natural or social sciences governing design requirements
4. Testable design product hypotheses	Used to test whether the meta-design hypotheses meet the meta-requirements
Design process	
1. Design method	A description of procedure(s) for artefact construction
2. Kernel theories	Theories from natural or social sciences governing the design process itself
3. Testable design process hypotheses	Used to verify whether the results of the design hypothesis-based method in an artefact are consistent with the meta-design

Source: Walls et al. (2004)

In addition, ISDT can involve the methodologies, guidelines, principles or tools that are used in the development of the artefacts (Gregor 2002), in order to accelerate the design process by restricting available options and thus reducing developers' uncertainty and leading to better development results (Markus et al. 2002). Furthermore, ISDT allows researchers to generate testable research hypotheses that can be empirically validated using both positivistic and interpretative research methods (Markus et al. 2002; Siponen et al. 2006). More precisely, ISDT draws on three interconnected elements—namely: 1) a set of user requirements; 2) a set of principles for selecting system features; and 3) a set of principles deemed effective for guiding the development process. Also, ISDT is based on a theory, which is also referred to as kernel theory, and provides more practical implementation methods to practitioners (Gregor 2002; Markus et al. 2002).

Many researchers have already used the components of an ISDT proposed by (Walls et al. 2004:Table 2) for emerging technologies (Jones et al. 2003; Kourouthanassis 2006; Markus et al. 2002; Siponen et al. 2006). Our study follows this trend and applies an ISDT for one RFID university-based laboratory.

RFID technology and RFID university-based laboratory

RFID technology as an emerging inter-organisational information system

RFID technology is an emerging inter-organisational information system (IOS) that uses radio frequencies to automatically identify individual items or products in real time in a given supply chain (Curtin et al. 2007; Poirier and McCollum 2006). It belongs to two main classes of technologies: 1) automatic identification and data capture (AIDC) technologies, such as barcodes, biometrics and magnetic stripes; and 2) wireless technologies such as local area networks and metropolitan area networks (for more details, see Fosso Wamba et al. 2008a).

RFID technology components

Any RFID system is a combination of three major technologies: 1) a tag—active, passive or semi-passive—which serves as an electronic source of data and can be attached to or embedded in a physical object to be identified; 2) a reader and its antennas that communicate with the tag without requiring line of sight; and 3) a host server equipped with software (middleware) that manages the RFID system, filters data and interacts with enterprise applications. The middleware is the backbone of any RFID system. Indeed, it is the place where all business decisions that are used to manage the entire RFID system are configured (Fosso Wamba et al. 2008b).

RFID tags have various sizes and functional characteristics; however, the most important are the following.

1. Power source: an active tag contains a tiny battery from which power is drawn, while a passive tag does not contain any power source. The semi-passive tag works as a passive tag, but has a power source that enables it to run an onboard sensor (Roberti 2006a).

2. Operating frequency: the low-frequency tag uses frequencies ranging from 125–134 kHz, the high-frequency tag uses the 13.56 MHz frequency, the ultra-high-frequency tag uses a frequency between 866 and 960 MHz, and the microwave tag works with frequencies ranging from 2.4 to 5.8 GHz.

3. Read range.

4. Data storage capacity and capability: the RFID tag can be either read only or read/write. The data transmission rates of active tags are higher than those of passive tags and, similarly, the data storage capacity of the latter is smaller than that of the former.

5. Operational life: owing to its power source, the active tag's operational life is shorter than that of the passive tag (depending on how the power source is being used).

6. Cost: as it lacks a power source, the passive tag is less expensive than the active tag (Asif and Mandviwalla 2005).

It should be noted that RFID readers: 1) can have a read or read/write capability (Ngai et al. 2007), which enables data to be read or read/written on RFID tags through radio frequencies when these tags are passed near the range of the reader; 2) can be configured to control the timing communication with the RFID tag (the reader talks first) or to react to messages from the tags (the tag talks first) (Asif and Mandviwalla 2005); and 3) can be a fixed or a mobile device.

RFID technology capability

RFID technology is capable of delivering precise and accurate data from any tagged products (at item, case or palette levels) in real time in a given supply chain, thus increasing information flow (Datta et al. 2007; Fosso Wamba and Boeck 2008; Riggins and Slaughter 2006) as well as improving supply-chain efficiency (Katina and Luke 2005; Loebbecke 2007). Moreover, the technology is 'expected to revolutionize many of the collaborative supply chain processes and to empower new collaboration scenarios, such as anti-counterfeiting, product recall and reverse logistics, collaborative in-store promotion management and total inventory management' (Bardaki et al. 2007:1). For example, when adapted to specific context, RFID technology allows a vast range of applications such as inventory management, access control, anti-counterfeiting, logistical tracking, and so on.

Despite its high potential, RFID technology is currently facing many problems that prevent its large-scale adoption. Among these problems are issues of standards, changing RFID middleware options, tag and reader performance (Riggins and Slaughter 2006), the lack of investment returns (Vijayaraman and Osyk 2006) and the requirement in terms of strategy redesign, business process redesign, IT infrastructure transformation and organisational structural transformation (Fosso Wamba et al. 2008a). These issues have led to the establishment of many RFID-based university laboratories, each of which is working on a specific area in order to provide some possible answers (Table 11.3).

Table 11.3 Some RFID university-based laboratories

University RFID lab	Purpose	Source
Auto-ID Labs 1. MIT, 2. University of Cambridge, 3. University of St Gallen, 4. University of Fudan, 5. Information and Communication University, 6. University of Adelaide, and 7. Keio University	Creating internet networks for things using RFID and wireless sensor networks Creating a global system for tracking goods using a single-numbering system called the electronic product code	Auto-ID Labs*
University of Nebraska-Lincoln	The university has an extensive RFID lab stocked with RFID and material-handling equipment that students use for coursework The course focuses on RFID, RFID in logistics and RFID in engineering and business classes	Burnell (2008)
Middlesex Community College in Massachusetts	Certificate program geared towards preparing students to install and service RFID equipment	Burnell (2008)
Boise State University and the University of Alaska Anchorage	A joint graduate certificate program in supply chain management with a strong RFID focus	Burnell (2008)
Alien's RFID Solutions Center (supported by five universities: Ohio State University, Ohio University Center for Automatic Identification, Wilberforce University, Wright State University and the University of Cincinnati)	Developing RFID curricula Enhancing RFID studies via student internships at the Solutions Center Facilitating faculty consulting engagements at the center and other joint projects	Roberti (2006b)
Oklahoma State University	Course focusing on RFID system applications in manufacturing and engineering systems A systematic statistical approach for experimental design of a developed RFID system. The research has yielded new principles for harnessing information on the complex (non-linear and stochastic) nature of the process underlying signals from RFID and other sensor networks	Burnell (2008)
Southern Alberta Institute of Technology	To foster innovation and to conduct applied research in RFID application technologies This leading-edge facility allows local and national enterprises from all sectors to implement RFID applications in areas such as supply-chain management, asset tracking, safety systems and process information analysis	SAIT (2008)

University RFID lab	Purpose	Source
Texas State Technical College RFID Training Center	Training facility for corporate and student education in RFID To provide state-of-the-art workforce training To serve as a centre of excellence devoted to facilitating the widespread adoption of RFID technologies	TSTC Waco (2008)
University of Pittsburgh	Serves as an international resource to academics and members of the business community	Mickle (2007)
ePoly Center at Polytechnic School of Montreal	Training facility for corporate and student education in RFID Course focused on RFID, RFID in logistics and RFID in engineering and business classes Evaluation of the impacts of RFID/EPC on supply-chain management in the context of B2B RFID project management	Fosso Wamba et al. (2008a, 2008b) Bendavid et al. (2007)
University of Wisconsin RFID Lab	Demonstration and education of RFID technology and applications	Burnell (2008)
University of Arkansas RFID Research Center	To create and extend knowledge in RFID utilisation and its impacts on business and society	RFID Research Center (2008)

* From the Auto-ID Labs web site: <http://autoid.mit.edu/cs/>

ISDT for an RFID university-based laboratory

This section deals with ISDT when applied to an RFID university-based laboratory (Table 11.2). The various components of ISDT are described below.

Meta-requirements

There are four main meta-requirements

- the first refers to all technology providers and is necessary for the set-up and running of the RFID-based laboratory
- the second refers to the profile of potential RFID university-based laboratory users (for example, industrial stakeholders, students, policymakers)
- the third refers to the RFID university-based laboratory support for the various RFID applications using different contexts (for example, manufacturing, retailing, and so on)

- the fourth is the ability of researchers working in the laboratory to quickly select RFID technology components and convert the requirements of potential users into decision rules to be implemented in the RFID middleware.

Regarding the set-up and the use of an RFID-based laboratory, the head of the research centre needs to create a network of all actors ranging from RFID technology providers (tag provider; reader provider; middleware provider and auxiliary RFID system provider of items such as stack lights, motion sensors, and so on; complementary software providers such as business process management system [BPMS] providers and enterprise resource planning [ERP] providers) to potential users (for example, students, industrial stakeholders).

Indeed, as any RFID system comprises three major technologies, the head of the RFID-based laboratory needs to establish a strong partnership with the firm involved in the design, testing and distribution of different RFID components. Through this partnership, the research centre could act as a bridge between all potential users and all RFID technology providers by putting together all pieces of equipment needed to test a specific application, by enabling potential users to test, learn and trial the technology and allowing the RFID technology providers to refine and adjust their offers to a potential RFID technology adopter. Moreover, the RFID-based laboratory could facilitate the creation of new partnerships between different RFID technology providers (tag provider with reader provider and middleware provider for a specific application), which leads to a bundled RFID system offer to potential customers. For example, some applications in the shipping industry could require RFID tags with higher frequencies for longer range, while RFID tags with low frequencies might be needed to access control applications (Asif and Mandviwalla 2005). To cope with the technological needs of potential users, the diversification issue has to be quickly addressed by the RFID-based laboratory through partnerships.

To be more efficient in this context, the head of an RFID-based laboratory needs to make some choice regarding specialisation. For instance, the University of Cambridge, which is part of the Auto-ID Labs, focuses on the integration of RFID and other identification technologies into industrial environments by developing specific research themes such as: 1) reduction in the uncertainty of RFID deployment; 2) methodologies for tracking and tracing objects; 3) management of product information networks; 4) quantification of the impact of RFID introduction; and 5) RFID integration with sensing and automation systems.[1] On the other hand, the University of Arkansas RFID Research Center (Table 11.3) is trying to use the laboratory to create and extend knowledge in

---

1 From Cambridge Auto-ID Lab web site: <http://www.autoidlabs.org.uk/>

RFID utilisation and its impacts on business and society. Specialisation could foster the development of RFID best practices by industry, sector and application, and thus enable comparisons through collaboration between laboratories.

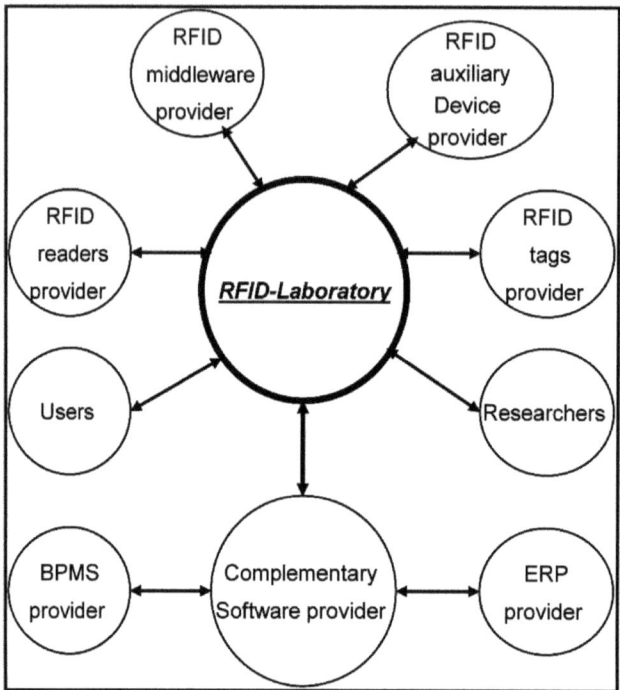

Figure 11.1 Potential stakeholders involved in the set-up and use of an RFID university-based laboratory

Meta-design

Researchers working in an RFID-based laboratory could be regarded as the designers or the integrators of the product artefact (RFID system). Indeed, they need to have the required knowledge to analyse users' needs, identify the required RFID system, install the system, test it and translate 'users' business requirements' into decision rules in the middleware. The key issue here is the designers' capacity to design a product artefact that is flexible enough to meet the various users' needs. For example, by using a motion sensor, designers could use the same gate equipped with an RFID reader to simulate a 'receiving process' (inbound) or a 'shipping process' (outbound) depending on the direction of the movement. Also, they could use BPMS to model and simulate different configurations of the RFID system in order to choose the optimal one. This could help accelerate and enhance the accuracy of component selection as well as the RFID system integration process. To achieve this, they need to rely on some basic communication quality so as to create fruitful exchanges with all RFID-based laboratory stakeholders.

Kernel theories

Given the emerging nature of RFID technology and the wish of stakeholders involved in the project to better understand the technology and assess its impact on their business processes, three theories that could apply to this ISDT have been identified

- business process re-engineering (BPR)
- IT business value and impacts
- IT diffusion theory.

Firms have been facing strong challenges such as market globalisation, aggressive competition, increasing cost pressures, the rise of customised demands with high product variance, the management of short shelf-life groceries and strict traceability requirements. In order to cope with all this, firms have been investing huge amounts of money in IT. These investments do not, however, always lead to improved organisational performance. This phenomenon is better known as the 'IT productivity paradox' (Brynjolfsson and Hitt 1996) and is due to the macroeconomic approach that is being used to assess the impact of IT investments (Oz 2005). Many authors call for the use of an alternative approach—known as the process-oriented approach—which emphasises the evaluation of IT investments at the locus of the impact: 'business process' (Zhu and Kraemer 2002).

'A business process is a set of interrelated activities which have definable inputs and, when executed, result in an output that adds value from a customer's perspective' (Al-Mudimigh 2007:869). BPR or business process management (BPM) aims to improve organisational performance in terms of cost, quality, service and speed (Hammer and Champy 1993; Ulbrich 2006). BPR is considered a key dimension in IT implementation (for example, ERP, integrated standard software packages and enterprise application systems). In fact, in order to grasp the real potential of an emerging IT, the current intra and inter-organisational business process needs to be redesigned before any implementation (Al-Mudimigh 2007). In the same light, Sarker and Lee (2002:10) state that 'IT is the central object of redesign in the redesign process'. Also, the transformational effects of IT investments need to be explored by taking into consideration the firm IT strategy, IT management capability and external environment and industry factors. IT diffusion theory offers important insights into the way in which, and the speed at which, an emerging technology is adopted by the members of a social system (Rogers 2003; Venkatesh et al. 2003)—by considering IT characteristics (for example, complexity, compatibility and relative advantage), organisations' characteristics and the factors that influence the adoption (for example, mandates, centralisation, organisational slack), diffusion process and contextual factors (for example, level of competitiveness, reputation, research and development allocation, technology standardisation) (Damanpour and Schneider 2006; Fichman 1992).

Design method

Many recent studies of RFID technology suggest that it is not a 'plug and play technology' (Fosso Wamba et al. 2008b). To grasp its impacts on firm performance, the integrator needs to focus on the product value chain of the firm, critical activities within that product value chain and core business processes associated with these activities. Based on these prerequisites, the first design method should be focused on the intensive use of a BPMS in order to propose various business process scenarios integrating RFID technology. This could help RFID laboratory integrators to easily transform firm business requirements into 'virtual' RFID laboratory component selection, thus reducing the cost associated with the simulation of each application in the laboratory. The second design method focus implies that integrators need to design the RFID laboratory to be as flexible as possible in order to handle various core business processes from various industries.

Testable design product and design process hypotheses

Based on the proposed kernel theories of this ISDT, the following hypotheses have been formulated

- the RFID university-based laboratory offers a vendor an independent environment for the testing and validation of various scenarios integrating RFID technology (H1)
- the RFID university-based laboratory is a viable means to evaluate the impact of RFID technology on supply-chain process performance (H2)
- the RFID university-based laboratory contributes to accelerating the adoption decision of RFID technology among potential adopters (H3)
- the RFID university-based laboratory acts as an enabler of knowledge transfer among potential users or adopters (H4)
- the RFID university-based laboratory contributes to assessing the user perception of RFID technology complexity (H5).

All these hypotheses can be empirically tested using positivistic and interpretative research methods (Markus et al. 2002; Siponen et al. 2006).

Validation

Our hypotheses have been tested in one RFID university-based laboratory (Figure 11.2). The laboratory uses components from various suppliers (Table 11.4).

On the left side of Figure 11.2, we have an RFID portal, including

- a photo eye (1) for automatic product detection and a trigger to activate two fixed antennas (2), allowing the antennas to be awakened and to transmit radio waves to a fixed reader (3) only where necessary
- the reader captures or updates the information written on the tags (4)
- a stack light (5) linked to the fixed reader allows the confirmation of the status of the readings as the products (or boxes) are passing on the conveyor belts (6).

On the right side of Figure 11.2 are

- an RFID portal (7) with four fixed antennas
- two photo eyes
- one fixed reader similar to those on the left side of Figure 11.2.

The third part of the laboratory comprises an ERP server provided by SAP (8d), two middleware servers where all the business rules are configured (8a, 8b) and one BPMS server from IDS Scheer AG (8c).

The three screens on the walls (9) are provided by the research centre. All the information resulting from transactions is projected here, allowing participants to follow the information flow in real time, as each transaction is automatically performed.

In the context of supply-chain applications, the RFID portal on the left side of Figure 11.2 could be used as the supplier's shipping dock and the RFID portal on the right side of Figure 11.2 as the retailer receiving dock.

This laboratory has been used for teaching purposes and for supply-chain redesign integrating RFID technology in the retailing and utility industries, thus demonstrating its high flexibility and adaptability (H4).

Regarding teaching, the laboratory has been used for courses at the undergraduate and postgraduate levels. The use of the laboratory at the two levels involved the tagging of various products with different characteristics (bottle with water, oil or cream, product with metal, and so on), the testing of the reader's reliability based on the type of product and the orientation of antennas, and the analysis of data capture by the reader in the middleware. Moreover, postgraduate students were involved in the data-collection process and validation. They were also involved in the mapping of existing business processes and the mapping of various scenarios integrating RFID technology using the BPMS tool. This exercise helps to validate the feasibility of business redesign processes integrating RFID technology, to assess their business value at different points of the supply chain and their technological feasibility through iterative discussion with key industrial and technological respondents. Finally, postgraduate students were involved in the demonstration of the integration of information systems (ERP and middleware) and optimisation of business processes in the laboratory. This step demonstrates that the implementation of RFID in the supply chain seems possible in terms of business and according to a technological perspective (H2).

Almost one-third of the students who undertook master's degree programs dealing with RFID technology have chosen to carry out their final projects on this topic. In addition, four of these students have decided to continue their doctoral studies on RFID technology, which highlights the importance of an RFID-based laboratory as a powerful teaching tool.

The laboratory has enabled the actors involved in different supply chains under study to identify opportunities for the optimisation of this technology. At the same time, it has raised the complementary investment that is needed to achieve the potential of RFID technology (IT and warehouse infrastructures, upgrading, employee training and change in management) and the limits of this technology in their specific context (standards, IT integration, security) (H5). After these studies were conducted in the laboratory the actors involved in the retail supply chain decided to conduct a pilot study in their setting (H3), but those from the utility industry were reluctant to move forward with a pilot study in their field. Indeed, the integration of the RFID-based infrastructure in the utility environment calls for a major redesign of their current IT infrastructure and the adoption of a 'new IT layer' from a vendor different to their current, traditional IT vendor. One of the managers involved in the project said: 'We are going to wait for the RFID package from our current IT vendor, so we'll not have to add a new IT layer into our infrastructure, and thus avoid the problems of integration, interoperability and security' (H1). Finally, the results of these studies were presented during numerous conferences, published in leading journals or integrated in book chapters (H4).

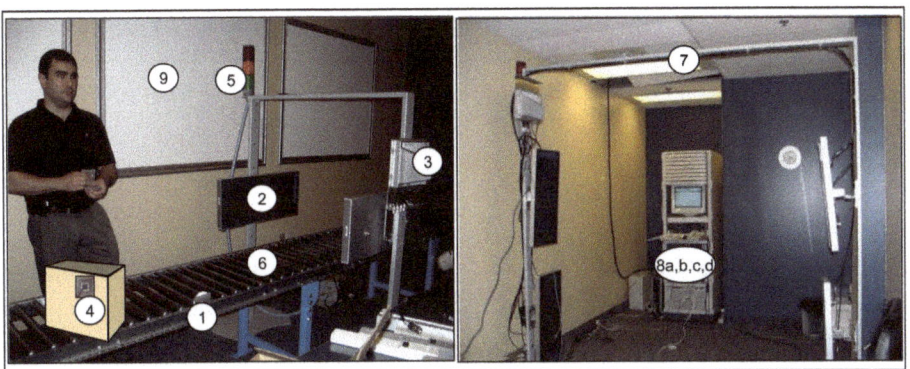

Figure 11.2 ePoly RFID Laboratory

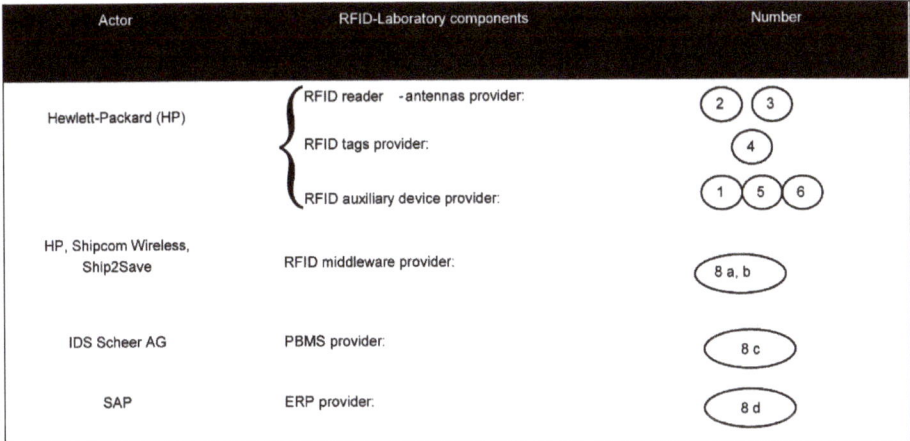

Table 11.4 Major suppliers of the ePoly RFID Laboratory equipment

Conclusion

In this chapter, an ISDT that is fit for the design, implementation and use of an RFID university-based laboratory is being used. The laboratory has been used for academic (teaching and research) and industrial (RFID application testing and validation) purposes. The study offers some insights into the set-up and use of an RFID-based laboratory in university settings and proposes a number of empirically testable hypotheses that are likely to be useful to researchers. The next logical step of this research work could be the validation of our hypotheses using empirical data from pilot studies conducted by firms involved in this study. Finally, in the context of the supply chain, RFID technology can also be considered an 'open innovation'. Indeed, to fully grasp the real value of RFID technology, we saw that members of the supply chain should establish co-development partnerships with various players in the RFID industry. In fact, co-development partnerships are viewed as 'increasingly effective means of innovating the business model to improve innovation effectiveness' (Chesbrough and Schwartz 2007:1).

Acknowledgments

This research has been made possible through the financial contribution of SSHRC, NSERC and FQRSC. We have benefited from the comments and suggestion of Dieudonné Toukam, MA. Also, the authors would like to thank the anonymous referee for his valuable input during the review process of the chapter.

References

Al-Mudimigh, A. S. 2007, 'The role and impact of business process management in enterprise systems implementation', *Business Process Management Journal*, vol. 13, no. 6, pp. 866–74.

Asif, Z. and Mandviwalla, M. 2005, 'Integrating the supply chain with RFID: a technical and business analysis', *Communications of the Association for Information Systems*, vol. 15, pp. 393–427.

Bapna, R., Goes, P. and Gupta, A. 2003, 'Replicating online Yankee auctions to analyze auctioneers' and bidders' strategies', *Information Systems Research*, vol. 14, no. 3, pp. 244–68.

Bapna, R., Goes, P., Gupta, A. and Jin, Y. 2004, 'User heterogeneity and its impact on electronic auction market design: an empirical exploration', *MIS Quarterly*, vol. 28, no. 1, pp. 21–43.

Bardaki, C., Pramatari, K. and Doukidis, G. I. 2007, 'RFID-enabled supply chain collaboration services in a networked retail business environment', *20th Bled eConference eMergence: Merging and Emerging Technologies, Processes, and Institutions*, 4–6 June, Bled, Slovenia.

Bendavid, Y., Lefebvre, É., Lefebvre, L. A. and Fosso Wamba, S. 2007, 'B-to-B ECommerce: assessing the impacts of RFID technology in a five layer supply chain', *Proceedings of HICSS, B-to-B E-Commerce Mini-Track*, Computer Society Press, IEEE, Hawai'i.

Brynjolfsson, E. and Hitt, L. M. 1996, 'Paradox lost? Firm-level evidence on the returns to information systems spending', *Management Science*, vol. 42, no. 4, pp. 541–58.

Burnell, J. 2008, 50+ RFID labs and test centers identified worldwide, <http://www.rfidupdate.com/articles/index.php?id=1528>

Chesbrough, H. and Schwartz, K. 2007, 'Innovating business models with co-development partnerships', *Research Technology Management*, vol. 50, no. 1, pp. 55–9.

Curtin, J., Kauffman, R. J. and Riggins, F. J. 2007, 'Making the most out of RFID technology: a research agenda for the study of the adoption, usage and impact of RFID', *Information Technology and Management*, vol. 8, no. 2, pp. 87–110.

Damanpour, F. and Schneider, M. 2006, 'Phases of the adoption of innovation in organizations: effects of environment, organization, and top managers', *British Journal of Management*, vol. 17, no. 3, pp. 215–36.

Datta, S., Granger, C. W. J, Barari, M. and Gibbs, T. 2007, 'Management of supply chain: an alternative modelling technique for forecasting', *Journal of the Operational Research Society*, vol. 58, pp. 1459–69.

Fan, M., Stallaert, J. and Whinston, A. B. 2003, 'Decentralized mechanism design for supply chain organization using an auction market', *Information System Research*, vol. 14, pp. 1–22.

Fichman, R. G. 1992, *Information technology diffusion: a review of empirical research*, Working Paper, MIT Sloan School of Management, Cambridge, Mass.

Fosso Wamba, S. and Boeck, H. 2008, 'Enhancing information flow in a retail supply chain using RFID and the EPC network: a proof-of-concept approach', *Journal of Theoretical and Applied Electronic Commerce Research, Special Issue on RFID and Supply Chain Management*, vol. 3, no. 1, pp. 93–105.

Fosso Wamba, S., Lefebvre, L. A., Bendavid, Y. and Lefebvre, É. 2008a, 'Exploring the impact of RFID and the EPC network on mobile B2B ECommerce: a case study in the retail industry', *International Journal of Production Economics, Special Issue on RFID: Technology, Applications, and Impact on Business Operations*, vol. 112, no. 2, pp. 614–29.

Fosso Wamba, S., Lefebvre, É., Bendavid, Y. and Lefebvre, L. A. 2008b, 'From automatic identification and data capture (AIDC) to "smart business process":

preparing for a pilot integrating RFID', in Syed Ahson and Mohammad Ilyas (eds), *RFID Handbook: Applications, technology, security, and privacy*, CRC Press Taylor & Francis Group, London.

Goldkuhl, G. 2004, 'Design theories in information systems—a need for multigrounding', *Journal of Information Technology Theory and Application*, vol. 6, no. 2, pp. 59–72.

Gregor, S. 2002, 'Design theory in information systems', *Australian Journal of Information Systems, Special Issue*, pp. 14–22.

Gregor, S. 2006, 'The nature of theory in information systems', *MIS Quarterly*, vol. 30, no. 3, pp. 611–42.

Hammer, M. and Champy, J. 1993, *Reengineering the Corporation*, Harper Business, New York.

Jones, D., Gregor, S. and Lynch, T. 2003, 'An information systems design theory for web-based education', *Proceedings of the IASTED International Symposium on Web-Based Education*.

Katina, M. and Luke, M. 2005, 'The pros and cons of RFID in supply chain management', *International Conference on Mobile Business (ICMB'05)*, pp. 623–629.

Kourouthanassis, P. E. 2006, A design theory for pervasive information systems, <http://www.eltrun.aueb.gr/eltrun/phd-studies/completed-phds/phd-thesis-title-a-design-theory-for-pervasive-information-systems-1/>

Levina, N. and Ross, J. W. 2003, 'From the vendor's perspective: exploring the value proposition in information technology outsourcing', *MIS Quarterly*, vol. 27, no. 3, pp. 331–364.

Loebbecke, C. 2007, 'Piloting RFID along the supply chain: a case analysis', *Electronic Markets*, vol. 17, no. 1, pp. 29–38.

Markus, M. L., Majchrzak, A. and Gasser, L. 2002, 'A design theory for systems that support emergent knowledge processes', *MIS Quarterly*, vol. 26, pp. 179–212.

Martin, A. 2004, 'Addressing the gap between theory and practice: IT project design', *Journal of Information Technology Theory and Application*, vol. 6, no. 2, pp. 23–42.

Mickle, M. H. 2007, 'Establishment of the University of Pittsburgh RFID Center of Excellence', *IEEE Applications and Practice Magazine*, vol. 45, no. 4, pp. 14–16.

Ngai, E. W. T., Cheng, T. C. E., Au, S. and Lai, K.-H. 2007, 'Mobile commerce integrated with RFID technology in a container depot', *Decision Support Systems*, vol. 43, no. 1, pp. 62–76.

Oz, E. 2005, 'Information technology productivity: in search of a definite observation', *Information & Management*, vol. 42, pp. 789–98.

Poirier, C. and McCollum, D. 2006, *RFID Strategic Implementation and ROI: A practical roadmap to success*, J. Ross Publishing, Fort Lauderdale, Fla.

RFID Research Center 2008, Mission, vision, history, <http://itri.uark.edu/118.asp>

Riggins, F. J. and Slaughter, K. T. 2006, 'The role of collective mental models in IOS adoption: opening the black box of rationality in RFID deployment', *Proceedings of the 39th Hawaii International Conference on System Sciences*.

Roberti, M. 2006a, 'Sensing new RFID opportunities', *RFIDJournal*, <http://www.rfidjournal.com/article/articleview/2081/>

Roberti, M. 2006b, 'Alien opens Dayton RFID Lab', <http://www.rfidjournal.com/article/view/2140/1/1>

Roberts, C. M. 2006, 'Radio frequency identification (RFID)', *Computers & Security*, vol. 25, no. 1, pp. 18–26.

Rogers, E. M. 2003, *Diffusion of Innovations*, The Free Press, New York.

SAIT 2008, New applications for radio frequency identification to be developed in SAIT's 'RAD Lab', <http://www.sait.ca/pages/research/index.shtml>

Sarker, S. and Lee, A. S. 2002, 'Using a positivist case research methodology to test three competing theories-in-use of business process redesign', *Journal of the Association for Information Systems*, vol. 2, no. 7, pp. 1–72.

Siponen, M., Baskerville, R. and Heikka, J. 2006, 'A design theory for secure information systems design methods', *Journal of the Association for Information Systems*, vol. 7, no. 11, pp. 725–70.

Srivastava, B. 2004, 'Radio frequency ID technology: the next revolution in SCM', *Business Horizons*, vol. 47, no. 6, pp. 60–8.

Subramani, M. R. 2004, 'How do suppliers benefit from information technology use in supply chain relationship?', *MIS Quarterly*, vol. 28, pp. 45–73.

TSTC Waco 2008, TSTC Waco receives $305 000 for RFID training facility, <http://www.waco.tstc.edu/ct/>

Ulbrich, F. 2006, 'Improving shared service implementation: adopting lessons from the BPR movement', *Business Process Management Journal*, vol. 12, no. 2, pp. 191–205.

Venkatesh, V., Morris, M. G., Davis, G. B. and Davis, F. D. 2003, 'User acceptance of information technology: toward a unified view', *MIS Quarterly*, vol. 27, no. 3, pp. 425–78.

Vijayaraman, B. S. and Osyk, B. A. 2006, 'An empirical study of RFID implementation in the warehousing industry', *The International Journal of Logistics Management*, vol. 17, no. 1, pp. 6–20.

Walls, J. G., Widmeyer, G. R. and El Sawy, O. 1992, 'Building an information system design theory for vigilant EIS', *Information Systems Research*, vol. 3, no. 1, pp. 36–59.

Walls, J. G., Widmeyer, G. R. and El Sawy, O. A. 2004, 'Assessing information system design theory in perspective: how useful was our 1992 initial rendition?', *Journal of Information Technology Theory and Application*, vol. 6, no. 2, pp. 43–58.

Wyld, D. C. 2006, 'RFID 101: the next big thing for management', *Management Research News*, vol. 29, no. 4, pp. 154–73.

Zhu, K. and Kraemer, K. L. 2002, 'E-commerce Metrics for net-enhanced organizations: assessing the value of e-commerce to firm performance in the manufacturing sector', *Information Systems Research*, vol. 13, no. 3, pp. 275–95.

Design Science in IS

12. An assessment of DSS design science using the Hevner, March, Park and Ram guidelines

DAVID ARNOTT
MONASH UNIVERSITY

GRAHAM PERVAN
CURTIN UNIVERSITY OF TECHNOLOGY

Abstract

Design science has been an important strategy in decision support systems (DSS) research since the inception of the field in the early 1970s. Recent reviews of DSS research have indicated a need to improve its quality and relevance. DSS design science has an important role in this improvement as design science can engage industry and the profession in intellectually important projects. The 2004 publication of the Hevner, March, Park and Ram (HMPR) guidelines for the conduct and assessment of information systems design science provides a vehicle for assessing DSS design science. This chapter presents research that uses bibliometric content analysis to apply the HMPR guidelines to a representative sample of DSS design-science papers in 14 journals. The analysis highlights issues that need attention—notably, evaluation, research design, strategic focus and theorising. Comments are also offered on the experience of applying the HMPR guidelines to a large body of research.

Introduction

Decision support systems (DSS) is the area of the information systems (IS) discipline that is focused on systems that support and improve managerial decision making in terms of contemporary professional practice. Arnott and Pervan (2008) identify seven DSS types that are separated by technology, theory foundations, user populations and decision tasks.

- *Personal Decision Support Systems (PDSS)* are usually small-scale systems that are developed for one manager, or a small number of independent managers, to support a decision task. Perhaps the oldest DSS type, PDSS remains important in practice, especially in the form of user-built models and data-analysis systems (Arnott 2008).
- *Group Support Systems (GSS)* 'consists of a set of software, hardware, and language components and procedures that support a group of people engaged in a decision-related meeting' (Huber 1984). GSS are typically implemented as electronic meeting systems (EMS) (Dennis et al. 1988) or group decision systems (GDS) (Pervan and Atkinson 1995).
- *Negotiation Support Systems (NSS)* are DSS that operate in a group context, but, as the name suggests, they involve the application of information technology (IT) to facilitate negotiations (Rangaswamy and Shell 1997). As the group members in NSS are opposing parties, NSS has had to be developed on a different theory foundation to that of GSS.
- *Intelligent Decision Support Systems (IDSS)* involve the application of artificial intelligence techniques to decision support. IDSS can be classed into two generations: the first involves the use of rule-based expert systems for decision support, and the second uses neural networks, genetic algorithms and fuzzy logic (Turban et al. 2005).
- *Knowledge Management-Based DSS (KMDSS)* are systems that support decision making by aiding knowledge storage, retrieval, transfer and application. KMDSS can support individual and organisational memory and inter-group knowledge access (Burstein and Carlsson 2008).
- *Data Warehousing (DW)* provides the large-scale data infrastructure for decision support. In general terms, a data warehouse is a set of databases created to provide information to decision makers. In practice, data warehousing includes enterprise data warehouses, data marts and applications that extract, transform and load (ETL) data into the data warehouse or mart (Watson 2001).
- *Enterprise Reporting and Analysis Systems (ERAS)* are enterprise-scale systems that include executive information systems (EIS), online analytical processing systems (OLAP), business intelligence (BI) and, more recently, corporate performance management systems (CPM). BI tools access and analyse data warehouse information using predefined reporting software, query tools and analysis tools (Nelson et al. 2005).

In the nearly four decades of its history, DSS has moved from a radical movement that changed the way information systems were perceived in business to a mainstream commercial IT movement that all organisations engage. During this time, DSS has continued to be a significant sub-field of IS scholarship.

Design science is an alternative—or a complement—to the natural science approach that is dominant in IS research. In design science, the researcher 'creates and evaluates IT artifacts intended to solve identified organisational problems' (Hevner et al. 2004:77). March and Smith (1995:253) clearly draw a distinction between natural and design science: 'Whereas natural science tries to understand reality, design science attempts to create things that serve human purposes.' Design science is particularly relevant for contemporary IS research because it could help researchers confront two of the major challenges of the discipline: the role of the IT artefact in IS research (Orlikowski and Iacono 2001) and the low level of professional relevance of many IS studies (Benbasat and Zmud 1999). The terminology of design science is gaining momentum in IS. March and Smith (1995) were the first major users of the term in IS, although 'design theory' was used earlier (Walls et al. 1992). The landmark publication is Hevner et al. (2004), who proposed a set of seven guidelines to assess design-science research in IS. The publication of the guidelines in *MIS Quarterly* is particularly symbolic. A prescriptive design-science methods paper in the most cited IS journal will be influential with journal editors and reviewers, and it is also likely to be used by PhD examiners for IS design-science theses.

DSS research has a long history of using design-science strategies and many of the early DSS projects involved designing and implementing innovative IT-based systems (for example, Meador and Ness 1974; Keen and Gambino 1983). General reviews of DSS research have pointed to a need to increase the rigour of DSS design-science research (Arnott and Pervan 2005, 2008). One way to improve the quality of DSS design science—and to improve its contribution to general IS research—is to systematically review published projects and identify strategies for improvement. That is the goal of this chapter.

Research method and design

There are two fundamental strategies for literature analysis. The first—thematic analysis—involves classifying and analysing papers according to themes that are relevant to the theory and practice goals of a research project (Webster and Watson 2002). Thematic analysis is by far the most common form of literature review in journal papers and theses. The second fundamental strategy is bibliometrics, which involves the measurement of publication patterns. The two most common bibliometric methods are citation analysis (Osareh 1996) and content analysis (Weber 1990). In DSS literature analysis, Sean Eom's series of studies has used citation analysis to analyse the intellectual structure of the field (Eom 1995, 1996, 1999; Eom and Lee 1990, 1993). In bibliometrics, content analysis involves the coding and analysis of a representative sample of research articles. In this approach, data capture is driven by a protocol that can have both quantitative and qualitative aspects. This form of data capture is a very labour-intensive process but it has the advantage that it can illuminate the deep structure of the field in a way that is impossible to achieve with other literature analysis approaches. This research adopted a content analysis method to help understand the nature of DSS design-science research and to assess its strengths and weaknesses.

The sample of articles for this project is DSS research published between 1990 and 2005 in the 14 journals shown in Table 12.1. We adopted a large set of quality journals as a basis of the sample because we believe that this best represents the invisible college of DSS research. Previous analyses of IS research have used a similar sampling approach (Alavi and Carlson 1992; Benbasat and Nault 1990; Pervan 1998; Chen and Hirschheim 2004). Alavi and Carlson (1992) used eight North American journals for their sample. Webster and Watson (2002) have, however, criticised the over emphasis on North American journals in review papers. In response, we included five European IS journals (*Information Systems Journal, European Journal of Information Systems, Information and Organization, Journal of Information Technology* and *Journal of Strategic Information Systems*) in our sample. Following Chen and Hirschheim (2004), the classification of a journal as US or European is based largely on the location of the publisher.

The quality of journals was classified as 'A' level or 'Other'. This classification is based on publications that address journal ranking (Gillenson and Stutz 1991; Hardgrave and Walstrom 1997; Hirschheim 1992; Holsapple et al. 1994; Mylonopoulo and Theoharakis 2001; Walstrom et al. 1995; Whitman et al. 1999) and on discussions with journal editors and senior IS academics. Another indicator of journal quality is the Thomson ISI journal impact factor. The 2006 impact factors for 13 of the 14 journals in the sample are shown in Table 12.1. *Information & Organization* is not in the Thomson ISI index.

The selection of the journal sample was the first stage in arriving at the DSS design-science sample. An overview of the sampling process is shown in Figure 12.1.

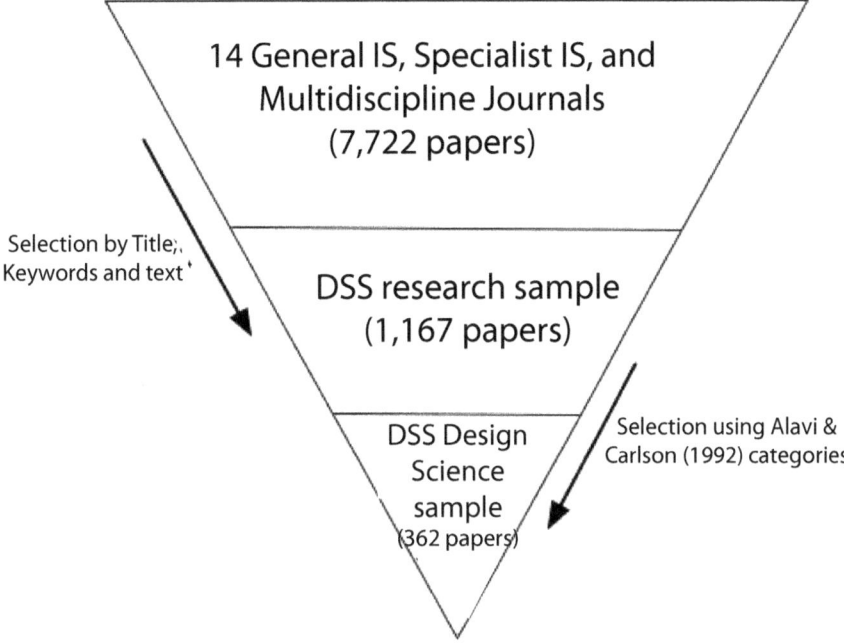

Figure 12.1 Arriving at the DSS design-science sample

The first stage of article sampling was to identify the DSS articles in the 14 journals. The papers were initially selected electronically by examining keywords and titles. A manual check was performed of the table of contents of each issue of each journal. In addition, the text of each potential article for analysis was examined to verify its decision support content in terms of definition of DSS provided above. This procedure identified 1167 DSS papers. Table 1.1 shows the distribution of the DSS papers in the sample by journal. Overall, 15.1 per cent of published papers in the 14 journals between 1990 and 2005 were in the DSS field. When only the general IS journals in the sample are examined, the proportion of DSS articles increases to 18.9 per cent. Each of these measures indicates that DSS is an important part of the IS discipline.

Table 12.1 DSS and DSS design-science article samples by journal

Journal	Origin	Ranking (ISI impact factor)	Journal orientation	No of DSS articles published	DSS design-science articles published	DSS design-science articles as a % of published DSS articles
Decision Sciences (DS)	US	A (1.620)	Multi-discipline	67	19	28.4
Decision Support Systems (DSS)	US	A (1.160)	General IS	500	247	49.4
European Journal of Information Systems (EJIS)	Europe	A (0.862)	General IS	25	5	20.0
Group Decision and Negotiation (GD&N)	US	Other (0.429)	Specialist IS	139	24	17.3
Information and Management (I&M)	US	A (2.119)	General IS	104	13	12.5
Information and Organization (I&O)	Europe	Other (not abstracted)	General IS	16	1	6.3
Information Systems Journal (ISJ)	Europe	A (1.543)	General IS	16	1	6.3
Information Systems Research (ISR)	US	A (2.537)	General IS	34	5	14.7
Journal of Information Technology (JIT)	Europe	A (1.239)	General IS	25	2	8.0
Journal of Management Information Systems (JMIS)	US	A (1.818)	General IS	84	18	21.4
Journal of Organizational Computing and Electronic Commerce (JOC&EC)	US	Other (0.500)	Specialist IS	73	12	16.4
Journal of Strategic Information Systems (JSIS)	Europe	Other (0.971)	General IS	8	1	12.5
Management Science (MS)	US	A (1.687)	Multi-discipline	41	13	31.7
MIS Quarterly (MISQ)	US	A (4.731)	General IS	35	1	2.9
Total				1167	362	31.0

12. An assessment of DSS design science using the Hevner, March, Park and Ram guidelines

Each of the 1167 papers was coded using the Alavi and Carlson (1992) taxonomy, as modified by Pervan (1998) to include action research and to distinguish between positivist and interpretative case studies. The result of this coding is shown in Table 12.2. The papers from the article types—'Tools, techniques, methods, model application', 'Conceptual frameworks and their application', 'Description of type or class of product', 'Technology, systems, etc.', 'Description of specific application, system, etc.' and 'Action rwesearch'—were inspected by both researchers to see if they met the design-science research definition of Hevner et al. (2004). In particular, each paper was inspected for a focus on an innovative artefact, rather than providing a description of an existing commercial product. This yielded a DSS design-science sample of 362 papers. This sample shows the importance of design science to DSS scholarship, as design science is the strategy of 31 per cent of DSS papers. To help identify trends in DSS design-science research, we divided the sample into four four-year eras: 1990–93, 1994–97, 1998–2001 and 2002–05.

The 362 DSS design-science papers were then coded using the protocol shown in Appendix 12.1. The protocol was based on the guidelines proposed by Hevner et al. (2004). The time taken to code each article varied from 20 minutes to more than one hour. To ensure coding validity, both researchers coded each paper; disagreements in coding were discussed and resolved. An important aspect of coding validity is that the two researchers have decades of experience in the DSS area, are experienced journal reviewers and editors and have published DSS design-science projects (for example, Arnott 2004, 2006).

Table 12.2 The DSS and DSS design-science samples by article type

		Article type	DSS (no.)	Papers (% of sample)	DSS (no.)	Design (% of sample)	Science (% of DSS)
Non-empirical	Conceptual orientation	DSS frameworks	53	4.5	0	0.0	0.0
		Conceptual models	30	2.6	0	0.0	0.0
		Conceptual overview	49	4.2	0	0.0	0.0
		Theory	22	1.9	0	0.0	0.0
	Illustrative	Opinion and example	22	1.9	0	0.0	0.0
		Opinion and personal experience	5	0.4	0	0.0	0.0
		Tools, techniques, methods, model applications	148	12.7	92	25.4	62.2
	Applied concepts	Conceptual frameworks and their application	69	5.9	41	11.3	60.3

Empirical	Objects	Description of type or class of product, technology, systems, etc.	39	3.3	27	7.5	69.2
		Description of specific application, system, etc.	215	18.4	199	55.0	92.6
	Events/ processes	Lab experiment	209	17.9	0	0.0	0.0
		Field experiment	19	1.6	0	0.0	0.0
		Field study	37	3.2	0	0.0	0.0
		Positivist case study	64	5.5	0	0.0	0.0
		Interpretative case study	37	3.2	0	0.0	0.0
		Action research	6	0.5	3	0.8	50.0
		Survey	77	6.6	0	0.0	0.0
		Development of DSS instrument	4	0.3	0	0.0	0.0
		Secondary data	28	2.4	0	0.0	0.0
		Simulation	34	2.9	0	0.0	0.0
Total			1167		362		31.0

An analysis of DSS design-science research

In this section, we present the analysis of the papers in the DSS design-science sample. First, some observations are made about the general nature of DSS design science. This is followed by a detailed analysis of the sample using the guidelines proposed by Hevner et al. (2004)—the 'HMPR guidelines'.

'Design science' in DSS design science

As mentioned in the introduction, the term 'design science' is relatively new to IS research. The definition used to identify DSS design-science research was taken from Hevner et al. (2004:77), who stated that the design-science researcher 'creates and evaluates IT artifacts intended to solve identified organisational problems'. March and Smith (1995) argue that design science must be technology oriented.

In terms of this project, authors do not need to explicitly call their research 'design science' for it to be retrospectively identified as design science. In our sample, only six papers (1.7 per cent) mentioned the term design science. This means that the authors of 356 papers (98.3 per cent) either were not aware of design science or did not identify their work as design science. Where authors did identify an overall research strategy, they mostly used terms such as 'description', 'development', 'design' and 'implementation', as shown in Table 1.3. The term 'development' was used in 18 of the 42 papers identified (either on its own or in combination with other terms, including 'implementation', 'design', 'description', 'assessment' and 'validation'). 'Description' was used in 13 papers (on its own or with 'demonstration', 'implementation' and 'development'). 'Design' was utilised in six papers, 'implementation' in four papers and 'demonstration/demonstrate' in three papers.

Table 12.3 Non 'design science' descriptors in DSS design-science research

	Frequency	Percentage of sample
Description	10	2.8
Development	7	1.9
Design	2	0.6
Development and implementation	2	0.6
Design and implementation	2	0.6
Design and development	2	0.6
Exploratory systems development	2	0.6
Action research	2	0.6
Description and demonstration	1	0.6
Description of implementation	1	0.3
Description of development	1	0.3
Design, development and assessment	1	0.3
Development and validation	1	0.3
Systems development	1	0.3
Theory development and implementation	1	0.3
Implementation	1	0.3
Demonstration	1	0.3
Propose-present-demonstrate	1	0.3
Application of model and method	1	0.3
Case study	1	0.3
Decision analysis	1	0.3
Total	**42**	**13.4**

To further understand this issue, we examined the citations in the sample of foundational design-science papers. The frequency of citation of these papers is shown in Table 12.4. This confirms the overall impression of the method identification statistics, with only 3 per cent of DSS design-science papers citing these foundational papers.

Table 12.4 Design-science citations in DSS research

Reference	Frequency
Simon (1996 or earlier), The Sciences of the Artificial	3
Walls et al. (1992), ISR	3
Gero (1990), AI Magazine	1
Hevner et al. (2004), MISQ	1
March and Smith (1995), DSS	1
Nunamaker et al. (1991), JMIS	1
Whyte (1989), Sociological Forum	1
None	351 (97%)
Total	362

The literature analysis suggests that the term design science has had little impact in DSS research. Even papers authored by researchers that are leading the design-science movement in IS have not cited design-science reference works or mentioned design science as the method (for example, Berndt et al. 2003). This could be an artefact of journal reviewing practices in which editors and reviewers prefer terms other than design science to describe a paper's overall research strategies.

HMPR guideline 1: the design artefact

The first HMPR guideline concerns the design artefact. Hevner et al. (2004:Table 1)—following the definitions of March and Smith (1995)—state: 'Design-science research must produce a viable artifact in the form of a construct, a model, a method, or an instantiation.' The coding of the DSS sample yielded 396 artefacts. Thirty-four papers contained significant secondary artefacts in addition to their primary products. The results of the coding are shown in Table 12.5.

Table 12.5 Design artefacts in DSS design-science research (primary and secondary)

Design artefact	1990–93		1994–97		1998–2001		2002–05		Total	
	(no.)	(%)	(no.)	(%)	(no.)	(%)	(no.)	(%)	(no.)	(%)
Construct	0	0.0	0	0.0	1	1.2	1	0.9	2	0.5
Model	7	9.3	9	7.1	5	5.9	7	6.4	28	7.1
Method	12	16.0	34	27.0	18	21.2	39	35.5	103	26.0
Instantiation	56	74.7	83	65.9	61	71.8	63	57.3	263	66.4
Total	75		126		85		110		396	

Clearly, the focus in DSS research over all periods has been on instantiations; they constitute close to two-thirds of all artefacts. High-quality examples of these instantiation artefacts include R-EIS, a repository-based executive information system (Chen 1995), and PUZZLE, a strategic business intelligence system

(Rouibah and Ould-ali 2002). In a positive sign of a maturing field, however, the development of methods has increased to 35.5 per cent of design artefacts in the most recent period. An example of a high-quality method artefact in this period is the multi-agent design for a DSS in Hall et al. (2005).

HMPR guideline 2: problem relevance

The second HMPR guideline addresses problem relevance. Hevner et al. (2004:Table 1) define the second guideline, saying that '[t]he objective of design-science research is to develop technology-based solutions to important and relevant business problems'. Unfortunately, Hevner et al. provide no guidance on how to assess or categorise the 'importance' and 'relevance' constructs.

To operationalise 'importance' in this project, we used the well-accepted concept of a hierarchy of management processes and activities (Anthony 1965). Anthony's framework divides management activities into a hierarchy of importance to the organisation from strategic, through tactical, to operational. Table 12.6 presents the primary focus of the DSS papers over time using Anthony's management activities. The table reveals that the focus has varied a little over time and has been mostly at the operational level (75.7 per cent). Overall, only 10.5 per cent of papers involved artefacts that had a strategic focus or impact.

Table 12.6 The importance of business problems in DSS design-science research

	1990–93		1994–97		1998–2001		2002–05		Total	
	(no.)	(%)	(no.)	(%)	(no.)	(%)	(no.)	(%)	(no.)	(%)
Strategic	3	4.2	12	10.4	14	18.2	9	9.2	38	10.5
Tactical	14	19.4	15	13.0	10	13.0	11	11.2	50	13.8
Operational	55	76.4	88	76.5	53	68.8	78	79.6	274	75.7
Total	72		115		77		98		362	

Further analysis of importance across DSS types revealed that the operational focus was consistently high across personal DSS, GSS, ERAS, IDSS and NSS. In contrast, however, KMS were mostly tactical (71.4 per cent). An example of design-science research with a tactical impact is KNOVA, a knowledge-based DSS for radiologists (Holden and Wilhelmij 1995–96). In concert with the general sample, few KMS were focused on the strategic level. A high-quality exception is an IDSS for strategic alignment in manufacturing (Kathuria et al. 1999).

The relevance of each paper was coded on a scale of high, medium and low. The relevance of DSS design-science research was assessed with respect to two main target audiences: IS practitioners and managerial users. In coding 'relevance', we erred on the generous side—that is, when a decision between categories was difficult, we coded the paper in the category of higher relevance. The result of the coding is shown in Tables 12.7 and 12.8.

Table 12.7 The relevance of DSS design-science research to IS practitioners

	1990–93		1994–97		1998–2001		2002–05		Total	
	(no.)	(%)	(no.)	(%)	(no.)	(%)	(no.)	(%)	(no.)	(%)
High	3	4.2	5	4.3	2	2.6	5	5.1	15	4.1
Medium	19	26.4	29	25.2	28	36.4	26	26.5	102	28.2
Low	50	69.4	81	70.4	47	61.0	67	68.4	245	67.7
Total	72		115		77		98		362	

Table 12.7 shows that the relevance scores for IS practitioners have been relatively stable over time. IS practitioner relevance was mostly low in the first period (69.4 per cent in the low-relevance category) and has remained at that level over time. Very few articles (4.1 per cent overall) were rated to be of high relevance to IS practitioners. The story for managerial users in Table 12.8 is a little better, with 23.8 per cent of the papers rated high in managerial relevance and 'only' 41.4 per cent coded as low relevance. The levels of managerial relevance have also been quite stable over time. A further cross-tabulation of IS practitioner relevance against managerial user relevance reveals that only nine of the 362 papers were highly relevant to both groups. The repository-based EIS, R-EIS (Chen 1995), is one example of this high-scoring group.

A further analysis of IS practitioner relevance over the different DSS types showed better relevance ratings for ERAS (53.8 per cent or seven-thirteenths of low relevance), DW systems (25 per cent or one-quarter low relevance) and KMS (28.6 per cent or two-sevenths low relevance)—although it should be noted that the number of papers of these types is quite small. A similar analysis of managerial user relevance revealed that papers on ERAS, KMS and NSS were of greater relevance to managerial users than other types of DSS.

Table 12.8 The relevance of DSS design-science research to managerial users

	1990–93		1994–97		1998–2001		2002–05		Total	
	(no.)	(%)	(no.)	(%)	(no.)	(%)	(no.)	(%)	(no.)	(%)
High	14	19.4	28	24.3	21	27.3	23	23.5	86	23.8
Medium	24	33.3	33	28.7	30	39.0	39	39.8	126	34.8
Low	34	47.2	54	47.0	26	33.8	36	36.7	150	41.4
Total	72		115		77		98		362	

HMPR guideline 3: design evaluation

The third HMPR guideline concerns the evaluation of the design artefacts. Hevner et al. (2004:Table 1) define this guideline, saying, 'The utility, quality, and efficacy of a design artifact must be rigorously demonstrated via well-executed evaluation methods.' The coding of the DSS design-science papers for this guideline was based on the evaluation taxonomy presented by Hevner et al. (2004:Table 2). The result of this coding is shown in Table 12.9.

Table 12.9 Evaluation methods in DSS design-science research

		1990–93		1994–97		1998–2001		2002–05		Total	
		(no.)	(%)	(no.)	(%)	(no.)	(%)	(no.)	(%)	(no.)	(%)
Observational	Case study	6	8.3	10	8.7	13	16.9	13	13.3	42	11.6
	Field study	1	1.4	0	0.0	3	3.9	3	3.1	7	1.9
Analytical	Static	0	0.0	0	0.0	1	1.3	0	0.0	1	0.3
	Architecture	0	0.0	1	0.9	0	0.0	0	0.0	1	0.3
	Optimisation	0	0.0	0	0.0	0	0.0	0	0.0	0	0.0
	Dynamic	0	0.0	0	0.0	0	0.0	0	0.0	0	0.0
Experimental	Controlled experiment	1	1.4	4	3.5	5	6.5	5	5.1	15	4.1
	Simulation	14	19.4	17	14.8	17	22.1	26	26.5	74	20.4
Testing	Functional	0	0.0	2	1.7	0	0.0	2	2.0	4	1.1
	Structural	0	0.0	0	0.0	0	0.0	1	1.0	1	0.3
Descriptive	Informed argument	0	0.0	3	2.6	2	2.6	2	2.0	7	1.9
	Scenarios	13	18.1	21	18.3	8	10.4	15	15.3	57	15.7
None		37	51.4	57	49.6	28	36.4	31	31.6	153	42.3

Surprisingly, overall, 42.3 per cent of papers were coded as 'none'. This means that the focus of the paper was the presentation and description of an artefact without any attempt to establish its worth, effectiveness or usefulness. This large proportion of un-evaluated projects is a major problem for DSS design science. Over time, the situation is improving—from 51.4 per cent coded as 'none' in the first period to 31.6 per cent in the most recent period. However, 31.6 per cent 'none' is still a very poor result for the discipline. A further analysis of evaluation method against DSS type revealed that 'none' was coded noticeably more often for GSS (54.9 per cent) but less often for IDSS (29.8 per cent).

Of the papers that did include an evaluation of the artefact, three approaches dominated: simulation at 20.4 per cent of the sample, scenarios at 15.7 per cent and case study at 11.6 per cent—with another, controlled experiment, significant at 4.1 per cent. The other evaluation approaches identified by Hevner et al. (2004) are either hardly used or not used at all. Interestingly, only 13.5 per cent of papers evaluated their artefacts in the field. A further analysis of evaluation method by DSS type was performed but was limited to studies where an evaluation was in fact undertaken. This analysis showed that

- PDSS were evaluated mostly by simulation (37.1 per cent) (for example, Hall et al. 2005), scenarios (28.9 per cent) (for example, Balbo and Pinson 2005) and case studies (18.6 per cent) (for example, Tavana and Banerjee 1995)
- GSS were evaluated mostly by case studies (34.8 per cent) (for example, Dennis et al. 2003; de Vreede and Dickson 2000),[1] controlled experiments (21.7 per cent) (for example, Zhang et al. 2005) and scenarios (17.4 per cent) (for example, Moreno-Jiminez et al. 2005)
- three of the ERAS papers from the eight evaluated used scenarios (for example, Chen 1995)
- for DW, only one study was evaluated and it used a case study (Sen and Sen 2005)
- IDSS were evaluated mostly by simulation (50 per cent) (for example, Walczak 2001), followed by scenarios (14.2 per cent) (for example, Kathuria et al. 1999)
- KMS (only four papers) were all evaluated by case studies (for example, Holden and Wilhelmij 1995–96)
- NSS (only six papers) were evaluated by scenarios (66.7 per cent) (for example, Kuula 1998) or case studies (33.3 per cent) (for example, Noakes et al. 2005).

The third HMPR guideline stresses rigour in evaluation via well-executed methods. Table 12.9 and the associated analysis by DSS type show the presence or absence of evaluation, but not the quality of evaluation. To analyse the quality of evaluation, each paper that undertook some form of evaluation was first coded for the appropriateness of the evaluation method to the objects of the study and the nature of the artefact. Second, the quality of the execution of the evaluation method in each paper was assessed on a scale of high, medium and low. Like the coding strategy used for Tables 12.7 and 12.8, here, evaluation method choice and execution quality were assessed generously. Tables 12.10 and 12.11 contain these assessments for those DSS papers in which an evaluation method was used.

---

1 Note that this paper in fact used an action research approach for evaluation but had to be classified as case study because the HMPR guidelines did not include action research as an evaluation method.

Table 12.10 The choice of evaluation method in DSS design-science research

	1990–93		1994–97		1998–2001		2002–05		Total	
	(no.)	(%)	(no.)	(%)	(no.)	(%)	(no.)	(%)	(no.)	(%)
Highly appropriate	16	45.7	25	43.1	36	73.5	38	56.7	115	55.0
Adequate	18	51.4	32	55.2	12	24.5	28	41.8	90	43.1
Poor	1	2.9	1	1.7	1	2.0	1	1.5	4	1.9
Total	35		58		49		67		209	

In each era, when evaluation did occur, the level of appropriateness of the evaluation method choice was at least 'adequate'. This indicates that researchers who evaluate artefacts are making reasonable choices in terms of method. Over time, the quality of the choice of evaluation method has been a little variable, but there is no significant trend in the coding.

Table 12.11 The quality of evaluation execution in DSS design-science research

	1990–93		1994–97		1998–2001		2002–05		Total	
	(no.)	(%)	(no.)	(%)	(no.)	(%)	(no.)	(%)	(no.)	(%)
High	5	14.3	16	27.6	13	26.5	23	34.3	57	27.3
Medium	17	48.6	24	41.4	26	53.1	34	50.7	101	48.3
Low	13	37.1	18	31.0	10	20.4	10	14.9	51	24.4
Total	35		58		49		67		209	

Table 12.11 shows that in each era, when evaluation was conducted, the quality of evaluation was mostly medium to high. This indicates that those researchers are doing a reasonable job in conducting the evaluation. Further, the proportion of low-quality execution has steadily decreased—from 37.1 per cent in 1990–93 to only 14.9 per cent in 2002–05.

The overall picture in relation to evaluation is that, surprisingly, more than 40 per cent of DSS design-science projects do not undertake formal evaluation of the artefacts. When artefact evaluation is performed, researchers generally make an appropriate choice of method. Further, the quality of the execution of evaluation is steadily, and significantly, improving.

HMPR guideline 4: research contributions

The fourth HMPR guideline concerns the research contributions of design science. Hevner et al. (2004:Table 1) define this guideline by saying that '[e]ffective design-science research must provide clear and verifiable contributions in the areas of the design artifact, design foundations, and/or design methodologies'. Each paper in the DSS sample was examined for its primary research contribution according to the HMPR definition. Secondary contributions were also recorded where they occurred. Among the 362 papers, the design artefact was the primary research contribution in 360 cases, with only one paper having design foundations and one having design methodologies as their primary research contribution. Only eight papers had a secondary research contribution: one in the design artefact, six in design foundations and one contribution to design methodologies.

There were a number of examples of high-quality research contribution through a design artefact. These included a repository-based executive information system (Chen 1995), a strategic business intelligence system (Rouibah and Ould-ali 2002) and a knowledge-based DSS for radiologists (Holden and Wilhelmij 1995–96). Two notable contributions to design foundations were a design theory for systems that support emergent knowledge processes (Markus et al. 2002) and a groupware-based business process re-engineering process (Dennis et al. 2003). An example of a high-quality contribution to evaluation methodologies is DeSanctis et al. (1994), who have developed a method for conducting a preliminary evaluation of an EMS. In particular, their method assesses the match between user and designer perspectives on system interface, functionality and holistic attributes.

HMPR guideline 5: research rigour

The fifth HMPR guideline concerns the rigour of design-science research. Hevner et al. (2004:Table 1) define this guideline, saying: 'Design-science research relies upon the application of rigorous methods in both the construction and evaluation of the design artifact.'

We operationalised this guideline using two constructs: the rigour of the theoretical foundations of the research and the rigour of the research methodology. Each construct was coded on a scale of strong, adequate or weak. As with other HMPR guidelines, here, the coding was generous with respect to assessments at category boundaries.

The rigour of theory foundations was coded by considering the use of appropriate reference theory—and in particular, argument as to why the reference theory was appropriate. The effective use of theory in evaluation and the discussion were coded highly, as was consideration of the limitations or weaknesses of the theory foundations. The result of the coding for the rigour of theory foundations is shown in Table 12.12. More than 80 per cent of papers were coded as either adequate or strong. This has been fairly consistent over time and represents a good result for the DSS discipline. A cross-tabulation of the rigour of theory foundations with DSS type found that the data in Table 12.12 were fairly consistent across DSS type.

12. An assessment of DSS design science using the Hevner, March, Park and Ram guidelines

Table 12.12 The rigour of the theoretical foundations of DSS design-science research

	1990–93		1994–97		1998–2001		2002–05		Total	
	(no.)	(%)	(no.)	(%)	(no.)	(%)	(no.)	(%)	(no.)	(%)
Strong	20	27.8	41	35.7	26	33.8	38	38.8	125	34.5
Adequate	38	52.8	47	40.9	42	54.5	46	46.9	173	47.8
Weak	14	19.4	27	23.5	9	11.7	14	14.3	64	17.7
Total	72		115		77		98		362	

The result of the coding of the rigour of research methodologies in the sample is shown in Table 12.13. The results are extremely disappointing, with 75 per cent of papers in the weak category and only 3.3 per cent coded as strong. Most of the papers in the 'weak' set did not mention research method and design at all. The time trend in the sample is for the less rigorous category to decrease substantially over time—a positive result for the field. Unfortunately, the improvement has been in the adequate and not in the strong category.

Table 12.13 The rigour of the research methodologies of DSS design-science research

	1990–93		1994–97		1998–2001		2002–05		Total	
	(no.)	(%)	(no.)	(%)	(no.)	(%)	(no.)	(%)	(no.)	(%)
Strong	0	0.0	6	5.2	2	2.6	4	4.1	12	3.3
Adequate	10	13.9	21	18.3	18	23.4	31	31.6	80	22.1
Weak	62	86.1	88	76.5	57	74.0	63	64.3	270	74.6
Total	72		115		77		98		362	

Table 12.14 contains a cross-tabulation of the rigour of the theoretical foundations against the rigour of the research methodologies. It reveals a strong association between the constructs (a correlation of 0.408, which is significant at the 0.1 per cent level). Also, the table reveals the direction of the association. In the 64 design-science DSS cases in which the theoretical foundations are weak, all 64 are weak in their research methodologies. This means that DSS design-science researchers who are not rigorous with their theoretical foundations pay little attention to research methodology issues.

Table 12.14 Theoretical foundations versus research methodologies

Research methodologies	Theoretical foundations							
	Strong		Adequate		Weak		Total	
	(no.)	(%)	(no.)	(%)	(no.)	(%)	(no.)	(%)
Strong	10	7.9	2	1.2	0	0.0	12	3.3
Adequate	52	41.3	28	16.3	0	0.0	80	22.1
Weak	64	50.8	142	82.6	64	100.0	270	74.6
Total	126		172		64		362	

HMPR guideline 6: design as a search process

The sixth HMPR guideline concerns the iterative search process that is characteristic of high-quality design. Hevner et al. (2004:Table 1) define this guideline as '[t]he search for an effective artifact [which] requires utilizing available means to reach desired ends while satisfying laws in the problem environment'.

Thirty-seven papers (10.2 per cent of the sample) decomposed the design problem into sub-problems, 23 papers (6.4 per cent of the sample) displayed iteration from the sub-problem solution to the overall problem solution and 10 papers (2.8 per cent of the sample) used 'satisficing' to decide on the solution convergence point. This analysis shows little support for an evident search process in DSS design-science research.

HMPR guideline 7: communication of research

The seventh, and final, HMPR guideline concerns the communication of research. Hevner et al. (2004:Table 1) define this guideline by saying: 'Design-science research must be presented effectively both to technology-oriented as well as management-oriented audiences.'

The effectiveness of communication was coded on a scale of high, medium and low, with the 'generous' approach of the coding of other constructs. Both coders have significant technical and managerial experience. The result of the coding is shown in Tables 12.15 and 12.16.

Table 12.15 The effectiveness of technology-oriented communication in DSS design-science research

	1990–93		1994–97		1998–2001		2002–05		Total	
	(no.)	(%)	(no.)	(%)	(no.)	(%)	(no.)	(%)	(no.)	(%)
High	17	23.6	29	25.2	28	36.4	41	41.8	115	31.8
Medium	43	59.7	61	53.0	41	53.2	48	49.0	193	53.3
Low	12	16.7	25	21.7	8	10.4	9	9.2	54	14.9
Total	72		115		77		98		362	

Table 12.16 The effectiveness of management-oriented communication in DSS design-science research

	1990–93		1994–97		1998–2001		2002–05		Total	
	(no.)	(%)	(no.)	(%)	(no.)	(%)	(no.)	(%)	(no.)	(%)
High	0	0.0	2	1.7	3	3.9	0	0.0	5	1.4
Medium	10	13.9	8	7.0	14	18.2	16	16.3	48	13.3
Low	62	86.1	105	91.3	60	77.9	82	83.7	309	85.4
Total	72		115		77		98		362	

The effectiveness of technical communication was reasonable, with 85.1 per cent of papers coded as medium or high. Further, the proportion of papers with high effectiveness increases with each period. The effectiveness of management communication is the reverse of technical communication, with 85.4 per cent of DSS papers coded as low effectiveness. Further, there is no significant improvement in the percentage of 'low' papers over time. Unfortunately, only 1.4 per cent of papers have high effectiveness in managerial communication.

The picture that emerges in Tables 12.15 and 12.16 is of a discipline with a strong technical focus but one whose papers are unlikely to influence managerial activities. Table 12.16 goes a long way towards explaining the perceived lack of relevance in DSS (and IS) research. Perhaps the table is a reflection of the nature of academic journals, in which the rigour of theory base, design and execution is rewarded by publication. The table is also influenced by the nature of the DSS design-science sample. There are no premier professional journals in the sample as the object of this chapter is to assess the quality of DSS design-science research. Had the *Harvard Business Review*, *Sloan Management Review* and *MIS Quarterly Executive* been in the sample, the statistics for the effectiveness of managerial communication could have been more encouraging. On the other hand, we suspect the number of DSS articles in these premier professional journals could be small.

Summary of the HPMR guideline-based analysis

Using the HPMR guidelines has provided an evidence-based understanding of the nature of DSS design-science research. The analysis shows that design science as a term has had little usage in DSS research and the current debate on design science is yet to impact on published DSS research. Despite this, design science is the strategy of 31 per cent of published DSS research since 1990. The focus in DSS design-science research over all periods has been on instantiations; they constitute close to two-thirds of all research artefacts. Methods are about one-quarter of DSS design-science artefacts. The 'artefact' is the major contribution of most DSS design-science papers, with few making design foundations or methodology contributions. DSS design science addresses problems at the lowest level of managerial impact; operational management support is the focus of 75 per cent of papers. The assessment of relevance shows that two-thirds of papers are of low relevance to IS practitioners. The assessment of relevance to managers is significantly better. Evaluation is a major problem area for DSS design science, with 42 per cent of papers not undertaking any form of evaluation. The rigour of the theory foundations of DSS design science is reasonable, but many papers do not explicitly address research design. In terms of the communication of results, the analysis shows a discipline with a strong technical focus but also one whose papers are unlikely to influence managerial activities.

Strategies for improving DSS design-science research

The analysis in the previous section provides a basis for considering how to improve the quality and impact of DSS design-science research. A word of caution is warranted before proceeding. Our aim is to identify major areas that can be improved in DSS design-science research. This identification can paint an overly negative impression of the field, which is not our intention. Further, the standard of IS research has improved significantly since 1990 and an assessment of older research from a 2008 perspective could be biased. It is important to remember that DSS design-science research has progressed in the 16 years of the sample period without the assistance of an agreed set of guidelines for what constitutes quality in design-science research. Nevertheless, the analysis in the previous section has highlighted four major areas that need serious attention. The areas identified overlap considerably and represent different levels of abstraction about the problems of DSS design-science research.

Evaluation

Evaluation is the biggest weakness in DSS design-science research. The focus of many papers is the description of an instantiation without any attempt at evaluation. The presence of rigorous and convincing evaluation is an important separator of consulting, professional design and design research. Some form of convincing evaluation should be mandatory for design-science research.

The analysis in this chapter shows that those researchers who have performed some form of evaluation usually choose an appropriate strategy but the quality of the execution of the evaluation needs significant improvement.

There is also a need to broaden the base of evaluation methods and techniques. Three methods currently dominate DSS research: simulation, scenarios and case studies—with experiments also significant. This is a very narrow methodological base. Other evaluation approaches in Hevner et al. (2004:Table 2) could be relevant and methods not in this table should be considered. These could include qualitative methods such as focus groups.

Research foundations and methodologies

The next major area of concern is with the theoretical foundation and research methodology of DSS design science. These are surprising concerns and are not explained by an averaging effect where, for example, poor foundations early in the sample are offset by strong foundations in papers later in the sample.

The most disappointing result in the analysis was that 75 per cent of papers were identified as being 'weak' with respect to research methods. Most of these papers did not mention research design at all. While the rigour of research methods was low, the effectiveness of managerial communication (Guideline 7) was even worse, with 85 per cent of papers coded in the poorest category. This implies that there is no trade-off between rigour and relevance in DSS design-science research.

We believe that researchers should focus on improving the rigour of all aspects of design-science research. It is the rigour of academic research that is most valued by practitioners. A greater focus on quality in research foundations and methods will also help build to a cumulative tradition in DSS design-science. We noticed during the coding, principally through the citation of DSS work, that although not covered by the HMPR guidelines, there is no general sense of published research building on previous DSS design-science projects.

Strategic focus

The analysis under Guideline 2—problem relevance—shows that 75 per cent of DSS design-science research has been focused on operational management problems. If DSS design science is going to have a major impact on the way managers work and make decisions, researchers need to increase the organisational importance of the tasks that are targeted. This is particularly important as the business intelligence movement has raised the visibility of, and demand for, decision support by senior managers and executives.

Theorising

The final major area of DSS design-science that we believe needs significant improvement is the level and quantity of theorising in published papers. This finding builds on the previous discussion regarding research foundations and methodologies. It is not related to a particular HMPR guideline but emerges from the overall analysis in section three.

We need to move beyond an instantiation as the primary focus in DSS design science. Gregor and Jones (2007) divide design artefacts into material or abstract artefacts. They argue that the abstract artefacts—constructs, models and methods—are theory or components of theory. One of the strongest findings in section three is that 66 per cent of design artefacts in DSS research are instantiations. It is clear that the DSS field needs to urgently emphasise theory and theorising in design-science projects. A key aspect of this improvement should be the explicit consideration of IS design theory in manuscripts (Walls et al. 1992; Gregor and Jones 2007).

Comments on the Hevner, March, Park and Ram guidelines

It is clear from the Thomson ISI citation count that the HMPR guidelines will be a major reference work for IS design-science researchers. In this section, we reflect on the effectiveness of the guidelines in assessing a large sample of design-science papers.

In general, the guidelines were relatively easy to apply. The major difficulty in the design of the content analysis was the lack of definition of the constructs for some guidelines. As described above, we operationalised these opinion-based constructs on three-point scales. This proved to be an effective approach to coding and there were few disagreements between the coders. We did find that it was important to keep rereading Hevner et al. (2004) during the coding process in order to remain calibrated to their definitions, constructs and meanings.

It was very difficult to assess Guideline 6—which relates to design as a search process—from the published papers. By their nature, journal papers are written in a linear style. Often the research design and the project description can appear more ordered, and more structured, than is in fact the case. This is not a criticism of these papers; it is an artefact of the publishing process. It does, however, create a problem for the assessment of the iterative search process of a piece of design-science research. As a result, the assessment of papers for HMPR Guideline 6 is difficult or biased unless the search process is explicitly addressed by the authors.

In response to one of the concerns in the previous section, we believe that Guideline 4—which relates to the research contributions of a paper—could be broadened to include an explicit contribution to theory.

Hevner et al. (2004:82) state: 'Following Klein and Myers (1999) we advise against mandatory or rote use of the guidelines.' Following the analysis of DSS design science, we believe that some of the guidelines should be mandatory—namely, Guideline 1, the design artefact; Guideline 2, problem relevance; Guideline 3, evaluation; and Guideline 5, research rigour.

Notwithstanding these concerns, using the HMPR guidelines to analyse a large set of DSS design-science papers did provide a clear idea of the state of the field. More importantly, they provide a clear idea of the areas that need significant improvement.

Concluding comments

This study is subject to a number of limitations. The first concerns the representativeness of the sample. The use of the Alavi and Carlson categories as the filters for the DSS design-science sample could underestimate the sample size as the coding was based on the focus or dominant method of the paper. Some papers that were coded as experiments could really have been design science but the published papers paid cursory attention to artefact construction. In particular, the journal reviewing practices early in the sample could have encouraged this style of write-up. Fortunately, the sample is large and this effect should be diluted.

The second limitation concerns the subjective nature of some of the coding. This is inevitable when interpreting guidelines that do not have well-defined constructs. We believe that researchers with considerable experience in DSS research and design science who used our protocol on our sample would generate similar data.

This study shows that design science is an important part—perhaps the major part—of DSS research. The lessons learned from the application of the HMPR guidelines should help to significantly improve DSS research. Our further research into the nature of DSS design-science research includes the use of the HMPR guidelines to develop a 'balanced scorecard' that will provide a quality measure of a piece of design-science research. A second strand of further research will attempt to distil the general design theories that have been used for DSS design science.

The stakes are high for DSS design science. If we get design science right, if it is relevant and rigorous, we will have increased influence in industry and the profession—much like what occurs in medicine. If we get it wrong, the disconnect between academe and practice will be amplified.

References

Alavi, M. and Carlson, P. 1992, 'A review of MIS research and disciplinary development', *Journal of Management Information Systems*, vol. 8, no. 4, pp. 45–62.

Anthony, R. N. 1965, *Planning and Control Systems: A framework for analysis*, Graduate School of Business Administration, Harvard University, Cambridge, Mass.

Arnott, D. 2004, 'Decision support systems evolution: framework, case study and research agenda', *European Journal of Information Systems*, vol. 13, no. 4, pp. 247–59.

Arnott, D. 2006, 'Cognitive biases and decision support systems development: a design science approach', *Information Systems Journal*, vol. 16, no. 1, pp. 55–78.

Arnott, D. 2008, 'Personal decision support systems', in F. Burstein and C. W. Holsapple (eds), *Decision Support Systems Handbook*, Springer-Verlag, Berlin, pp. 127–50.

Arnott, D. and Pervan, G. 2005, 'A critical analysis of decision support systems research', *Journal of Information Technology*, vol. 20, no. 2, pp. 67–87.

Arnott, D. and Pervan, G. 2008, 'Eight key issues for the decision support systems discipline', *Decision Support Systems*, vol. 44, pp. 657–72.

Balbo, F. and Pinson, S. 2005, 'Dynamic modeling of a disturbance in a multi-agent system for traffic regulation', *Decision Support Systems*, vol. 41, pp. 131–46.

Benbasat, I. and Nault, B. 1990, 'An evaluation of empirical research in managerial support systems', *Decision Support Systems*, vol. 6, no. 3, pp. 203–26.

Benbasat, I. and Zmud, R. W. 1999, 'Empirical research in information systems: the question of relevance', *MIS Quarterly*, vol. 23, no. 1, pp. 3–16.

Benbasat, I. and Zmud, R. W. 2003, 'The identity crisis within the IS discipline: defining and communicating the discipline's core properties', *MIS Quarterly*, vol. 27, no. 2, pp. 183–94.

Berndt, D. J., Hevner, A. R. and Studnicki, J. 2003, 'The catch datawarehouse: support for community health care decision-making', *Decision Support Systems*, vol. 35, no. 3, pp. 367–84.

Burstein, F. and Carlsson, S. A. 2008, 'Decision support through knowledge management', in F. Burstein and C. W. Holsapple (eds), *Decision Support Systems Handbook*, Springer-Verlag, Berlin, pp. 103–20.

Chen, M. 1995, 'A model-driven approach to accessing managerial information: the development of a repository-based executive information system', *Journal of Management Information Systems*, vol. 11, no. 4, pp. 33–63.

Chen, W. S. and Hirschheim, R. 2004, 'A paradigmatic and methodological examination of information systems research from 1991 to 2001', *Information Systems Journal*, vol. 14, no. 3, pp. 197–235.

Dennis, A. R., Carte, T. A. and Kelly, G. G. 2003, 'Breaking the rules: success and failure in groupware-supported business process reengineering', *Decision Support Systems*, vol. 36, pp. 31–47.

Dennis, A. R., George, J. F., Jessup, L. M., Nunamaker, J. F. jr and Vogel, D. R. 1988, 'Information technology to support electronic meetings', *MIS Quarterly*, December, pp. 591–624.

DeSanctis, G., Snyder, J. and Poole, M. S. 1994, 'The meaning of the interface: a functional and holistic evaluation of a meeting software system', *Decision Support Systems*, vol. 11, pp. 319–35.

de Vreede, G.-J. and Dickson, G. 2000, 'Using GSS to design organizational processes and information systems: an action research study on collaborative business engineering', *Group Decision and Negotiation*, vol. 9, pp. 161–83.

Eom, S. B. 1995, 'Decision support systems research: reference disciplines and a cumulative tradition', *Omega: The International Journal of Management Science*, vol. 23, no. 5, pp. 511–23.

Eom, S. B. 1996, 'Mapping the intellectual structure of research in decision support systems through author cocitation analysis (1971–1993)', *Decision Support Systems*, vol. 16, no. 4, pp. 315–38.

Eom, S. B. 1999, 'Decision support systems research: current state and trends', *Industrial Management and Data Systems*, vol. 99, no. 5, pp. 213–20.

Eom, H. B. and Lee, S. M. 1990, 'A survey of decision support system applications (1971–1988)', *Interfaces*, vol. 20, no. 3, pp. 65–79.

Eom, S.B. and Lee, S. M. 1993, 'Leading universities and most influential contributors in DSS research: a citation analysis', *Decision Support Systems*, vol. 9, no. 3, pp. 237–44.

Gero, J. S. 1990, 'Design prototypes: a knowledge representation schema for design', *AI Magazine*, vol. 11, no. 4, pp. 26–36.

Gillenson, M. L. and Stutz, J. D. 1991, 'Academic issues in MIS: journals and books', *MIS Quarterly*, vol. 15, no. 4, pp. 447–52.

Gregor, S. and Jones, D. 2007, 'The anatomy of a design theory', *Journal of the Association for Information Systems*, vol. 8, no. 5, pp. 312–35.

Hall, D., Guo, Y., Davis, R. A. and Cegielski, C. 2005, 'Extending unbounded systems thinking with agent-oriented modelling: conceptualizing a multiple perspective decision-making support system', *Decision Support Systems*, vol. 41, pp. 279–95.

Hardgrave, B. C. and Walstrom, K. A. 1997, 'Forums for MIS scholars', *Communications of the ACM*, vol. 40, no. 11, pp. 119–24.

Hevner, A. R., March, S. T., Park, J. and Ram, S. 2004, 'Design science in information systems research', *MIS Quarterly*, vol. 28, no. 1, pp. 75–106.

Hirschheim, R. 1992, 'Information systems epistemology: a historical perspective', in R. Galliers (ed.), *Information Systems Research: Issues, methods and practical guidelines*, Blackwell Scientific Publications, Oxford, pp. 28–60.

Holden, T. and Wilhelmij, P. 1995–96, 'Improved decision making through better integration of human resource and business process factors in a hospital situation', *Journal of Management Information Systems*, vol. 12, no. 3, pp. 21–41.

Holsapple, C., Johnson, L., Manakyan, H. and Tanner, J. 1994, 'Business computing research journals: a normalized citation analysis', *Journal of Management Information Systems*, vol. 11, no. 1, pp. 131–40.

Huber, G. P. 1984, 'Issues in the design of group decision support systems', *MIS Quarterly*, vol. 8, no. 3, pp. 195–204.

Kaplan, R. S. and Norton, D. P. 1996, *The Balanced Scorecard: Translating strategy into action*, Harvard Business School Press, Cambridge, Mass.

Katerattanakul, P. and Han, B. 2003, 'Are European IS journals under-rated? An answer based on citation analysis', *European Journal of Information Systems*, vol. 12, pp. 60–71.

Kathuria, R., Anandarajan, M. and Igbaria, M. 1999, 'Linking IT applications with manufacturing strategy: an intelligent decision support system approach', *Decision Sciences*, vol. 30, no. 4, pp. 959–91.

Keen, P. G. W. and Gambino, T. J. 1983, 'Building a decision support system: the mythical man-month revisited', in J. L. Bennett (ed.), *Building Decision Support Systems*, Addison-Wesley, Reading, Mass., 133–72.

Keen, P. G. W. and Scott Morton, M. S. 1978, *Decision Support Systems: An organisational perspective*, Addison-Wesley, Reading, Mass.

Klein, H. K. and Myers, M. D. 1999, 'A set of principles for conducting and evaluating interpretive field studies in information systems', *MIS Quarterly*, vol. 23, no. 1, pp. 67–94.

Kuula, M. 1998, 'Solving intra-company conflicts using the RAMONA—interactive negotiation support system', *Group Decision and Negotiation*, vol. 7, pp. 447–64.

Land, F. 1992, 'The information systems domain', in R. D. Galliers (ed.), *Information Systems Research: Issues, methods and practical guidelines*, Blackwell Scientific, Oxford, pp. 6–13.

Lee, A. 2001, 'Editor's comments', *MIS Quarterly*, vol. 25, no. 1, pp. iii–vii.

March, S. and Smith, G. F. 1995, 'Design & natural science research on information technology', *Decision Support Systems*, vol. 15, no. 4, pp. 251–66.

Markus, M. L., Majchrzak, A. and Gasser, L. 2002, 'A design theory for systems that support emergent knowledge processes', *MIS Quarterly*, vol. 26, no. 3, pp. 179–212.

Meador, C. L. and Ness, D. N. 1974, 'Decision support systems: an application to corporate planning', *Sloan Management Review*, vol. 15, no. 2, pp. 51–68.

Moreno-Jiminez, J. M., Joven, J. A., Pirla, A. R. and Lanuza, A. T. 2005, 'A spreadsheet module for consistent consensus building in AHP decision making', *Group Decision and Negotiation*, vol. 14, pp. 89–108.

Mylonopoulos, N. A. and Theoharakis, V. 2001, 'On-site: global perceptions of IS journals', *Communications of the ACM*, vol. 44, no. 9, pp. 29–33.

Nelson, R. R., Todd, P. A. and Wixom, B. H. 2005, 'Antecedents of information and system quality: an empirical examination within the context of data warehousing', *Journal of Management Information Systems*, vol. 21, no. 4, pp. 199–235.

Noakes, D. J., Fang, L., Hipel, K. W. and Kilgour, D. M. 2005, 'The Pacific salmon treaty: a century of debate and an uncertain future', *Group Decision and Negotiation*, vol. 14, pp. 501–22.

Nunamaker, J. F. jr, Chen, M. and Purdin, T. D. M. 1991, 'Systems development in information systems research', *Journal of Management Information Systems*, vol. 7, no. 3, pp. 89–106.

Orlikowski, W. J. and Iacono, C. S. 2001, 'Research commentary: desperately seeking the "IT" in IT research—a call for theorizing the IT artifact', *Information Systems Research*, vol. 12, no. 2, pp. 121–34.

Osareh, F. 1996, 'Bibliometrics, citation analysis and co-citation analysis: a review of literature I', *Libri*, vol. 46, pp. 149–58.

Pervan, G. P. 1998, 'A review of research in group support systems: leaders, approaches and directions', *Decision Support Systems*, vol. 23, no. 2, pp. 149–59.

Pervan, G. P. and Atkinson, D. J. 1995, 'GDSS research: an overview and historical analysis', *Group Decision and Negotiation*, vol. 4, no. 6, pp. 475–85.

Rangaswamy, A. and Shell, G. R. 1997, 'Using computers to realize joint gains in negotiations: toward an "electronic bargaining table"', *Management Science*, vol. 43, no. 8, pp. 1147–63.

Rouibah, K. and Ould-ali, S. 2002, 'PUZZLE: a concept and prototype for linking business intelligence to business strategy', *Journal of Strategic Information Systems*, vol. 11, no. 2, pp. 133–52.

Sen, R. and Sen, T. K. 2005, 'A meta-modeling approach to designing e-warehousing systems', *Journal of Organizational Computing and Electronic Commerce*, vol. 15, no. 4, pp. 295–316.

Simon, H. A. 1996, *The Sciences of the Artificial*, Third edition, MIT Press, Cambridge, Mass.

Tavana, M. and Banerjee, S. 1995, 'Strategic assessment model (SAM): a multiple criteria decision support system for evaluation of strategic alternatives', *Decision Sciences*, vol. 26, no. 1, pp. 119–43.

Turban, E., Aronson, J. E. and Liang, T.-P. 2005, *Decision Support Systems and Intelligent Systems*, Seventh edition, Pearson Education, Upper Saddle River, NJ.

Walczak, S. 2001, 'An empirical analysis of data requirements for financial forecasting with neural networks', *Journal of Management Information Systems*, vol. 17, no. 4, pp. 203–22.

Walls, J. G., Widmeyer, G. R. and El Sawy, O. A. 1992, 'Building an information systems design theory for vigilant EIS', *Information Systems Research*, vol. 3, no. 1 (March), pp. 36–59.

Walstrom, K. A., Hardgrave, B. C. and Wilson, R. L. 1995, 'Forums for management information systems scholars', *Communications of the ACM*, vol. 38, no. 3, pp. 93–107.

Watson, H. J. 2001, 'Recent developments in data warehousing', *Communications of the Association for Information Systems*, vol. 8, pp. 1–25.

Weber, R. P. 1990, *Basic Content Analysis*, Second edition, Sage, Newbury Park, Calif.

Webster, J. and Watson, R. T. 2002, 'Analyzing the past to prepare for the future: writing a literature review', *MIS Quarterly*, vol. 26, no. 2, pp. xiii–xxiii.

Whitman, M. E., Hendrickson, A. R. and Townsend, A. M. 1999, 'Research commentary: academic rewards for teaching, research and service: data and discourse', *Information Systems Research*, vol. 10, no. 2, pp. 99–109.

Whyte, W. F. 1989, 'Advancing Scientific Knowledge Through Participatory Action Research', Sociological Forum, vol. 4, no. 3, pp. 367-385.

Zhang, P., Sun, J. and Chen, H. 2005, 'Frame-based argumentation for group decision task generation and identification', *Decision Support Systems*, vol. 39, pp. 643–59.

Appendix 12.1

Article coding protocol

Guideline 1: the design artefact

1.1 Type of artefact   1. Construct   2. Model   3. Method   4. Instantiation
1.2 What was the artefact?

Guideline 2: problem relevance

2.1 Importance of business problem   1. Strategic   2. Tactical   3. Operational
2.2 Relevance to IS practitioners   1. High   2. Medium   3. Low
2.3 Relevance to managerial users   1. High   2. Medium   3. Low

Guideline 3: design evaluation

3.1 Type of evaluation

    Observational   1. Case study   2. Field study
    Analytical   3. Static   4. Architecture   5. Optimisation   6. Dynamic
    Experimental   7. Controlled experiment   8. Simulation
    Testing   9. Functional (black box)   10. Structural (white box)
    Descriptive   11. Informed argument   12. Scenarios
                13. None

3.2 Choice of evaluation method   1. Highly appropriate   2. Adequate   3. Poor choice
3.3 Quality of execution of evaluation   1. High   2. Medium   3. Low

Guideline 4: research contributions

4.1 Contribution area   1. The design artefact   2. Foundations   3. Design methodologies

Guideline 5: research rigour

5.1 Theoretical foundations   1. Strong   2. Adequate   3. Weak
5.2 Research methodologies   1. Strong   2. Adequate   3. Weak

Guideline 6: design as a search process		
6.1 Decomposition into sub-problems	Yes	No
6.2 Iteration from sub-problem solution to overall problem solution	Yes	No
6.3 Satisficing used to decide on solution convergence point	Yes	No

Guideline 7: communication of research			
7.1 Effectiveness of technology-oriented presentation	1. High	2. Medium	3. Low
7.2 Effectiveness of management-oriented presentation	1. High	2. Medium	3. Low
8.1 Did the paper mention 'design science'? Yes	No		
8.2 If 'no', what did it call it? Or 'nothing'			

9. Design science reference citations

1	March and Smith (1995), *DSS*
2	Markus et al. (2002), *MISQ*
3	Nunamaker et al. (1991), *JMIS*
4	Simon (1996 or earlier), *The Sciences of the Artificial*
5	Walls et al. (1992), *ISR*
6	Hevner et al. (2004), *MISQ*
7	Other
8	None

10. Free text comments on the paper

13. Design science in IS research: a literature analysis

MARTA INDULSKA
UNIVERSITY OF QUEENSLAND

JAN RECKER
QUEENSLAND UNIVERSITY OF TECHNOLOGY

Abstract

The publication of the work on design science by Alan Hevner and his colleagues has fostered much discussion on what is and what is not considered to be design science in information systems (IS) research. Anecdotal evidence suggests that some authors claim design science as a methodology in their work, without much consideration of theoretical or methodological aspects or the appropriateness of their artefact. Also, it would appear that design-science papers have been proliferating rapidly of late. Accordingly, we were interested to identify the proliferation, nature and quality of design-science research in IS conference publications since the publication of Hevner et al.'s work in 2004. We examine design-science articles published at five major IS conferences in the past three years. We subject 83 articles—identified as relevant via a rigorous analysis process—to three types of analysis: statistical, thematic and methodological. The results of these analyses indicate that design science appears to be a growing stream of research in IS. We also found design-science research to be strongly prevalent in the research domains of process, knowledge and information management. The most interesting results stem from our methodological analysis, which suggests that only a small percentage of the papers discuss a concise and consistent implementation of the design-science methodology suggested by Hevner et al.

Introduction

Recent years have seen an increased interest in topics associated with design science or design research within the information systems (IS) community. Most of this interest emerged after the publication of Hevner et al.'s (2004) paper on design science. Since then, some the most prestigious IS journals have launched special issues on design science. These include the *Journal of Information Technology Theory and Application* (*JITTA*) in 2004, the *Journal of the Association of Information Systems* (*JAIS*) in 2007 and, most recently, *MIS Quarterly* (*MISQ*), in 2008. Some of the most prominent IS conferences—for example, the Americas Conference on Information Systems (AMCIS) and the International Conference on Information Systems (ICIS)—also now feature tracks dedicated to design-science research. New conferences on design science in IS, such as the International Conference on Design Science in Information Systems and Technology (DESRIST), have likewise been introduced in the past few years. Last, but not least, the online forum ISWorld now features a web page on design science. The dedicated page includes details of the design-science methodology and a list of other related resources (for example, publication outlets) (<http://www.isworld.org/Researchdesign/drisISworld.htm>). All of these efforts show an increasing interest in design science within the IS research community.

The main motivation behind the emergence of design science as a research paradigm in IS was to complement the 'mainstream' behavioural orientation of IS research with more design-oriented science research (Hevner et al. 2004; March and Smith 1995; Walls et al. 1992). This move sought to address lack of relevance in the field of IS (Applegate and King 1999; Benbasat and Zmud 1999; Rosemann and Vessey 2008).

Clearly, the emerging discussion about design aspects in IS should be seen as encouraging. In the end, IS research is concerned with the design, development, implementation and use of socio-technical systems in organisational contexts (Zmud and Boynton 1991). With the emergence of design science, however, and its surrounding discussions, a number of questions and issues surface. Some researchers argue a lack of defined scope and boundaries for the design-science approach in IS (for example, Carlsson 2005b). Others are concerned about the unclear philosophical presuppositions of design science (for example, Niehaves 2007). More generally, a wide range of scholars lament a lack of clarity in the understandings of, and endeavours in, design science (for example, McKay and Marshall 2005). These, and similar, arguments often tap into the issue of the difference between high-quality professional design and design-science research (Gibson and Arnott 2007).

While design science, or design theory, was discussed as early as 1992 (Walls et al. 1992), and further developed in the mid-1990s (March and Smith 1995) and the new millennium (Markus et al. 2002), it was the Hevner et al. (2004) publication that propelled design science out of its niche into the headlights of the IS community. In their paper, Hevner et al. (2004) argue that design science in IS attempts to create and evaluate IT artefacts intended to solve identified relevant organisational problems. They go on to suggest seven guidelines for the conduct, evaluation and communication of design-science research in IS.

Notwithstanding earlier or other contributions to design-oriented research in IS (for example, March and Smith 1995; Markus et al. 2002; Walls et al. 1992), the motivation of this chapter is to study the progress of design-science research in IS in the years that have followed the publication by Hevner et al. (2004). To this end, we carry out a literature analysis of work published at five prominent academic IS conferences in 2005, 2006 and 2007. The conferences considered include: Australasian Conference on Information Systems (ACIS), Americas Conference on Information Systems (AMCIS), European Conference on Information Systems (ECIS), International Conference on Information Systems (ICIS) and Pacific-Asia Conference on Information Systems (PACIS). In our literature analysis, we focus on relevant design-science papers within these conferences and we wish to address the following questions.

- What proportion of papers at IS conferences pertains to design-science research?
- Is the focus on design science in IS publication outlets increasing in recent years?
- What are the main thematic foci of IS design-science papers?
- Is design science in IS concentrated within schools in specific geographical areas?
- To what extent do design-science papers discuss the seven guidelines specified by Hevner et al. (2004) and how are these guidelines implemented?

We proceed as follows. Section two presents the methodology we employed to ensure a rigorous and unbiased analysis process. The descriptive statistics from our publication analysis are presented in section three. In section four, we review the extent to which published design-science work discusses and implements design-science methodologies, following the seven guidelines suggested by Hevner et al. (2004). Section five discusses our thematic analysis of the papers, aided by the use of the Leximancer analysis tool. We conclude in section six with a discussion of our findings and some recommendations for the road ahead.

Methodology

As a first step, we took as our data set the collection of papers published at the five main AIS-sponsored IS conferences—namely, ACIS, AMCIS, ECIS, ICIS and PACIS. We considered papers in the years 2005–07 (that is, papers that followed the publication of the design-science paper by Hevner et al. [2004]). With this specific focus, we do not wish to discredit other work on design science in IS but rather seek to enable meaningful and focused analysis in our study. We specifically focus on conferences as publication outlets, as opposed to journals, due to the relatively short period from idea conception to publication. The conference paper data set consists of 3284 papers, which was prepared and indexed for a full text search.

From the 3284 papers, we extracted 94 papers that matched the search term of 'Hevner' and a further 129 papers that matched the search term of 'design science' in a full text search. After eliminating duplicate papers from the search results, the final data set for the subsequent analysis consisted of 142 papers. Two researchers carried out the searches and identification of duplicate papers independently. The researchers then met to consolidate the result sets, with no identified inconsistencies.

The search terms restrict the set of papers to those that either directly follow the Hevner et al. study or refer to design science. While this choice limits the scope of our study, it also enables a focused analysis. Other search terms (for example, 'design theory') can also be used and could potentially yield different results. Those terms (for example, 'design theory') did not, however, always imply that a design-science methodology was followed, which was why we opted not to include this search term.

The set of 142 selected papers was subjected to a categorisation of design-science contribution into four categories, *viz.*—methodology, discussion, application and other.

- *Methodology:* Papers that discussed the conduct of design science in specific IS research domains, such as systems analysis and design (Tan et al. 2007), or that discussed the combination or role of the design-science methodology with other approaches to IS, such as focus groups (Gibson and Arnott 2007) or action research (Purao et al. 2005). Three such papers were identified from the set of 142 publications.

- *Discussion:* Papers that discussed the design-science approach from a variety of angles, including its epistemological presuppositions (Niehaves 2007), its previous applications in IS (McKay and Marshall 2005), its combination with paradigms such as critical realism (Carlsson 2005a) and others. Fourteen such papers were identified.

- *Application:* Papers that reported on the implementation of the design-science approach in their respective domains of study. Fifty-seven such papers were identified.
- *Other:* This cluster contains another nine papers, of which seven feature only a brief mention of design science, and two refer to design science in their outlook to future work.

At this stage of the analysis, we identified a number of papers (59 in total) that had to be eliminated from the analysis due to lack of relevance to the theme 'design science'. A variety of reasons for exclusion were encountered

- a paper was published in a 'design-science' track but did not in fact cover design science in the understanding relevant to this chapter
- a paper referred to, or referenced, 'design science' without making a contribution to design science itself
- a paper used the classification of artefacts suggested by Hevner et al. (2004) for a study other than design science
- a paper was a panel discussion.

Two researchers independently performed the analysis of paper relevance and then met to revise their classification. Four inconsistencies (3 per cent) were found and were resolved before further analysis was carried out. This stage of the analysis narrowed the data set down to 83 design-science papers.

The next stage of the analysis process involved classification of papers that belonged to the 'application' category. The main aim of this stage was to gain an insight into the extent of design-science contribution within those papers. More specifically, we were interested in whether, and to what extent, published design-science papers followed the seven methodological guidelines suggested by Hevner et al. (2004). The categories emerged during the first round of analysis and were refined by the two researchers before the second round of analysis was carried out. The final set of categories used was as follows: 'merely states that it follows design-science guidelines', 'focuses on one guideline', 'focuses on some but not all guidelines', 'focuses on all guidelines without elaborating on their implementation', 'elaborates on the implementation of all guidelines', 'merely states that it belongs to design-science research' and 'states that it uses design science in combination with other methodologies'. A further discussion of these classifications is provided in section four.

The final stage of the data analysis was concerned with the identification of themes in the set of relevant papers. To this end, we used a data-mining tool, Leximancer, in order to generate automatically themes from the data. The details of the analysis are presented in section five.

Publication analysis

The analysis and categorisation of publications identified 83 papers relevant to the analysis of design-science research. The results are summarised—per conference and per year—in Table 13.1. The table also shows the total number of papers over the three-year period for each conference, allowing the calculation of the ratio of papers focusing on design science.

Table 13.1 Design-science papers published in AIS conferences during 2005–07

	ACIS	AMCIS	ECIS	ICIS	PACIS	Total
2005	4	4	3	2	0	13
2006	4	13	3	7	1	28
2007	6	17	13	4	2	42
Total	14	34	19	13	3	83
Total of all published papers, 2005–07	336	1578	568	376	426	3284
DS papers to published papers	4%	2%	3%	3%	1%	3%

The results show that, while design-science research published at IS conferences still represents a very small percentage of the total number of papers published at such venues (3 per cent of all published papers), it is on the increase. Of 1037 papers published at the considered conferences in 2005, 13 were concerned with design science (1.3 per cent). This ratio increased to 2.5 per cent (28 of 1108 papers) in 2006 and 3.7 per cent (42 of 1139 papers) in 2007. A Kruskal-Wallis one-way analysis of variance showed this increase to be significant at $p=0.001$. This result indicates that, over recent years, significantly more design-science papers have been published at IS conferences (confirmed by a second ANOVA analysis).

Figure 13.1 shows the number of design-science publications at the five considered conferences per annum. ACIS and PACIS show a steady but slow increase in design-science papers. ECIS shows a significant increase of design-science papers in 2007 relative to its previous years. We can only speculate that this increase could be related to the conference's theme in that year ('Relevant Rigour—Rigorous Relevance'), the fact that the conference featured a panel discussion on design science or the fact that Alan Hevner was the keynote speaker. AMCIS and ICIS, on the other hand, featured *dedicated* design-science tracks in 2006 and 2007. Interestingly, however, we note a decrease in design-science papers in 2007 at ICIS while the share of design-science papers at AMCIS continues to increase.

13. Design science in IS research

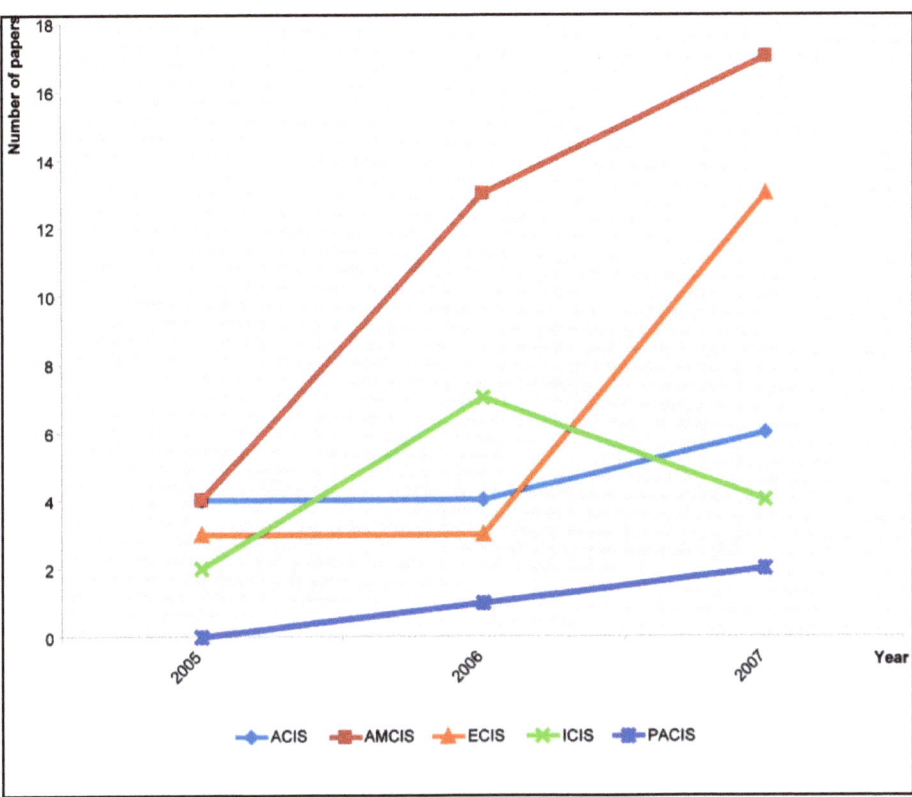

Figure 13.1 Longitudinal display of number of publications at AIS conferences per annum

In carrying out our analysis, we also recorded the country of origin of the first publishing author. From this data, Figure 13.2 shows the geographical distribution of publications. More than 39 per cent of publications originate from departments within the United States (39.76 per cent), closely followed by Europe (33.73 per cent). Authors from IS departments in the Asia/Pacific Rim (Australia, Hong Kong and New Zealand) are responsible for 19.28 per cent of design-science publications. Contrasted with other literature studies—most notably Lyytinen et al. (2007)—the geographical distribution of design-science researchers appears to deviate from the distribution of IS scholars publishing in high-impact journals.[1]

---

[1] This statement has to be approached with caution. The Lyytinen et al. (2007) study concerns journal articles and the time frame of 2000–05, while our study concerns conference papers during 2005–07.

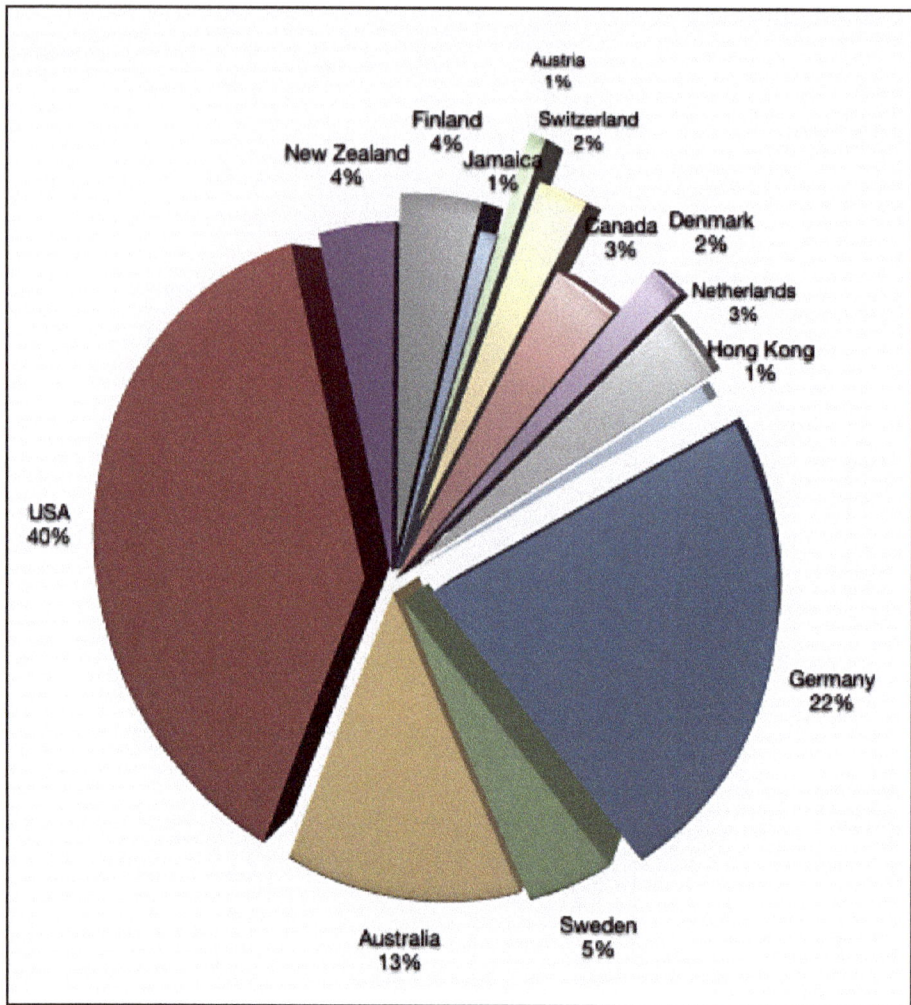

Figure 13.2 First author's country of origin

Based on the statement by Lyytinen et al. (2007)—that 25 per cent of all IS scholars work in European IS departments—we note an over-proportional share of design-science contributions from European IS scholars. This could be seen as evidence for the prevalent view that European IS scholars often view IS as an applied discipline with a strong focus on practical relevance and design constructions—the tool/method-first contribution (Lyytinen et al. 2007). Statements about Asia/Pacific Rim scholars are hard to make due to lack of statistics on the proportion of scholars in comparison with Europe or North America. We speculate, however, that the share of design-science contributions identified (19.28 per cent) is proportionally high.

Methodological analysis

One of the continuing debates about design science in IS concerns the real procedure by which design-science research is executed (for example, McKay and Marshall 2005; Niehaves 2007). More precisely, McKay and Marshall (2005:7) lament that while Hevner et al. (2004) 'articulate some guidelines for design science research, stemming from its problem solving orientation, and then list some appropriate approaches for the evaluation of the designed artefact: they do not, in fact, propose a method or process for the conduct of design research'.

In light of these debates, we examined the set of papers in respect to whether, and how, IS scholars conducting design-science work implemented and executed the seven guidelines suggested by Hevner et al. (2004) and shown in Table 13.2. Through this analysis, we can identify: 1) whether or not design-science scholars follow the suggestions of Hevner et al. (2004); and 2) how they go about implementing the guidelines through appropriate research methods, tools or techniques. To that end, we scrutinised 57 papers that we identified as being 'application' papers and coded each of the papers using the seven classifications of guideline referral described in section two.

Table 13.2 Design-science research guidelines

Guideline	Description
Guideline 1: Design as an artefact	Design-science research must produce a viable artefact in the form of a construct, a model, a method or an instantiation.
Guideline 2: Problem relevance	The objective of design-science research is to develop technology-based solutions to important and relevant business problems.
Guideline 3: Design evaluation	The utility, quality and efficacy of a design artefact must be rigorously demonstrated via well-executed evaluation methods.
Guideline 4: Research contributions	Effective design-science research must provide clear and verifiable contributions in the areas of the design artefact, design foundations and/or design methodologies.
Guideline 5: Research rigour	Design-science research relies on the application of rigorous methods in both the construction and the evaluation of the design artefact.
Guideline 6: Design as a search process	The search for an effective artefact requires utilising available means to reach desired ends while satisfying laws in the problem environment.
Guideline 7: Communication of research	Design-science research must be presented effectively to both technology-oriented and management-oriented audiences.

Source: Hevner et al. (2004:83)

Our analysis yields a number of interesting results. Table 13.3 shows the frequency count of papers we classified in the seven categories. We note that the largest share of papers (36.8 per cent) claims to follow the design-science guidelines without elaborating on how the seven guidelines apply to their work or how they implemented and/or executed the guidelines. Of these, some papers discuss some of the original guidelines—for instance, foundations, relevance, rigour or evaluation—without elaborating on their application in the research domain at hand, while others merely state 'the methodology used is essentially design science, though the proposed model still needs validation'.

Table 13.3 Results from the methodological analysis

Coding category	Number of papers within category
Merely states that it follows design-science guidelines	21 (36.8%)
Focuses on one guideline	13 (22.8%)
Focuses on some but not all guidelines	4 (7.0%)
Focuses on all guidelines without elaborating on their implementation	0 (0.0%)
Elaborates on the implementation of all guidelines	11 (19.3%)
Merely states that it belongs to design-science research	4 (7.0%)
States that it uses design science in combination with other methodologies	4 (7.0%)

An additional 7 per cent of papers claimed affiliation to design science through statements such as 'this paper can be classified as empirically founded design science' or 'it provides an apt illustration of design science in information systems research'.

Of the papers that focused more deeply on one, several or all of the guidelines (28 in total), 46.4 per cent (22.8 per cent of all papers) focused on one guideline. At times, this was due to the early stage of the research progress ('we are still in the "Generate design alternatives" phase of Simon's Generate/Test Cycle'). The one guideline most frequently mentioned in the 13 papers focusing on one guideline only was that of 'design evaluation' (nine referrals in total). Of the papers that focused on more than one guideline, we found that the guidelines of problem relevance, research rigour and design evaluation were mostly present.

Eleven papers elaborated in a comprehensive manner on their consideration of the seven guidelines—mostly in the form of a table that summarised the implementation of the guidelines (see, for instance, Klose et al. 2007; Knackstedt et al. 2007). Notably, the one guideline receiving the weakest attention was that of 'communication of research'. Interestingly, the six papers that were found to discuss the implementation of the seven guidelines well all originated from Germany.

Of the papers that combined design science with other approaches to IS research (four papers in total), we found that grounded theory, experiments and action research were approaches of choice.

Thematic analysis

In a last step, we were interested in the types of content, subject area and/or topic discussed in design-science research articles. To that end, we subjected all identified papers to a thematic analysis procedure using the content analysis tool Leximancer.[2]

Leximancer allows users to analyse large amounts of text quickly. The tool performs a full text analysis both systematically and graphically by creating a map of the concepts and themes reappearing in the texts—a so-called document map. The concepts are displayed in such a manner that links to related subtext can subsequently be explored. Each of the identified concepts is placed on the map in proximity of other concepts in the map through a derived combination of the direct and indirect relationships between those concepts. Essentially, Leximancer employs a machine-learning technique based on the Bayesian approach to prediction. The procedure used for this is a self-ordering optimisation technique (unlike neural networks). Once the optimal weighted set of words is found for each concept, it is used to predict the concepts present in fragments of related text. In other words, each concept has other concepts that it attracts (or is highly associated with contextually) as well as concepts that it repels (or is highly disassociated with contextually). The relationships are measured by the weighted sum of the number of times two concepts are found in the same 'chunk'. An algorithm is used to weight them and determine the confidence and relevancy of the terms to others in a specific chunk and across chunks.

We used Leximancer as a qualitative data-analysis tool for several reasons

- its ability to derive the main concepts within text and their relative importance using a scientific, objective algorithm
- its ability to identify the centrality of concepts
- its ability to assist in applying grounded theory analysis to a textual data set
- its ability to assist in visually exploring textual information for related themes.

To prepare the data set for Leximancer analysis, we used the categorisation of the papers discussed earlier and created two main data sets: 1) *application* papers

---

2   For more information about the Leximancer tool, please refer to <http://www.leximancer.com>

(57 in total); and 2) *methodology and discussion* papers (17 in total). These were created for each conference under consideration, with the exception of PACIS, at which no design-science methodology or discussion papers were published in the past three years.

Leximancer analysis was performed separately for each 'application' and 'methodology and discussion' set of papers at each of the five conferences. In each case, after one Leximancer pass, the list of automatically generated concepts was edited to remove the concept terms 'Hevner', 'March', 'Information_Systems' (which appears due to URL references in many of the papers) and 'Quarterly'. These concepts were removed because they did not add to the understanding of the content of the paper (given the already narrowed data set of papers) and would only clutter and dominate the generated theme map. The analyses uncovered subtle differences in design-science themes discussed at the various conferences. Due to lack of space, we omit these results here and present the overall thematic analysis findings.

Following the individual conference analyses, we ran separate Leximancer analyses of all methodology and discussion papers, all application papers and the overall set of papers. In these analyses, the additional concept of 'paper' was removed before running the analysis a second time, due to the frequency of the term across the whole data set.

The analysis of the methodology and discussion papers identifies a number of central themes, as shown in Figure 13.3. The strongest recurring theme is that of 'research', which includes the analysis of existing research and available data, and is closely related to analysis and evaluation of methods. Other strong themes in the paper set include those of 'design' and 'systems', which indicate a proportionately significant amount of discussion about the real design of artefacts and a discussion of the field of IS and related technical development. Overall, the concept map in Figure 13.3 indicates that the continuing debate on design-science research in IS focuses on themes such as its role in the IS discipline, the choice of appropriate research methods and theories in conjunction with design science, and the question of the underlying paradigm(s) of design science.

An analysis of the set of application papers, on the other hand, shows a very different set of themes within the research (see Figure 13.4). Within this set of papers there are a number of very strong recurring themes emerging, *viz.*—design, process, data, knowledge and information. The strength of the 'design' theme is perhaps not surprising, since the majority of papers develop some type of artefact. The 'information' theme suggests a focus on information management and requirements elicitation, which is closely related to the IS implementation concept. A surprising theme is that of 'process', with a strong concept of 'business processes', 'model' and 'management' within it. This theme indicates that a significant proportion of papers concentrates on the application of design science in the area of process modelling, analysis and design of process-aware information systems, and business process management in general. A similar situation was found for the research domains concerning 'data' and 'knowledge', indicating that a large number of research efforts were dedicated to contributing designs in the form of data management or knowledge management systems and/or services.

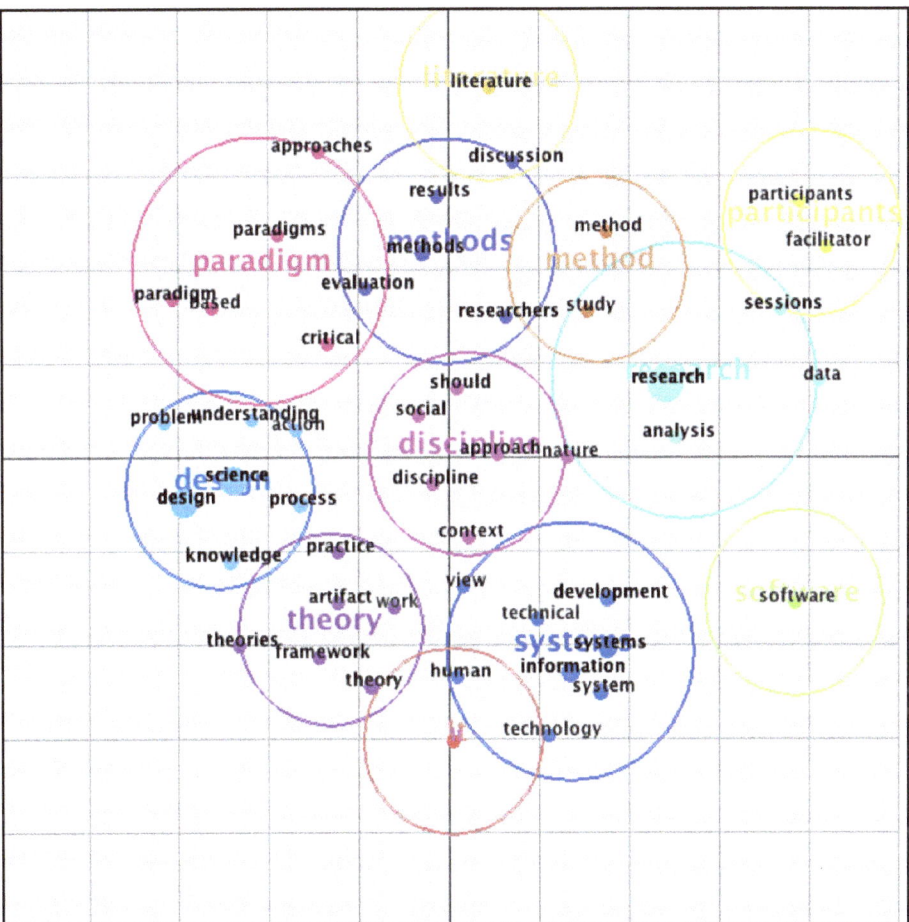

Figure 13.3 Themes identified in methodology and discussion papers

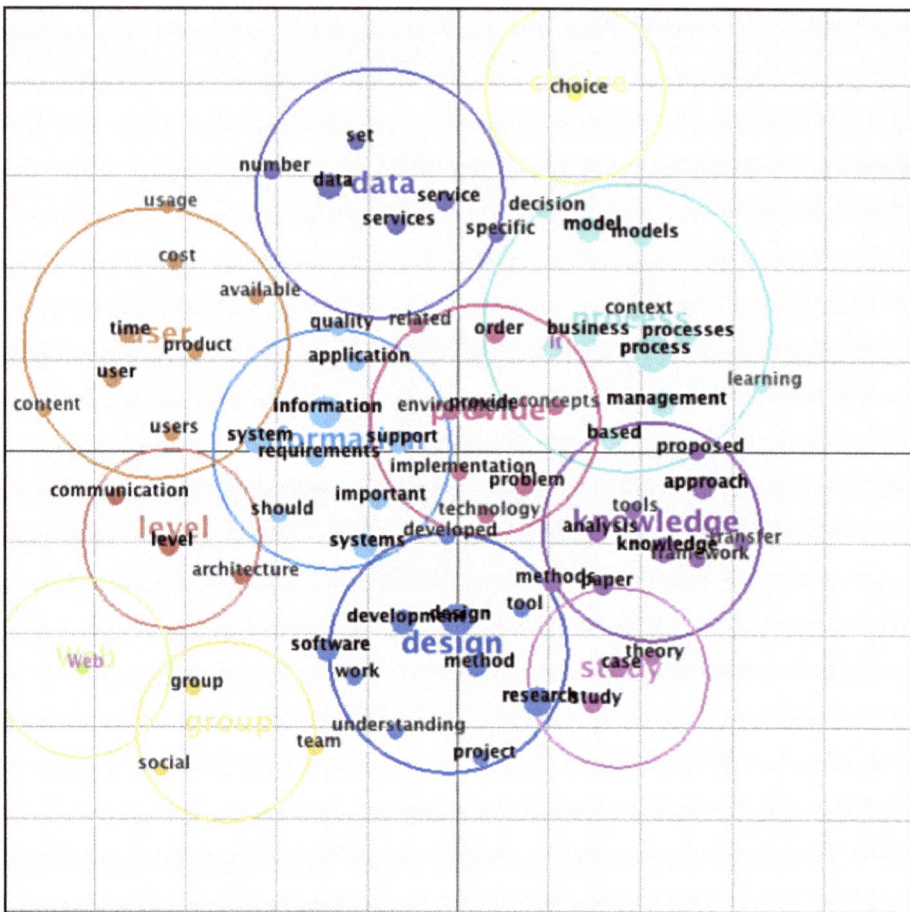

Figure 13.4 Themes identified in application papers

As a last step, to complement our methodological analysis (see section four), we conducted a seeded analysis of the application papers, looking for concepts that could be associated with the seven guidelines of design science suggested by Hevner et al. (2004). Two researchers individually analysed the automatically generated list of most frequently occurring concepts within the application paper set. From this list, a set of concepts was selected that we considered to be related to the design-science guidelines. The list of concepts was then used for the analysis of the 'application' data set, with automatic concept generation disabled. In other words, instead of using Leximancer's set of automatically generated concepts, we seeded the analysis with a smaller set of concepts that was identified by the two researchers to be of relevance to any of the seven guidelines. This seeded analysis provided an insight into the design-science guidelines that are commonly discussed within the application papers. Figure 13.5 shows the theme map generated from this analysis.

Figure 13.5 suggests that the main emphasis of the design-science application papers is on the guidelines of *development* and *evaluation*—a finding that supports our methodological analysis presented in section four. Evaluation in particular is often empirical in nature—testing as one approach denotes a central concept in its own right. The themes of 'design' and 'evaluation' include the guidelines set out by Hevner et al. (2004) as strong concepts, indicating the centrality of these guidelines for design science conducted in IS. The analysis also shows, to a lesser extent, the feature of other guidelines in the paper set, including the communication of results and the issue of utility and relevance of the artefact. The non-centrality of these concepts could be seen as an indication that more guidance is required for IS scholars on how to address concepts of communication, relevance or utility.

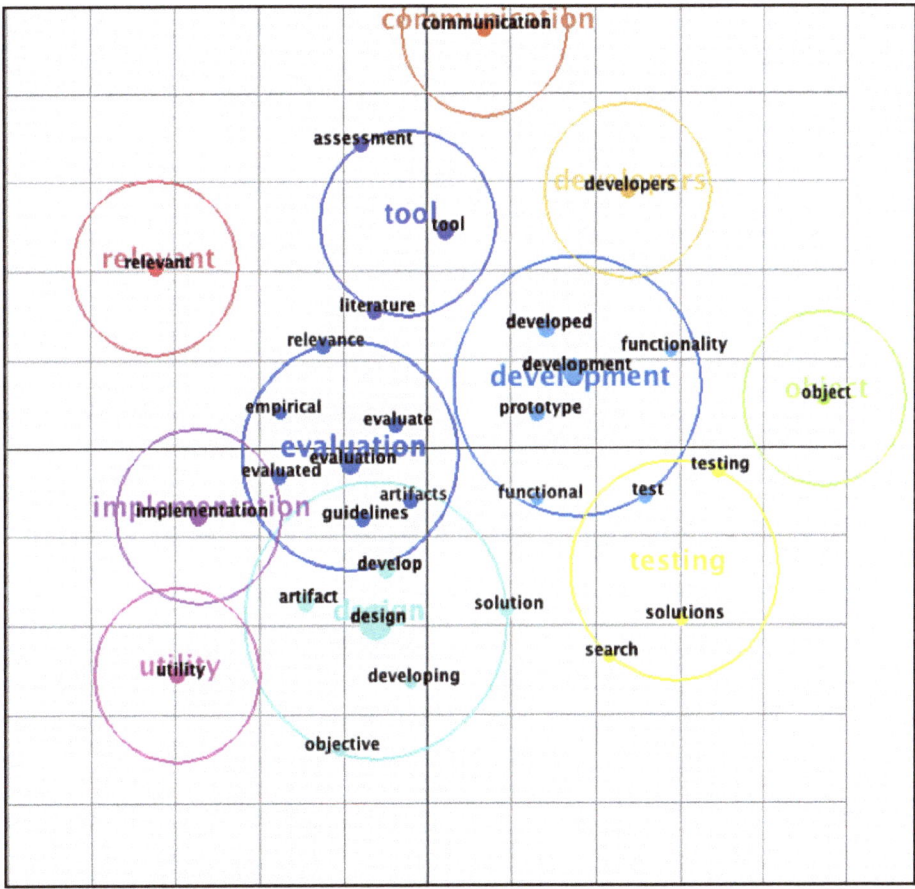

Figure 13.5 Themes related to design science guidelines in application papers

Discussion and conclusions

In this chapter, we present an analysis of design-science publications at five prominent IS conferences—namely, ACIS, AMCIS, ECIS, ICIS and PACIS—in the period 2005–07. Our analysis is motivated by a perceived increase in design-science research in IS and the continuing discussion within the IS research community on the appropriateness, methodology and scope of design science. We use the set of published papers at these conferences as our data set and narrow it down to a set of papers that is relevant to the design-science theme, using the Hevner et al. (2004) article as a reference benchmark for our selection. We then subject the papers to a statistical, methodological and thematic analysis.

Our findings provide a number of interesting insights. First, we identify a statistically significant increase in design-science papers in the period 2005–07. Our findings also indicate that the majority of design-science research originates from schools in the United States (39.76 per cent). European researchers, however, appear to have an over-proportional share of design-science contributions (33.73 per cent). Second, we find that the methodological guidelines suggested by Hevner et al. (2004) have had limited overall impact on how published design-science work has been carried out to date. Only 19.3 per cent of all papers elaborate on their consideration of the Hevner et al. guidelines. We argue that this finding indicates a need for further guidance on the conduct of design-science research. To that end, we agree with McKay and Marshall (2005:7) that the original guidelines require further details on operationalisation and instantiation so that they can be of more help to design-science efforts. We also argue that a number of design-science efforts in IS fail to attain strong methodological rigour, which calls for more contributions in this area to rectify this lack. Third, our thematic analysis indicates that design science is prominent in certain domains of IS research, such as process modelling, knowledge management and tool design.

While all care has been taken to design a methodology that increased the rigour and objectivity of this study, we identify the search terms and the methodological analysis as sources of limitation of our work. In the analysis, we considered only papers that used the term 'Hevner' and/or 'design science'. This means that papers that *do* design science without referencing the seminal work or without identifying the work as design science are not considered in this study. At IS conferences, however, authors generally elaborate on the employed methodology. Accordingly, we consider the percentage of such potentially omitted papers to be small. In our future work, we intend to widen the scope of our analysis by including other search terms, such as 'design theory'. In a related manner, our methodological analysis was based on the authors' description within the chapter. Accordingly, if a guideline (for example, evaluation) was not articulated or was not implied in the paper then it was assumed it had not been followed in the published research.

Regarding methodological contributions to design science, we suggest as a step forward works such as Gregor and Jones's (2007) research on the anatomy of design theory in which they identify six core and two additional components for design theory work, or the work by Niehaves (2007), who shows how the seven guidelines could, in theory, be executed following an interpretative epistemology. In light of the recent emergence of methodological contributions to design science, we can put forward the hope that we will see an increase in methodologically sound, theoretically strong and methodically well-executed design-science contributions to IS research in the future.

References

Applegate, L. and King, J. L. 1999, 'Rigor and relevance: careers on the line', *MIS Quarterly*, vol. 23, no. 1, pp. 17–18.

Benbasat, I. and Zmud, R. W. 1999, 'Empirical research in information systems. The practice of relevance', *MIS Quarterly*, vol. 23, no. 1, pp. 3–16.

Carlsson, S. A. 2005a, 'Design science research in information systems: a critical realist perspective', in B. Campbell, J. Underwood and D. Bunker (eds), *Proceedings of the 16th Australasian Conference on Information Systems*, Australasian Chapter of the Association for Information Systems, Sydney.

Carlsson, S. A. 2005b, 'Developing information systems design knowledge: a critical realist perspective', *The Electronic Journal of Business Research Methodology*, vol. 3, no. 2, pp. 93–102.

Gibson, M. and Arnott, D. 2007, 'The use of focus groups in design science research', in M. Toleman, A. Cater-Steel and D. Roberts (eds), *Proceedings of the 18th Australasian Conference on Information Systems*, University of Southern Queensland, Toowoomba, Qld, pp. 327–37.

Gregor, S. and Jones, D. 2007, 'The anatomy of a design theory', *Journal of the Association for Information Systems*, vol. 8, no. 5, pp. 312–35.

Hevner, A. R., March, S. T., Park, J. and Ram, S. 2004, 'Design science in information systems research', *MIS Quarterly*, vol. 28, no. 1, pp. 75–105.

Klose, K., Knackstedt, R. and Beverungen, D. 2007, 'Identification of services—a stakeholder-based approach to SOA development and its application in the area of production planning', in H. Österle, J. Schlep and R. Winter (eds), *Proceedings of the 15th European Conference on Information Systems*, University of St Gallen, Switzerland, pp. 1802–14.

Knackstedt, R., Winkelmann, A. and Becker, J. 2007, 'Dynamic alignment of ERP systems and their documentations—an approach for documentation quality improvement', *Proceedings of the 13th Americas Conference on Information Systems*, Association for Information Systems, Keystone, Colo.

Lyytinen, K., Baskerville, R., Iivari, J. and Te'Eni, D. 2007, 'Why the old world cannot publish? Overcoming challenges in publishing high-impact IS research', *European Journal of Information Systems*, vol. 16, no. 4, pp. 317–26.

McKay, J. and Marshall, P. 2005, 'A review of design science in information systems', in B. Campbell, J. Underwood and D. Bunker (eds), *Proceedings of the 16th Australasian Conference on Information Systems*, Australasian Chapter of the Association for Information Systems, Sydney.

March, S. T. and Smith, G. F. 1995, 'Design and natural science research on information technology', *Decision Support Systems*, vol. 15, no. 4, pp. 251–66.

Markus, M. L., Majchrzak, A. and Gasser, L. 2002, 'A design theory for systems that support emergent knowledge processes', *MIS Quarterly*, vol. 26, no. 3, pp. 179–212.

Niehaves, B. 2007, 'On epistemological diversity in design science: new vistas for a design-oriented IS research?', *Proceedings of the 28th International Conference on Information Systems*, Association for Information Systems, Montreal.

Purao, S., Sein, M. K., Rossi, M. and Cole, R. 2005, 'Being proactive: where action research meets design research', in D. E. Avison and D. F. Galletta (eds), *Proceedings of the 26th International Conference on Information Systems*, Association for Information Systems, Las Vegas, Nev.

Rosemann, M. and Vessey, I. 2008, 'Toward improving the relevance of IS research to practice: the role of applicability checks', *MIS Quarterly*, vol. 32, no. 1, pp. 1–22.

Tan, X., Siau, K. and Erickson, J. 2007, 'Design science research on systems analysis and design: the case of UML', *Proceedings of the 13th Americas Conference on Information Systems*, Association for Information Systems, Keystone, Colo.

Walls, J. G., Widmeyer, G. R. and El Sawy, O. A. 1992, 'Building an information systems design theory for vigilant EIS', *Information Systems Research*, vol. 3, no. 1, pp. 36–59.

Zmud, R. W. and Boynton, A. C. 1991, 'Survey measures and instruments in MIS: inventory and appraisal', in K. L. Kraemer (ed.), *The Information Systems Research Challenge: Survey research methods*, Harvard Business School, Boston, Mass., pp. 149–80.

www.ingramcontent.com/pod-product-compliance
Lightning Source LLC
Chambersburg PA
CBHW040545220526
45473CB00017B/3030